Routledge H
Education in India

This comprehensive handbook introduces the reader to the education system in India in terms of its structural features, its relations with society and culture, and the debates that have shaped the present-day policy ethos. Expert scholars provide a lucid analysis of complex themes such as the equal distribution of educational opportunities, legal provisions shaping the opportunity structure, and curricular issues in major areas of knowledge. The volume provides a general overview of India's education system and examines key and current issues that face higher and school education, the examination system, disciplines of social sciences, curriculum, teachers, law, coaching, and unemployment.

This handbook will serve as a valuable resource and guide to anyone seeking authentic information about India's contemporary educational challenges in relation to its society, economy, and politics. It will be useful to scholars and researchers of education, public policy and administration, sociology, and political studies, as well as practitioners, think-tanks, those in media, government, and NGOs.

Krishna Kumar is former Professor of Education, University of Delhi and former Director, National Council of Educational Research and Training (NCERT), India.

Routledge Handbook of Education in India

Debates, Practices, and Policies

Edited by Krishna Kumar

Routledge

Taylor & Francis Group

LONDON AND NEW YORK

First published 2018 by Routledge

2 Park Square, Milton Park, Abingdon, Oxfordshire OX14 4RN

52 Vanderbilt Avenue, New York, NY 10017

Routledge is an imprint of the Taylor & Francis Group, an informa business

First issued in paperback 2019

British Library Cataloguing in Publication Data
A catalogue record for this book is available from the British Library

Library of Congress Cataloging in Publication Data
A catalog record has been requested for this book

ISBN: 978-1-138-09161-0 (hbk)
ISBN: 978-0-367-34544-0 (pbk)

Typeset in Bembo
by Wearset Ltd, Boldon, Tyne and Wear

MIX
Paper from
responsible sources
FSC
www.fsc.org   FSC™ C013985

Printed in the United Kingdom
by Henry Ling Limited

Contents

Contents

Figures

Tables

Contributors

Philip G. Altbach is Research Professor and founding Director of the Center for International Higher Education at Boston College, USA. He has taught at Harvard University, University of Wisconsin, and State University of New York at Buffalo. He is the author of *Global Perspectives on Higher Education* (2016), *Student Politics in America: A Historical Analysis* (1997), *Turmoil and Transition: Higher Education and Student Politics in India* (1969), among other books.

Karuna Chanana is a former Professor and taught Sociology of Education and Gender at the Zakir Husain Centre for Educational Studies, School of Social Sciences, Jawaharlal Nehru University, New Delhi, India. She is the author of *Interrogating Women's Education: Bounded Visions, Expanding Horizons* (2001), and has published in several national and international academic journals and books.

Pankaj Chandra is Professor of Operations and Technology Management at Ahmedabad University, Gujarat, India. He is former Director of the Indian Institute of Management – Bangalore, India and has held full-time faculty positions at the Indian Institute of Management, Ahmedabad and McGill University, Canada. His areas of research are manufacturing management, building technological capabilities and hi-tech entrepreneurship, and governance in knowledge organisations.

Satish Deshpande teaches Sociology at the University of Delhi, India. He is the author of edited volumes *The Problem of Caste* (2014), *Beyond Inclusion: The Practice of Equal Access in Indian Higher Education* (2013), and *Contemporary India: A Sociological View* (2003), among others.

Jane Dyson is Lecturer at the School of Geography, University of Melbourne, Australia. She is author of many articles and books, including *Working Childhoods: Youth, Agency and the Environment in India* (2014). She has also produced an award-winning short documentary film on her scholarly work, available at www.lifelinesfilm.com.

Nidhi Gaur is a doctoral student at the Central Institute of Education, University of Delhi, India. She completed her post-graduation in Sociology and Education, and graduated in Elementary Education from the University of Delhi. She briefly taught in a private school in Delhi before joining Nirantar, an NGO that works in the area of gender and education.

Latika Gupta teaches Educational Theory and Pedagogy at the Central Institute of Education, University of Delhi, India. She is a bilingual writer and has worked for the National Council for

Educational Research and Training (NCERT), contributing to the development of social and political life textbooks for the upper-primary grades.

Craig Jeffrey is Director of the Australia India Institute, New Delhi, India and a former Professor at the University of Oxford, UK. He is author of many books on India, including *Timepass: Youth, Class and the Politics of Waiting in India* (2010) and *Keywords for Modern India* (with John Harriss, 2014).

Nalini Juneja is Professor at the National University of Educational Planning and Administration, New Delhi, India and heads the Department of School and Non-Formal Education. She has also been a Visiting Professor at the Center for the Study of International Cooperation in Education, Hiroshima University, Japan. She is the author of 'Primary Education for All in the City of Mumbai, India: The Challenge Set by Local Actors' (UNESCO, 2001).

Krishna Kumar is former Professor of Education, University of Delhi and former Director of the National Council for Educational Research and Training (NCERT), India. Recipient of several international fellowships, he was awarded the Padma Shri in 2011 by the President of India. The same year, the Institute of Education, University of London awarded him an Honorary DLitt for his contribution to the discipline of Education. His recent books include *Prejudice and Pride: School Histories of the Freedom Struggle in India and Pakistan* (2001), *Battle for Peace* (2007), *Politics of Education in Colonial India* (2013), *A Pedagogue's Romance* (2016), and *Education, Conflict and Peace* (2016). He has co-edited (with Joachim Oesterheld) *Education and Social Change in South Asia* (2006) and (with Edward Vickers) *Constructing Modern Asian Citizenship* (2015). Several of his books are in Hindi, the latest being *Choori Bazaar mein Larki* (2013), an award-winning analysis of girls' upbringing and education. A columnist and a short story writer, he also writes for children.

Chaise LaDousa is Associate Professor of Anthropology at Hamilton College, New York, USA. He has authored several articles and books including *Hindi is Our Ground, English is Our Sky: Education, Language, and Social Class in Contemporary India* (2014) and *House Signs and Collegiate Fun: Sex, Race, and Faith in a College Town* (2011).

Shobhit Mahajan is Professor at the Department of Physics & Astrophysics, University of Delhi, India. Apart from his research work in cosmology and theoretical particle physics, he has written two textbooks and several books on popular science. He is also the author of a report on science education for the Observer Research Foundation, Mumbai.

Manabi Majumdar is Professor of Political Science at the Centre for Studies in Social Sciences, Kolkata, India. She has worked extensively on the broad themes of politics of education, child labour, local democracy and capability deprivation and its measurement. Her recent publications include *Education and Inequality in India: A Classroom View* (with Jos E. Mooij, 2011).

Archana Mehendale is Professor at the Centre for Education Innovation and Action Research, Tata Institute of Social Sciences (TISS), Mumbai, India where she co-leads the Research Group of Connected Learning Initiative (CLIx), a multi-partner initiative of TISS, Massachusetts Institute of Technology, USA and Tata Trusts. She has been involved in several law-making processes during her tenure at the National Law School of India, Bengaluru, India.

Disha Nawani is Professor and Chairperson, Centre for Elementary Education, School of Education, Tata Institute of Social Sciences, Mumbai, India. She teaches, researches and writes on curricular, pedagogic and assessment-related issues in elementary education.

Kumkum Roy teaches Ancient Indian History at the Centre for Historical Studies, Jawaharlal Nehru University, New Delhi, India. Her areas of interest include gender, political institutions and pedagogical practices. She is also a Fellow at the Nehru Memorial Museum and Library, New Delhi.

Padma M. Sarangapani is Professor of Education, Tata Institute of Social Sciences, Mumbai, India. Her current areas of work and research include teacher education, quality in education, elementary education and the use of ICTs in curriculum and teacher professional development and education and culture/indigenous education. She was a member of the Steering Committee of the National Curriculum Framework 2005 and the National Council of Teacher Education (2013–2016).

Milind Sohoni, a computer scientist and mathematician, teaches at the Indian Institute of Technology – Bombay, India. He has been a Visiting Researcher at the University of Chicago, USA; Kyoto University, Japan; Max Planck Institute, Germany; and Zakir Husain Centre for Higher Education, Jawaharlal Nehru University, India. He also works as a development researcher with the Government of Maharashtra.

Hari Vasudevan is Professor at the Department of History, Calcutta University, India. He has been involved in syllabus production and textbook development at the universities of West Bengal, Delhi and Indira Gandhi National Open University (IGNOU). He was Chairman of Syllabus and Textbook Development Committees for Social Science for the National Council for Educational Research and Training (NCERT) from 2005 to 2009.

Virginius Xaxa is Professor and Deputy Director at the Tata Institute of Social Sciences (Guwahati Campus), India. He has taught Sociology at the Delhi School of Economics, University of Delhi and North-Eastern Hill University, Shillong. He is the author of several books including *Economic Dualism and Structure of Class: A Study in Plantation and Peasant Settings in North Bengal* (2002) and *State, Society and Tribes: Issues in Post-Colonial India* (2008).

Preface

Reading about education always intrigues me more than writing about it. As a reader, one is alert to the different ways in which people use the word 'education'. When you are writing, you are preoccupied with the meaning it has for you, that too in the immediate context. While editing this handbook I have often wondered how its readers will cope with the many different ways in which its contributors have used the keyword 'education'. Their locations, backgrounds, disciplines and expertise have shaped the ways in which they look at education in today's India. I hope readers of the handbook will notice the variation in the terminology the contributors have used to describe and examine the nature of the problems facing the system of education India has.

To the usual complexity involved in social inquiry of any aspect of Indian society, a significant addition has been made by the fast-paced but not necessarily planned changes introduced in the recent past. These changes are related to the economic policies associated with liberalisation and globalisation. No sector or stage of education is untouched by this policy. The impact is so deep and regionally so varied that 'liberalisation' as a common label seems much too compressed and inadequate to describe the policy to which the impact is attributed. And there is reasonable ground to wonder whether there is any policy at all. India's socio-political ethos defies sober reflection on the meaning that liberalisation might have for education. But the absence of a discourse or policy has not hampered the growth of market forces in education. If the size of this volume were to be increased to three or four times of what it is, the full picture of education in the era of liberalisation might still prove elusive in some details. Therefore, I see no harm in feeling content with the illustrative glimpses this volume provides. Someone eager to grasp how to make sense of education in present-day India will find plenty to ponder on.

Right from the start of this project I faced the question: 'How many areas can it cover?' One part of the answer was: 'Not all.' And the second part of this answer was: 'Coverage is no substitute for analytical depth.' The choice of topics was constrained by availability of existing contemplative literature that the contributors and I might draw on. There are more than a few critical areas of education in India that, for one reason or another, have not attracted scholarly attention. In some cases, the attention given is not commensurate with the significance or gravity of the problem these areas pose. One can cite secondary schooling, medical education and private universities as three topics deserving more and deeper attention than they have so far received. Readers who miss these topics in the table of contents will perhaps find some solace in the collateral insights provided, respectively, in the chapters covering the examination system, engineering institutes, and management education. Quite the contrary is the case for issues pertaining to the pursuit of equality. It is a major theme for anyone interested in India and its system of education, and this handbook provides extensive and varied coverage of this issue in different parts and chapters. This coverage is quite wide and it takes note of the systemic resistance and reaction that the pursuit of equality has met. These tendencies, as expressed by the coaching or private tuition industry and publicly sung sagas of institutionalised nepotism, are seldom permitted to enter the discourse of research on education. I hope the contributions included in this handbook on these themes will arouse interest and encourage further study.

I would like to acknowledge with gratitude the warm readiness with which all the authors I approached agreed to contribute. All but three chapters included in the handbook have been freshly written. I am thankful to Professor Philip Altbach and Professor Satish Deshpande for permitting me to include their papers originally prepared for publication elsewhere. My own chapter on the Vyapam scam was written for the *Economic and Political Weekly*. Finally, I wish to acknowledge the help Ms Ritu Pandey gave me in copy-editing the volume.

Introduction

Krishna Kumar

Education impacts people, both in the way they live and the way they interact with the world. The collectives of nation, state, and family and how they manifest are a result of these larger interactions between individuals while following group norms. Any inquiry into education can help make sense of the role it plays in shaping the larger collective in which the life story of an individual unfolds.

In order to probe the role of education in individual lives, we can look at the knowledge and the skills that schools, colleges, and universities promise to provide and the opportunities they open up thereby. The other role of education, i.e. in the collective life of the young, can be studied by looking at its relation with our system, to the economy, politics, and culture. This handbook aims at enabling readers to recognise and pursue both of these dimensions of education. It may look like a tall order, given the modest space that educational studies occupy in the wider field of social sciences in India at present. It is a relevant point to make. But this handbook draws upon the corpus of knowledge available within India and elsewhere about education. As a field of study, education in India has joined the social sciences quite late, and its entry is still disputed over matters of turf, status, methodology, and institutional space. It remains poorly understood and unappreciated despite being a subject of much public concern. Education is widely believed to be a means of social change, but this belief hasn't translated into adequate efforts to grasp the nature of the change that it has brought about and is going to encourage further.

The growth of educational studies in India as a whole has been sluggish and the overall body of knowledge generated so far is neither balanced nor adequately contemporary. Relatively more research exists on elementary education than on secondary and higher education. Much of the research now available on elementary education relates to the significant changes and reforms that have taken place since the 1990s. The economic reforms that started in the 1990s have resulted in changes at all levels of education, including elementary, but the scholarship that explores the complex and varying relationship between the new economy and education is limited. Attempts to analyse the new economic policies or reforms have seldom included a serious engagement with education, both in terms of policy and details of execution. The National Policy on Education (NPE), originally drafted in 1986, did not explicitly anticipate the new economic agenda; rather, it carried an agenda to address the contradictions and contrary demands on education that had been growing since India's independence from colonial rule in the mid-twentieth century. In any case, in the late 1980s, no one could have guessed the implications that the new economic policy would have on children, youth and their education. Between then and now, the unfolding of the economic scenario has significantly affected education, but this has not received the kind of research that would illuminate the two dimensions of education mentioned earlier, i.e. its meaning in an individual life and its impact on the collective. Moreover, education presents a paradox for someone attempting to study it. If we isolate it as a focus of study, we miss its dynamic relationship with structures and circumstances, particularly economic circumstances. On the other hand, if we view it as an outcome of circumstances, we miss its own power to make a long-term impact on the context. Educational inquiry can neither afford to get subsumed in a general study of society, nor should it risk its own reduction to the regurgitation of dominant schlock.

Using this handbook

The readers of this handbook can use it in two different ways. First, it can serve as a means of exposure to significant issues that India faces at different levels of its system of education. It is convenient to make this use of the handbook because most of its contributors focus either on schools or on colleges and universities. The overlap between the two levels is important too, particularly in terms of knowledge and procedures of evaluation. In the areas of science, mathematics, and the social sciences, therefore, the handbook provides the opportunity to examine the overlap or continuity between the school and the university. Nearly all authors have used some amount of historical information to develop an explanatory framework. This general approach will help the readers recognise, in the context of the stage that might interest them, where things are 'now' and how they got 'here'.

Second, this handbook can be used for locating the major debates that have shaped India's educational climate. As a democratic country with a vast, highly diverse and stratified population, India is a land of debates, and education is both a major site and subject of debates. The quest for equality and justice underlies the daily bustle of collective life, and educational activities occupy a sizeable part of this bustle. In education, key debates are over the meaning of equality and ways in which institutions pursue or hinder this important modern value. Knowledge, its design and distribution, acquire a central place in the larger debate over equality. Readers will notice that the relation between knowledge and the struggle for equality forms the underlying theme of several chapters. The list of references given by their authors will assist the readers to track this meta-theme of educational writings and debates.

Readers will also find in its chapters a considerable diversity of style and approach. This is because the contributing authors are located in diverse disciplinary and institutional settings and the subject matter of their contributions requires specialised treatment. In a few cases, a survey of existing knowledge is necessary; in other cases, the reader's interest is best served by narrating a trajectory that explains the present. Why science education in India is not as popular as one might expect or why engineering education does not address community needs are questions that require both systemic and historical knowledge. It is expected that readers will find the insights provided in one chapter useful for reading others. The distribution of the chapters into five parts is meant mainly to draw attention to the commonality of concerns. Thus, the examination of the Right to Education law will enable the reader to appreciate the challenges posed by older laws that govern urban planning. Contributors who have dealt with curricular concerns have been placed in a single part. One part is devoted to a sample of higher professional education in engineering, management, and teaching. Chapters concerning the structure of higher education and its capacity to address social inequalities, specifically those related to caste, tribal groups and women, are placed together. The final part consists of chapters dealing with the underbelly of the system – where activities conducted with limited legitimacy proliferate.

The range of disciplinary orientations reflected in the handbook is quite wide. It includes history, sociology, anthropology, law, engineering, management, science, and education itself. Despite the variety of themes and disciplinary specialisation of the authors, the handbook can hardly claim to be exhaustive. It is neither a compendium nor a comprehensive guide. Were it either of these, it would reduce a subject like education in contemporary India to jargon and numbers. The handbook aims at arousing the reader's curiosity about education in a country as deeply diverse and as politically charged as India is. To make sense of the experience called learning in such a society, one needs conceptual tools and information drawn from different disciplines. One also needs examples of expert handling of such tools. This is what the handbook attempts to offer – a sample of discussions with the fluidity necessary to mix different insights and develop new ones. As the editor of this volume, I was anxious to spare the reader the burden of absorbing too many statistics about a system that has been expanding quite rapidly, thereby rendering all statistics of transitional value. Only essential statistical information is provided; otherwise, the emphasis is on theory-building to interpret and to explain progress towards unequivocally set goals, and the problems that resist solutions.

Schools

The role of education in shaping childhood is a story of historic importance in modern India. Although historical scholarship on pre-British education for children remains sparse and some of the debates surrounding this research are far from being settled, there is consensus on the view that the nineteenth century forms a watershed in the history of Indian education (Kumar 2014; Shahidullah 1984). The varied schools and systems that existed across India prior to British colonial rule did not survive the new institutional order that took shape in the middle decades of the nineteenth century. What replaced it is usually referred to as the 'modern' system of education. How modern it was, in a normative sense, cannot be easily judged, but it did encourage both economic and geographical mobility, and triggered the articulation of demand for social justice by the lower-placed groups in the complex caste system. This impact of education needs to be studied with careful consideration of socialisation processes operative at the level of the family and kinship. And socialisation is inevitably an inter-generational story. The economic and cultural functions of education are normally associated with the advent of modernity in India's mainly agrarian society, and they have continued to shape the experience of childhood and schooling ever since they set in. The social and cultural turmoil that characterises India's everyday political life can be seen as an outcome of the expansion of access to education over a period spanning the last seven generations. Without studying education, both as it is individually experienced and as a system closely interacting with the economy, we cannot make much sense of contemporary India's public life. Nor can we assess the plausibility of the pronouncements made about the future by specialists of economy and politics.

As an institution dispensing knowledge, skills, and opportunities, the school is no single institution. Unlike many countries where the school creates bonds of commonality, the school in India reinforces existing groups and strata, and then permits the schooled members of these groups to compete for opportunities for further education and employment. The school as a state institution continues to coexist with the school as a social institution, implying thereby that the hierarchical caste system that characterises the Indian social order is not necessarily threatened by the dispersal of new forms of knowledge and skills that permit members of essentially unequal groups to compete with each other. The socialisation of children that the school brings about avoids a direct conflict with their socialisation – into caste and religious identities and gender roles – at home. Thus, schooling performs, in some of its roles, the function of bringing about modern forms of contest among different strata, while, in some of its other roles, it allows the maintenance and reproduction of stratifying social institutions.

As an institution of the state, schooling of children partakes of the vision encoded in the Constitution that took effect after the end of British rule some seven decades ago. The vision was egalitarian and transformative, but initially it had little legal force. It has taken the parliament exactly six decades after the promulgation of the Constitution in 1950 to modify it in 2009 so as to make eight years of elementary education a fundamental right of every child. Archana Mehendale examines this important change in terms of the challenges new laws face in influencing the reality on the ground. Undoubtedly, this will be a prolonged process, and this chapter helps us grasp the reasons why the process cannot be smoother or more predictable. The reasons analysed in this chapter are the ones entrenched in the system itself. But there are others that have to do with social conditions, such as poverty that encourages child labour and sharp regional variance in the economy that compels the rural poor to migrate to big cities. Nalini Juneja looks at the historical legacy that dominates provision for schooling in urban India. Her chapter shows why privatisation of schooling is common in cities and how it affects the children of the poor. Padma Sarangapani presents the main findings of her study aimed at explaining differential quality in schools in the city of Hyderabad. Her chapter demonstrates that schools functioning in a stratified social environment pursue different aims. These aims derive from the school owners' view of the needs and priorities of the particular stratum they serve.

The impact of modern education in rural India over the last 150 years has not been studied as such, but it has been a major theme in literature. The young hero's desire to return to the village and improve life there after receiving higher education is a prominent theme in modern fiction. Hindi novelist Phanishwar Nath Renu's 1955 novel, *Maila Anchal*, offers a richly emotive portrayal of this theme in the character of a doctor. General education is conventionally believed to alienate village youth and encourage migration to cities. Shrilal Shukla's *Raag Darbaari* (1968), a voluminous satire, deals with this theme in a compressed story of a young educated man's visit to his village during vacation. At the end of his visit, during which he gets a thorough exposure to the murky world of local politics, the hero wants to run away back to the city although he has been offered a job at the local intermediate college. These two fictional accounts indicate how crucial education has been to the village: whether we see it from the perspective of state-sponsored 'rural development' or as proof of its irrelevance to the village (Kumar 2015; Thakur 2014). The latter perspective informed Mahatma Gandhi's *Nai Talim* (literally, new education) and constituted a major critique of modern colonial education. Schooling based on Gandhi's ideas was highly innovative and continues to be practised in a few institutions. Nidhi Gaur presents a glimpse of one such institution in her chapter.

Colleges and universities

How the system of education works at higher levels demands a grasp of the historical conditions in which the present institutional order originated and the shape it acquired under those conditions. We need to refer specifically to the middle decades of the nineteenth century. Prior to the creation of the first three universities in 1857 in Calcutta, Madras, and Bombay, bachelor-level courses in arts, i.e. BA courses, had started in a handful of colleges. The newly set-up universities were meant to affiliate these existing colleges for the purpose of examination. This architecture of an examining body holding together a number of affiliated colleges suited a society characterised by vast and varied geography. Means of transport were scarce, and aspirations of the higher strata to gain eligibility to the new modes of salaried employment under the expanding colonial state apparatus were high. Affiliated colleges were to prove a lasting feature of the Indian higher education system. Despite being criticised in every major review report commissioned by the state, they have proliferated, apparently because they are rooted in India's varied regional and economic geography.

Contributions covering higher education look at the Indian scenario from the perspective of changes that are shaping the global picture, especially the economy. As a large economy, and one that is widely believed to share, with China, a crucial space and role in the world economy, India naturally arouses the expectation that its policies in higher education, particularly in research and advanced technology, will reflect its global status. Comparative research has pointed out that China and other East Asian countries have taken education as a whole, and higher education in particular, far more seriously than India has. In this volume, Philip Altbach draws on this comparative knowledge to point towards the considerable gap between the space that India occupies in the global economy and its educational preparedness to maintain that. Altbach believes that higher-order centres of research are necessary for India to stay competitive, especially in science and higher technology. He also points out the inefficiencies that are built into the administrative structure of Indian higher education, i.e. in the vast component of affiliated colleges controlled by a relatively small number of universities. Altbach also discusses why privatisation has so far failed to provide a credible alternative. In the specific context of science and technology, this volume has two comprehensive contributions that explain the nature of the problem Altbach has pointed out.

Social inclusion is an important concept that provides us the means to notice a different kind of systemic imbalance. How higher education could be made inclusive has been a subject of considerable debate. This debate has by and large focused on issues pertaining to access, and has remained somewhat oblivious to issues that relate to the character of knowledge and intellectual training that higher education is supposed to provide. It is not surprising that access has served as the core of the debate on inclusion, considering how major and how visible access as an aspect of institutional life at any level of education is. At another level, the debate on inclusion has remained concerned mainly with ways to provide greater access to marginalised sections of society, such as the Scheduled Castes and Scheduled Tribes, religious minorities (particularly Muslims) and women. Ways to overcome regional disparities have also been a concern addressed under the debates on inclusion. Relatively less attention has been paid to issues pertaining to teacher–student relations, the character of knowledge imparted in courses, and the ethos of institutions. Under the policy of reservation, institutions of higher education have attempted to provide proportionate representation to marginalised groups in enrolment. Close to half the available seats in public institutions are routinely filled by candidates who belong to the three major categories covered under the quota system; namely, the Scheduled Castes, the Scheduled Tribes, and the Other Backward Classes. Procedures of ensuring that all reserved seats are duly filled have stabilised over the years in all major universities. From this point of view, one can say that Indian universities have a more inclusive look today than they did half a century ago.

If we go beyond admission or enrolment, and look for deeper signs of inclusivity, we come across a reality that frequently erupts across the routine life of Indian academia, sometimes causing national-level upheavals of the kind that occurred in Hyderabad Central University recently. In this episode, a Dalit research scholar committed suicide after facing expulsion from hostel and other common facilities in a case where it is difficult to separate ideological issues from purely administrative ones. In his chapter on the reservation policy for the Scheduled Castes, Satish Deshpande raises a wide range of issues that make the policy in its present form look rather nominal. Virginius Xaxa has similarly examined the progress made in the context of the Scheduled Tribes, the other major grouping of the intended beneficiaries of the reservation policy in higher education. The analysis offered by Deshpande and Xaxa indicates that progress towards the goal of making Indian universities and colleges inclusive has been confined mostly to access. In terms of achieving retention and success of students from the reserved categories, significant obstacles remain and many of them have not been recognised. Discrimination on the basis of caste is perhaps just as widespread in Indian campuses as it is in elementary and secondary schools. The only difference between the school and higher levels is that at the former level it has been recognised and certain measures, however inadequate, have been taken to prevent it.

Knowledge and the curriculum

This handbook introduces the reader to curriculum policies and wars in Indian education as a major theme across different levels of the system. Several chapters throw light on the struggles over the choice of appropriate knowledge that the system of education has witnessed. In this respect, professional higher education offers no exception. Why knowledge has proved to be so contested a domain of education can be understood in the context of the colonial rule under which the system was born and shaped. What deserves to be examined and grasped with deeper interest and attention is the range of reasons that have blocked or, in some cases slowed down, reform in curriculum since the end of colonial rule. India's difficulties in this respect were perhaps not as great as Africa's. There, as Mamdani (2007) has interpreted, the legacy of colonial rule meant a vacuum at higher levels in many independent colonies. The Indian story started, so to speak, with the construction of a higher education system before there was a primary school system in any substantial sense. This did, to an extent, solve the problem of knowledge choices, but only to an extent. Needs of the colonial state placed the general arts degree at the commanding and popular height of the new system. A surfeit of BA pass or fail youth perhaps gave a sobering factor to society as a whole, though it also brought an endemic kind of educated unemployment. The term 'sobering' is meant to convey the accumulated impact of prolonged exposure to language, literature and subjects like history, politics, geography and economics. The higher education system that the British created and promoted in the second half of the nineteenth century was mainly an examining and certifying system, but it served several other purposes and had consequences that may not have been part of the original design. As a means of certifying individuals for eligibility for various jobs and careers that the new colonial state was going to offer to Indians (who would work for lower salaries than Englishmen with similar qualifications), higher education accommodated new aspirations among the colonised. It set the targets for school education to achieve at different levels both in terms of the content of knowledge to be expected and the skills and aptitudes to be cultivated. While office skills, such as précis making, would be more common among the educated class of Indians, mathematical skills and the capacity to learn basic technical skills would also be imparted to a smaller segment, to be employed in the slowly expanding engineering apparatus of the colonial state through departments like public works, railways, police, and the armed forces.

Science and technology are two major areas of knowledge and skill where modern education systems carry the burden of national development, and not merely social demand. This was apparent enough in the early days of independence, and the Kothari Commission (1964–66) was an epic articulation of this expectation. Two chapters illuminate these areas in a critical manner. Shobhit Mahajan's chapter deals with science and mathematics in secondary and tertiary education, and Milind Sohoni's chapter examines engineering education. Some aspects of the analysis these two chapters offer are similar, but several crucial aspects apply very differently to the two areas. The obvious difference lies in the types of institutions where education in these areas is provided. Mahajan's focus is on science in undergraduate colleges, while Sohoni's chapter concerns professional colleges and institutes of engineering. In many colleges that offer science at the undergraduate level, classroom teaching is poorly served by functional laboratories. The reasons lie in financial and institutional capacity as well as in procedural constraints. Sohoni's chapter, interestingly, reminds us of the conceptual constraints that have their roots in colonial history and relations of knowledge. They form a web of factors, including social and political, that we need to take into account in order to grasp why engineering education is now so widespread, yet so barren in terms of its capacity to address social and economic needs. If we combine the insights of Sohoni's chapter with a picture of the inner workings of a teacher training institution drawn by Latika Gupta, we can comprehend and assess the constraints that a poorly functioning system of higher professional education places upon the productivity of education itself and of the economy.

These chapters also indicate how tough and prone to distortion and corruption the official attempts to control and regulate the higher, including professional, education system can be in an era of state withdrawal and growth of private commercial interests. Engineering and teacher education are among more than a dozen areas of higher professional education that the government attempts to regulate and control by means of powerful statutory councils. The malfunctioning and failure of these councils have been evident for quite some time, but the regulatory procedure has by itself become a factor of vested interest. The regulatory system overlaps with the older affiliating system, and together they choke what little urge any single institution might have for innovation and change. The central government's mechanism of regulating the flow of funds and policies through the University Grants Commission has also evoked considerable criticism since the 1980s (Singh 1988). Its role overlaps with that of the Ministry of Human Resource Development that has been found, rather frequently in the recent past, to be involved in cases where affairs of a central university indicated a crisis of one kind or another. A parallel and somewhat different kind of case is presented by Pankaj Chandra in his chapter on management education. This is an area of knowledge and professional training marked by an absence of colonial legacy. This fact can be rightly perceived as a major factor of the ostensible vibrancy of management education in India, at least among the top-end institutions. Yet, as Chandra points out, the adverse effects of the regulatory system are beginning to surface in management courses too. Readers of the handbook might find a deeper question worth contemplating with regard to management education and its availability at a so-called world-class level of quality in at least the apex institutions set up to provide it. The deeper question is why the knowledge and training these institutions have been imparting did not influence the structures and procedures designed in the state's capacity to govern universities, colleges, and schools. If the reason lies in the orientation of management education towards private business, the cause of this orientation can be traced to the influence of American institutions and advisers from the earliest days of this sector. Attempts to tilt management education towards public governance at the grassroots level needs to form an important segment of the history of this sector even though these attempts are not part of its active memory. The Jawaja experiment spearheaded by Ravi Mathai was a major innovation in management education (Mathai 1985). It is true, of course, that this remarkable experiment could not influence, let alone alter, the general character of management education or the teaching of social sciences in India at the higher level. Hari Vasudevan's chapter on social sciences alludes to the pedagogic constraints of this vast area of undergraduate and later education.

Systemic imbalance

The growth of access to different stages or levels of education is one of the important factors shaping the systemic organisation and the relation between education and economic opportunities. The overall balance in terms of size and quality at different stages not only explains the functional efficiency of a system of education, but also the nature of its relationship with the social and cultural milieu in which the young live and study. Problems arising from systemic imbalance have, therefore, been of great interest to scholars of education in different countries. In India, however, the issue has not received much scholarly attention, although the Kothari Commission's report had drawn attention to the various kinds of gaps that it had noticed between school education and the higher education system. The gaps this commission had noticed, and that many educational planners of the 1970s had warned against, have grown wider over the last three decades, thereby exacerbating the problems caused by systemic imbalance. In a country with a vast population deprived of literacy, one might expect the primary level of education to grow more rapidly than higher education. But progress of primary education remained sluggish during the early decades after India gained independence. The number of institutions serving higher education multiplied, and not surprisingly, many of these institutions faced serious problems in maintaining their quality. This situation became more serious when, from the 1980s onwards, elementary education witnessed a rapid increase in both its public demand and in the state's response to it. Over the last decade, significant pressure has built up on the secondary stage of school education and on institutions of higher education. If we isolate higher education as a sector and notice the growth of institutions within itself, we might get the impression that their number has multiplied quite remarkably. Within itself, secondary and higher secondary education may create a similar impression. These impressions are erroneous because neither of the two stages have grown at a pace sufficient to accommodate the far higher growth in the number of children crossing elementary education. Although India's case is not as extreme as that of Sri Lanka, where primary education became universal while secondary education remained limited, the Indian story does represent a case of serious systemic imbalance. Up until the 1980s, dropout rates at the primary level were high, so the pressure on secondary education remained weak. That scenario has changed, and now the pressure of a radically expanded base level is manifesting at each level placed above it.

The pressure of numbers on the infrastructure of educational institutions has remained a constant object of concern for administrators and planners of higher education in India. Insufficient financial resources to cover all different aspects of institutional needs has been consistently cited, since colonial days, as a major reason why the system does not reach general levels of excellence. This line of argument is reflected in a great deal of writing on the two major functions of higher education, namely teaching and research. That India does not spend public funds comparable to many other countries is mentioned as a refrain, and the reference point of this refrain is the recommendation made by the Kothari Commission half-a-century ago that India should spend at least 6 per cent of its GDP on education. This has not happened. Both the advocacy for exhorting the state to remember that goal and the debate over state vs private financial responsibility have remained alive. If one views the state's priorities and decisions as a reflection of the social world, then it is not difficult to see that the state–private debate has effectively kept the planners' demand or pressure to increase public expenditure somewhat weak. Not just the debate, the economic and social divide that exists in India between the better-off and articulate upper caste strata and the poorer lower caste society also diffuses the pressure that might build up for rational or sensible public expenditure on education from time to time. Additionally, there is the culturally embedded suspicion of the state and doubt about the integrity of its institutions. This doubt has historically nourished an attraction for private provision and a cynical mindset towards government institutions. Certainly, the post-1980s phase of development has boosted this mindset, leading to an increase in the layers of privately managed institutions at all levels of education.

These socio-cultural factors are not particularly palpable, and in a climate dominated by a neo-utilitarian ideology, it is politically incorrect to mention these factors. Indeed, the mention itself bolsters privatisation by way of casting doubt on the state's capacity to improve its efficiency. So, private provision has been growing – and much of it is commercial in nature – by leaps and bounds, in all sectors of education, including English-medium schooling and general as well as professional higher education. The market is truly the dominant player in this story. It has altered the meaning of quality in education, by commoditising it so as to make it measurable in different ways. The state's role is now believed to be mainly of a regulatory nature, and the Indian experience so far suggests that regulatory institutions in the field of education are either irrelevant or corrupt. Thus, the federal regulatory body, the UGC, has become irrelevant to the growth of private universities approved by provincial assemblies. In vocational or professional education, private finance now covers a far bigger proportion of enrolment. The state is unable to keep pace with this growth even with the basic function of maintaining an official registry or count. In a rare case, the Supreme Court brought to light the scale of the growth of private university when it struck down the validity of nearly 200 such so-called universities in the small state of Chhattisgarh. The case was initiated in the public interest by Yash Pal, whose great stature as a scientist and visionary educationist imparts to this episode the extraordinariness that makes it virtually irreplaceable and, therefore, somewhat marginal to currently dominant trends. Since the early 1990s, privatisation has grown at a rapid pace, not merely in professional and vocational areas, but in general education as well. Private colleges presently constitute 75 per cent of the total number of institutions offering higher education in different areas of knowledge and skill, accounting for about 65 per cent of the total enrolment. On its own, this reality may not carry the same negative value for all observers. There are perhaps as many enthusiasts of privatisation as there are strong critics. This is simply one more site of sharp disagreement and polarised debate in contemporary India.

References

Kumar, Krishna (2014) *Politics of Education in Colonial India* (New Delhi: Routledge).

Kumar, Krishna (2015) 'Education and Modernity in Rural India' in Edward Vickers and Krishna Kumar (eds) *Constructing Modern Asian Citizenship* (London: Routledge) pp. 31–49.

Mamdani, Mahmood (2007) 'Higher Education, the State and the Marketplace', *Indian Educational Review* 43(1): 134–143.

Mathai, Ravi J. (1985) *The Rural University: The Jawaja Experiment in Rural Innovation* (New Delhi: South Asia Books).

Shahidullah, Kazi (1984) *From Pathsalas to Schools* (Calcutta: Bagchi).

Singh, Amrik (ed.) (1988) *Higher Education in India* (New Delhi: Konark).

Thakur, Manish (2014) *Indian Village: A Conceptual History* (Jaipur: Rawat).

Part I
Logic of access

The opening section of this handbook focuses on access to education. As a term, 'access' generally refers to availability of an opportunity. In the context of education, access depends on provision, implying the availability of institutions where education is available. The core idea for any discussion of access to education is the state, its policies and the will to execute them by providing for appropriate institutions within the reach of families and children. Geography of institutional provision, by itself, would mean little for assessing the adequacy of access unless it is matched with the economic condition of families and the age of children for whom the provision is being made. This is why the question of access has proved so difficult for India. Despite the fact that India has a political system based on the principles of liberal democracy, making primary education available to all children has taken a hundred years – after it was first attempted – to be accepted as a legal goal. The term 'primary' is currently being replaced by 'elementary', referring to a recently enacted central law that makes education from the age of six to fourteen a fundamental right of every child. The first chapter in this handbook examines the complexities of this law, including the problems its execution is likely to face. Archana Mehendale, the author of this chapter, discusses the background of this law by taking the reader into the implications of federal governance in children's education. She also helps the reader to examine the new law in the context of poverty, especially the widely prevalent use of children as a source of income for the family.

The second chapter, by Nalini Juneja, takes us into the tangled issues of poverty and schooling in the urban context. Her analysis reveals how urban demography intersects with spatial planning and the political economy of privatisation of education. This subject rarely figures when policies of education per se are discussed. How the land demarcated for schools in model plans made for urban development passes into the hands of private bodies is a story that normally does not belong to educational research. But it is a highly relevant narrative today because privatisation of education is occurring at a rapid pace at all levels of education, including the higher ones. The value of education as a saleable commodity is rising fast in response to the current tendency in the state to withdraw and transfer its educational responsibility to private providers. In turn, the status of private schooling – and now, universities too – is impelling the state to proceed more adroitly in this direction. This is a theme many readers will recognise as a global phenomenon, rooted in the ideological formation known as neo-liberalism. Global though it is, the phenomenon needs to be analysed in local contexts of nations and regions if one wants to study the modus operandi of the capture of children's education by private capital.

Though the term 'private' distinguishes fee-charging schools from the ones run by the government, there are sharply differentiated schools within both categories. While state schools differ on many counts such as 'central' and 'state' (i.e. provincial) and within each of these, private schools also differ on several counts, such as the fees they charge, the language they use as a medium of teaching, and the types of bodies that run them. Padma Sarangapani studied these different types in the city of Hyderabad. Her chapter attempts to develop a typology, then relate it to the question of quality and unravel the concept of quality. The chapter makes us aware of how problematic it may be to simplify the Indian urban educational scene, especially if we conflate private schooling with quality. This assumption has consistently gained popularity over the past three decades. During this period, 'quality' has emerged – or has been propagated – as a discourse. It has helped to deepen the reach of the neoliberal framework of analysis and its influence on state policy. In educational theory too, the discourse of quality has enabled a stolid perspective to gain currency.

How does the system of education, with such bewildering variety of schools and diversity of policies in 29 states, function and survive? How does it accommodate the expectations of a sharply stratified society? The answer to these questions is: 'With the help of a public examination culture.' Although public examinations are part of the system of education, they have served the system for well over a century by imparting to it a firm, annually reinforced coherence. This is why it is correct to call the public examination system a cultural construct that has its own customs and rituals recognised and observed across India's vast geography. The most important among the various examinations that Indian children take through their educational career is the Grade XII 'Board' examination. This exam ends the higher secondary stage, and it serves to dispense eligibility for further education. Those who appear in it are already stringently filtered, so to speak, by the Grade X examination, traditionally known as the 'high school' exam. Both of these examinations are taken by 'Boards', an institution that exercises tremendous power over the curriculum, how it finds expression in syllabi and textbooks, but most importantly, how teachers teach in the classroom. The 'Boards' that arrange or 'take' the exams are of two types. One category functions in 29 states of India; the other category has just two, the 'central' board that affiliates the few schools run by the central government all over India and a much greater number of private schools with a certain elite status. The complex story of the examination system is presented in the last chapter of this part. Disha Nawani, the author, offers a historical background to the secondary examination system, and also presents valuable statistics showing the 'results' of each Board in the past few years. These data enable us to get a glimpse into the magic of the exam system, its capacity to allocate success and failure on the basis of a one-time performance, and thereby to offer a meritocratic handle to the social system to manage diversity of backgrounds, interests, and aspirations.

The various systemic and social factors that shape the logic of access to different stages of education are mentioned and discussed in other sections of this handbook as well. While access at the elementary level is now a legal right, going beyond this level involves competitive capacity and socio-economic wherewithal. Thus, the crucial transition from Grade VIII to IX contains, as an object of inquiry, a complex story in which social stratification in terms of caste and income levels, and gender, play crucial roles in shaping individual educational mobility. These factors accumulate greater power as an individual looks towards higher education. Access at these higher levels is no longer just about the availability of a college to enrol in; it is also about the capacity to face a mixture of systemic and social factors. These factors form the subject matter of the chapters included in Part IV. These chapters enable us to realise how important it may be to comprehend systemic resistance to social inclusivity in the Indian society.

1

Compulsion to educate

Archana Mehendale

The Constitution is regarded as a 'superior or supreme law' (Wheare 1966) that reflects the normative structure and ideology of a sovereign and guides the state's relationship with its citizens. The Indian Constitution is 'partly flexible and partly rigid' (Kashyap 1986), allowing it to be amended through its representative democracy. The Constitution (86th Amendment) Act, 2002 (hereafter referred to as the 86th Amendment) was a significant milestone. Adopted after both Houses of Parliament had unanimously voted in its favour and receiving the President's assent thereafter, the amendment inserted a new Fundamental Right, amended a Directive Principle of State Policy and inserted a new Fundamental Duty.

The new Article 21A under Part III Fundamental Rights of the Constitution, states: 'The State shall provide free and compulsory education to all children of the age of six to 14 years in such manner as the State may, by law, determine.' The revised Article 45 under Part IV Directive Principles of State Policy states: 'State shall endeavour to provide early childhood care and education for all children until they complete the age of six years.' The new Article 51A (k) under Fundamental Duties recognises the duties of 'who is a parent or guardian to provide opportunities for education to his child or, as the case may be, ward between the age of six and 14 years'. The enactment of The Right of Children to Free and Compulsory Education Act, 2009 (hereafter referred to as the RTE Act) and its coming into force in 2010, operationalised the fundamental right to education for children between the ages of six and 14 years. The RTE Act is a central legislation on a concurrent subject, and state governments are empowered to formulate rules to execute the legislation. Using these delegated legislative powers, the state governments have prepared rules which are applicable in their jurisdiction and are meant to guide the implementation of the RTE Act. These are subordinate to the RTE Act and are thus expected to adhere to the provisions of the RTE Act.

Being a justiciable Fundamental Right, the government is now legally bound to provide free and compulsory education to children, and ordinary citizens can directly approach the High Court or the Supreme Court if the government fails to fulfil its mandate. Such a firm legal accountability of the government was missing before the amendment when it was classified as a non-justiciable Directive Principle of State Policy. This recent law-making on education has percolated into public imagination and discourse through a new acronym, 'RTE', which has become the new reference point of education policy, a new peg on which all ideological, pedagogical, administrative, and social questions related to education and educational spaces are left to hang. The 'RTE' pitch has been extended to areas that are not technically covered by the 86th Amendment, the RTE Act, or the rules notified by the state governments. Regulation of fee hikes in private schools is one example where the RTE Act does not directly make any provision, but it is drawn upon to justify arguments for lower fees. The RTE buzzword is periodically used by education administrators and teachers to draw attention to the changed regime within which education has to be transacted and their roles enacted.

The chapter first describes the context within which the right to education became a constitutional and a statutory right in India by highlighting its historical, administrative, and legal significance. The idea of compulsion implied in the right is then explored in order to locate the contradiction within historical and contemporary ideas surrounding free and compulsory education. The chapter concludes with a brief account of the contestations and debates on various legal provisions, which point to the gaps and issues that remain unresolved within the official agenda and public discourse.

Context and significance of the legislation

The framers of the Indian Constitution had committed to providing free and compulsory education to children below the age of 14 years within ten years of commencement of the Constitution (see Article 45 before it was amended in 2002). Although this commitment was placed under Part IV Directive Principles of State Policy, this was the only provision that had a time frame of ten years mentioned in the Constitution. This commitment was neither taken seriously nor was there any kind of parliamentary review or debate in 1960 when the goal was supposed to have been achieved. The increase in the illiterate population during this decade from 294.2 million in 1951 to 325.5 million in 1961 confirms that elementary education was not a political priority.

Context

The National Policy on Education (1968) and the National Policy on Education (1986) were also committed to universalisation of free and compulsory elementary education in a time-bound manner, but they failed to meet their targets. The first official recommendation to include the right to education under the Fundamental Rights was made by the Acharya Ramamurti Committee (Ramamurti 1990), which was constituted to review and recommend policy revisions. But these recommendations were ignored and the revised policy of 1992 stated 'it shall be ensured that free and compulsory education of satisfactory quality is provided to all children up to 14 years before we enter the 21st century'. In the early 1990s, three different factors influenced the decision to make education a fundamental right in India.

First, the Education for All Initiative, which was kick-started during the World Conference on 'Education for All (EFA): Meeting Learning Needs' held at Jomtein, Thailand in March 1990, saw the adoption of the 'World Declaration on Education for All' along with the 'Framework for Action to Meet Basic Learning Needs'. It held that 'education is a fundamental right for all people, women and men, of all ages, throughout the world' (Inter Agency Commission 1990). The initiative was significant in the Indian context because it opened the possibility of external donor assistance for basic education. The government, which had deliberately opted not to seek external financing for primary education till then, sought external funds from the World Bank for supporting its new programme, called the District Primary Education Programme. The EFA also started a new era of international monitoring through observable and measurable targets, thereby placing the government under pressure to demonstrate its commitment to international observers. Second, judicial directions in two landmark cases related to the role of the state in higher education actually paved new jurisprudence on the right to education. In 1992, while hearing a case of capitation fees in professional colleges, in *Mohini Jain v. State of Karnataka*,[1] the Supreme Court held that 'right to education' is concomitant to fundamental rights enshrined under Part III of the Constitution and that 'every citizen has a right to education under the Constitution'. In 1993, a five-member bench of the Supreme Court in the landmark case of *Unnikrishnan, J.P. v. State of Andhra Pradesh*[2] reviewed the earlier judgment and held that 'though right to education is not stated expressly as a fundamental right, it is implicit in and flows from the right to life guaranteed under Article 21 … [and] must be construed in the light of the Directive Principles of the Constitution'. Thus,

> right to education, understood in the context of Article 45 and 41 means: (a) every child/citizen of this country has a right to free education until he completes the age of 14 years and (b) after a child/citizen completes 14 years, his right to education is circumscribed by the limits of the economic capacity of the State and its development.

Third, large-scale mobilisation and civil society advocacy drew upon the Supreme Court judgments and demanded that the right upheld by the judiciary be enshrined in the Constitution to give it political and legal permanence.

Significance of a justiciable right

In their recent work on studying Constitutions of 191 countries, Heymann *et al.* (2014) found that 81 per cent of the countries recognised the right to primary education and 53 per cent of them provided it free at the primary stage. The newer Constitutions, particularly those adopted in the developing and middle-income countries since the 1990s, were more likely to include the right to education.[3] Legislation in countries like China, Japan, and the United Kingdom imposes obligations on the state to provide funds for free and compulsory education.[4] International human rights law classifies education as an economic, social, and cultural right that can be attained as per the maximum availability of states' resources and in a progressive manner.[5] India, as we discussed earlier, was committed to providing free and compulsory education since 1950, but it was only in 2002 that this was elevated to a justiciable right. The significance of making education a justiciable right can be accounted for at historical, administrative, and legal levels.

The division of justiciable and non-justiciable rights under Part III and Part IV respectively of the Indian Constitution builds on the idea of a hierarchy of rights that makes the first generation of civil and political rights privileged because they are legally enforceable, while the second generation of social, economic, and cultural rights are meant to direct the governance and state policy and be progressively realised. Juneja (2003) has argued that the Constituent Assembly debated about the inclusion of education up to the age of 14 years as part of Fundamental Rights, but this was relegated to the Directive Principles. The amendment reinstates the right under Part III on Fundamental Rights of the Constitution after it remained unimplemented as a Directive Principle of State Policy. It is also historically significant given that it is the first time that a positive right having significant resource implications has been introduced under Part III of the Constitution. By inserting it as Article 21A, it has reinforced the Supreme Court observations in *Unnikrishnan*, where the right to education was linked to Article 21 on right to life.

At an administrative level, having a central legislation on a concurrent subject has opened newer challenges to federal relations. There are significant inter-state variations in terms of economic, political, and education levels, and state governments are faced with a number of challenges while implementing centrally laid norms. The dependence of the state governments on the central funds, particularly funds allocated through the District Primary Education Programme (DPEP) in 1994 and the Sarva Shiksha Abhiyan (SSA) in 2003 while trying to retain their autonomy in policy matters such as teachers' appointments, service conditions, curriculum and assessments, is one example. Even after the RTE Act came into force, state governments expressed their inability to adhere to its mandate without the financial support of the central government. Significant funding from the central government for over a decade of DPEP and SSA has neither resulted in achievement of goals on access and quality of education,[6] nor has it enabled the state governments to deliver the programme on their own. Concurrency of education has largely tilted towards a centralising trend putting the principles underlining the federal structure under strain. Evidently, a number of state governments have not made use of their available jurisdiction to formulate state-specific policies. For instance, rules notified by some state governments under the RTE Act are replicas of the rules framed by the central government. The state curriculum frameworks also do not express the distinct imaginations of state governments on education and its aims and are closely modelled on the National Curriculum Framework. Another area of administrative significance is that of decentralisation in education. The RTE Act provides for decentralisation by outlining duties of the state governments and local authorities. Additionally, state governments have notified rules that further elaborate on the roles mandated for sub-statal bodies. Although education was required to be decentralised by state governments after the 73rd and 74th Amendments to the Constitution, state governments had not devolved funds, functions, and functionaries to the local levels. By providing a uniform minimum framework of sharing of duties among the state and the local authorities, the RTE Act effectively suggests a top-down approach of decentralisation.

The third area where the RTE Act has necessitated administrative changes is that of the implementation mechanism. Since the early 1990s, the governments have adopted a 'mission mode'[7] style of functioning that runs parallel to the education departments, and is designed to ensure greater efficiency and streamlined implementation. The RTE Act requires that the focus is shifted again to the education departments and goes beyond a programmatic mode of realising a fundamental right. Although the Anil Bordia Committee (Ministry of Human Resources Development 2010) suggested a revised framework for the Sarva Shiksha Abhiyan (SSA) that was aligned with the RTE Act, the implementation of the Act requires state departments to perform their conventional functions of funding, provisioning and regulation, that are not limited to the scope and tenure of the SSA. In other words, RTE would require state education departments to be present, and rebuild their administrative capacities and orientations to deliver on the legal mandate.

The legal significance of education as a justiciable right is that violation of rights or its inadequate protection can be challenged in the courts. This itself has resulted in the interpretation of the scope and applicability of various provisions. One of the significant legal features introduced by the RTE Act is that of horizontal application of rights. In a general sense, fundamental rights are enforceable only against the state and are meant to protect citizens from the actions of the state. Thus, if a fundamental right is being violated, action would rest against the state as it is duty bound to protect these rights. Article 21A does not refer to the private institutions in any way. However, Section 12(1)(c) requires private unaided schools to provide 25 per cent of their total seats to children from disadvantaged and weaker sections. The horizontal application of rights which extends the duties created under the RTE Act to non-state actors was challenged by private schools in the Supreme Court.[8] The apex court said that the principle of reasonable restriction on the right to carry out business or profession (Article 19 (1)(g))[9] is not an absolute right and the state can restrict it in the interest of the general public (Article 19 (6)).[10] Thus,

Section 12(1)(c) provided under the RTE Act that flows out of Article 21A would justify restriction on the right to carry on business that is enjoyed by the private schools as per Article 19(1)(g). One of the earlier drafts of the constitutional amendment bill had specifically prohibited the state from making 'any law, for free and compulsory education … in relation to the educational institutions not maintained by the State or not receiving aid out of State funds'. However, the provision was removed as it was considered fit to leave it to the judiciary to decide on the scope and width of Article 21A and the extension of duties to private institutions. This unique legal feature of the RTE Act has also been a subject of legal contestation requiring the judiciary to comment on the hierarchy of fundamental rights.

Nature of compulsion

The international legal framework on human rights recognises the right to education, which encompasses an entitlement to free and compulsory education at the primary school level. This is enunciated in the Universal Declaration on Human Rights (1948), International Covenant on Economic, Social and Cultural Rights (1966) and the United Nations Convention on the Rights of the Child (1989).

In the General Comment No. 11 of the International Committee on Economic, Social and Cultural Rights (1999), the term 'compulsory' has been explained to refer to the 'fact that neither parents, nor guardians, nor the State are entitled to treat as optional the decision as to whether the child should have access to primary education'. It also notes that the provision of compulsory primary education in no way conflicts with the right of parents and guardians to choose for their children schools other than those established by the public authorities. Thus, a reference to 'compulsion' in the expression of the human right to education is not new and hints at the legacy of compulsory education in Western countries that had helped to establish universal education systems in those regions; an approach that was forwarded and reaffirmed as a universal method of respecting and fulfilling the right to education.

The idea of compulsion

Compulsion is linked with the idea of duty and has typically been used with a connotation of 'enforcement' by the state on its citizens. Similar ideas of compulsion are related to compulsory conscription for military service in some countries, compulsory licencing (regulation) of enterprises, compulsory taxation, and so on that are practised in democratic societies. However, given the inherent conflict between human rights and the state's exercise and imposition of its authority, compulsion has been questioned on the grounds of infringement of personal freedom and liberty, while arguing that public interest alone cannot justify making certain actions compulsory. For instance, voting, although necessary for a healthy functioning democracy, is not made compulsory because it is seen as an imposition that goes against the exercise of fundamental freedoms. When the compulsion is on the state, it is seen as an extension of the duty of the state. However, questions related to the nature of compulsion – what does it require of the parties on whom it is imposed? Who imposes compulsion? Is it adequate to realise the right? – remain largely unanswered even in the international normative articulations.

What has compulsory education meant in India?

The earliest effort to introduce free and compulsory education was Gokhale's bill in the Imperial Legislative Assembly in 1911, which proposed abolition of child labour among boys and imposed taxation to provide free education for poor families. This was defeated because it would create a problem of availability of cheap agricultural labour. Moreover, the elite did not support the taxation of the rich for the education of the masses (Kumar 1991). The origins of legislation on compulsory education can be traced to the colonial period when, like other British colonies, India also adopted legislation on free and compulsory education almost alongside legislation outlawing employment of children in factories and mines. These were promulgated at the provincial level and worked on a schema wherein local authorities had the discretion to notify the applicability of free and compulsory education in their jurisdiction. In some provinces, local authorities could put in place exemptions on the basis of gender or other criteria. These legislations were modelled on truancy law and compelled children to attend school. Parents and employers could be penalised for keeping children away from school. The legislation provided bureaucratic procedures including issuance of show-cause notices to parents and levying fines and penalties against them. Although this idea of compulsion was linked with imposition of force and authority, the legislation also provided for 'reasonable excuses for non-attendance' that allowed children to stay away from school. These included lack of educational facilities, conditions of physical and mental disability, and other circumstances that may require children to stay at home.

After Independence, these legislations remained in force in several states,[11] but their implementation remained weak (Law Commission of India 1998: 70). Weiner (1991) explained this lack of implementation as being a result of the deeply entrenched caste system. He argued that by not providing free and compulsory education, differentiation among social classes was being maintained with the aim of preserving the existing social arrangements. Weiner's main theory about lack of political will to implement free and compulsory education legislation can be summarised as:

> India's low per capita income and economic situation is less relevant as an explanation than the belief systems of the state bureaucracy, a set of beliefs that are widely shared by educators, social activists, trade unionists, academic researchers, and, more broadly, by members of the Indian middle class. These beliefs are held by those outside as well as those within government, by observant Hindus and by those who regard themselves as secular, and by leftists as well as by centrists and rightists. At the core of these beliefs are the Indian view of the social order, notions concerning the respective roles of upper and lower social strata, the role of education as a means of maintaining differentiations among social classes, and concerns that 'excessive' and 'inappropriate' education for the poor would disrupt existing social arrangements.
>
> *(Weiner 1991: 5)*

Juneja (1997) showed how the officials responsible for enforcing the legislation were not aware of the provisions and their mandate and how the enforcement of compulsory education was 'actively discouraged' from the early 1960s. In other words, free and compulsory education failed to have any impact in India and compulsion on parents and employers was rarely enforced. What is important to note is that the state itself was not duty-bound to provide education in any way, and the legislation was merely enabling in nature.

The 86th Amendment and the RTE Act brought a paradigm shift in the schema of the legislation, although the phrase 'free and compulsory education' continues to be used. The considerable confusion that surrounds the use of rather contradictory terms such as 'right' and 'compulsory' can be attributed to the ambiguity related to the nature of compulsion imagined in the legislation. When the Parliamentary Standing Committee (1997) deliberated on an early draft of the constitutional amendment bill, it held that reference to compulsion in the language of a fundamental right can cause confusion and there is a need to clarify on whom does the compulsion lie under the 'fundamental right to compulsory education'. It recommended that the compulsion should lie on the state, which is duty-bound to fulfil and protect a fundamental right. The Saikia Committee (1996) had earlier observed that if compulsion is placed on the state, it will open the floodgates for litigation and state education departments will be overburdened with court cases. The Law Commission of India, in its 165th report (1998), had recommended a different approach to compulsion and the legislation as a whole. It had suggested that the central government adopt a minimal skeletal legislation leaving the state governments with guidelines to amend existing state legislations or enact new ones. It recommended making it compulsory for the parents and guardians to send their children to school. Furthermore, it recommended that the state legislation should provide for 'permissive compulsion', which would allow state governments and local authorities to enforce the law selectively in a phased manner, grounds for exemption from compulsory schooling, and minimum and maximum punishments that can be imposed on defaulting parents. It observed that persuasion and incentives are not enough and some amount of compulsion is necessary. It clarified that 'a statute imposing compulsion is no encroachment on any fundamental right, for no one has any right to remain ignorant and illiterate'. The report also extended the idea of compulsion to obligation on the state, parents, and society as a whole. These ambiguities around the nature and meaning of compulsion continued to remain unaddressed even in the legislation itself.

It is argued that the state that had failed to enforce compulsory education through its local authorities and attendance authorities would be ineffective in discharging its duties of providing education to all. Yet, compulsion has been imposed on the state. As the explanatory note provided under Section 8(1) of the RTE Act clarifies, the compulsion is on the state and not on the parents. Since the local authorities are required to ensure free and compulsory education of all children, it is not clear how the local authorities will ensure that all the children are in school without bringing in an element of compulsion. The new legislation works on the assumption that all children, if given a chance, would like to be in school, that children have stability in their lives and have a place to stay, and that they are interested in formal schooling and investing in their future. Moreover, there is no reference to the child and her agency. The legislation, which provides children a right, does not factor in possibilities that children may exercise their agency and not wish to attend school. Therefore, children effectively are also under the compulsion to attend schools.

Is compulsory education free?

National and international law prescribe that compulsory education is also 'free'. This implies that while parents are under the compulsion to send their children to school, the state is under the obligation to provide such education free of charge. Even though 'right to free and compulsory education' is a universally established legal norm, Tomasevski (2006) argues that in developing and transition countries, up to 35 per cent of the cost of education is borne privately. This goes against the principle that education should be free for the users because getting educated is mandatory for all children. Her review of education law and practice in 170 countries shows that more than 20 different charges can be imposed on children, and children are pushed out of schools as the costs of schooling increase. Wherever countries have compensated families for lost revenue in sending children to school, there has been better retention of children in education. Even though India has the highest number of child labourers in the world, the notion of free education in India does not include the idea of compensating parents for the opportunity costs involved in sending their children to school instead of sending them to work as wage labour.

Free education has meant that government schools would not charge fees at the elementary level. Tilak (1996) shows how this entitlement of free education even in a restricted sense is violated by government schools. Using National Sample Survey Organisation (NSSO) data, he shows that households spend large sums of money on acquiring primary education, and students pay tuition fees, examination fees and other fees even in government primary schools, and incentives are not available for all students. Against this background, it is pertinent to note that Section 3(2) of the RTE Act provides that 'no child shall be liable to pay any kind of fee or charges or expenses which may prevent him or her from pursuing and completing the elementary education'. This is applicable in government schools and in unaided non-minority private schools for children admitted under the provisions of Section 12(1)(c),[12] unlike the colonial education legislation which guaranteed free education only in government schools. Although state rules have reiterated that no charges or fees should be levied by private schools on children admitted through this provision, evidence shows that schools have imposed various kinds of fees on these children. Furthermore, most private schools have not received timely and complete reimbursements from state governments, resulting in the schools passing on these charges to the children (Mehendale et al. 2015; Sarin and Gupta 2014). An important underlying principle on which the provision of free education rests is the premise that education is a charitable activity and cannot be run as a profit-making enterprise.[13] Yet, the RTE Act shies away from applying this principle in the regulation of private schools and does not deal with the issue of high fees charged by private schools.

To summarise, the 86th Amendment and the RTE Act use the term 'free' and 'compulsory' in a manner very different from the colonial legislation on free and compulsory education. The entitlement to free education is now extended to unaided non-minority private schools, but what constitutes 'free education' in these private schools is left widely open-ended. While the compulsion was clearly on the parents (and partially on the employers) in the older legislation, the new legislation places compulsion primarily on the state (at all three levels – centre, state, and local authorities), on private schools, parents, and effectively also on children. The idea of compulsion does not fit into the new vocabulary of rights and entitlements. The term is a superfluous remnant. As the legislation provides for duties of the state, it was not necessary for the legislation to carry the term compulsory in order to convey that the compulsion is on the state. On the other hand, by keeping an anachronous term such as compulsion, it has left room for ambiguities in interpretation and subtly underlined the idea of 'shared compulsion', wherein the compulsion is in fact placed on not just the state but also on the private entities (schools as well as parents) and the children themselves.

Gaps and issues

The process of policy-making is essentially a political one, which entails balancing and mediating between contesting interests, values, and priorities. This is true of the process of law-making in India, wherein democratic processes such as expression of political contestation do not come to a close with the formulation of legislation, but carry over and resurface during the continuous processes of interpretation and implementation. A number of ambiguities (both conceptual and normative), gaps, and questions that remained unsettled, negotiated, and ignored during the process of formulation of RTE, have surfaced between 2010 and 2015, a period when RTE was being tested as a 'lived document'. The scope and applicability of the RTE, its limits and significance, the meaning of its provisions, and its relation to other legislative norms have been elaborated upon by all three arms of the government. Parliament amended the RTE Act in 2012 and specified a definition of children with disabilities, their right to home-based schooling, private unaided schools, and minority institutions with School Management Committees playing an advisory role. The state legislature of Rajasthan and Karnataka have contemplated amending the RTE Act for their respective states.[14] Five years after having supported the adoption of the original Act, these state governments are considering amendments that will address their specific requirements and concerns about the RTE Act. The proposals for such amendments underline the fact that RTE is subject to testing and amendments through a process of continued contestations among various stakeholders. The executive has utilised its powers to give directions under Section 35(1) and has issued a number of explanatory advisories and guidelines on matters such as neighbourhood schools, screening procedures, grievance redress by local authorities, and so on. These directions have intended to clarify the scope of specific provisions and put some of the controversies to rest. The third arm of the government, the judiciary, has played a crucial role in interpreting the scope of duties and rights enunciated in the RTE Act, particularly the exclusion of minority-run schools from the purview of the RTE Act.[15] This brief comment on the role of the three arms of the government in dealing with enduring tensions and contestations about the RTE Act reflects the discordance that prevails between these institutions. For instance, executive actions (and inactions) pertaining to Teachers' Eligibility Tests have been challenged in the Courts.[16] Although the legislature intended that certain provisions such as recognition of private schools[17] and provision of qualified teachers[18] be time bound, the state governments have not implemented these provisions within the stipulated timeframe, thereby diluting the legislative intent.

While the RTE Act passes through a course of re-interpretation and revisions, two distinct streams are evident. The first stream consists of different issues and questions pertaining to the legal provisions that are on the 'official agenda'. These are questions and problems that the government itself recognises as being worthy of review and reconsideration. These are backed by interest groups and stakeholders, including school managements, parents, teachers, and others. These issues straddle and find space between the official agenda and review as well as the public discourse, which is largely shaped by the media. One example of the issues falling under the first stream is that of the application of the RTE Act to the minority-run institutions, which was not mentioned in the legislation itself. Given that religious and linguistic minority schools have a constitutional right to establish and administer institutions without state interference (Article 30 of the Constitution), the imposition of, particularly, Section 12(1)(c) requiring private schools to offer admission to children of disadvantaged and economically weaker backgrounds was challenged in the courts. In a way, the silence of the legislation on this matter necessitated the courts to interpret and settle it.[19]

Another example is that of quality of education, which is not explicitly defined although all schools are required to ensure particular standards of infrastructure, duration of class hours, qualified teachers, curriculum, and evaluation (Mehendale 2014). In a system governed by the principles of New Public Management and goal-driven regulation (Dale 1997), quality is construed as production of minimum learning outcomes; the fact that the RTE Act does not guarantee these measures of quality is being questioned. Data from the National Achievement Survey (Government of India, n.d.) and Annual Status of Education Reports (ASER 2014) show that a large number of students are unable to demonstrate minimum competencies in language and mathematics, and it is contended that the RTE Act is unable to address this paradox. States like Gujarat and Kerala have tried to bring in references to learning outcomes and independent assessments within the state rules, thereby attempting to guarantee right to 'quality' education.[20]

The issue of corporal punishment in schools found a place on the official agenda, with the guidelines issued by the National Commission for Protection of Child Rights in response to increasing cases of corporal punishment in schools. Being a recommendatory body, the enforceability of these guidelines is limited, yet it has brought to light the inadequacy of existing legal provisions on corporal punishment. Not only is there no separate offence under the Indian Penal Code on corporal punishment meted out by those who are *in loco parentis*, but in fact it takes a lenient view, with Sections 88 and 89 providing immunity to a person inflicting corporal punishment on a child if such punishment is inflicted 'in good faith for the child's benefit' (NCPCR, n.d.). There has been a lot of contention around the no-detention provision and the requirement of continuous and comprehensive evaluation (CCE), bringing these matters back to the drafting table. The Gita Bhukkal Committee (Ministry of Human Resources Development 2014) objected to these provisions and recommended that learning outcomes are measured in schools, that 'performance-driven culture' is catalysed in the schools, and no-detention is implemented in a phased manner.[21] The Central Advisory Board on Education (CABE), the highest federal advisory body on education, recommended that the no-detention policy under the RTE be revoked.[22] The state of Rajasthan has proposed to amend the RTE Act to delete the no-detention clause in its application within the state.[23]

The second stream consists of issues and questions pertaining to the RTE Act that remain on the periphery and have not yet become part of the official agenda. Despite the backing of interest groups and civil society organisations, these issues have neither received serious attention and consideration of policy-makers, nor have they been at the forefront in the public discourse and media coverage. They continue to remain on the periphery as 'gaps' or agenda issues-in-waiting. For example, the definition of teacher and her status is not included in the RTE Act. In fact, it remains silent on who is a teacher, particularly with reference to her status and position within the school, the education system and effectively within society as a whole. Although it specifies the minimum qualifications that a teacher has to fulfil and the duties she is bound to perform, it does not deal with the differentiated working realities of elementary school teachers in India. The presence of various categories of teachers, referred to by different names, appointed by different authorities (both public and private), on different service terms and conditions, with different kinds of job requirements, has not been acknowledged by the RTE Act. The fact that the state governments are primarily responsible for decisions on teachers' service matters has been a convenient 'escape hatch' for the central government.

Another example is that of the rights of young children to early childhood care and education, which was debated during the formulation of the RTE Act, but was included only as a discretionary obligation of state governments. Since then, the issue has remained on the periphery despite advocacy groups demanding its inclusion through an amendment. Given that different parent ministries are responsible for school education and early childhood care and education, the matter has remained unresolved within the government itself. Similarly, lack of inter-ministerial coordination around child-related legislation, particularly children with disabilities, child labourers, children in need of care and protection, and children allegedly in conflict with the law, has pushed the right of education of these categories of children to the margins. Even though these categories together account for the majority of out-of-school children and hence deserve to be seen as primary beneficiaries of the right to education, the existing legal provisions are inadequate in addressing their actual needs. Another key matter that has seen state indifference is the establishment of effective mechanisms for grievance redress and monitoring. The local authorities and the Commissions for Protection of Child Rights at the central and state levels, although meant to dispense with cases and violations under the RTE Act through a more accessible administrative channel, have remained non-functional, thereby leaving the right-holders with the sole option of taking a judicial recourse. Given that such an option of approaching the High Court or Supreme Court is beyond the reach of those whose rights stand violated, the right remains largely unexercised by the primary right-holders.

The location of issues in either stream is not on account of their 'merit' in terms of how critical they are to the fulfilment of the objects of the RTE Act. On the other hand, they reflect the political process of balancing between the competing interests that continue to be determined by complex factors. In a democratic society, the constant shaping and re-shaping of public opinion and political preferences and the slow, iterative response of policies/legislation to such processes ensures that no change is drastic and unimplementable. The RTE Act, although appearing only as an aspirational piece of legislation, shows the way in which school reforms are headed.

Conclusion

The recognition of the right to education as a justiciable Fundamental Right is a milestone in the history of education in India because of its legal, political, and administrative significance. It has heralded a significant departure from the earlier colonial legislation in terms of the way in which 'free' and 'compulsory' have been understood and defined. This corresponds to the changing education scenario and emerging role of private actors in education provision, which the new legal regime tries to simultaneously accommodate and regulate. The process by which the right to education became a constitutional right and the ensuing enactment and implementation of the RTE Act manifest the underlying contestations and tensions. A selective surfacing of some of the issues on the official agenda, while sidelining other critical ones and the resulting reviews, revisions, and reimagination of the original legislative intent indicates that the RTE Act remains a constantly negotiated instrument. Lack of acknowledgement of the complexity of implementation and the resulting slow pace at which the legal provisions are interpreted and mediated at the local level could result in summarily dismissing the workability of specific legal provisions or the legislation itself. Given the significance of this Fundamental Right, there is a need to guard against any such premature dismissal of the established statutory norms.

Notes

1 AIR 1992 SC 1858.
2 (1993) 1 SCC 645.
3 For example, the South African Constitution, which provides for the right to basic education, including adult education.
4 The Compulsory Education Law of People's Republic of China (1986, revised in 2006) provides nine years of free and compulsory education and mandates the state to guarantee funds. The Japanese Constitution and the Basic Act on Education (2006) and the Basic Plan for Promotion of Education guarantee nine years of free and compulsory education. In the UK, the Education and Skills Act, 2008 was amended so as to guarantee state-provided free and compulsory education to children of 5–18 years.
5 See Article 2 of the International Covenant on Economic, Social and Cultural Rights, 1966 and the UN Committee on Economic, Social and Cultural Rights (CESCR), *General Comment No. 13: The Right to Education (Art. 13 of the Covenant)*, 8 December 1999, E/C.12/1999/10, available at: www.refworld.org/docid/4538838c22.html (accessed 27 October 2015).
6 The Performance Audit Report (Report no. 15 of 2006) of the Comptroller and Auditor General of India highlighted that

> the objective of SSA was to enroll all out of school children in school, education guarantee centres, alternate schools and back to school camps by 2003. The date was revised to 2005 only in March 2005. However, out of 3.40 crore children (as on 1 April 2001), 1.36 crore (40 per cent) children in the age group of 6–14 years remained out of school as on March 2005 four years after the implementation of the scheme and after having incurred an expenditure of Rs. 11133.57 crore.

> (Para. 7.3.2)

7 'Mission mode' refers to projects such as Sarva Shiksha Abhiyan that have clearly defined objectives, scope, implementation timelines and milestones, as well as measurable outcomes and service levels. These were donor-supported and were implemented by a structure that ran parallel to the state structure in terms of funding, accounting, and monitoring, but was run with members from the state education department and consultants.

8 *Society for Unaided Private Schools of Rajasthan v. Union of India* (2012) 6 SCC 1.

9 Article 19(1)(g) is a fundamental right which provides freedom to practise any profession, or to carry on any occupation, trade, or business.

10 Article 19(6) is a fundamental right which states that nothing provided for in Article 19(1)(g) can prevent the state from making any law imposing, in the interests of the general public, reasonable restrictions on the exercise of the right conferred by said subclause.

11 Nineteen states and Union Territories had legislation on free and compulsory education as per the 165th report of the Law Commission of India (para. 6.2). These were adopted between 1917 and 1995 and were loosely modelled on the Delhi Education Act, 1960 with some state-level variations. See also Juneja (2003) for a list of pre-Independence and post-Independence legislation on compulsory education.

12 Section 12(1)(c) provides that private schools should allocate 25 per cent of their seats starting Grade 1 or preschool, whichever is earlier, to children belonging to disadvantaged and economically weaker sections. This is supplemented by Section 12(2) which mandates state governments to compensate the private schools to the extent of per-child expenditure incurred by the state or the actual amount charged due to the child, whichever is less.

13 See Supreme Court decision in *P.A. Inamdar v. State of Maharasthra* decided on 12 August 2005 and reported in (2005) 6 SCC 537.

14 State amendment of a central legislation is possible within the framework of Article 254 of the Constitution. States can bring in an amendment as education is a concurrent subject, but they will have to seek the President's assent if it has to survive a challenge of repugnancy with the Central Law as per Article 254(2). If they don't seek the President's assent, the bill will be hit by Article 254(1) and can be challenged on grounds of repugnancy. The proviso of Article 254(2) allows Parliament to bring in legislation that can even repeal such a legislation brought by the state.

15 See *Pramati Educational & Cultural Trust v. Union of India* (2014) 8 SCC 1.

16 A large number of cases filed at the High Court level come from aggrieved candidates who are challenging the state decisions on eligibility criteria, relaxation of norms on pass percentage, declaration of results, and appointments.

17 As per Section 19 of the RTE Act, schools were given three years after the commencement of the Act to meet the infrastructure norms as specified under the Schedule of the Act.

18 As per Section 23(2) of the RTE Act, state governments were given five years after the commencement of the Act to put in place adequate teacher educational institutions in the state.

19 See *Pramati Educational & Cultural Trust v. Union of India*.

20 Rules notified by Gujarat and Kerala both refer to provision for independent periodic assessments to present school quality reports (Gujarat Rule 27 and Kerala Rules 7(i) and 20(3)). Gujarat allows schools seeking recognition to relax the infrastructure norms as long as they are able to demonstrate learning outcomes (Rule 15). Kerala only prescribes setting up of norms and standards on quality (Rule 7a).

21 Opinions of experts and politicians were divided on this crucial issue.

22 This recommendation was made during the 63rd meeting of the CABE held on 19 August 2015.

23 See The Right of Children to Free and Compulsory Education (Amendment Bill), 2015 (Bill no. 34 of 2015), introduced in the Rajasthan Legislative Assembly.

References

Annual Status of Education Report (ASER) 2014. New Delhi: ASER Centre (accessed at http://img.asercentre.org/docs/Publications/ASER%20Reports/ASER%202014/National%20PPTs/aser2014indiaenglish.pdf on 22 June 2015).

Dale, R. 1997. The state and governance of education: an analysis of the restructuring of the state–education relationship. In *Education: Culture, Economy, Society*, edited by A.H. Halsey, Hugh Lauder, Philip Brown, and Amy Stuart Wells. Oxford: Oxford University Press.

Government of India (n.d.) National Achievement Survey. (accessed at http://mhrd.gov.in/?q=nas on 22 June 2015).

Heymann, J., Raub, A., and Cassola, A. 2014. Constitutional rights to education and their relationship to national policy and school enrolment. *International Journal of Educational Development* 39: 131–141.

Inter-Agency Commission. 1990. World declaration on Education for All and framework for action to meet basic learning needs.

Juneja, N. 1997. Right of the Child to Education and issues in implementation of compulsory education: perceptions of education administrators. *New Frontiers in Education*, 27(1).

Juneja, N. 2003. Constitutional amendment to make education a fundamental right: issues for a follow-up legislation. Occasional Paper 33. New Delhi: NIEPA.

Kashyap, S.C. 1986. *Constitution Amendment in India*. New Delhi: Lok Sabha Secretariat.

Kumar, K. 1991. *Political Agenda of Education: a Study of Colonialist and Nationalist Ideas*. New Delhi: Sage Publications.

Law Commission of India. 1998. *165th Report on Free and Compulsory Education for Children*. New Delhi: Law Commission of India.

Mehendale, A. 2014. The question of 'quality' in education: does the RTE Act provide an answer? *Journal of International Co-operation in Education*, 16(2): 87–103.

Mehendale, A., Mukhopadhyay, R., and Namala, A. 2015. Right to Education and inclusion in private unaided schools. *Economic & Political Weekly*, 50(7): 43.

Ministry of Human Resources Development. 2010. Report of the Committee on Implementation of The Right of Children to Free and Compulsory Education Act, 2009 and the resultant revamp of Sarva Shiksha Abhiyan.

Ministry of Human Resources Development. 2014. Report of CABE Sub-Committee on Assessment and Implementation of CCE and No-Detention Provision (under RTE Act, 2009) (accessed at http://mhrd.gov.in/sites/upload_files/mhrd/files/document-reports/AssmntCCE.pdf on 15 October 2015).

National Commission for Protection of Child Rights (NCPCR). n.d. Eliminating corporal punishment in schools (accessed at www.ncpcr.gov.in/view_file.php?fid=108, on 15 October 2015).

Ramamurti, A. 1990. *Report of the Review Committee on the National Policy on Education 1986*. New Delhi: Government of India.

Sarin, A. and Gupta, S. 2014. Quotas under the Right to Education. *The Economic & Political Weekly*, 49(38): 65.

Supreme Court of India. 2008. Judgment, *Ashok Kumar Thakur v. Union of India*, 10 April.

Tilak, J.B.G. 1996. 'How free is free primary education in India'. *The Economic and Political Weekly*, 31(5): 355–366.

Tomasevski, K. 2006. *The State of the Right to Education Worldwide. Free or Fee: 2006 Global Report*. Copenhagen: n.p.

UN Committee on Economic, Social and Cultural Rights, *General Comment No. 11: Plans of Action for Primary Education (Art. 14 of the Covenant)*, 10 May 1999, E/1992/23 (accessed at www.refworld.org/docid/4538838c0.html on 1 June 2015).

Weiner, Myron. 1991. *The Child and the State in India: Child Labor and Education Policy in Comparative Perspective*. Princeton: Princeton University Press.

Wheare, K.C. 1966. *Modern Constitutions*. London: Oxford University Press.

2

Education in urban areas

Nalini Juneja

The urban population worldwide exceeded, for the first time, its rural population in 2009. In India, although only 27.8 per cent of the population is as yet 'urban', the growth of urban population also exceeded rural growth for the first time in the Indian Census of 2011. Theoretically this urban population is spread among 7,935 towns.[1] In reality, however, the distribution is 'top heavy' (Kundu 2014: 202), with about a quarter of the urbanites concentrated only in five 'mega' cities – Mumbai, Delhi, Kolkata, Chennai, and Bengaluru. The rest are distributed among towns and cities of varying sizes. Fifty-three of these cities are large enough, with populations exceeding one million, to be called metropolitan cities.

In India, urban areas are generally assumed to be well resourced and privileged – a logic which suggests that policy interventions might be more useful if focused on the *real* problems of education of those residing in villages. Any 'theory' of rural location of educational problems would soon find itself at odds when confronted with the enrolment data of urban schools (Table 2.1), showing that their share of enrolment in the private sector (comprising the aided, unaided and unrecognised) far exceeds enrolment in government ones. Among them, unaided schools have the largest share of both schools and enrolment, while the enrolment share of aided schools (18 per cent) is remarkable in comparison to their much lower share of schools (11 per cent).

Table 2.1 is also testimony to 'trouble in (the urban) paradise', for it shows that privately managed schools, which nationally constitute only 23 per cent of all schools in India,[2] constitute over 63 per cent of all schools in urban areas, and accommodate over 70 per cent of enrolment. In the 'believed-to-be-privileged' urban areas, government schools – which are the only ones providing free and accessible education to the poorest – are far fewer than fee-charging private schools, despite 26.4 per cent of the urban population (in 2011–12) estimated to be living below the poverty line (Rangarajan 2014: 5) and the presence of huge slum populations. According to the 2011 census, the slum population is estimated to be 41.3 per cent of all households in Mumbai; 29.6 per cent in Kolkata (Municipal Corporation (MC)); 28.5 per cent in Chennai (MC).

The Census information, along with Table 2.1, provides a glimpse of much that one might expect to see in cities in India – high population density, congestion, large numbers living in poverty, slums, a disproportionate ratio of free government schools to fee-charging private schools – and hence, inequity and disparity next to abundance for some.

Table 2.1 Elementary education: urban schools and enrolment 2014–15

Management	Schools	Enrolment
Government	83,320 (36.3%)	21,169,853 (29.8%)
Private aided	25,196 (11.0%)	12,793,024 (18.0%)
Private unaided	111,419 (48.5%)	35,489,823 (49.9%)
Others (Madrasas, recognised and unrecognised; unrecognised schools)	9,559 (4.2%)	1,655,665 (2.3%)
Total	229,494 (100%)	71,108,365 (100%)

Source: As on 30 September 2014. Table obtained by special request to DISE, NUEPA.

In order to understand the origin of some current issues in education belonging uniquely to the city in India, this chapter will take a brief look at the developmental history of Indian cities with a focus on education. From this perspective, in subsequent sections it will first attempt to present as inevitable the growing stratification among schools; it will then highlight the consequences of a unique and surviving pattern of education imposed on the 'presidency cities' during the British Raj; and finally, it will throw light on the effects of city master plans on the education scene and on the RTE Act of 2009. At the outset, however, this chapter attempts to clarify the terms 'urban schools' and 'urban education', which in American educational journals may carry a meaning rooted in the history of US cities, but are interpreted and used very differently in India and in this chapter.

'Urban education' (USA)

The terms 'urban schools' and 'urban education' carry different meanings in the USA and India. In the American context, reference is made to 'inner city schools' attended by children of the poorer sections, usually of 'colour' (a euphemism for African-Americans and Asians) and migrants, whereas the better schools attended by the socio-economically privileged usually lie outside the city 'in the suburbs'. In Indian cities, on the other hand, it is the poor who tend to live on the outskirts of cities in slums, while the so-called posh areas and the 'best' schools may be found in the heart of the city. These differences might be ascribed to the processes of urbanisation and to the funding pattern of schools in the USA.

Public schools in the USA were truly public in the way they served their local communities and, at least initially, were usually financed by voluntary contributions and later through local property taxes. 'This tradition had real advantages because many families were living in small, relatively isolated communities with similar standards of living' (Biddle and Berliner 2002: 49). With increasing urbanisation, people from these small communities moved to cities. When these cities became overcrowded, those who were well-off moved to the expanding suburbs and in doing so reduced the tax base of the cities. It was at this point, according to Biddle and Berliner, that the system developed faults:

> Parents who moved to affluent suburbs were generally willing to fund well-equipped, well-staffed public schools for their own children, but – familiar only with the tradition that public schools should be funded locally – they saw little reason to pay additional taxes to fund equivalent schools for the impoverished students left behind in city centres or rural towns.
>
> *(Biddle and Berliner 2002: 49)*

With those who were better-off moving to the more desirable living environments of the suburbs, the 'urban schools', as the schools in the cities came to be known, were left to serve neighbourhoods 'in which there were high concentrations of poverty ... accompanied by the concentration of undesirable conditions to which children were exposed, such as education failure, violence, crime, welfare dependency, and family disruption' (NCES 1996: 3).

Adding insult to injury as it were, 'children raised in these surroundings were labeled "deprived" or "disadvantaged" and ... depicted as requiring special educational interventions' (Rury and Mirel 1977: 61).

One may wonder if it is merely a coincidence that the term used in the Sarva Shiksha Abhiyan (SSA) for children needing special educational interventions in cities in India is 'urban deprived', whereas there is no corresponding label for children needing special interventions in rural areas.

Development of cities and education in India

The process of India's urbanisation differed from that of the West. Patel (2006) points out that cities were first developed by the colonial state, and later through the intervention of the independent nation state. Under the British Raj, caste and hierarchy in new forms were created when the traditionally landed elite became the propertied class in the new cities as well (Patel 2006). Thus cities like Calcutta, Bombay, and Madras 'became the prime cities which were also the seats of imported culture' (Das 1981: 54).

In the creation of these cities, the intention of the colonial rulers, according to Kundu (2014), was to provide high-quality civic amenities to themselves, to the elites linked to them, and to those who could afford high prices. Consequently 'public facilities were concentrated in towns and cities and were available to the privileged sections of the urban community with access to the rural population being negligible' (Kundu 2014: 194). Cities in India continue to have better social and physical infrastructure, including more educational facilities,

> as is reflected in a higher percentage of literate and educated persons in these cities and [they] are also able to attract educated migrants from all over the country seeking higher education or skilled employment in modern and capital-intensive activities that have grown significantly in recent years.
>
> *(Kundu 2014: 209)*

Schools, concentrated in urban areas, underwent an administrative change when the management of government schools, following the recommendation of the Indian Education Commission (1881–82), was transferred to district and municipal boards with the view that primary education of the masses should be the first charge in the care of the state, while all government secondary schools should be transferred to local, native management. Soon, under a system of grants-in-aid, the government devolved greater responsibility of the direct management of education by handing over its primary schools to municipalities and the secondary ones to private institutions in the urban areas. At that time, the large municipalities were those of the presidency cities of Bombay, Madras, and Calcutta.

From the presidency cities, this pattern of municipal primary followed by private-aided provisioning of secondary education spread to all municipal corporations in the provinces in which these cities were located, and continued thus even after Independence. For example, primary education first became a municipal function in the presidency city of Bombay, then in all other municipal corporations in the province of Bombay (which at one time included Gujarat); and ultimately after the reorganisation of states, this pattern continued in all municipal corporations in both Gujarat and Maharashtra, even though the arrangement outside of such cities was different. Thus, in some cities, the educational devolution to municipal corporations had been a reality for almost 100 years by the time primary education was devolved to rural local bodies.

After Independence, one of the features distinguishing cities as they evolved was the idea during the third plan period that their spatial development should be guided by a 'master plan'. The city master plans that evolved during this period created a rightful place, literally, for schools within the planned cities by providing for land allotments, virtually free of cost, for public purposes such as schools (Juneja 2005a).

Today, as will be seen in the sections that follow, these historical characteristics of cities continue to bear on education in the urban context in India.

Section I

Stratification

Despite the global trend towards the adoption of market-led ideas and growing popularity of private schools, Table 2.1, showing the share of private schools to be over 63 per cent of all urban schools in India and their enrolment share to be exceeding 70 per cent of all urban enrolment, does indeed generate concerns for equality and equity of educational opportunity, especially in cities where private schools are concentrated. Cities especially have seen increasing economic differentiation, linguistic dichotomisation, and segregation among schooling opportunities. In its largest cities, the variety of schools to be seen in India perhaps leaves behind almost every city in the world. The variation among schools has been oft described and commented upon by Juneja (2003, 2005a, 2010, 2014).

The type of school attended, and the medium of instruction, apart from being signifiers of status, have important implications for life outcomes, a fact well-recognised by 'the affluent and the middle class [who] had forsaken state-run schools in the 1960s and 1970s' (Farooqui 1998: 329), and increasingly by the poor seeking to enrol their children in one of the 'mushrooming private schools, aimed at the urban poor whose key selling point is often the provision of English as a medium of instruction' (Miller 2005: 115); or in an elite private school through admission by lottery under the quota reserved under Section 12(1)(c) of the RTE Act 2009.

English has been the language of power since colonial times; even now, with market forces and globalisation, since 'English functions as a major business tongue' (Nilekeni 2009: xii) and is seen as key to economic success and getting a good job; this trend, Miller (2005) notes, has continued and even been reinforced in post-colonial India, especially in large urban centres, as confirmed empirically by Munshi and Rosenzwieg (2006) in the city of Mumbai.

Private schools

Private schools can range from the large elite ones to unrecognised, low-fee ones in the bylanes. The elite schools, many set up before Independence, were once usually either missionary schools or the 'public schools' established in the colonial tradition to 'adapt the good things of British public school life and administration to the Indian ways of life' (Srivastava 2005: 3). In cities like Delhi, according to Farooqui (1998), even in the 1960s 'private enterprise in a key area like school education was a reality of life long before liberalisation became fashionable' (p. 328). Now, increasingly the most prestigious schools in cities tend to belong to national or even international chains of schools, and could even be affiliated to foreign boards such as the International Baccalaureate

(IB) and Cambridge International Examination (CIE). Such is the popularity of these international schools that their numbers have seen tenfold growth in the past decade (Panda 2015).

Low-fee private and unrecognised schools

Not all of the urban children attending private schools are enrolled in elite schools. Of late, a large number of new, non-elite, low-fee, and often unrecognised private schools have arisen in cities, towns, and even in rural areas to accommodate the demand that government schools cannot or do not meet. De et al. (2002), in a study conducted in three northern states, found that 117 (70 per cent) of the 167 unaided private schools that had come up in recent years were in urban areas, where 'in the last 10 years, no new government schools have been set up' (De et al. 2002: 5231). These schools served the less privileged sections of the population who were left with little choice because 'government schools are few in number and hard to find' (Noronha et al. 2005: 107). In urban areas especially, they held the government to blame for the spawn and spread of private schools:

> What children have today in these towns is a government primary system in which little investment is being made, in spite of the new demands of Education for All. Schools are dwindling in quantity and often in quality, ignoring the problems of constant inmigration to urban areas. It is no wonder that children are flocking to the new private cram schools.... All kinds of shoddy arrangements are flowering in the name of private schools.
>
> *(Noronha et al. 2005: 111)*

A study by Juneja (2001a) bears out the tardy pace of growth in government provisioning in cities. This study found that in Kanpur, over a four-year period, no new government school had come up although 80 new private schools had been established. Similarly, in Surat, 81 per cent, in Nagpur 70.6 per cent, and in Indore, 55 per cent of new schools were in the private sector.

A major attraction of these low-fee private schools is that they purport to teach in English as a medium of instruction; Noronha et al. (2005) report 'much imitation of elite private schools not only in belts and ties and benches but also in the teaching of English' (p. 105), a finding supported by other researchers on private schools in towns and cities across India (Miller 2005; Ohara 2012; Srivastava 2008; Tooley 2009; Tooley and Dixon 2003). Nilekeni (2009: xii) sees in the low-fee private schools an instrument 'for not just more choice, but also greater power'.

Although schools in India are 'non-profit' organisations, or at least by law they are supposed to be, efforts are reportedly underway to study how low-fee private schools catering to the city poor can function as tools of 'social capitalism'.[3] Research by Tooley and Dixon (2003) and Tooley (2009) made no secret of their profit motive and their search for a business model for use across India and in other developing countries. Similar research in other parts of India and advocacy of for-profit private schools for the poor through state-supported vouchers to enable children to access schools of their choice has also grown – a phenomenon perceived by Nambissan and Ball (2010) and Nambissan (2015) as part of organised attempts to 'institutionalise market principles in education' and to create 'pressure for legal changes for for-profit schooling and vouchers' (Nambissan and Ball 2010: 17).

As it is, about 4 per cent of urban schools were identified in Table 2.1 as 'unrecognised' – i.e. not registered by local authorities. (Madrasas are included in that category on account of their exemption from registration under the RTE Act 2009.) It is generally believed, however, that the number of unrecognised schools is far greater than officially estimated, and the fact that these schools are able to attract students further testifies to the ability of such schools to cater to demand not met by the government despite the RTE Act 2009.

'Quasi government' schools

Another category of schools identifying themselves neither as straight-forwardly 'government' nor plainly 'private' has emerged in the past few decades. These could be referred to as 'quasi-government' (Juneja 2010: 21) which, despite the availability of schools under the cantonment board and central government for children of transferable employees (these schools now increasingly being left to the patronage of lower ranks) were established by registered societies for children of 'officers' of the defence, police, and civil services.

Government schools and differentiation

The label 'government school' too can cover a broad range of schools, often in the same city. Of late, even government schools have been diversifying and differentiating hierarchically in an unconcealed mimicry of 'public' (elite private) ones. In Delhi, for example, 'Sarvodaya Vidya-layas' were created after the fashion of private whole schools with the justification of providing education from grades 1 to 12 'under one roof *as is being provided in the private public schools*'.[4] Then in 1996, 'In order to have at least some government schools, to begin with, having standards *comparable to those available in the so-called better public schools*',[5] the government provided one Rajkiya Pratibha Vidyalaya in each of the districts of the state to which children were admitted at primary by selection. The differential infrastructure, finances, clientele, and even the prestige enjoyed by these different types of government schools ensures they have little in common other than the label 'government school'.

Absence of a 'school map'

The presence and functioning of such a large and differentiated variety of schools each catering to a niche clientele inevitably precludes the possibility of the operation by educational authorities of a 'school map' which determines 'school zones' and restricts schooling choices, if any, to within these zones. Consequently, it is common in all towns and cities in India to find large numbers of children being ferried from one end of the city to the other in order to attend the school chosen by their parents, or as is more likely to be the case, the school to which they have been able to secure admission. 'It is not uncommon for children to daily traverse a distance of 50 kms to and from school' (Farooqui 1998: 328).

This large-scale movement of children has in turn given rise to yet another set of phenomena related uniquely to education in the city, namely the school transport lobby, road accidents, and toxic fumes causing lung diseases among children.

School transport lobby

According to a news report of Delhi (Bhatnagar 2013), an estimated 4,200 school buses are involved in the daily task of ferrying 1.6 million children, using enormous amounts of fuel and time. This does not include the numbers of children who use other means of transport such as public buses, vans, cars, taxis, autos, two wheelers, rickshaws, etc. to reach school – a task which 'often acquires greater significance than the activity related to actually imparting education and the charges for which far exceed tuition fees – which are by no means nominal in private schools' (Farooqui 1998: 328).

Road accidents

The costs of lack of operation of school catchment areas are not limited to time and money alone. According to the *Global Status Report on Road Safety 2013* (WHO 2014), India has the highest number of road accidents in the world. Most of these accidents happen in cities. Despite an estimated 30 per cent of accidents going unreported, the child traffic death rate in India is 4–5 times higher than in other developed nations; 41 per cent of child deaths every year are in transportation accidents (Mahajan 2014). These alarming statistics are despite the fact that these do not take into account injuries or cases in which death occurred a few days after the accident.

Toxic fumes and lung diseases

According to the WHO, 13 of the 20 most polluted cities in the world are in India, with Delhi being the worst among them (CSE 2014; WHO 2014). Children are at greater risk as their vital organs are not mature enough to deal with it, the worst affected being those who commute in unpacked (open) vehicles as they are more exposed to dust particles in the air. A recent report in 2015 on child lung health found that about 35 per cent of all school children tested across metropolitan cities in India fared badly in screening tests, indicating poor air quality across India ('Delhi's children have the weakest lungs' 2015).

Section II

Devolution of upper primary to the private sector

The pattern of provision of education can differ from that of the state in many cities. These cities are mainly those which owed their educational pattern to the 'presidency city' tradition – under which, as presented earlier, in addition to devolution of primary education to municipal bodies, post-primary education was similarly devolved to private schools with grant-in-aid from the government. Consequently in such cities, a transition[6] to the private-aided secondary schools was (and still is) required of all children for the completion of elementary education – now their fundamental right. It was neither noted nor studied until recently that such a pattern could be implicated in the large-scale decline of primary school enrolments in cities (Juneja 2005b, 2007).

The blocked chimney syndrome

Juneja (2001a; see Figure 2.1) noted in studies from nine metropolitan cities in a research project coordinated by her that trends of enrolment in government primary schools were positive in some cities (Delhi, Indore, Jaipur, Coimbatore, and Gwalior), but negative for the other cities (Mumbai, Nagpur, Surat, and Vadodara). These inconsistent growth trends defied conventional explanation such as of differential demographic growth.

History and serendipity led to the realisation that negative trends corresponded to the 'presidency city pattern' of 'municipal primary–private aided post primary' education, whereas in cities with a positive primary trend the secondary schools were run directly by the government

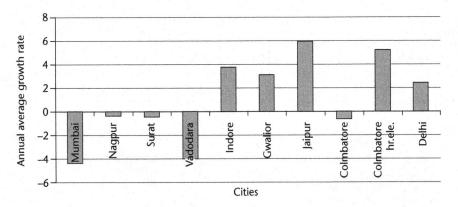

Figure 2.1 Government primary school enrolment trends in cities.
Source: Juneja 2001a.

and not devolved to the private sector. In the absence of state intervention to ensure access to subsidised private-aided secondary schools, children left free municipal schools for the fee-charging primary stage of aided secondary schools. A study of Calcutta (Nambissan 2003) also confirmed a much lower dropout rate among children in schools offering classes beyond the primary stage.

This phenomenon was termed by Juneja (2005b) as the 'Blocked Chimney Syndrome' (using the metaphor of smoke in a chimney, which tends to 'back flow' (dropout) if its upward path is blocked).

The city of Delhi, on the other hand, after a Delhi High Court Order in 2002 (CWP 4400/1997) has designated all municipal primary schools as 'feeder schools' to a 'parent' government secondary school within a neighbourhood admission plan. Now, every child completing grade five in a municipal school, knows she has a secured seat in grade six of a nearby state government secondary school.

However, despite the RTE Act 2009, there is still no such transition plan operational for children in the municipal schools of Mumbai, or other such cities where primary education has been devolved to the municipal corporations, even though the state continues to pay for secondary education in its aided schools. Kingdon (1996) had raised the issue of misplaced subsidies as early as 1996. Kamdar (2002) too had raised this question for, in a situation where the poor do not complete primary education, it also means that the poor do not benefit from subsidies to secondary and tertiary education.

Juneja (2011) conducted a study in Delhi and in Mumbai to find out whose education was being subsidised in private-aided schools if the poor are not able to take advantage of these (see Figure 2.2). In both of these cities, primary education is provided by municipal corporations but, as seen above, the Delhi government provided secondary education but, unlike Mumbai, had also instituted a transition plan. Data from 4,100 children in 42 secondary schools showed that the children in grade six in government secondary schools in Delhi (where a transition plan had been operationalised) came predominantly (almost 85 per cent) from its municipal schools where they had availed of free education. In Mumbai, however, instead of the imagined large-scale crossover of children from the municipal schools to the private-aided sector, less than 15 per cent in grade five (the first post-primary grade) came from municipal primary schools.

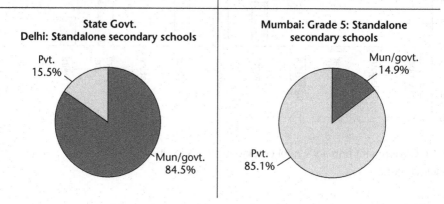

| Delhi: children from municipal schools constitute 84.5 per cent of enrolment in the post-primary grade of state-provided secondary schools. | Mumbai: children from municipal schools constitute less than 15 per cent of enrolment in post-primary grade of state-provided secondary schools. |

Figure 2.2 Children from municipal primary schools in Delhi and Mumbai in the lowest grade of state-provided secondary schools.

Source: Juneja 2011.

Section III

City master plans

City master plans are another distinct and historical feature of Indian cities. The first 'model' master plan of Delhi (1960) envisaged an egalitarian and an integrated society, as did the Educational Commission (1964–66), which had expected education to bring 'different social groups and classes together' (Educational Commission 1966: para 1.36).

The preparation and implementation of the 'model' master plan was supported by foreign experts, bylaws, and regulations for implementation (Das 1981; Shaw 1996; Wood 1958). The foreign professional planners, according to Shaw (1996: 225) had a distaste for congestion, crowded cities, and 'an obsession with order and homogeneity ..., [and a tendency] to erase slums because of their unsightly presence and the preference for low-density spread out cities'. Nevertheless, the demarcation of land for different planned activities created spaces also for schools – both government and private.

This section briefly touches upon issues in education arising out of such notions of legitimacy, and then goes on to a more recent bequest of master planning in India – Section 12(1)(c) of the RTE Act 2009, better known as the clause that sought to reduce educational segregation by making it mandatory for every private school to admit and give free education to 25 per cent of its enrolment from economically weaker sections and disadvantaged groups.

Land and privilege

Today, the spread of slums beyond planned city boundaries is calling into question the planning models borrowed from the West. As cities grew, they tended to become more segregated, and as seen in the previous section, so did the schools. Many schools in the heart of the city now occupy valuable real estate, while increasing land prices have relegated the poor that would attend the government schools in the cities to its peripheries. Even the SSA does not seem immune to the idea of the city as a legitimate space only for the privileged. Against all norms of holistic planning, the SSA 'city plan' appears to be an exercise not of mapping all educational provisioning in the city, but to devise innovative schemes for the education of those arbitrarily categorised as 'urban deprived', and therefore living not in 'the city' but in its slums and on the streets.

Slums, the poor, and education

While finding land for school sites poses a problem in cities, so does the problem of what to do with emptying schools in the heart of cities whose clientele has moved to cheaper housing on the city outskirts. On the other hand, classes become overcrowded in the few schools that come up on the fringes of the city, and teachers who normally come from a different socio-economic background are reluctant to be posted to new schools (Juneja 2001a).

In Delhi, Tsujita (2013) found schools to be situated outside slums, but all children from the same slums do not necessarily attend the same school, and hardly any children from slums attend private schools.

Banerji (2000), in her study of Mumbai slums, found that the 'non legal' nature of slum dwellings adds to the precariousness of existence for the poor and keeps children away from schools, while teachers are less than supportive of their problems. Even those who do attend schools often find no peaceful place to study because of constant noise and sounds (Desai 1989). Similar findings continue to be echoed in the work of Tsujita (2013) in relation to children living in slums; the work of Monika Banerjee (2014) in the context of the SSA and children of the urban poor; and of Ramachandran (2005), Mooij (2008), and Dalal (2015) in the context of teacher social distance and its manifestations in classroom situations.

Street children, children out of school

As if born of the city, some children are known as 'street children' and are a common sight even today in almost all cities in India. They are engaged in occupations such as rag picking, street vending, begging, and working in roadside repair shops and *dhabas* and in manufacturing units (Bhaskaran and Mehta 2011; Kaur and Javed 2015). Notoriously numerically underestimated, a recent study (Bhaskaran and Mehta 2011) found only 50,923 such children in Delhi. 'Street children' are not necessarily without families, nor do all of them live on the street. Typically these children, as found by Bhaskaran and Mehta (2011), are not even literate (50.5 per cent), although about one-fifth of them had had some formal education, while one-quarter had received some kind of non-formal education.

Exclusive 'colonies'

Despite the lofty ideals of master plans and education policies, 'planned' colonies and private schools in cities share in common the belief that neither are for the poor. An RTI supplication[7] in 2012 revealed, for example, in the case of Faridabad, one of the oldest planned cities in India, that across three planned 'sectors' for the privileged, the only school accessible for free to children of domestic servants and petty tradesmen who serviced the posh houses was a three-roomed dilapidated primary one about 3 km away, while all the school sites in the sectors had been given to fee-charging private schools.

Similarly, in a colony in Delhi with 12 elite private schools there was not a single municipal primary school to be found in any of the 'sectors' of the colony. One of the highest officers of the municipal corporation revealed under conditions of anonymity that they had indeed planned to set up municipal primary schools in the sectors, but the RWAs (Resident Welfare Associations) told them not to do so, for they did not want the presence of the children of the poorer sections of society causing 'disturbances' in their colony when none of 'their own' children would attend such schools. The municipal primary schools were finally set up only in the urban villages in that area.

School land/valuable real estate

A recent news report (Siddiqui 2015) tells of school land being grabbed in the outskirts of Kanpur by land mafia, of chopping down of trees in the yard, uprooting of swings in the playground, and intimidation of children and parents, resulting in the school having a deserted look as the children stay away in fear.

Another rare instance of documentation of diversion of school land for commercial ventures, as city land prices escalated, was reproduced by Verma (2004) in her blog, quoting from a booklet produced by activists protesting against closure of schools in the heart of Indore city:

> Well-attended and well-equipped schools have been closed down for merger in the name of 'rationalisation' in areas where, incidentally, massive commercial development is proposed. Commercialisation of school premises has been trumpeted as a necessary 'radical' way of raising resources for education, even as state allocations for the purpose have lapsed and earlier similar exercises have not ploughed profits back to schools. And for doing all this, the administration has won plaudits simply because it has 'opened 103 new schools' in the city's slums by writing 'school' in chalk on the door of each of the existing community halls.
>
> *(Verma 2004)*

From master plan to RTE Act: breaching the barriers of private schools

The city master plans, implemented by the urban development authority of the state, provided for the allotment of free land to educational institutions subject to terms and conditions specified in the land allotment letter (Juneja 2005a, 2007, 2014). One of these conditions was that schools receiving free land would admit and give free education to 25 per cent of their enrolment.

From the late 1960s until January 2004, although schools continued to obtain land, the existence of the conditional clause appeared to have been forgotten till the matter was brought up in a public interest litigation (PIL) in 2002.

The issue of cheating the poor out of the seats due to them being in private schools made newspaper headlines and ultimately influenced the insertion of a similar clause mandating inclusion of the poor into private schools all over India – see Section 12(i)(c) of The Right of Children to Free and Compulsory Education Act 2009. This clause in the national Act has evoked enormous research interest (Juneja 2014; Mehendale *et al.* 2015; Sarin and Gupta 2013).

Section IV

Researching the city

Research with an educational policy focus is limited; policy research on education in urban areas even more so. There could be at least three reasons for this. First, as mentioned at the beginning of this chapter, urban areas are generally assumed to be privileged, and not so much in need of research as the rural where the *real* problems in Indian education may be found.

Urban: not seen as a 'problem'

Support for the unassailability of such rationale comes from the exclusively rural focus of 'the state', as seen for example in the educational data presented through the official educational statistics system, 'DISE' – an acronym for District Information System for Education. This rural focus of DISE constitutes the second impediment to educational policy research in towns and cities. DISE, save for two separate publications on aggregated 'urban' and 'rural' educational data, disaggregates its sub-district data on its 'School Report Cards' site only by levels of rural habitation and rural administration, while ignoring their urban equivalents. Similarly, centrally sponsored educational schemes such as the DPEP and the SSA are 'district' focused. (Although the latter did concede an arbitrarily defined segment called 'urban deprived' as a component for funding within the district plan.)

Confusion between 'urban' and 'city/town' statistics

The average researcher, attempting to study *education in cities*, such as Indore, may find confusing the fact that the Census of India offers population statistics for the district using four different terms. There are data for 'Indore District', 'Indore District Urban', 'Indore Urban Agglomeration', and 'Indore (M.C.)' (Table 2.2; Figure 2.3).

'District urban' comprises the total population of all the towns of various sizes within Indore District, separated by rural areas – represented in Figure 2.3 by blobs of different sizes. The implications of this diagrammatic representation becomes meaningful when one realises that from the child's perspective, aggregating information for separate towns even within one district is of little value considering that for most children schools are accessible, or not, only within a 'local area' within easy access.

Lack of disaggregated educational data

The third problem is presented by the type of *educational* data available. According to the Census of India, 'Village or Town is recognised as the basic area of habitation. In all censuses throughout the world this dichotomy of Rural and Urban areas is recognised and the data are generally presented for the rural and urban areas separately.'[8] Official educational statistics (from DISE), on the other hand, publish educational data for national, state, and district levels only, while 'School Report Cards' data can be aggregated online for state, district, block, a special SSA

Table 2.2 Population Indore 2011

Indore population	2011
Indore District	3,276,697
Indore District Urban	2,427,709
Indore Urban Agglomeration	2,170,295
Indore (M.C.)	1,964,086

Source: www.census2011.co.in/census/metropolitan/242-indore.html.

Nalini Juneja

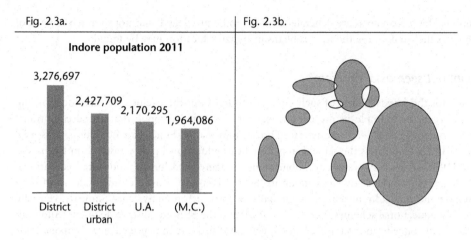

Figure 2.3 (a) Showing difference between populations of district, district urban, urban agglomeration, and municipal corporation areas. (b) Diagrammatical representation of
Indore District Urban comprising 11 towns.

Source: www.census2011.co.in/census/metropolitan/242-indore.html.

categorisation known as a 'cluster', and for the village level, but not for *urban* sub-district levels
such as towns and cities. Thus the official presentation of educational statistics in India permits
only the rural to be observed, while rendering towns and cities invisible.

Had data been readily available for towns and cities, 'the blocked chimney syndrome' that
could manifest itself in city data but is subsumed when aggregated with district data, might have
revealed itself much earlier.

Town-/city-specific data are important for use within districts. Private schools are concentrated in cities. For example, a study of Indore showed that while district educational statistics
revealed the share of government schools in Indore *district* to be 73 per cent, in Indore *city* the
share of government schools was only 33 per cent due to the greater concentration of private
schools (Juneja 2001b). The same study also found that there was little increase in the number
of government schools within the city, whereas at the district level government schools showed
a healthy growth in the same period.

Some districts in India are fully urban and could spell hope for the urban researcher.
Unfortunately, this hope is belied if trying to study Mumbai, comprising two fully urban
districts in the Census – Mumbai and Mumbai Suburban. For DISE, however, 'Mumbai
Suburban' is not a 'district' but a *code*, and contains data not of schools in the Mumbai subur-
ban area, but only of *municipal schools across both districts*. Similarly, for reasons best known to
itself (and kept to itself, for nowhere is this 'coding system' revealed), for DISE 'District
Mumbai' contains data of *private* schools, i.e. schools recognised by the State Directorate of
Education *in both districts*.

Thus, even the organisation of official educational statistics can put a spanner into the works
for educational policy research efforts in urban areas.

Conclusion

The vicious cycle of assumptions of 'all is well' in education in urban contexts diminishes the likelihood of research attention to towns and cities, and reinforces the disinclination to provide disaggregated urban educational data. This cycle impacts ultimately the availability of research on towns and cities, thus reinforcing and perpetuating the belief that all is indeed well in urban areas. Schooling problems are therefore believed to be negligible here except perhaps for problems of a segment known as the 'urban deprived' – already being ably addressed by the SSA.

However, as seen in this chapter, the concept of the 'urban deprived' is imported and ill-fitting when viewed in the historical context of educational development in cities under colonial rule in India – a policy path that continues to shape education in cities today. The remarkable diversity of schooling opportunities masks the disparity of availability, accessibility, and affordability of these schools, while contributing to stratification and inequity in education. The right to choice enjoyed only by some adds risk to children's lives and lungs due to accidents and toxic fumes caused in the process of mass transportation to schools at the far end of towns.

Devolution of responsibility for post-primary education to the private sector in presidency cities, under British rule (seen also as the first public–private partnership in education once grant-in-aid was instituted) continues, as seen in this chapter, to affect children's access to free primary education on the one hand, and the perception of municipal primary schools as failing on the other.

City master plans demarcated school spaces and made land available to schools, both government and private, in cities. Even so, lands and schools continue to be at risk due to tendencies towards segregation and greed, while forces which rose up to counter them gave birth to a revolutionary clause for inclusion of the poor and private schools in the 2009 historic legislation for the right to education in India and continue to be a beacon of hope in the neoliberal, privatised educational cityscape.

Notes

1 Analogous to 'village', which is the basic unit of rural habitation; 'town' is the basic unit of urban habitation. In terms of population, habitations having at least 5,000 inhabitants, living in densities of at least 400 persons per square kilometre with 75 per cent of males engaged in non-agricultural occupations may be classified as urban.

2 http://dise.in/Downloads/Trends-ElementaryEducation-2014-15/AllIndia.pdf.

3 A term said to have been used by Bill Gates to describe 'the use of the profit motive to solve social problems' (Ball et al. 2015: 22).

4 www.edudel.nic.in/welcome_folder/aboutdep.htm (accessed 19 April 2015).

5 Cabinet Note No. F.DE-15/Act/140/97 dated 27 March 1997 of the Government of National Capital Territory of Delhi (GNCTD), quoted in the High Court of Delhi CM No. 5202/2012 in W.P.(C) No. 7796/2011. http://delhicourts.nic.in/July12/Social%20Jurist%20Vs.%20govt.%20of%20NCT.pdf (accessed 19 April 2015).

6 The term *transition* is applied only for change of *stage* of education such as between the terminal stage of primary to the beginning of the upper primary stage; between the terminal stages of secondary to the beginning of the tertiary stage, etc. Thus it usually refers to movement of a whole class (i.e. cohorts) of children, or groups of children rather than one child. For this reason, 'transition' requires planning and monitoring in order to ensure successful transition at critical points such as between sub-cycles in elementary education, using indicators of transition such as 'Transition Rate'.

7 Appeal Case No. 5016 of 2012: letter No. RTI/13/357 dt.4.7.13.

8 http://censusindia.gov.in/Data_Products/Library/Indian_perceptive_link/Census_Terms_link/censusterms.html.

References

Ball, S., Junemann, C., and Santori, D. 2015. *Following policy: global educational policy networking the case of low fee private schools*. London: Institute of Education.

Banerjee, M. 2014. 'Elementary Education of the Urban Poor'. *The Economic & Political Weekly*, 49(37), 33.

Banerji, Rukmini. 2000. 'Poverty and Primary Schooling: Field Studies from Mumbai and Delhi'. *The Economic and Political Weekly*, 35(10), 795–802 (accessed on 12 September 2011 from www.jstor.org/stable/4408991).

Bhaskaran, R., and Mehta, B. 2011. *Surviving the streets: a census in Delhi*. New Delhi: Institute for Human Development and Save the Children.

Bhatnagar, Gaurav Vivek. 2013. 'School Bus Operators Threaten to go Off Delhi Roads from March'. *The Hindu*. 16 February (accessed on 5 May 2015 from http://m.thehindu.com/news/cities/Delhi/school-bus-operators-threaten-to-go-off-delhi-roads-from-march/article4421800.ece).

Biddle, B.J., and Berliner, D.C. 2002. 'Unequal School Funding in the United States'. *Educational Leadership*, 59(8), 48–59.

CSE. 2014. 'WHO Says India Ranks Among the World's Worst for its Polluted air. Out of the 20 Most Polluted Cities in the World, 13 are in India'. 8 May (accessed on 5 May 2015 from www.cseindia.org/content/who-says-india-ranks-among-world%E2%80%99s-worst-its-polluted-air-out-20-most-polluted-cities-world-).

Dalal, J. 2015. 'The Indelible Class Identity'. *The Economic & Political Weekly*, 50(8), 37.

Das, B. 1981. 'Urban Planning in India'. *Social Scientist*, 9(12), 53–67 (accessed on 5 May 2015 from www.jstor.org/stable/3517133).

De, A., Noronha, C., and Samson, M. 2002. 'Private Schools for Less Privileged'. *The Economic and Political Weekly*, 37(52), 5230–5236.

'Delhi's Children Have the Weakest Lungs as Compared to Kids from Other Metros'. 2015. *India Today*. 5 May (accessed on 6 May 2015 from http://indiatoday.intoday.in/story/delhi-pollution-children-air-weakest-lungs-metros/1/433663.html).

Desai, Armaity S. 1989. 'Education of the Child in Urban Slums: An Overview of Factors Affecting Learning and Responsive Action Through Social Work.' *The Indian Journal of Social Work*, 1(4).

Education Commission. 1966. *Education and Development: Report of the Education Commission 1964–66*. New Delhi: National Council of Educational Research and Training [Reprint 1971].

Farooqui, A. 1998. 'How the City Devours its Children'. *The Economic and Political Weekly*, 33(7), 328–330.

Juneja, N. 2001a. *Primary Education for All in the City of Mumbai, India: The Challenge set by Local Actors*. Paris: International Institute for Educational Planning.

Juneja, N. 2001b. *Metropolitan Cities in India and Education of the Poor: Case Studies of Education of the Poor in Ten Metropolitan Cities in India*. Research Report. NIEPA. (Mimeo).

Juneja, N. 2003. 'Education of the poor in metropolitan cities – an issue of concern'. *Perspectives in Education*, 19 (2); April 2003.

Juneja, N. 2005a. 'Exclusive Schools in Delhi: Their Land and the Law'. *The Economic and Political Weekly*, 40(33), 3685–3690.

Juneja, N. 2005b. 'Is a "Blocked Chimney" Impeding Access to Secondary Education in Some Cities and Inducing Dropout in Municipal Primary Schools?' Occasional Paper No. 35. National Institute of Educational Planning and Administration.

Juneja, N. 2007. 'Private Management and Public Responsibility of Education of the Poor: Concerns Raised by the "Blocked Chimney" Theory'. *Contemporary Education Dialogue*, 5(1), 7–27.

Juneja, N. 2010. 'Access to What? Access, Diversity and Participation in India's Schools' (accessed from www.create★rpc.org/publications/ptas/).

Juneja, N. 2011. *Report of a Study of Transition between Sub Cycles of Elementary Education in Diverse Contexts of Educational Administration*. Research Report. New Delhi: National University of Educational Planning and Administration. (Mimeo).

Juneja, N. 2014. 'India's New Mandate Against Economic Apartheid in Schools'. *Journal of International Cooperation in Education*, 16(2), 55–70.

Kamdar, Sangita. 2002. 'Grants in Aid in Secondary Education: The Case of Maharashtra'. Study sponsored by the National Institute of Educational Planning and Administration New Delhi, April 2002.

Kaur, S.K., and Javed, M. 2015. 'Profile of Activities Performed by Street Children in Ludhiana'. *Agricultural Research Journal*, 52(1), 84–88.

Kingdon, G.G. 1996. 'Private Schooling in India: Size, Nature, and Equity-Effects'. *The Economic and Political Weekly*, 31, 3306–3314.

Kundu, A. 2014. 'India's Sluggish Urbanisation and its Exclusionary Development'. In Gordon McGranahan and George Martine (eds) *Urban Growth in Emerging Economies: Lessons from the BRICS* (pp. 191–232). London: Routledge.

Mahajan, N. 2014. 'India Needs Tougher Road Safety Laws'. *Taaza Khabar News*. 7 February (accessed on 5 May 2015 from http://taazakhabarnews.blogspot.in/2014/02/india-needs-tougher-road-safety-laws.html).

Mehendale, A., Mukhopadhyay, R., and Namala, A. 2015. 'Right to Education and Inclusion in Private Aided Schools: An Exploratory Study in Bengaluru and Delhi'. *The Economic and Political Weekly*, 7, 43–51.

Miller, S. 2005. 'Language in Education: Are We Meeting the Needs of Linguistic Minorities in India'. In R. Banerji and S. Surianarian, *City Children, City Schools: Challenges of Universalising Elementary Education in Urban Areas* (pp. 114–138). New Delhi: Pratham Resource Centre/UNESCO.

Mooij, J. 2008. 'Primary Education, Teachers' Professionalism and Social Class: About Motivation and Demotivation of Government School Teachers in India'. *International Journal of Educational Development*, 28(5), 508–523.

Munshi, K., and Rosenzweig, M. 2006. 'Traditional Institutions Meet the Modern World: Caste, Gender and Schooling Choice in a Globalising Economy'. *American Economic Review*, 96(4), 1225–1252.

Nambissan, G.B. 2003. 'Educational Deprivation and Primary School Provision: A Study of Providers in the City of Calcutta'. IDS Working Paper No. 187. Institute of Development Studies.

Nambissan, G.B. 2015. 'Poverty, Markets and Elementary Education of the Poor'. TRG Poverty and Education Working Paper Series.

Nambissan, G.B., and Ball, S. 2010. 'Advocacy Networks, Choice and Private Schooling of the Poor in India'. *Global Networks*, 10(3).

NCES. 1996. *Urban Schools: The Challenge of Location and Poverty*. Washington, DC: NCES.

Nilekeni, N. 2009. 'Foreword'. In J.P. Tooley, *The Beautiful Tree*. New Delhi: Penguin.

Noronha, C., De, A., and Samson, M. 2005. 'The New Private Schools'. In R. Banerji, and S. Surianarain, *City Children, City Schools: Challenges of Universalising Elementary Education in Urban India* (pp. 95–113). New Delhi: Pratham Resource Centre/UNESCO.

Ohara, Y. 2012. 'Examining the Legitimacy of Unrecognised Low-Fee Private Schools in India: Comparing Different Perspectives'. *Compare*, 42(1), 69–90.

Panda, Pranati. 2015. *A Study of International Schools in India*. Research Report. New Delhi: National University of Educational Planning and Administration. (Mimeo).

Patel, S. 2006. 'Urban Studies: An Exploration in Theory and Practices'. In S. Patel and K. Deb (eds), *Urban Studies Reader in Sociology and Social Anthropology*. Delhi: Oxford.

Ramachandran, V. 2005. 'Why School Teachers are Demotivated and Disheartened'. *The Economic and Political Weekly*, 40, 2141–2144.

Rangarajan, C. 2014. *Report of the Expert Group to Review the Methodology for Measurement of Poverty*. Planning Commission. New Delhi: Government of India.

Rury, J.L., and Mirel, J.E. 1977. 'Political Economy of Urban Education'. *Review of Research in Education*, 22, 49–110.

Sarin, A., and Gupta, S. 2013. *Quotas Under RTE: Leading Towards an Egalitarian Education System?* Ahmedabad: Indian Institute of Management.

Shaw, A. 1996. 'Urban Policy in Post-Independent India: An Appraisal'. *The Economic and Political Weekly*, 31(4), 224–228.

Siddiqui, F.R. 2015. 'Kanpur Land Sharks Grab School Land'. *The Times of India*, 21 February (accessed on 27 March 2015 from http://timesofindia.indiatimes.com/city/kanpur/Kanpur-land-sharks-grab-school-land/articleshow/46316063.cms).

Srivastava, P. 2008. 'The Shadow Institutional Framework: Towards a New Institutional Understanding of an Emerging Model of Private Schooling in India'. *Research Papers in Education*, 23(4), 451–475.

Srivastava, S. 2005. *Constructing Post-Colonial India: National Character and the Doon School*. New Delhi: Routledge.

Tooley, J. 2009. *The Beautiful Tree: A Personal Journey into how the World's Poorest People are Educating Themselves*. New Delhi: Penguin.

Tooley, J., and Dixon, P. 2003. *Private Schools for the Poor: A Case Study from India*. Reading: Centre for British Teachers.

Tsujita, Y. 2013. 'Factors That Prevent Children from Gaining Access to Schooling: A Study of Delhi Slum Households'. *International Journal of Educational Development*, 33(4), 348–357.

Verma, Gita, D. 2004. *Indore Zila Sarkar's Interventions in School Education: Betraying Our Children in the Name of Decentralization and Universalization of Education.* New Delhi: Architexturez Imprints (accessed on 5 May 2015 from http://architexturez.net/doc/az-cf-21855).

WHO. 2014. 'Air Quality Deteriorating in Many of the World's Cities' (accessed on 5 May 2015 from www.who.int/mediacentre/news/releases/2014/air-quality/en/).

Wood, J. 1958. 'Development of Urban and Regional Planning in India'. *Land Economics*, 34 (4), 310–315.

3

Institutional diversity and quality

Padma M. Sarangapani

The research and discussion on quality in Indian education has been disproportionately shaped by the government vs private school war and focused on primary schools for the 'poor'. We have little or no formal knowledge of the vast and growing private sector of schools. A few surveys conducted on schools that cater to the middle class segment, such as the ones carried out by magazines like *Education World* and *India Today* from time to time are more in the nature of being marketing exercises of quality reputation, and are based on self-reporting and perceptions, which reveal more about what the middle-class values in its schools. In contrast, key studies on schools catering to the lower socio-economic segment that have informed our understanding of this sector have either taken learning outcomes and parental choice or else have chosen a few input parameters as metrics and proxies of quality (see, for example, Centre for Civil Society 2015; Jalan and Panda 2010; Karopady 2014; Mehrotra 2005; Tooley *et al.* 2007). These studies tend to 'plug into' and add grist to the government vs private schools war with assumptions on how quality is produced by the state (bureaucracy) vs the market, highlighting features such as teachers' accountability and cost efficiency/value for money or what is to be valued as an education outcome.

For the moment let us set aside the effects these studies intend to have on the government vs private schools for the poor debate, and take the findings of the studies at face value. What we have are segmented and partial pictures that do not tessellate to cover the landscape – we are not able to understand the schools as a part of a societal ecosystem within which they function in relation to each other. This partial picture of the landscape allows stereotypes to persist which draw on and reify prejudices regarding the culture of schools, of teachers and their work (see, for example, Centre for Civil Society 2015). Apart from anecdotal personal knowledge, we don't know of the types of institutions that exist, how diverse they are, and if this diversity is of any educational consequence in terms of meriting attention and explanation or having an explanatory potential. We have little comprehensive knowledge on what their education qualities are, or what diversity exists in 'quality' and why. We don't know who goes where or what kinds of teaching take place in different settings. We don't know what typology may be most useful to characterise and explain the diversity of quality, and how these qualities are produced and maintained.

In this chapter I propose answers to some of these questions through an analysis of data that was gathered in a survey of *all* schools in one education block of the city of Hyderabad, Telangana (Sarangapani *et al.* 2013; forthcoming). The survey was designed to gather data collected by trained education researchers on every single school in the block. The block was selected as it had a demographic range from slum areas to upper middle-class localities, and a relatively high concentration of schools of all types including aided, private, government (Telugu and Urdu medium) and madrasas (according to DISE[1]). The survey design was aimed at understanding the school: management and finances, clientele, and 'quality'.

The concept of 'quality' was operationalised as a 'master concept' following the works of Naik (1975) and Winch (1996). Elsewhere I have noted how their construction and commentary on 'quality', although set apart by close to 30 years, in different social and historical milieu, and in response to different issues, are remarkably similar in scope (Sarangapani, unpublished note). Based on this work we developed the concept of quality as having six dimensions that need assessment and comment in order to be able to judge and compare quality of education of schools in a public school system. The six dimensions that enable a comprehensive understanding of quality when taken together include (1) aims and relevance; (2) provisioning (infrastructure and staffing); (3) curriculum; (4) pedagogy; (5) standards and outcomes; and (6) efficiency and accountability. In this chapter I will be examining school diversity through the lens of aims and pedagogy.

The city of Hyderabad and Block A

The city of Hyderabad, with a 400-year history, has become well known in education and development literature through the studies of James Tooley, who has written extensively and appreciatively of the low-fee-paying schools that cater to the poor, particularly in the Muslim-dominated parts of the old city (see for example, Tooley and Dixon 2003; Tooley *et al.* 2007). About 30 per cent of the city's population is Muslim, with Urdu as its mother tongue.[2] From 2003 onwards Tooley conducted a series of studies and surveys through which he claimed to have gathered evidence that private schools for the poor fared better than government ones, even if the private schools were not recognised. Such schools, it is being claimed, produce better value for money than the government schools on account of the market discipline that makes them oriented to meeting parents' expectations for quality and keeping the wages of teachers low (Tooley 2009).

In 2003, when Tooley began his work in the city, Hyderabad had already disproportionately benefited from about ten years of an IT-savvy chief minister who was able to draw several IT businesses into the city, convey a climate of receptivity to business, corporate houses and the World Bank, and deregulate services such as health and school education (Mooij 2003). The 1993 School Regulation Act[3] deregulated salary fixation for teachers, requiring only that a private unaided school must earmark 50 per cent of its income for staff salary and an additional 15 per cent for the Provident Fund and health insurance. The state already had a booming, successful chain of coaching classes training students for a range of competitive examinations involving science and mathematics, engineering, medicine, and pharmacology, etc. From 1993 onwards, many of these institutions had re-invented themselves as schools. At the time of our survey, the city had several such chain 'corporate schools' – which typically admitted students in middle school and combined state board studies with high-intensity study of mathematics and science problem-solving and speed-oriented coaching.

Mandal 'A' (Figure 3.1) is known by a busy retail commercial hub nestled in it. A few arterial roads run through the Mandal, connecting the centre of Hyderabad city to an industrial estate, to new development to the north, and to the city of Secunderabad to the north-east. The area includes a range of socio-economic groups from upper middle classes – professional, bureaucrats, and police etc. – to lower middle class, working class and a few slums with migrants from

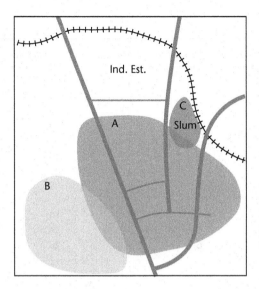

Figure 3.1 Sketch of Block A.
Source: rough sketch (not to scale) by author.

North Telangana. Sections of the population include old residents of the city, Muslim and Dalit-Christian residential areas, and also newer migrant communities from diverse linguistic and regional backgrounds.

Driving through these roads it is difficult to miss the schools and coaching and tuition centres amidst the shops and restaurants, all crowded along the main roads. With their brightly coloured walls and hoardings advertising the school's name with photographs of their top student ranks from the most recent class X examinations, the schools seem to have positioned themselves so that they can catch the eyes of passers-by, like any shop selling its wares in the marketplace.

Between July and October 2011, 84 schools were identified and surveyed by a group of 12 trained researchers, using tools developed for this purpose. This chapter presents findings from the survey in three parts. In the first part, the schools are introduced. In the second, the 'education market' is introduced based on a discussion of the management and the clientele of the schools. The third part discusses quality, drawing on findings pertaining to 'aims' and 'pedagogies' of these schools.

An introduction to school diversity

Of the 84 schools surveyed (see Table 3.1), 71 were in Mandal A. Additionally, eight schools (including six unrecognised) were in the areas between Mandal A and B and of uncertain jurisdiction, and five were in a large slum area bordering Mandal A.

Conventionally used typology – Government, Aided, Private Unaided Recognised, Private Unaided Unrecognised, and Madrasa – reflects first the 'ownership' of the school, i.e. its key management/decision making – government or private/non-government – and second the core financing of the school – government funded or not receiving government funds/supported directly.[4] This categorisation is useful for a majority of government purposes around financing and regulation. Literature discussing school quality has tended to follow this categorisation. The main effect of this categorisation is that only funding and regulation emerge as the key (explanatory)

Table 3.1 Schools surveyed

Management type and funding	Mandal A	Mandal A/B	Mandal C	Grand total
Government	8		1	9
Aided	5			5
Government aided	3			3
Government aid and charities (religious mission/CSR/grants)	2			2
Private unaided recognised	45	2	1	48
Charities (religious mission/CSR/grants)			1	1
Fees and charities (religious mission/CSR/grants)	2	1		3
High-fee-based	10			10
Low-fee-based	33	1		34
Private unaided unrecognised	12	6	2	20
Charities (religious mission/CSR/grants)	1		1	2
Fees and charities (religious mission/CSR/grants)	1		1	
High-fee-based	6			6
Low-fee-based	5	5	1	11
Madrasa (unrecognised)	1		1	2
Grand total	71	8	5	84

Source: data for all tables in this chapter are compiled by the author.

variables when comparisons between schools are made. This is convenient for neoliberal institutional theorisation of the school, which approaches school functioning with the assumption that 'accountability' and 'value for money/cost optimisation' are adequate to explain what schools do or don't do, what they do well or do poorly and which schools 'succeed' or 'fail'. In what follows, I introduce the 84 schools, drawing attention to additional distinctions that bring to the fore characteristics that give a more differentiated sense of the educational range and types of schools.

The nine government schools included six primary and three high schools (grades six to ten). Of the five aided schools, three were managed by religious trusts.

There were a total of 48 private recognised schools: ten were high-fee charging, 33 were low-fee charging, three included support from charities along with their fee and one was CSR (corporate social responsibility) funded. There were 20 private unrecognised schools of which two ran on charities, one had a combination of fee and charities, six were high-fee charging, and 11 were low-fee charging. Two madrasas, both unrecognised, were funded fully by religious charity. Of the schools that were run by a combination of fee and charity, two in Mandal A were partially supported by religious missions. Three others (of which two were not recognised) were special schools – dealing with impairments and with learning difficulty.

Fifty-five per cent of schools could be accessed and studied with great ease, accepting us at face value or after seeing our official letters; 19 per cent required an official introduction by the Mandal officers; 15 per cent of schools, even after such an introduction and a great deal of time, were obstructionist and gave us limited access or made access difficult and took up a lot of time and repeated visits; 11 per cent obstructed our entry through various tactics of excuses, delay, rudeness and in a few cases point blank refusal. In the case of the Central Board of Secondary Education (CBSE) affiliated schools, the Mandal Education Officers said they were helpless;

these elite schools refused to deal with the local education authorities, claiming that their affiliation to the CBSE gave them this immunity.

The schools were unevenly spread over the area of the Mandal – in what seemed to be related to their potential clientele base; 57 per cent of the schools were located in residential areas; 33 per cent in commercial areas; and 7 per cent in slums. The schools along the main road seemed to be vying for attention from passers-by.

The schools were established in the block from the 1930s onwards. The oldest schools in the area were two for girls, established by a Hindu reformist mission in the 1930s with the aim of promoting girls' education in the memory of the daughter of a founding trustee. Both of these, after Independence, became aided schools. One, however, closed down the previous year, and the other continued under a new related 'Marwari women's trust' that had expanded to vocational training, a pre-university (PU) college for girls, and had recently also established a fee-paying English-medium school for low-income children in the same premises. Between the 1950s and 1970s, most schools in this Mandal were government and government-aided ones. After the 1980s, no new government or government-aided schools were added to the Mandal. Instead there was a rapid expansion of private ones, with as many as 16 from the 1980s and growing at a steady rate, with over ten being added each decade. In the year of our survey as many as seven new schools were added to the Mandal, of which six were 'high-fee paying'. The emergence of relatively more high-fee-based schools from 2010 onwards was indicative of the new and changing aspirations of the residents of the area.

A few new primary government schools were added in the decade of the 2000s under the Sarva Shiksha Abhiyan Mission (SSA) in the slum areas of the block. A number of low-fee-based private unrecognised schools at the time of the survey were in existence from the 1980s onwards.

Ninety-three per cent of the schools were *coeducational*. One Madrasa was only for boys and one had segregated classes for boys and girls. The other coed segregated school was also one based on Islamic faith values. The other three girls-only schools were all run by religious missions (two by a convent). In all the coed schools, boys and girls were seated in separate sections of the class. One recognised school and three unrecognised schools catered to children with *special needs*.

English-medium education was offered in 90 per cent of the schools – 100 per cent of the private recognised schools and 90 per cent of the unrecognised private schools were all English-medium only. Additionally, eight of the nine government schools offered English-medium teaching in addition to Telugu- and Urdu-medium teaching. This was following a recent government policy decision. The teachers told us that admission into the English-medium section was based on parental choice. We found equal class strengths in both English- and Telugu-medium sections of the schools. The teachers told us that there were parents who had decided against English medium as they felt that they may not be able to cope with its needs. Aided schools were required to be only Telugu medium. The management of three of these five aided Telugu-medium schools had also begun an English-medium fee-paying branch. *There were only four other schools that were not English medium – all funded by charities.* Two of these were Urdu madrasas, one Telugu-medium school was an evening school centre funded by a Christian mission, while another Telugu-medium school was a Shishu Mandir, affiliated to the RSS and funded by a Hindu mission for whom education in the mother tongue was an ideological choice.

The *sizes of the schools* varied widely, from fewer than 50 students (five schools) to very large schools with 2,000–3,000 students (one school). Twenty per cent of schools that were surveyed had enrolments of fewer than 100 (35 per cent with enrolments of fewer than 150). These small schools are of interest as the small size raises questions about their stability. About 20 per cent of schools in the area had enrolments between 150 and 400. *An enrolment of about 400 seemed to be a 'tipping' number for stability*, giving an average class size of 33 in 12 levels starting from pre-school to class X. Thirty-eight per cent had enrolments of more than 400, with three schools being very large with enrolments of more than 1,500.

Based on the reports of the heads of these schools, their enrolment trends were noted: in 15 per cent the enrolment was growing and the institutions were sought after and well established. Forty-two per cent were steady; 25 per cent were struggling to keep their enrolment intact and to survive with regular fee collection; 14 per cent were shrinking and steadily losing their clientele.

Seventy per cent were neighbourhood schools drawing their catchment from surrounding areas; this included all the low-fee-paying schools. About 15 per cent drew children from a wider area and ran school buses and vans. Eleven per cent of schools, almost all from the high-fee-paying group, drew their clientele from the entire city. One exceptional case was that of a high-fee-paying school whose catchment was largely the neighbourhood and area. This had been established by a reputable and charismatic maths and science teacher who had become very successful and had built up a reputation for the school – it was among the older private schools of the area and had secured the patronage of established professionals living there. The special school and its unrecognised branch centre drew clientele from very far, clearly on account of the exclusive service they provided.

Forty-nine of the 84 schools (58 per cent) had the full range of levels from pre-primary to secondary school. All of the private recognised schools except for three followed this model, with pre-primary also being the key stage for admissions. The three exceptions had only upper primary and secondary (i.e. classes VI to X) and were among the 'coaching type' schools with a focus on class X exam results in mathematics and science. The government and aided schools did not have a pre-primary grade and were from class I onwards. Three primary government schools included a pre-primary cohort; this group sat in the corridor and was minded by a teacher funded by an NGO. (This enrolment has not been included in the figures). The government high schools were from grade VI to X. Urdu sections in particular in the government school were multigraded, with only two teachers for classes I to V.

Twenty-eight were classed as 'small schools' with an enrolment of fewer than 150. Of these, 17 were low-fee-based, of which seven were recognised and the remaining ten were unrecognised (accounting for 90 per cent of all unrecognised low-fee-based schools). In other words, low-fee-based, unrecognised schools in the area were very small (average enrolment fewer than 100). Twenty-one out of the 29 small schools (with enrolments fewer than 150) were found to be struggling to survive or with shrinking enrolments – this included all 17 small low-fee-based schools. The only small schools that were steady or even growing were the ones that were government funded or which had the support of charities. Aided schools, which had not secured any other source of funding, were struggling and shrinking.

Fifteen of these small schools which were running on fees had children in a range of grades – all the way from PP till secondary school. The class cohorts were not mono-graded; there were not enough students or teachers for this. These schools had multigraded classes: a teacher would be surrounded by students from different grades sitting in groups, who she taught, rather than tutored, by turns.

The education market: school management and their clientele

The government schools in the Mandal were all under the District Education Officer (DEO) of Hyderabad and managed by the systems of the DEO. On a day-to-day basis they were under the supervision of the Block Education Officer, who had an office in the campus of one of the government schools of the block. Each school had a headmistress (HM; primary school) or principal (high school) who was appointed to this post, or the acting HM who was from among the senior most teachers of the school. All other recognised schools that were not directly under the Department of Education were required legally to be under the management of a trust or society with education in its mandate. This included the aided institutions and the fee- or non-fee-paying institutions. However, in reality many schools were not managed by collectives of trustees or office bearers, but by individuals or families. Some were created by and managed in the style of 'corporates'. Schools were legally required to be 'not-for-profit', but understandably for all schools, finances were important. Fee-based schools had to be more concerned about *fixing the level of the fee as well as ensuring the regularity of monthly collection* as the fee was the only source to finance various expenses of the school. For non-fee-based schools also, managing with the available resources was a concern, because the loss of all clientele would lead to closure of the institution – an undesirable eventuality for those whose livelihoods depended on it. However, in addition to finances, there were other considerations that were also found to inform each institution's educational ideals and the design of its offerings and provisions – i.e. its unique academic identity and the qualities of the education it offered.

Managements

In addition to the Department of Education, ten distinctive types of private management forms were identified which were found to be useful in understanding aspects of the financing, academic identity, and education qualities of schools (Table 3.2). *Each of these management forms represented a distinct education ideology – defining their purpose in being in education and their educational imagination and their intentions. Inherent was also an imagination of their clientele – as representing either*

Table 3.2 Types of management

	Type of management	Classification	Total number	Break-down
1	Department of Education (District Education Office)	Government	9	
2	Corporate social responsibility (CSR) trust	CSR philanthropy	1	
3	Non-government organisation (NGO)	NGO or expert specialised group	2	
4	Charity (linked to religious group)	Religious organisations	12	1
5	Mission (religious – Hindu, Christian, Islamic)			5
6	Religious trust			6
7	Family trust	Family trusts	7	
8	Teacher entrepreneur	Individual entrepreneurs	41	19
9	Tuition teacher–entrepreneur			5
10	Entrepreneur			17
11	Corporate	Corporates	12	
	Total		84	

a particular community (socio-economic ('poor' and in need of charity) and/or religion) which they wished to serve and/or a particular economic group defined by the amount and regularity with which they would be able to pay a fee.

The 12 corporate management schools in the Mandal were all branches of statewide chains (in two cases nationwide), and were known for competitive examination coaching. Corporate management was characterised by hierarchical control in matters such as teacher appointments, curriculum, textbook selection, assessment and reporting, and even daily lesson plans, across all branches from the central control office. New corporate schools were professionally run, while old corporate schools used family to extend and keep control of finances, fee collection, and parent relations. There were three such family-based corporates in the block. The professionally managed groups had refined their 'product' beyond engineering competitive exams towards higher-level aspirations in the competitive coaching space – oriented to very high-stakes competitive examinations such as the IIT entrance, private 'Olympiads', and a global competitive world. These institutions used IT in their management more intensively.

Family trust-run schools were among the oldest in the area. Some of these institutions had been started by individuals with close involvement in the national movement and who regarded education as important in developing their communities – Muslim, Hindu, and Dalit-Christian. They had been active in local politics, and began these institutions at a time when there were few schools in the area. Two family trust schools were relatively new and established in the 1980s, and both had grown into successful large schools, one of which was CBSE affiliated and had a strong Hindutva character. Most of these older family trust schools were now managed by the second generation of the families and also included some family members who had qualified as teachers and were active in teaching and managing the schools as head. If not, the families kept direct control of the school through their presence on a daily basis.

Fifty per cent of all schools (61 per cent of all fee-based) were started as *entrepreneurial ventures*. Almost all of the entrepreneurial schools were low-fee-based. Nineteen (i.e. 23 per cent of all schools) were by *teacher-entrepreneurs*. Typically they had started their career as teachers in the same local area and had decided to set up their own school. They frequently cited the desire 'not to work for someone else and to be independent' as the key motivation for this move. Eight of these teachers had established their reputation as maths and science tutors at the time they took this leap. Having an established tuition clientele seems to have given them the confidence that they could run their own establishment. Four of these teacher-entrepreneurs were women who had decided to establish their own school so that they could run it according to their education ideals. Eight of the schools started by teachers were stable, having achieved a size of 400 pupils or more.

Schools that had been established by *tuition teachers* and *business-entrepreneurs* tended to cater to the lowest socio-economic groups (mostly groups 4 and 5). Such schools tended to be very small and were run like home tutorials. Seventeen such schools were started as businesses by entrepreneurs, including three women. Most opted for the school business on the advice of family and friends, thinking it would be easy for them to establish and run, and because they had an apartment or house as an initial investment. One had seen an advertisement for a school for sale in the newspaper and had decided to buy it. There were at least seven such cases of the school registration and recognition having been bought by the current management. A few entrepreneurs held more than one school registration, but ran only one school, leading to anomalies between the DISE record and reality on the ground. In the low-fee-charging group, 19 were managed by families – husband-and-wife teams who had to run the school like a family enterprise in order to manage funds and make ends meet. They struggled as they could not raise the fee too much and at the same time had to collect it regularly from parents. Some reported that when parents could not afford the fee any more, they simply stopped sending their child to the school and sought admission elsewhere.

A total of 28 schools in the Mandal had distinctive religious affiliations and to varying degrees incorporated religious instruction directly into the curriculum. At the very least they included religious prayers at assembly and had displays of religious symbols prominent in the school. These included Christian, Islamic, and Hindu religions.

Twelve of these schools had *religious purposes and ideals*. These institutions drew from religion and connection. For 11 of these their own religious community was their primary focus. Only one Christian charity served the poorest of the poor working children through an evening school. Five institutions were directly under a religious mission – a Christian convent, mosque (madrasa), and the RSS (Saraswati Shishu Mandir); these institutions had a religious purpose and offered religious instruction along with formal schooling. One of the two madrasas provided only religious instruction. The teachers of the madrasa schools, the charity school, and the Shishu Mandir (all very small unrecognised ones) were inspired by their religious ideology to work for the local poorest of the poor of their community. The two Christian convent schools had minority status. Six schools were run by religious trusts. These aimed to offer modern schooling, but drawing on and informed by faith – Hindu and Islamic – in their educational ideals. These institutions were thus deeply committed to serving their religious constituency and community through education. Religion was also evident in as many as 16 of the entrepreneur-run schools: four had a Christian affiliation, five had Islamic affiliation, and one was linked to a gurudwara. Six had Hindu affiliation: in two, students were even expected to participate in *pujas* that were held in the school, and one of them actively discouraged Muslim parents from admitting their wards to his school, saying that this enabled him to appeal to Hindu parents.

There was a professionally run non-fee-paying school run by a CSR-funded trust with a non-religious approach to working with the poorest of the poor. This school had many branches all over the city. There were two 'NGO' special schools – so designated as it was a specialised expert group offering education to children with a disability. These schools were run by an expert who raised funds and research grants from numerous sources and involved parents of the children and volunteers in running the school.

As can be seen from the above description, the niche occupied by the school was a combination of considerations of relevance to a particular clientele group (its needs and aspirations) and extent of dependency on fee, in turn leading an assessment of ability to pay, and being able to pay regularly. To convey relevance and desirability, a range of considerations were invoked or cultivated involving school financing and client–vendor relationship management: being English medium; being a known successful neighbourhood tutor with a reputation; being an institution with an association with a religion; offering maths and science competitive exam preparation; offering special education; or serving to enable children to pass.

Clientele

The socio-economic characteristics of the clientele were constructed based on detailed accounts of management on the occupations of the parents. Five groups were constructed based on these occupations: Group 1 comprised professionals, doctors, bankers, IT professionals, and government administrators; Group 2 comprised small businessmen, lawyers, and shop and hotel owners; Group 3 comprised clerks, teachers, accountants, and electricians; Group 4 comprised domestic workers, watchmen, auto-drivers, fruit vendors, bakery workers, carpenters, and mechanics; Group 5 comprised rag pickers and scavengers. Group 5 represented the poorest of the poor in the area, and included migrants from Dalit communities with 'polluting' occupations and extremely poor Muslim families living in slum areas surrounding a mosque.

Schools in general had a noticeable homogeneity in clientele (see Table 3.3). Mostly this was a homogeneity of socio-economic classes as represented by the occupational groups. Only two schools had clientele from socio-economic groups 1, 2, 3, and 4. This was the Christian evening centre and the NGO centre for children with a learning disability. Two schools had clientele from Groups 2, 3, and 4 (white-, pink-, and blue-collared groups): one was the recognised special school run by a disability-focused NGO and the other was a religious Islamic school. The special school earlier used to admit children without disability but was subsequently prevented from continuing this practice by the government on the grounds that they were recognised as a 'special school'.

Most schools catering to the high socio-economic groups were large ones with 400 pupils or more (14 out of 18), while the four schools catering to the low socio-economic group (i.e. which included Group 5) were all small and had enrolments of 150 or fewer. Fifteen schools had clientele from Group 3. A total of 35 private fee-based schools had clientele from the socio-economic Group 4. Twenty-four schools catered to children coming from Groups 1 and 2. This included all the CBSE and ICSE board-affiliated schools.

The schools that catered to children from Groups 4 and 5 were of special interest as these were the groups who are at the centre of the government vs. private school debates – i.e. parents who worked in irregular and manual work including domestic help, etc. This group patronised a range of schools – including government, the aided, private recognised, and private unrecognised. A total of 53 schools admitted students from Group 4. Twenty-five of these were unaided recognised schools of which six were small, with enrolments between 100 and 150 students. Ten were unrecognised and all were very small schools with enrolments of fewer than 100 (including two with fewer than 20). Fourteen private unaided recognised schools had enrolments between 400 and 1,500, which may be regarded as fairly large. All of these schools had a clientele from Groups 3 and 4, rather than only 4 or 4 and 5. Eleven of these schools had been established in the 1980s and 1990s and were among the older and more established ones of the area. Government schools tended to cater to Groups 4 and 5.

Ten schools catered to the poorest of the poor, of which only two were government and one aided, started by a Christian charitable trust. Two were private recognised schools: the first, which was fee-based, had started to shrink when the second, which was CSR-funded, came up. There were five unrecognised schools, started and managed by religious organisations/organisations with strong religious connections, all catering to this segment. One was a Christian evening learning centre, another was a Shishu Mandir; three others had Islamic support (including two madrasas). Thus the majority of the schools serving this group were charitable and had a strong religious backing from all three major faiths.

In as many as 20 of these, teachers reported that the children worked before and after school hours. Girls mainly assisted their mothers as domestic workers and all had duties at home, including sibling care and cooking. Boys often worked as mechanics, delivering newspapers, or vending fruits and vegetables, and in local hotels.

Quality

As noted in the introduction to the chapter, quality has been taken as a 'master concept' involving six dimensions. The literature has largely discussed the dimensions of provisioning, outcomes, and accountability for the schools catering to Groups 4 and 5. In this last section, I discuss diversity in school 'quality' in relation to two of the quality dimensions: educational aims

Table 3.3 School clientele

	Groups 1 and 2	Group 2	Groups 2 and 3	Groups 1–4	Group 3	Groups 2–4	Groups 3 and 4	Group 4	Groups 4 and 5	Group 5	Ni
Charities (religious mission/CSR/grants)									4	1	
Private unaided recognised									1	1	
Private unaided unrecognised									1	1	
Madrasa									2		
Government funded								7	1	1	
Government								7	1	1	
Government aided								2			
Aided								2	1		
Government aid and charities (religious mission/CSR/grants)							1	1			
Aided							1	1			
Fees and charities (religious mission/CSR/grants)			1	1		1	1				
Private unaided recognised											
Private unaided unrecognised			1	1		1	1				
Low-fee-based	3	4	2		2	1	9	21	2		1
Private unaided recognised	1	4	2		2	1	9	14	1		
Private unaided unrecognised	2							7	1		1
High-fee-based	13	2					1	1			
Private unaided recognised	7	2					1	1			
Private unaided unrecognised	6										
Grand total	**16**	**6**	**3**	**1**	**2**	**2**	**12**	**31**	**7**	**3**	**1**

and pedagogy. Examining aims and how they vary across schools invites attention to the relationship between quality, clientele type, management form and school finances for survival and profitability in explaining this variation, and in reflecting on the consequences of the variation. Pedagogy involves looking at how institutions shape teachers and their practices through interpretation of educations aims and the expectations and assumptions schools have regarding home support for schooling.

Educational aims and the school business plan

Most schools had a narrative that established the unique niche they saw themselves occupying in terms of what they aimed to achieve for their students and what they had to offer as institutional objectives. While overall educational aims were formulated in general terms, institutions reflected more specifically on what they offered to parents – their 'unique selling proposition' which defined their academic identity both for themselves and for their clientele – i.e. how they represented themselves and how they were viewed. Usually the school's business plan was formed around this 'USP', which defined its attraction and desirability for its clientele, and additional activities and services it provided usually from a financial angle. Such narratives became available to us from more than one source: the head of the institution (leadership/management), senior teachers, school documents such as the school diary, magazine, and publicity materials, and their website.

Eleven schools *did not articulate or formulate any specific educational ideal* to define them (eight recognised and three unrecognised). All of these were struggling and shrinking, low-fee-based schools run by entrepreneurs and tuition–teacher entrepreneurs. Several of these schools were facing management crises following family problems: in one case the head had run into debt after investing in a film production that starred her son. In others, there were inheritance disputes. Four schools were being run by naïve entrepreneurs who were new to the business and seemed clueless. Three ran tutorial centres, with flexible timing for students and teachers based on mutual convenience, and multi-grade grouping based on how many teachers and how many students turned up. Only one actively pursued fee collection from parents; the others had trouble with even this; they were struggling to simply retain their students, as with any talk of fee they stood to lose the students altogether. All the schools catered to children from Group 4 (and one included Group 5). The only aim seemed to be to stay afloat by functioning within means. As one of the entrepreneurs put it, with this fee no good education can be provided.

For eight schools, the *raison d'être* derived from *serving a particular 'community' group*: in the case of three it was 'girls from poor families' and for five it was 'community needs/poorest-of-the-poor of that community'. These schools serving the Muslim community wanted to provide modern education opportunities with Islamic values. The social learning component was also important in the case of the madrasas which served the poorest of the poor (Group 5) – and strived to offer an education opportunity of privately passing exams, along with learning '*hukumat* and manners' for both boys and girls. The Dar-ul-Uloom Madrasa was not offering the community a modern education opportunity, but was serving the religious needs of the community through a purely religious education. In the case of the girls' schools, two wanted to provide a Christian education through which girls would become God-fearing and Jesus-loving: one in Telugu medium serving lower socio-economic status groups and one in English medium for higher socio-economic status groups. The third (also aided Telugu medium) drew from early nationalist ideas of citizenship and patriotism appropriate to girls from poorer sections of society. The management said that they had limited ability to offer good education as they could not press parents to pay fees beyond a point and lose them, as it was important for them to serve their community.

Nineteen schools drew their educational identity and unique purpose from the fact that their clientele was poor. These schools were *oriented to serving the needs of the poor* as interpreted by them. For eight of these schools, access to modern education was central to the needs of the poor. For two – one recognised and one unrecognised, both of which ran on fees – the focus was on providing English-medium education in which the students would succeed. They functioned like tutorials and were flexible in their timings to enable participation. They also prepared students to take examinations privately. Both schools were very small and with multigraded classes. The remaining six ran on aid or charity and spoke of the importance of giving the poor an opportunity to succeed with modern education that stressed upon overall values and character, particularly traits such as resilience, self-confidence, autonomy, independent thinking and problem solving. Three of these institutions were run by religious missions and linked the development of these attributes to being rooted in the community, religious value education and education in the mother tongue. One, which was a CSR-supported English-medium school, aimed at providing social mobility through education which prepared poor students to succeed in examinations but with all-round development of understanding and self-confidence.

In the three government primary schools (two of which were in slum areas and of SSA origin), the aims of education were dominantly of 'domestication' and 'civilising the poor'. The school teachers here spoke of the poor needing education in order to become 'civilised'. In eight schools – government and aided – multiple aims seemed to be in operation, and were dependent on the views of individual teachers regarding the social situation of their students. Teachers of the Urdu-medium sections regarded the aim of education to be domestication and their own work as 'service to their community'. A few teachers of grade 1 particularly focused on domestication and conventional rote-based literacy instruction. Other teachers aimed at learning with understanding and students becoming self-confident, self-reliant, and independent. In three schools, the key focus was on learning social norms – to adjust to society, to be God-fearing, and to learn to live with others. These were run by entrepreneurs – in two cases the schools were not recognised.

'Affordable and good education' was the aim of 13 private low-fee-based schools. 'Unlike corporate schools, we want to give a good education … we want to develop children to do something for the country.' 'English and marks. This is what parents want.' 'We give duller success. Hard work and discipline leads to success.' With the exception of three of this group which were struggling to retain their client base, with a focus on negotiating fees and cajoling parents to pay, these schools had achieved a 'steady' state of loyal parents. Some of these schools resorted to humiliating children in various ways for non-payment of fees, including making them miss their examinations, or standing outside their class. What chiefly distinguished this group of schools was that they did not promise high results in maths and science. At the low end, these schools supported 'weak' students and ensured they passed the examinations. They explained that they admitted children who were rejected by other schools and enabled them to study and pass exams by focusing on their self-confidence and character. They spoke of values such as punctuality and regularity and character building. At the upper end of the spectrum, the aims were elaborated beyond 'good education' and 'values' to include 'all-round development' of children, learning English, and becoming able to secure a job. A second group of schools aimed to provide affordable maths and science scores and exam success. These schools had been started by successful maths teachers. Twelve of the schools in this group had been started by teachers and were managed by teacher entrepreneurs or family trusts. At least four of the schools in this group were anxious about the emergence of the new corporate schools that were threatening their client base. They complained that these schools lured their best students away.

A group of nine 'corporate' schools all aimed to make students *successful in science and mathematics-based competitive examinations*. Unlike the affordable group that only promised results in the high school maths and science exams, this group aimed at the competitive examinations. One 'old' family-run corporate school, which ran as a chain, was focused on entrance exam success. Other new corporate schools combined the importance of success in these engineering exams with 'all round development'. With the exception of one, all of these schools were part of multi-institutional chains that had started as coaching schools – mostly at the state level, but also including national coaching schools for elite engineering entrance exams. 'The vision to prepare students for professional courses at the school level itself.' 'Imparting concept based analytical thinking.' 'National building through science and mathematics.'

Nine schools emphasised *all-round development with success in examinations* as their key aim, adding the importance of values as well as coaching to succeed in examinations as their USP. These schools were all oriented to educating children from Groups 1 and 2. They emphasised values such as obedience, respecting elders, being God-fearing, cultivating love for the country, and being able to stand on their own feet. The schools in this group aimed to achieve this through investing in curriculum. Most schools in this group said they preferred the CBSE for this reason. 'We develop personality through scientific testing', was the claim of another. The claim 'Not an engineer or doctor but an IAS officer who can hire any engineer or doctor' suggested that these schools were preparing students for a wider range of white-collar employment opportunities. Table 3.4 offers a summary.

While there is a diversity in educational aims, this diversity was *across* schools catering to different social groups/classes. More 'progressive' and 'holistic' aims of education were found in schools catering to the highest income bracket, while lower down the spectrum the focus shifted to very discipline-based rote learning for either exam success or to be able to learn English. Teacher entrepreneur-run schools attempted to move pedagogy and aims in the direction of textbook learning with understanding as compared with other management types. The only exception was in the case of schools dealing with children with disability or in the lowest socio-economic group where the aim was for all-round development and autonomy and self-reliance – but this seems to be linked to the expectation that these children would not gain

Table 3.4 Aims of education

Aspects of aims	Groups 4 and 5	Groups 3 and 4	Groups 1 and 2
'Domestication'/'Civilising' mission	X		
Social learning, social norms	X		
Citizenship and patriotism	X	X	
Values – respect, punctuality, working hard	X	X	
Values – religious	X	X	X
Autonomy, resilience and independence	X		X
'All round development' – personality and interests, self confidence, 'soft skills'	X		X
English	In a few cases	X	Taken for granted
Science and Mathematics (high school exam)		X	
Science and Mathematics (competitive exams)		X	X
Securing a job/being employable		X	
Having a career			X

access to 'mainstream' channels of employment and success and would need to chart their own way. There was relatively limited diversity seen within social groups.

Pedagogy

The processes of teaching and learning that were being followed attempted to achieve the educational aims of the institution, but also specific educational purposes that the teachers intended. An understanding of the distinctive work being carried out in each classroom was characterised by drawing on five dimensions: (1) teachers' expectations and intended aims of education for the children they were teaching and what they expected them to achieve; (2) their expectations of the home, particularly in terms of support for schooling; (3) a 'method' they employed for teaching; (4) the 'method' that they intended by which students would learn; and (5) the method of discipline/moral regulation that was prevalent in the school. The composite of these five dimensions was reviewed and again synthesised into seven broad types of pedagogy. It was found that pedagogy was characteristic of a school, rather than of an individual teacher – the only exception being the government school where, as in the case of educational aims, there was a great deal of variation from teacher to teacher.

Teachers' *expectations about learning* referred not generally to expectations of some abstract learner, but more specifically to expectations about what these children who she was expected to teach could be and should be expected to learn. This constituted an educational aim that informed her pedagogic focus and effort. *These ranged from expectations that were teacher-referenced to those that were textbook-referenced to those that were society-referenced.* Minimal expectations took the form of the teacher-controlled and -defined learning of literacy and obedience, or expecting children to learn answers *as defined by the teacher.* The textbook-centric expectations involved learning answers to questions in the textbooks – from exact reproduction of textbook answers moving to answers which reflected the understanding of concepts and comprehension of the textbook. A last group referenced expectations of learning that was more widely valued in society, beyond school: learning of concepts and solving competitive exam papers, and in a few cases also the production of reasoning, independent autonomy, creativity, and novelty, reflecting understanding.

With regard to *expectations about home-support*, teachers had an implicit or explicit understanding of the home cultural and economic resources that supported the child's ability to learn school knowledge. At the lowest end, teachers had no expectations of home and viewed a child's home circumstances with empathy; in others a tense relationship prevailed vis-à-vis a child's home, particularly where there were difficulties in securing the school fee. The home of the child was viewed negatively as contributing problems that had to be countered in school and where no support could be expected. In a middle group, the sense was that although the home could not directly contribute useful things on its own, it could be influenced to support the child and the school and they could together support children towards meeting more and more expectations. Finally, there were institutions in which there was a cultural continuity between the home and school, in which the home provided valuable cultural capital – particularly knowledge of English. *The expectations about home support thus varied on an axis of expecting none in a situation of cultural division to full support in a situation of cultural continuity.*

Method of 'teaching': the dominant pattern of teaching in Indian schools is 'whole-class instruction', where the teacher engages and addresses the whole class and the entire group is basically doing the same thing. Also, following a set lesson is the dominant trend. Within this, variations were noted in the extent to which teachers did not give explanations, asked questions from children, and expected them to either repeat what was said, articulate in their own words, and expected and allowed children to ask questions – moving from overall silence in children to more dialogic situations with them. *Teaching varied from massified to approaches which focused on individual learners.* In the former, where there was little or no differentiation and engagement with what children were understanding, teachers primarily defined the objects of learning by marking portions and items to be learned without any discussion or explanation. The teachers here rarely made eye contact with the children and would ignore them even if they said something. In approaches where teaching was more *individualised*, teachers tried to monitor individual children's learning of prescribed knowledge in overall competitive settings. There were many schools, particularly the new corporate-managed ones, where pedagogy was scripted and tightly controlled by a centralised office. Here, teachers followed a detailed microplan and had fixed targets to meet in each lesson. The participation of children in these classes was also part of a script. There were schools where the teaching seemed to demand higher-order thinking from children and a few which were more dialogic and individualised. Children were often heard saying things on their own and asking questions. It seemed that their understanding was appreciated and their independent contributions valued and incorporated into an ongoing lesson.

Method of learning: a method of learning also was a part of the pedagogy. Each teacher seemed to be functioning with an implicit view of how children would learn and remember what there is to be learned or what they had been taught. *These ranged from learning by rote – i.e. repetition – to learning by thinking, understanding, and review.* This was a part of the pedagogy adopted by all teachers, where making sure that children had learned by testing and making them learn by spending time in the class on this was a part of their overall pedagogy. In other words, completing the time and effort in 'teaching' was time and effort spent also on 'making children learn': practice, rehearsal, assessment, and feedback. This ranged from rote memory-based learning methods in which the children were expected to repeat – and the teacher made them repeat over and over again – to making children think and express in their own words, revise, and attempt to apply their knowledge to answer new types of questions.

A *disciplinary culture* underlined the pedagogic work and in a sense the pedagogy only assumed and worked on this moral regulation. Pedagogy and its effects were believed to be as much about moral learning as they were about knowledge and skill development. The latter would follow from the former. Thus pedagogy was about shaping both the moral and epistemic capability and potential and identity of the student. At the lowest end, discipline was imposed through very visible forms involving corporal punishment and physical control. A second level was the use of guilt and conveying inadequacy arising out of moral failure. While there was no physical punishment, this discipline was also very visible. As the disciplinary cultures moved towards more invisible forms they could take the form of micro-control through rigorous timetabling and control of space and time of the student, in some cases for very extensive hours from early morning till late at night. Religion and religious values were also invoked in establishing invisible controls. In a few cases, control was expected to take the form of self-control through the use of reason. *The axis of variation was visible – external control of the body – to invisible – internal control through reason.*

Pedagogic types

Almost without exception a pedagogic form of the types described above marked the entire institution – the institution was broadly united in its educational identity and aims; as it was homogenous, it was largely oriented to the same educational aim and aspiration for the group that it served. There was a common view of the home and its resources to support the work of the school, as well as to contribute to its financial viability. The main areas in which variation was noted were the perspectives of individual teachers in schools – this was mainly in the dimensions of teaching and learning. Some variability from 'drill-and-repetition' in primary classes to more elaborate teaching in high school was noted particularly in the English-medium schools catering to Groups 3 and 4. Here, the initial years were more narrowly focused on teaching in the English medium to non-English-speaking students and moving to higher expectations when there was a higher level of fluency and comprehension of English. In five schools, a very wide variation was seen within the school between teachers. Some taught with high-level expectations and for higher-order cognition, while others adopted a domesticating pedagogy or drill. On one occasion, the same teacher exhibited dual pedagogy within a class, teaching one group in a more elaborate manner and another in a drill fashion. The schools with variations in pedagogy from teacher to teacher were schools for Groups 4 and 5, and were either government or aided schools. Table 3.5 offers a summary.

The low-fee-based private unaided unrecognised schools dominantly had 'domesticating pedagogies' (in 7 of 11 such schools). The key focus of these schools was on 'disciplining' children and keeping them quiet. The teachers felt that these children of the poor needed school in order to become civilised, and citizenship consisted of obedience. Textbooks were of no importance in these classes – the teacher defined what was to be learned and how, and was the final arbitrator in whether something had been learned or not. Discipline was mostly corporal and arbitrary. Children were constantly reminded that they were poor and that the best they could achieve was to remain silent.

Twenty-five of the 34 low-fee-based recognised schools had pedagogies involving rote and drill. The teacher-entrepreneur schools paid greater attention to ensuring that *each* child learned. A lot of time was spent on drill and repetition, mostly in a chorus learning manner, but teachers kept a strict watch on the children and from time to time would single-out individuals and check that they could repeat on their own.

In the entrepreneurial schools (11 of which were struggling and shrinking and seven of which had very small enrolments), classes were multigraded and teachers did little more than supervise this rote learning. The discipline in these schools was often both corporal and psychological. The classrooms were small and shared – children were squeezed in on benches. They often had their large bags on their laps and their books on top. They got into skirmishes with each other – knocking or jabbing each other. Keeping discipline and maintaining order in an overall noisy crowded environment seemed to be uppermost on the teachers' minds. When they taught they made children repeat the spellings of each word and rote learn answers.

Pedagogies that favoured higher-order cognitive capabilities, conceptual understanding, and independent thinking and writing answers in one's own words were both in textbook referenced pedagogies (type 4) as well as in more out-of-textbook and progressive pedagogies (types 6 and 7). Here, teachers allowed far greater self-expression of students and seemed to be oriented to their 'all-round development' and life outside the textbook and school. Pedagogy type 4 was constructed around enabling children to understand and engage with textbook knowledge. School seemed to be central to person formation in this pedagogic form. Many of the schools with pedagogy type 4 also had more diversity in the curriculum and, while being mostly low-fee-based, were aimed at giving children opportunities for all-round development and whole-school activities, including sports. The disciplinary cultures of these schools was based on middle-class values. While some of these schools tried to combine success in examinations and mathematics and science, this was not so in all.

Pedagogy types 6 and 7 differed in one important respect. Pedagogy type 6 catered to children from the highest socio-economic group of the area. These were children who all had

Table 3.5 Pedagogic types in relation to clientele type and management type

	Group 1: doctors, software professionals	Group 2: businessmen, lawyers, shop owners	Group 3: teachers, electricians, shop assistants	Group 4: domestic workers, mechanics, manual labour, fruit vendors	Group 5: rag pickers, scavengers, unemployed	
P1: Domestication and obedience-alphabetisation					DEO and entreprenuer (unrecognised)	12
P2: Rote learning of answers to pass examinations				Entreprenuer		21
P3: Drill learning of textbooks to do well in examinations			Teacher entreprenuer			13
P4: Textbook learning with understanding		Teacher entreprenuer, family trusts				7
P5: SWOT success in high-stakes competitive exams	Corporates					11
P6: All-round development and exam success	Religious and family trusts					3
P7: All-round development and self-reliance					Aided, government, charitable	7
Others (religious and special education)						3
No information						7

English spoken at home and parents pursuing elite careers – anticipating the future careers and aspirations of the children. The schools were run by very different management types – one a national religious mission trust, another a 'corporate' chain, and yet another a family trust. All of these schools had ample space for a diverse curriculum. *In pedagogic type 7, children were mostly from the poorest of the poor and did not have any home support for schooling.* The medium of instruction was the mother tongue. The teachers in these schools were keen to develop children's self-confidence and ability to learn to help them stand on their own feet. For these teachers, often the ability to read and understand any new text was an important aim as they felt these children had to rely on their own abilities in order to make something of their lives – they had neither any cultural capital at home nor parental resources to get them ahead in life. At the same time, these teachers did not seem to be preparing the children to succeed in life through a school examination and selection process. They would probably need to find opportunities and enter the workforce early. This included specific government school teachers.

SWOTT type pedagogy '5' was unique to Telangana/Andhra Pradesh – nine corporate-run schools and two established by successful math and science teacher entrepreneurs. Here, the ethos was heavily oriented towards success in the elite engineering examinations, with curricula that drew directly from the competitive exams. Conceptual understanding was greatly valued, but along with speed and accuracy developed out of drill and focused study to the exclusion of all else. Learning was heavily scripted and with frequent tests and analysis of the test results. The atmosphere was intensely competitive. In most of these schools order was built into the regime. One of these schools had a discipline coach posted on each floor. In this pedagogic form, success in competitive examinations was the aim and students were being trained for this. For the families of the students, maintaining and advancing one's current social status was crucially dependent on examination success. The pedagogy was thus not oriented towards the textbook per se, but to a world beyond. Conceptual learning was also valued, but only as it aided solving new and unknown problems that may appear in these examinations.

The relationship between social class and pedagogic form was striking – as the clientele of schools changed from Group 5 to Group 1, the dominant pedagogy also changed from pedagogy type 1 (or domesticating type), through which children were expected to learn obedience and to stay in their place on the lowest rung of society, to pedagogy types 5 and 6, which aimed at locating them in a wider social plane beyond the textbook and the school.

Conclusion

The heterogeneity and diversity of schools in Hyderabad city seems to be developing on account of both features of the state system as well as the market – indeed, on account of the complementary action of the two sectors. The 1970s to the 1980s was a turning point, with the cessation of state investment to open government schools or new aided schools and the beginning of the growth of private schools. Today there is heterogeneity and diversity seen in the schools, but this maps closely onto the socially stratified character of Indian society; the market has grown around class and community stratification; added to which we see a new strata – children with disabilities (impairments or learning difficulties) and 'dullers' (i.e. 'lower' intelligence). Clientele stratification is suggestive of an inherent segregation taking place in school selection along class and community lines, as well as exclusion of children with special needs, separating them into a class of their own. (This study was conducted before the RTE 25 per cent clause was operationalised in Telangana schools and it would be of interest to see whether in future this homogeneity is disrupted.) English medium is the default language option and opportunities for education in the mother tongue (Telugu and Urdu) are severely limited and only for the poorest of the poor, in either government or charitable settings.

Schools for the poor run by entrepreneurs and unstable small schools are mostly 'shrinking', raising questions regarding their stability. Pedagogic cultures in these schools are 'domesticating' or 'drill' based. Relationships with the home on the whole are tense and combative, with the schools having to balance keeping an upper hand over the parents and extracting fees with not losing their clientele. Those that are able to set aside such considerations are the ones that have a community religious affiliation with their clientele. Teacher–entrepreneur-run schools have less rote-based pedagogies, and although they are textbook cultures, these enable thinking and have expectations of concept development. While there are several schools for the poor which rely on shaming students – domesticating them or treating them as immoral – there also seems to be a widespread desire and parental investment in the ones that put students through a diffi-cult regimen to prepare them for competitive examinations. These schools seem to be more desirable. On the whole, there seems to be an invisible segregation operating in which the more competent students, or at least those who can cope with the regimen, are put into high-pressure schools while the less competent ones – the dullers – are sent to the schools that will coach them sufficiently to pass examinations. The poorest of the poor are served by charitable institutions. These, along with some of the aided schools and government school teachers, also espouse pedagogies that promote autonomy, thinking, and student confidence, all practised in the mother tongue.

This diversity of school types suggests the variables in the production of education quality in these institutions: aims which are derived from the socio-economic and community identity of the clientele, school financing and the type of management. There are multiple niches in the market ecosystem that these schools occupy. It is these considerations rather than 'private vs aided vs government' or 'recognised vs unrecognised' that provide us with a greater insight into the educational purposes and activities of these schools. Within any given bracket, being recog-nised vs being 'unrecognised' per se does not help distinguish any aspect of education quality between schools. However, it is instructive that such 'unrecognised' schools are found either at the 'top end' or the 'bottom end'; both these groups seem unconcerned about and are immune to the effects of the state or its need and ability to regulate.

The types of non-state interests in starting schools has evolved over the decades. Largely community-oriented initiatives until the 1970s gave way to entrepreneurship from the 1980s onwards. However, even in this group we see differences of quality even in the single dimen-sion of educational aims – between schools established by teacher–entrepreneurs and business entrepreneurs. Given how many of these schools are small and struggling, not only their quality, but also their institutional formation and stability cannot be ignored as issues when questions of their ability to serve the needs of the poor are debated. Moreover, in addition to the level or quantum of the fee charged, the ability to collect fees regularly is a major concern for these institutions, leading to their tense relationships with parents and having to resort to shaming children as a way of 'disciplining' parents. Fee collection tensions are mitigated usually on account of the simultaneous operation of charitable and communitarian considerations.

Religiously motivated trusts and institutions figure dominantly in the 'private' schools space. Also, it is instructive to note that the poorest of the poor may not be getting served by the gov-ernment institutions!

Contrary to common perception, all government schools do not have apathetic cultures, nor are all low fee-paying private schools hives of industrious effort. The diversity of institutional forms and qualities can be understood only by unpacking the categories of 'private' and 'govern-ment' to reveal the nature of their management/leadership, their reasons for being in the business of running schools, their educational aims, and the core finances of their operations. The school ethos evolves in relation to these considerations within the specific niche that it occupies and creates for itself, in the market ecosystem. Pedagogic cultures are determined at the institutional level even though they are realised through the practice of individual teachers. The stratification of school quality as manifested in its pedagogic form and educational aim is suggestive of the role of schools in the stratification of the formation of consciousness and agency (Bernstein 1977). The stratification between rather than within schools also provides conditions for the pedagogic messaging to be more intense, and minimises the opportunity for children to be exposed to different messaging. Surely this will have a cost for the society in which children grow up without having made friends or having been in the company of people who are different from them.

Notes

1 www.schoolreportcards.in.
2 Census2011.co.in, Hyderabad religion 2011, accessed on 14 November 2015.
3 Andhra Pradesh Educational Institutions (Establishment, Recognition, Administration and Control of Schools Under Private Management) Rules, 1993, in http://cdn.cfbt.com/~/media/cfbtcorporate/files/research/2003/r-private-schools-for-the-poor-india-2003.pdf.
4 Schools may be benefiting from indirect government funding. For example, in Delhi many 'private' schools have benefited from a land grant/lease. Now with the RTE fee reimbursement policy, a school stands to benefit for up to 25 per cent of its fee collection.

References

Bernstein, B. 1977. *Class Codes and Control Volume III*. London: Routledge and Kegan Paul.
Centre for Civil Society. 2015. Meta-Study of Literature on Budget Private Schools in India (www.ccs.in, accessed on 14 November 2015).
Jalan, Jyotsna and Panda, Jharna. 2010. *Low Mean and High Variance: Quality of Primary Education in Rural West Bengal*. Calcutta: Centre for Studies in Social Sciences.
Karopady, D.D. 2014. Does school choice help rural children from disadvantaged sections? *The Economic and Political Weekly* 49(51): 46–53.
Mehrotra, Santosh (ed.). 2005. *The Economics of Elementary Education in India: The Challenges of Public Finance, Private Provision and Household Costs*. New Delhi: Sage.
Mooij, Jos. 2003. Smart governance? Politics in the policy process in Andhra Pradesh, India. Working paper 228. London: Overseas Development Institute.
Naik J.P. 1975. *Equality, Quality and Quantity: The Elusive Triangle of Indian Education*. Bombay: Allied Publishers.
Sarangapani, P.M. (forthcoming) Hyderabad's education market. In *School Education in India: Market, State and Quality*, eds Manish Jain, Archana Mehendale, Rahul Mukhopadhyay, Padma M. Sarangapani and Christopher Winch. New Delhi: Routledge.
Sarangapani, P.M., Manish Jain, Rahul Mukhopadhyay and Christopher Winch. 2013. Baseline survey of the school scenario in some states in the context of RTE: study of educational quality, school management, and teachers. Andhra Pradesh, Delhi, and West Bengal, unpublished report submitted to the Sarva Shiksha Abhiyan, MHRD, New Delhi.
Tooley, James. 2009 *The Beautiful Tree: A Personal Journey into How the World's Poorest People Are Educating Themselves*. Washington, DC: Cato Institute.
Tooley, James, and Dixon, Pauline. 2003. Private schools for the poor: a case study from India. London: CfBT Research and Development (accessed from http://cdn.cfbt.com/~/media/cfbtcorporate/files/research/2003/r-private-schools-for-the-poor-india-2003.pdf on 12 September 2015).
Tooley, James, Dixon, Pauline, and Gomathi, S.V. 2007. Private schools and the millennium development goal of universal primary education: a census and comparative survey in Hyderabad, India. *Oxford Review of Education* 33: 539–560.
Winch, C. 1996. *Quality in Education*. Oxford: Blackwell Publishers.

4

Examination for elimination

Celebrating fear and penalising failure

Disha Nawani[1]

Assessment of students forms an integral part of all educational processes. The form, nature, and timing of such assessments varies, depending perhaps on the structure and formality of the learning spaces they are situated in and the foci and explicitness of specified objectives, learning or otherwise. Therefore, what has been *taught*,[2] especially in the context of formal school education, needs to be not only *learned* but get manifested, reported, and assessed as well, in some form or other. The purpose of student assessment could be either to gauge the acquisition of desired learning over a specified period of time or to use the assessment results to assist students in their learning (Pellegrino *et al.* 2001). It could even be to examine the effectiveness of syllabus, teaching/learning resources and pedagogic experiences in achieving the desired learning objectives (Tyler 1949) or be something totally extraneous to learning, serving perhaps as a legitimate screening device for selecting and discriminating between candidates for distributing or withholding of certain rewards.

Curriculum, teaching/learning resources, and assessment share an intricately intertwined relationship with one another. The manner in which this relationship unfolds is contingent on several factors. For instance, in school systems, where textbooks are prescribed by the state, textbook content often determines the 'what and how' of assessment (Kumar 1991). On the other hand, there are instances where the 'form and nature of assessment' guides the selection of curricular resources and pedagogic processes adopted in the classrooms. This in turn influences the meaning assigned to 'learning' and the way students approach learning (Willis 1993). Assessment is also inextricably linked with the location and positioning of teachers and students vis-á-vis each other and important others (textbook designers, policy-makers, inspecting officials, etc.) in the educational hierarchy.

These and several related issues gain prominence in the context of the Indian education system, which was significantly influenced by the educational policies of the British colonial era. Evaluation of students' learning acquired a definite meaning, shape, and aura, both distant from the traditional curricular, pedagogic, and assessment practices (Kumar 1991), as also deeply resilient and stubborn. The external nature of a written examination system, regulatory role and public use of its results, introduction of bureaucratic processes laced with formal rituals, uniformity in treatment of students, non-transparency in the process of evaluation, underlying pervasiveness and association of 'fear' with learning and a complete distrust of teachers in assessing students taught by them are some of the features discussed in this chapter as it attempts to trace and examine the history, structure, and implications of the contemporary examination system in India.

This chapter reiterates that assessment of students' learning need not only be understood in a pedagogic context as an objective and benign evaluation of students' competence, but needs to be placed in a larger societal context in which it often plays an important role in maintaining societies and even establishing order in them. This chapter has been organised into three sections. The first traces the institutionalisation of examinations in the colonial period, consolidation in independent India, and its implications. The second section discusses examination-related concerns and recommendations of various committees set up to examine the prevailing education system both before and after Independence. The third section traces the debate around specific assessment-related reforms initiated by the Right of Children to Free and Compulsory Education Act, 2009 (RTE) and aims to understand its ramifications for the disadvantaged child in Indian society.

Institutionalisation of the examination system in India: history, structure, and implications

This section briefly explains the origin, institutionalisation, and consolidation of the examination system in India. Situating the Board Examinations in a structural context, it explains the regulatory role played by them, placed as they are at the transitional stage between school and higher education. Finally, it highlights the impact of their institutionalisation on the meaning and purpose of learning as well as educational lives of teachers and students.

Brief historical overview

The process of institutionalisation of examinations in India is closely linked to the setting up of three universities in Calcutta, Bombay, and Madras in 1857. Set up in accordance with the Woods Despatch, 1854, these universities were entrusted with the task of conducting examinations, ascertaining candidates' proficiency, and screening their eligibility for government service. The institutionalisation process was strengthened after the Indian Education Commission of 1882 linked the grants-in-aid to schools to their examination results. Under 'payment-by-results', the system adopted by the Hunter Commission, grants to schools were given in proportion to the success and failure of students in the matriculation examination (Arasarkadavil 1963: 32). Over time, a condition was imposed based on the recommendations of the Universities Commission, 1902, under which secondary schools came under the purview of universities. This meant that for these schools to be entitled to register their students for the Secondary School Leaving Certificate (SSLC) examination, they needed to be recognised by universities, wherein individual school examination results played a key role in securing such recognition. In addition, every student desirous of entering college was required to complete secondary school as well as pass the SSLC examination. By 1904, the character of examinations thus became highly centralised (ibid.).

The nature of these examinations was significantly affected by the framework of education governed by Macaulay's Minutes of 1835. One among the several aims of the British to educate Indians was to train them for clerical jobs with the government. Since recruitment to service was related to an exam result, the concept of a minimum standard of proficiency and, hence, the concept of *pass* and *fail*, automatically crept in. In all these examinations, the stress was on memory and this was accentuated by the general background of our own teachers, traceable to the old *pathshala*[3] technique (NCERT 1971: 12) where teachers taught orally and students, in the absence of much written text, rote-learned the knowledge thus communicated to them. Another reason for this mechanical selection was the sheer number of candidates, which made it difficult to give any importance to other aspects of students' personality and the percentage of marks scored in such exams became the sole criteria for their selection (ibid.: 13).

Examining the manner in which this kind of examination system gained wider social acceptance can help us understand the validation and contestation around the social functions that examinations performed, placing them within the complex matrix of state and society. Most of the pupils studying in the secondary schools of the colonial period belonged to the educationally advanced classes of society, whose main objective was to obtain employment under the government. Gradually most of the secondary schools also came to be managed by the educationally advanced classes themselves (Naik and Nurullah 1974). As the examination system served the interests of this group, it gained social acceptance and became entrenched. However, there was another dynamic at work as well. Being part of the colonial education system, the examination system also represented the colonial state. It became a vehicle for the colonial state to express the principles that it claimed to represent. In the colonial imagery, Indian society was divided along caste and religious lines. The colonial state claimed that by virtue of its foreignness, it stood above these different groups, mediated between them, and was neutral in its approach towards them. Setting up of question papers and evaluation of students by people other than teachers who taught them was one such measure of expressing its neutrality. Phule's submission to the Hunter Commission helps one notice how he viewed colonial education, of which examinations were an important part, as promoting equity and fairness in a sharply stratified society:

> The withdrawal of Government from schools or colleges would not only tend to check the spread of education, but would seriously endanger that spirit of neutrality which has all along been the aim of the Government to foster, owing to the different nationalities and religious creeds prevalent in India.
>
> *(Phule 1882: 9)*

This perhaps also explains why the public exam system got so entrenched and acquired lasting social sanction in India.

Structure and role of Boards of Secondary Education in independent India

The first University Education Commission appointed after 1947 under the Chairmanship of S. Radhakrishnan gave priority to higher education. The Secondary Education Commission, headed by A.L. Mudaliar in 1952, specifically examined problems of secondary education. It gave a good deal of attention to matters concerning examinations. The Kothari Commission (1964–66; Ministry of Education 1966) recommended that each state should have a Board of Secondary Education (BSE). Till then, while some of the states did have such Boards, others did not. Owing to the pressure of increasing student population, universities withdrew from the job of the management and control of matriculation examinations. Thus, separate and autonomous BSEs came up in most states. The few that existed before 1947 (the precise number being two) took over the job of conducting matriculation examinations. Beginning with the 1920s, when Intermediate Boards were set up in several provinces, intermediate (and also matriculation) examinations came to be handled by them. Most of these Boards were examining Boards and did not perform any academic function, which meant that universities continued to dominate secondary school education until the 1960s, after which it began to get diluted. As the number of students increased at a phenomenal rate, the School Boards became more important and continue to be so, especially in the conduct of examinations and declaration of results on time. The practice of screening large numbers of students and selecting only a few, to match the number of seats available, is followed in most states (Singh 1997a).

Secondary education, as compared with higher, professional, and elementary education, received far less attention, even after Independence. While the states' priorities kept fluctuating between these sectors, secondary education was never looked upon as an independent sector of education (Singh 1997b). Interestingly, secondary education in India enjoys a peculiar relationship with college education, where the former, instead of being seen as a terminal stage of school education, is seen as a precursor to college education. The Board Examinations organised at the Secondary (Class X) and Higher Secondary (Class XII) levels therefore acquire special significance in such an educational context. Given the absence of alternative avenues of employment, when students choose to enter a college, generally speaking, it is mainly to defer unemployment; postponing the evil day, as it is called (Singh 1997b: 882). One can see a continuity in examination results serving as a criteria for limited opportunities (both admission to institutions of higher learning or employment) in colonial as well as independent India. The data in the following section show how aspirations of millions of students are thus scuttled and controlled by examination results (read: failure).

However, before presenting the statistics pertaining to performance of students across states in Class X and XII examinations, it may be pertinent to briefly examine the BSE operating in India at present. There are several educational Boards at present in the country – Central Board of Secondary Education (CBSE), Council for the Indian School Certificate Examinations (CISCE), which is an umbrella term for ICSE (Indian Certificate of Secondary Education for Class X) and Indian School Certificate (ISC for Class XII), National Open School (NOS), and numerous State Boards.

The CBSE is the oldest and most prestigious Board in India and comes under the central government. Schools recognised by CBSE fall into three categories – schools established by the central government under its various schemes, schools run by the Delhi government, other state governments, or by private agencies in those states, and private schools located in Delhi and various Union Territories.

While CBSE and NOS are government-sponsored and government-run, CISCE is a non-government body. Whereas CBSE and all other Boards generally follow the curriculum laid down by NCERT, the Council follows a different pattern of academic organisation.

While most private and prestigious public schools are affiliated to CBSE and CISCE and enjoy a superior status, State Boards are placed low in the hierarchy. They are set up by individual state governments in different states and follow their own syllabi and grading patterns. They are aimed at promoting regional language and culture and regarded as being relatively easier than other Boards.

Presenting board examination results (2009–2011)

This section presents data pertaining to results of Board examinations for Classes X and XII across three variables – states (State Boards versus CBSE, ICSE/ISC), gender (girls versus boys), and enrolment type/category of students (regular versus private) for 2009, 2010, and 2011.

A very preliminary examination of the data reveals how every year a large number of students are unable to pass these terminal examinations (Tables 4.1 and 4.2). It is not surprising that the failure rate is much higher among private students (more than 50 per cent) as compared with regular[4] students (varying between 20 and 30 per cent). Thus, students who for various social, cultural, and economic reasons are already outside the formal school system get eliminated completely by failure in Board Exams.

Table 4.1 Result of BSEs (2009–11): Class X

Year	Students appeared		Students passed	
	Regular	Private	Regular	Private
2009	13,257,089	1,845,177	94,66,126 (71.40%)	769,649 (41.71%)
2010	14,529,898	1,618,217	10,647,530 (73.28%)	772,904 (47.76%)
2011	14,556,735	1,320,628	10,178,487 (69.92%)	553,934 (41.94%)

Source: this is a consolidated summary of all students appearing in different state and central Board examinations held for that year. These data have been provided by Council of Boards on Secondary Education (COBSE).

Table 4.2 Result of senior secondary boards of examination (2009–11): Class XII

Year	Students appeared		Students passed	
	Regular	Private	Regular	Private
2009	7,011,131	1,026,703	5,568,157 (79.42%)	453,233 (44.14%)
2010	8,434,002	1,043,680	6,578,797 (78%)	493,725 (47.30%)
2011	10,173,781	1,180,096	7,616,545 (74.86%)	530,780 (44.98%)

Source: this is a consolidated summary of all students appearing in different state and central Board examinations held for that year. These data have been provided by the COBSE.

Tables 4.3 (Class X) and 4.4 (Class XII) show pass percentages of students across different Boards, including gender and enrolment category/type of students. There are significant variations in the pass percentages of students across State Boards. In Table 4.3, one can see states like Chhattisgarh and Madhya Pradesh consistently lagging far behind other states. Southern states like Tamil Nadu, Karnataka, Kerala, and Andhra Pradesh perform better, with ICSE and CBSE being among the top scorers. Children studying in schools affiliated to CBSE and ICSE belong to relatively privileged social backgrounds as compared to children studying in schools affiliated to State Boards. There are significant differences in the pass percentages of private and regular students, even in CBSE and ICSE. Results of private students are abysmally low across states. On average, girls perform better than boys. One can notice no significant changes in trends in data across three years. Similar trends can be seen in data for Class XII as well (Table 4.4). While failure in Class X ensures the exit of students midway through, failure in Class XII exams prevents those who manage to clear the first hurdle from joining colleges (professional and general) for higher learning. While for the majority of school students it is a two-hurdle race, some states previously had Board examinations even as early as class V.

A more sophisticated analysis of the data is required to arrive at a nuanced understanding of the implications of these scores, which is not within the scope of this chapter. However, the data point out: (1) the performance of the students in schools generally and exams specifically may depend on several variables external to the individual and cannot therefore always be seen as a direct outcome of one's competence and effort; and (2) the significant social function that such exams perform every year, of discriminating between students into pass and fail categories. While the pass category students continue to chug along in the system, without any guarantee of success, for the failed students the doors of formal education and associated rewards are forever closed – and that for seemingly *legitimate* reasons.

Table 4.3 Result of secondary examination of different boards (2009–11): pass percentage – Class X

No.	Name of board	2009 Regular			2009 Private			2010 Regular			2010 Private			2011 Regular			2011 Private		
		Boys	Girls	Total	Boys	Girls	Total	Boys	Girls	Total	Boys	Girls	Total	Boys	Girls	Total	Boys	Girls	Total
1	Board of Secondary Education, Andhra Pradesh	78.58	79.10	78.83	41.42	49.83	44.29	81.27	82.01	81.63	39.59	48.46	42.54	82.71	83.52	83.10	12.34	17.70	14.10
2	Board of Secondary Education, Assam	65.81	59.03	62.39	62.79	52.48	58.00	66.70	59.72	63.21	48.25	51.74	50.05	73.42	67.39	70.38	44.22	47.49	45.92
3	Bihar School Examination Board	65.84	60.65	63.76	72.24	68.11	70.55	71.97	67.37	70.06	78.63	73.86	76.70	71.33	59.94	66.39	77.89	62.84	71.83
4	Bihar State Madrasa Education Board	86.75	86.55	87.59	N.R.	N.R.	N.R.	89.57	92.19	90.65	38.68	32.29	36.00	98.33	98.98	98.59	23.26	19.99	22.04
5	Central Board of Secondary Education	89.26	91.23	90.07	44.61	36.19	40.97												
6	Chhattisgarh Board of Secondary Education	54.34	55.41	54.84	38.06	40.79	39.21	54.61	55.57	55.07	38.17	40.90	39.29	52.38	51.40	51.90	33.88	34.13	33.99
7	Council for Indian School Certificate Exam, Delhi	97.82	98.69	98.20	60.96	54.05	59.06	98.11	98.87	98.44	67.91	72.47	69.54	98.31	99.22	98.71	65.82	72.79	68.36
8	Goa Board of Secondary & HS Education	77.40	76.84	77.11	32.00	33.79	32.88	79.54	78.61	79.08	100.00	0.00	100.00	81.31	80.26	80.80	33.33	0.00	20.00
9	Gujarat Secondary and HS Education Board													73.48	79.66	75.85	47.03	61.09	50.75
10	Board of School Education, Haryana	84.00	85.00	84.00	45.00	40.00	44.00	79.23	80.94	79.98	67.45	75.00	70.16	64.16	69.54	66.57	60.69	65.00	62.36
11	Himachal Pradesh Board of School Education	55.44	58.11	55.75	54.82	45.48	50.18	62.3	64.18	63.19	65.29	65.79	65.53	62.01	62.42	62.20	64.09	63.75	63.92
12	Jharkhand Academic Council	81.57	76.72	79.47	75.94	72.19	74.48	79.48	76.32	78.07	70.72	67.31	69.34	74.71	69.47	72.25	58.12	55.31	56.87
13	Board of School Education, J&K	59.50	58.11	58.22	20.75	0.00	20.75							0.00	0.00	58.33	0.00	0.00	0.00
14	Karnataka Secondary Education Exam Board	74.45	77.30	75.83	12.19	23.57	14.80	66.71	71.00	68.81	5.45	14.16	7.32	78.86	82.90	80.85	8.97	21.27	11.69
15	Kerala State Board of Public Examination	89.74	93.99	91.92	N.R.	N.R.	N.R.	88.99	92.42	90.12	0.00	0.00	0.00	89.71	93.01	91.36	45.32	52.72	47.54
16	Board of Secondary Education, Madhya Pradesh	34.09	37.19	35.33	8.38	9.96	8.90	46.65	50.31	48.15	19.85	19.82	19.84	53.85	55.79	54.68	24.01	23.82	23.94
17	Maharashtra State Board of S&HS Education	80.39	82.98	81.55	38.49	43.78	40.09	78.25	82.50	80.17	36.00	43.83	38.34	70.34	74.93	72.42	31.58	41.03	34.42
18	Board of Secondary Education, Manipur	85.80	54.10	60.14	35.50	28.40	31.46	67.00	55.30	61.33	0.00	0.00	0.00	0.00	0.00	0.00	0.00	0.00	0.00
19	Meghalaya Board of Secondary Education	78.62	74.16	76.29	26.53	27.06	26.80	76.53	70.83	73.53	25.07	24.90	24.99	0.00	0.00	0.00	0.00	0.00	0.00
20	Mizoram Board of School Education	76.12	71.01	73.50	28.88	25.30	27.10	83.54	78.23	80.84	39.48	30.71	35.11	81.65	78.05	79.83	36.84	28.51	32.55
21	Nagaland Board of School Education	72.45	67.47	69.98	71.58	68.45	69.77	68.13	64.15	66.17	26.80	25.33	26.01	72.87	70.39	71.64	32.26	26.76	29.34
22	National Institute of Open School	0.00	0.00	0.00	33.40	37.84	34.75												
23	Board of Secondary Education, Orissa	51.73	49.42	50.38	40.14	43.78	41.60	72.38	69.35	70.86	53.48	56.66	54.84	66.59	63.78	65.21	33.71	36.52	34.91
24	Punjab School Education Board	77.40	79.29	78.07	9.35	10.67	9.92	75.59	82.67	78.80	61.76	72.06	66.04	67.84	73.66	70.57	41.28	54.27	46.73
25	Board of Secondary Education, Rajasthan	78.67	84.29	81.53	N.R.	N.R.	N.R.	77.05	77.41	77.18	9.38	10.56	9.92	75.54	76.12	75.76	8.58	9.85	9.19
26	Tamil Nadu State Board of Secondary Education				N.R.	N.R.	N.R.	79.33	85.45	82.45	8.60	11.38	9.43	82.28	88.15	85.28	0.00	0.00	0.00
27	Tripura Board of Secondary Education	62.11	54.57	58.65	37.04	35.43	36.36	63.71	55.82	60.05	34.77	34.78	34.77	65.03	58.64	62.07	24.61	26.22	25.38
28	UP Board of Intermediate and High School Education	49.00	68.10	57.29	43.60	62.96	50.59	64.52	77.76	71.35	64.21	77.29	70.79	66.83	77.55	71.66	57.56	63.05	59.11
29	Board of School Education, Uttarakhand	63.17	68.67	65.73	37.34	40.68	38.34	63.74	74.85	69.04	36.56	46.59	39.82	65.84	63.51	64.75	36.93	45.40	39.76
30	West Bengal Board of Secondary Education	86.82	76.32	81.74	55.55	52.50	53.85	86.05	77.43	81.78	38.59	32.25	35.34						
31	West Bengal Board of Madrasah Education	71.91	61.14	65.30	N.R.	N.R.	N.R.												
	Total	69.27	74.06	71.40	38.58	47.53	41.71	71.08	76.02	73.28	45.76	51.07	47.76	73.89	77.10	69.92	40.81	43.83	41.94

Source: these data have been provided by the COBSE.

Table 4.4 Result of senior secondary examination of different boards (2009–11): pass percentage – Class XII

Name of board	2009 Regular Boys	2009 Regular Girls	2009 Regular Total	2009 Private Boys	2009 Private Girls	2009 Private Total	2010 Regular Boys	2010 Regular Girls	2010 Regular Total	2010 Private Boys	2010 Private Girls	2010 Private Total	2011 Regular Boys	2011 Regular Girls	2011 Regular Total	2011 Private Boys	2011 Private Girls	2011 Private Total
1 Board of Intermediate Education, Andhra Pradesh							62.49	67.28	65.68	31.49	38.23	33.82	48.04	66.43	55.49	25.92	31.52	27.87
2 Assam Higher Secondary Education Council	74.15	74.06	74.87	48.57	53.58	50.98	73.57	73.21	73.39	53.19	54.20	53.66	78.06	76.44	77.27	62.25	64.11	63.12
3 Bihar School Examination Board	89.52	89.08	89.43	79.38	78.14	79.14	89.80	89.51	89.69	85.15	84.23	84.59	89.44	91.01	90.06	83.24	82.13	82.17
4 Central Board of Secondary Education	79.14	87.51	82.69	46.37	52.19	49.76	78.16	87.09	81.97	39.37	47.26	42.25	79.10	88.43	83.04	42.17	49.32	44.68
5 Chhattisgarh Board of Secondary Education	74.54	80.02	76.79	51.86	57.76	53.86	76.35	81.09	78.37	45.17	52.16	47.63	70.98	77.40	73.81	40.32	45.96	42.15
6 Council for Indian School Certificate Exam, Delhi	98.99	98.48	97.67	74.43	69.42	73.46	96.98	98.54	97.69	77.56	80.88	78.34	96.94	98.71	97.74	83.57	82.19	83.23
7 Goa Board of Secondary & HS Education	77.09	85.94	81.39	19.05	10.00	16.13	74.63	81.43	78.11	0.00	0.00	0.00	76.15	80.34	78.34	11.12	0.00	9.38
8 Gujarat Sec & Hr Sec Education Board	84.38	91.54	87.20	50.04	57.70	52.20	88.60	94.10	89.30	62.30	74.60	65.10	79.03	88.17	83.21	47.28	60.42	50.33
9 Board of School Education, Haryana	90.00	96.00	93.00	51.00	56.00	52.00	89.00	95.00	92.00	0.00	0.00	0.00	63.00	80.93	70.85	54.03	66.82	56.65
10 Himachal Pradesh Board of School Education	68.37	72.25	70.25	44.88	48.94	45.53	64.91	68.00	65.63	36.65	53.45	50.16	59.33	62.58	60.92	44.04	48.63	45.98
11 Jharkhand Education Council	81.57	76.72	79.47	75.94	72.19	74.46	48.54	60.48	53.52	32.64	40.90	35.05	45.80	58.99	51.48	34.42	42.15	36.96
12 Board of School Education, J&K	48.25	48.84	47.63	24.90	25.98	25.33	54.61	65.39	60.14	20.79	30.06	23.76	0.00	0.00	38.54	0.00	0.00	0.00
13 Dept. of Pre-University Education, Karnataka	44.40	55.07	49.75	23.35	28.68	25.12							53.64	64.32	59.07	20.56	30.66	23.69
14 Kerala State Board of Public Examination													76.61	87.00	82.21	28.08	48.44	36.72
15 Board of Secondary Education, Madhya Pradesh	62.87	74.01	67.13	28.01	34.73	30.20	66.01	76.11	69.87	33.91	39.72	35.78	61.79	70.07	65.02	28.34	33.71	30.09
16 Maharashtra State Board of S&HS Education	76.89	83.93	79.89	47.97	55.31	50.02	69.92	78.35	73.54	43.55	51.73	45.72	62.05	73.32	66.85	39.15	49.20	41.86
17 Council of Higher Secondary Education, Manipur	71.70	69.67	70.75	30.43	31.47	30.86	80.32	78.35	79.39	21.74	50.00	30.30						
18 Meghalaya Board of Secondary Education							60.82	69.89	65.75	21.30	21.24	21.27	66.77	74.62	70.14	48.22	55.76	51.06
19 Mizoram Board of School Education	69.88	68.94	69.39	26.35	22.71	24.88	76.87	70.91	73.82	32.28	23.76	28.55	75.18	74.20	74.65	32.37	29.86	31.29
20 Nagaland Board of School Education	77.15	78.18	77.66	47.83	51.92	49.59	72.04	72.31	72.19	34.87	34.95	34.91	69.57	73.39	71.51	54.16	55.43	54.77
21 National Institute of Open School	0.00	0.00	0.00	35.13	38.71	36.22							37.63	42.20	39.02	0.00	0.00	0.00
22 Orissa Council of Higher Secondary Education																		
23 Punjab School Education Board	95.15	97.83	96.02	30.95	36.33	32.89	65.77	78.72	71.94	42.95	60.25	50.47	68.74	83.33	75.64	41.63	67.64	53.44
24 Board of Secondary Education, Rajasthan	75.41	80.25	82.83	NA	NA	NA	93.07	97.35	94.56	24.29	32.06	27.28	90.29	95.69	92.21	26.52	34.14	29.66
25 Tamil Nadu State Board of Secondary Education	NA	NA	NA	NA	NA	NA	81.93	87.98	85.15	27.74	40.63	33.16	82.33	89.04	85.92	0.00	0.00	0.00
26 Tripura Board of Secondary Education	68.42	64.09	66.45	26.16	22.94	24.88	72.18	68.88	70.77	36.38	36.52	36.44	72.27	71.94	72.13	33.3	28.85	31.39
27 UP Board of Intermediate and High School Education	73.92	89.19	80.36	64.85	77.41	68.23	74.35	90.23	81.52	67.89	80.94	71.75	71.25	91.19	80.99	63.89	82.37	69.64
28 Board of School Education, Uttarakhand	70.85	81.65	76.19	38.92	50.45	42.84	69.36	84.05	76.59	46.96	63.25	53.60	74.32	83.21	78.42	49.70	57.08	52.56
29 West Bengal Council of Hr Secondary Education	79.25	64.48	77.79	N.R.	N.R.	N.R.	81.42	77.95	79.88	62.04	59.53	60.93	75.97	74.54	75.33	65.62	67.48	66.49
Total	76.72	83.06	79.42	42.14	46.63	44.14	74.81	82.00	78.00	44.11	52.91	47.30	70.18	81.43	74.87	43.55	54.56	44.98

Source: these data have been provided by the COBSE.

The introduction of such an examination system in the Indian school education system brought about some significant long-lasting changes, a few of which are highlighted here.

Pedagogic and sociological implications

The institutionalisation of exams not only led to the setting up of infrastructural prerequisites for conducting examinations (setting question papers, supervising examination halls, correcting answer scripts, etc.), but most importantly led to a complete distrust and disempowerment of teachers (Kumar 1991). The alienation, distancing, and disregard of the teacher formed part of the larger rejection/distrust of all that was indigenous/native (Elphinstone 1824).

Since textbooks were prescribed by the Director of Public Instruction (the highest official in the administrative hierarchy) and examinations were almost entirely based on them, textbooks emerged as the de facto curriculum (Kumar 1991) and the educational lives of students and teachers began to revolve around them. Learning began to be equated and restricted to memorisation of textbook content. Further, since these examinations were centralised, the questions on which all students were tested could only be very general in nature. This also meant that examinations provided no scope for testing knowledge specific to individual children's milieu and experiences (Kumar 1992).

External examinations increased the distance between teachers and students. The idea of impartial assessment, where the 'assessed' was not known to the 'assessor', besides leading to public and written examination at the end of the course, also led to on-the-spot testing of students by inspecting officials. With its aura of secrecy, strictness, and uniform treatment of all examinees, the examination system played an important role in the development of a bureaucratic system of education. To the English administrator, examinations like textbooks were a means of norm-maintenance. As Shukla has pointed out, colonial policy used written examinations to evolve a bureaucratic, centralised governance of education (Shukla 1978, cited in Kumar 1991). The official function of the examination system was to evolve uniform standards for promotion, scholarship, and employment. This function had a social significance in as much as it enhanced the public image of colonial rule as being based on just principles and impartial procedures. The secrecy maintained over every step, from the setting of papers to the final announcement of the result, gave a dramatic expression to the image of the colonial government as a structure that could be trusted.

Another important implication of the pervasiveness and centrality of Board examinations in students' lives was the grounding of fear as being integral to school learning. The fear associated with non-learning was unique to colonial times as it began to be associated with denial of several rewards that Western education brought along with it. There was only one road block in the way to people's aspirations being fulfilled and that was failure in those examinations.[5] Entrance to school meant being gradually initiated into a world of fear, where all that mattered was success in examinations, especially terminal ones. The fear of failure and associated shame and humiliation became part of the lore of childhood and adolescence (Kumar 1991). Munshi Premchand's *Bade Bhai Saheb* (*My Elder Brother*), written in 1910, is a classic story that conveys the anguish of a student who repeatedly fails in exams (Premacanda 1986). However, this story is not just about his frustration at failing, but makes a sharp comment on the irrelevance and futility of the education and examination system prevalent in those times.

The feeling of fear associated with school learning did not dissipate with the attainment of Independence, but was further strengthened. That is the reason why students are often found flocking to temples especially during exam time, seeking divine interventions, wearing religious markers, and making religious symbols on their answer scripts. Popular literature and culture continue to echo similar sentiments where the relevance of learning an alien curriculum is also questioned. An old song from a Hindi film, *Anpadh* (1962), conveys the feeling quite well, *Sikander ne Porus se kee thee ladhai toh main kya karoun* ... (If Alexander fought with Porus, why do I care?). One has also grown up hearing phrases like *padogey likhogey toh banogey nawaab, khelogey kudogey to banogey kharaab* (If you study, you will do well and if you play, you will get spoilt). Social sciences typically were loaded with lots of information for students to memorise, hence became the butt of jokes, *History Geography badi bewafa, raat ko rato, subah safaa* (History Geography are not to be trusted, you learn them at night, by morning they disappear).

Reminiscing about his childhood days, the famous sociologist T.N. Madan, born in 1933, writes about the fear he experienced when, after five years of home-based education, he was to join a school in Class VIII. As he was presented before the Inspector of Schools in his big office, he sweated and trembled with fear: 'I was however, oppressed by the fear of the upcoming examinations ... the entry into school ended my childhood, bringing with it many anticipated joys, but also unknown fears, including the examination blues' (Madan 2010: 192–193).

To conclude, the public, external exams that were introduced by the colonial system of education presented themselves as providing a 'neutral and fair' criteria for awarding limited employment opportunities to those aspiring for it. The same practice continued in independent India, where secondary education, instead of being perceived and developed as a terminal stage of education, was seen as a transitional stage where Board Exams performed the important role of filters. A system that was marked by uniformity, secrecy, and impartiality could hardly be faulted and students' success and failure in examinations was justified as the presence or absence of individual effort and talent. Thus the structural inadequacies of the system in being unable to either provide seats in institutions of higher learning or employment in the market was masked behind the superbly efficient system of examination in successfully eliminating a large number of job seekers/aspirants. Teachers and students both became pegs in such a system, which was dictated by fear and desperation to do well, while the bitter pill of failure was swallowed unques-tioningly as being caused due to one's own inability and incompetence.

Prevailing examination system: concerns and recommendations

It is interesting to note that no sooner was the system of external examinations introduced in India, than educationists and policy-makers began to recognise its limitations. Commission after commission pointed out the malaise afflicting the Indian education system, particularly exami-nations and the deleterious impact that they were having on the meaning of education at large and school education in particular.

Pre-Independence period

Criticisms levelled against external examinations in the pre-Independence period essentially focused on excessive importance being given to examinations causing enormous stress to both teachers and students, forcing them to channel all their energies into clearing exams, killing any kind of meaning making and creativity in the process. Other criticisms were imposition of the uniform textbook/curriculum across diverse school contexts, confinement of instruction to the rigid curricular framework, neglect of all education/training which could not be tested, the lit-erary character of courses of study to the exclusion of practical skills, prioritising rote memorisa-tion over other higher-order skills, and mechanical repetition and memorisation of textbook content (or even guides) (*Interim report of the Indian Statutory Commission 1929; Post-war Educa-tional Development in India 1944; Report of Calcutta University Commission, 1917–19; Report of*

Indian Education Commission, 1882–83; Report of Indian Universities Commission, 1902; Report of the Zakhir Husain Committee and the Detailed Syllabus, 1938; Resolution of Government on Educational Policy 1904).

Independent India

Interestingly, almost every commission/committee (Mudaliar in 1953; Radhakrishnan in 1948) bemoaned problems raised earlier and suggested more comprehensive ways of assessing students' learning. The Radhakrishnan Commission reiterated the pernicious manner in which the exams had become the aim and end of education, to the detriment of all initiative among teachers and students. Similarly, the Mudaliar Commission commented on the overwhelming influence of external exams, restricting and nullifying the real purpose of education. The Kothari Commission in 1964–66 upheld the importance of a written exam as a reliable and valid measure for judging educational attainment but also proposed inclusion of other techniques to measure those aspects for which the written test was not appropriate.

Similarly, the National Policy on Education, Programme of Action (NPE POA) of 1991 proposed the value of continuous institutional evaluation of scholastic and non-scholastic achievements of students but upheld the continuation of public examination for classes X and XII. However, it suggested measures that could make the examination process less taxing and more meaningful, such as provisions for clearing examinations in parts and innovative ideas like open-book examinations. It strongly articulated the need for assessing students by teachers who taught them (Government of India 1991: 150–151).

Perhaps one of the most comprehensive and simple yet enlightening reports on the malaise affecting Indian school education is the Yashpal Committee Report (YCR), also called *Learning Without Burden* (MHRD 1993). According to this report,

> the biggest defect of the examination system in its present form is that it focuses on children's ability to reproduce information to the exclusion of the ability to apply concepts and information to unfamiliar, new problems, or simply to think.
>
> *(MHRD 1993: 6)*

The National Curricular Framework (NCF) of 2005, drawing from the insights of YCR, reoriented the educational discourse towards focusing on problems of curricular failure and inability of schools to provide relevant and meaningful educational experiences to children, which led to their failure and subsequent dropout from schools. It was the first time a curricular or policy document challenged the objective and validity of conducting public examinations such as the Boards. It stated that there was an urgent need to revise the public examinations at the end of Class X and XII, whose quiz-based and text-based question–answer format caused inordinate anxiety to students. It also regarded the uniformity in such examinations as being unfair and discriminatory to a majority of students who were not placed in conducive teaching/ learning environments. In fact, it reconceptualised the role played by Boards to change from direct testing at present to careful and rigorous validation of school-based, teacher-conducted assessments. It also suggested that Class X Board Examination should be made optional and tenth-graders who wished to continue into the eleventh grade at the same school, and did not need the Board certificate for any immediate purpose, should be free to take a school-conducted exam instead of the Board exam (NCERT 2005, 2006).

However, it must be noted that apart from suggesting curricular and specific examination-related reforms, it also urged for reforms in other related areas like improvement of teacher-training, teacher quality, and teacher–student ratios, and making textbooks more relevant, interesting, and challenging, among others.

The next section focuses on measures initiated under the RTE Act and the discomfort expressed around them.

Contextualising contemporary examination reforms

Despite meaningful suggestions made repeatedly by various commissions set up for the purpose of reviewing the examination system in India, precious little has been done to ameliorate the ills plaguing it.

Right to Education Act, 2009

The RTE gave teeth to the reforms proposed in earlier review documents/policy formulations, the most recent being NCF 2005. The specific measures mandated in this regard are-

1   No child admitted in a school shall be held back in any class or expelled from school till the completion of elementary education (non-detention policy (NDP)).
2   Continuous and comprehensive evaluation (CCE) of a child's understanding of knowledge and his or her ability to apply the same.
3   No child shall be required to pass any Board Examination till completion of elementary education.

These measures pose a fundamental challenge to the existing examination practices, sharpening the dichotomy between a one-off examination and detaining children on the basis of its results, *and* regular assessment of students and not penalising them even upon failure. The subsections below present an elaboration of the first two provisions (since they are the ones being contested) including challenges associated with their use.

The NDP is not new, and existed at various levels (I–II, I–V, I–VII) in 28 states of India even before the passing of the RTE Act. Some states had a few conditions attached to it, like minimum attendance. The rationale behind mandating this provision in the RTE is that by creating a non-threatening teaching/learning/assessment environment in school, it essentially responds to the challenges confronted by the disadvantaged child, who struggles to come to school and strives even harder to stay on in school. On failing and being detained in the same class, such a child faces humiliation, gets demotivated, and often drops out of the school system. The Act recognises the importance of addressing the conceptual lags of children promoted under this policy and the need for giving them additional support beyond classroom hours. However, it is not difficult to imagine the inability of the already burdened school teacher teaching children who have little or no support at home to find additional time to achieve this.

The idea of CCE, similarly, is not new, but found mention in several commission reports and policies much before it took a formal shape in this Act. 'Continuity' in examination was supposed to ward off the evils associated with a singular exam on which hinged a child's future. 'Comprehensiveness' sought to give legitimacy to developing and assessing the overall personality of a student. The idea was to take away the fear associated with performance in a one-off terminal examination, and reinstate faith in the agency of the teacher to assess her students on a regular basis using multiple modes of assessment.

CCE is an umbrella term and there is no uniform model of CCE in the country. NCERT, CBSE, and different states, some with the help of non-government organisations (NGOs) and others with the help of private organisations and individuals, have evolved their own models of CCE. Besides several problems with these varied conceptualisations (Nawani 2013), CCE is grappling with multiple challenges at the level of implementation (Srinivasan 2015). While teachers are being given some basic training in most states, fuzziness abounds on what and how children are to be assessed and the way in which these results are to be used for their further growth. Teachers[6] have also complained of CCE adding to their woes of maintaining registers, filling up assessment formats, tracking students' growth, collecting evidence, and writing detailed descriptive portfolios, etc. The teachers perceived that as a result of CCE, the focus has shifted from teaching to maintaining assessment-related records. They also felt pressurised to project an inflated progress of the students over the course of the year to ensure that their own performance appraisal was not adversely affected.

With several states voicing their discontent with assessment-related reforms introduced under the RTE and the challenges faced by their schools, the Ministry of Human Resource and Development (MHRD) in 2012 set up the Central Advisory Board of Education (CABE) Sub-Committee to examine 'Assessment and implementation of CCE in the context of the No-Detention Provision of the RtE 2009' (MHRD 2014). This Committee was set up under the Chairmanship of Geeta Bhukkal, former Education Minister of Haryana.[7]

Two central concerns that informed this Committee's analysis of the provisions under study were: (1) declining learning level outcomes (LLOs)[8] of government-school children; and (2) migration of children from government schools to private schools, as reported by the Annual Status of Education Reports (ASER 2012).

The root cause identified by the Committee for declining LLOs of children is the NDP, which in most cases is misunderstood as no assessments. It further asserts that non-detention de-motivates both students and teachers; reduces teacher accountability; increases multi-level classrooms; and eventually increases teachers' burden. Moreover, it felt that this policy is implementable only in an ideal system – where there are optimal resources at every level (sufficient number of teachers), seamless processes (CCE), and a supportive ecosystem (engaged parents/community who ensure full attendance of children, driving and supporting students towards academic excellence).

The assertions made by the Committee and their implications need to be understood since they echo the popular perceptions about these provisions. The objective behind NDP is to remove the fear of failure from those students' minds that are most likely to fail and leave the system. This is achieved by de-linking 'promotion to next grade' from students' results. If it is being felt that this de-linking has led to a lackadaisical attitude towards learning on part of both teachers and students, then there is a clear problem with the kind of learning one is trying to promote and the reasons for which one is in school. Moreover, this provision neither de-emphasises learning nor assessments; it simply allows the potential dropout to stay a little longer in school than she otherwise would.

On the one hand is the claim that government schools largely cater to children whose parents are unable to support their children, while on the other hand lies the claim that NDP negatively impacts their motivation to attend school and do well. It is difficult to imagine how a detention policy will motivate these children to strive to perform well if they are both irregular in attending school and constrained in getting parental support. The NDP, on the contrary, tries to make the school less threatening for these very children, who are likely to fail and leave, never to return.

Multi-grade environments exist not only because of NDP, as is being asserted, but because of shortage of teachers, varying numbers of students in schools, and differential needs and support available to children either at home or in school. NDP does not by itself promote under-learning. It hinders the failing and incessant detention of children. In any case, even if 'failing' children were detained and held back, besides being demotivated, they would still continue to struggle in the same class unless substantial need-based support was provided to them. Children's failure also becomes compounded by poor quality of pre-service and in-service training and on-site support to teachers.

The last point is a classic case of the chicken-and-egg problem. There is no denying the fact that meaningful reforms cannot be seen in isolation and need several other processes to be in place, but then does it also mean that all such measures should be thwarted/postponed till every single variable in the education system is in order? The RTE Act in fact reiterates the need for several other rights-based provisions – adequate school infrastructure, minimum qualifications for teachers, pupil–teacher ratio, no non-academic activity for teachers, child-friendly curriculum, CCE and teacher-training education, etc., which need to be initiated simultaneously.

Both CCE and NDP, despite facing severe and real challenges, are based on sound principles that need to be recognised and supported rather than being dismissed in haste. To hold the child responsible for not attending school regularly when the school in question does not inspire the child in any manner and detains him for 'not knowing adequately enough', when the system is probably at fault in delivering, may not be an appropriate solution for the malaise. By blaming the child or the teacher alone, one personalises a structural malaise and shifts the onus entirely on them to perform. It is more important to create a system which supports teachers to teach and students to learn rather than creating a system based on fear of chastisement and failure leading to detention.

Concluding insights

Examinations serve a highly important function of controlling social conflict in situations where there is a mismatch between number of candidates appearing for exams and number of rewards contingent on their results. In a stratified society like India, social goods such as even education are not equitably distributed. While the right of citizens to elementary education was finally recognised in 2009, secondary education still remains outside its orbit.

Since their introduction, the purpose of Board examinations in India has not changed. It continues to filter a large number of aspirants, and thereby control aspirations for upward social mobility and curbs social dissent in circumstances where they remain unfulfilled. It is in this larger context that provisions such as school-based reform and non-detention of students should be seen. Related to this is also the increasing disempowerment of teachers where lowly paid, under-qualified, contractual teachers are being considered not just cost-effective but efficient. This is a reflection of the deeper educational malaise that our society is grappling with. An environment where accountability of both the teacher and the student is singularly linked with failure/non-performance (purely in terms of students' exam results), bereft from an understanding of the actual situations which they work in, can only promote detention of students and celebrate en masse failure in examinations.

Most importantly, the Boards of school education also need to broaden their vision and enlarge their role and not merely serve as examining bodies responsible for conducting examinations. Better linkages also need to be established between different agencies responsible for school education – organisations responsible for framing curricula, designing syllabi and developing textbooks, training and supporting teachers, and even inspecting schools. Until such a time that exams stop being viewed as tools by Boards of education to merely test students linked to some extraneous presentation/denial of reward and all economic benefits are restricted to a privileged few in the name of 'efficiency and meritocracy', all attempts at initiating reforms in this space will meet with resistance.

Notes

1 I would like to acknowledge the support of Manish Jain, Anisha George, and Suresh Reddy in developing this chapter.
2 The terms taught and learned (teaching and learning) may acquire different meanings depending on the underlying theory of learning, which defines learning and associated pedagogic processes in a particular educational context.
3 School in Hindi.
4 Regular candidate means a student enrolled in a school who has pursued a regular course of study and is entitled to appear for the Board exam that his school is affiliated to. A private candidate is one who is not a regular candidate but, under the provisions of bylaws, is allowed to undertake and/or appear in a given Board examination. Such students come from relatively disadvantaged backgrounds and find it difficult to study/continue in formal schools.
5 It is not uncommon to hear middle-class parents tell their children that if you do not study you will have to wash utensils and sweep floors in other people's houses.
6 This was revealed in interviews with several teachers, both government and private, as part of a study on CCE.
7 The Committee examined the existing literature on implications of non-detention and detention of students for their learning and also collected first-hand information from important stakeholders. It administered questionnaires to several states, incorporating questions for parents, teachers, and administrative staff. Thirteen states filled in those questionnaires, while 12 other states submitted separate reports sharing their experiences and voicing their concerns with regard to these provisions. In addition, the Committee also visited schools in several states and had conversations with teachers, students, parents, and other community members.
8 Several national, private, and international organisations have of late been assessing learning levels of children in schools. ASER is a survey conducted since 2005 by Pratham, an NGO working in the education space.

References

Annual Status of Education Report (Rural) (ASER) (2012). New Delhi: Pratham Resource Centre.

Arasarkadavil, D.J. (1963). *The Secondary School Leaving Examination in India: A Case Study of the Validity of the Examination in Kerala State*. Calcutta: Asia Publishing House.

Elphinstone, M. (1824). Minute on education by Mounstuart Elphinstone, March 1824. In G.W. Forrest, *Selections from the Minutes and Other Official Writings of the Honourable Mounstuart Elphinstone* (pp. 79–116). London: Richard Bentley and Son.

Government of India. (1904). *Resolution of Government on Educational Policy (1904)*. Calcutta: Superintendent, Government Printing.

Government of India (1991). *Report of the Committee for Review of NPE: Towards an Enlightened and Humane Society*. New Delhi: MHRD, Department of Education.

Government of India (2009). *The Right of Children to Free and Compulsory Education Act*. New Delhi: Ministry of Law and Justice, Legislative Department, Government of India, Retrieved from http://mhrd. gov.in/sites/upload_files/mhrd/files/rte.pdf.

Interim report of the Indian Statutory Commission (1929). London: HMSO.

Kumar, Krishna (1991). *Political Agenda of Education: A Study of Colonialist and Nationalist Ideas*, 2nd edition. New Delhi: Sage Publications.

Kumar, Krishna (1992). *What is Worth Teaching*, 4th edition. New Delhi: Orient Blackswan.

Madan, T.N. (2010). Between the braying pestles and the examination blues: the childhood years. In Malavika Karlekar and Rudrangshu Mukherjee (eds), *Remembered Childhood: Essays in honour of Andre Beteille*. New Delhi: Oxford University Press.

MHRD (1993). *Learning Without Burden: Report of the National Advisory Committee Appointed by MHRD*. New Delhi: MHRD.

MHRD (2014). *Report of CABE Sub-Committee on Assessment and Implementation of CCE and NDP (under the RtE Act, 2009)*. New Delhi: MHRD.

Ministry of Education (1966). *Education and National Development, Report of Education Commission* (1964–66). New Delhi: Government of India.

Naik, J.P. and Nurullah, S. (1974). *A Students' History of Education in India, 1800–1973*. New Delhi: Macmillan India Ltd.

Nawani, D. (2013). Continuously and comprehensively evaluating children. *Economic & Political Weekly*, 48: 33–40.

NCERT (1971). *Report of the Committee on Examinations, CABE, Ministry of Education and Social Welfare, India*. New Delhi: NCERT.

NCERT (2005). *National Curriculum Framework 2005*. New Delhi: NCERT.

NCERT (2006). *Position Paper: National Focus Group on Examination Reforms*. New Delhi: NCERT.

Pellegrino, J.W., Chudowski, N., and Glaser, R. (2001). *The Nature of Evidence and Reasoning from Evidence*. Washington, DC: National Academy Press.

Phule, J. (1882). Memorial addressed to the Education Commission. Retrieved from https://drive.google.com/file/d/0BwW2WP5670PqN2Q0ZTExZGQtMDEwZS00MmFjLTkyMGMtMmJlZTE1MjdjNGFj/view.

Post-war Educational Development in India (Sargeant Report) (1944). Delhi: Manager of Publications.

Premacanda (1986). *Stories from Premchand*. New Delhi: Madhuban Educational Books, Vikas Publishing House Pvt Ltd.

Report of Calcutta University Commission (1917–19) (1977). In *S.C. Ghosh Selections from Educational Records*, New Series, Vol. 2, New Delhi: Zakhir Husain Centre for Educational Studies.

Report of Indian Education Commission, 1882–83 (1884). Calcutta: Government Printing Press.

Report of Indian Universities Commission (1902) (1977). In *S.C. Ghosh Selections from Educational Records*, New Series, Vol. 2. New Delhi: Zakhir Husain Centre for Educational Studies.

Report of the University Education Commission, Aug–Dec 1948 (1949). Vol I. Delhi: Manager of Publications.

Report of the Zakhir Husain Committee and the Detailed Syllabus (1938). Wardha: Hindustani Talimi Sangh.

Shukla, S. (1978) 'Education, economy and social structure in British India'. *Varanasi National Journal of Education*, 1(1–2): 112–125; 7–80.

Singh, A. (1997a). *Remodelling of School Education Boards: Report of the Task Force on the Role and Status of Boards of Secondary Education*. New Delhi: MHRD.

Singh, A. (1997b). The place of secondary education. *Economic & Political Weekly*, 32: 880–883.

Srinivasan, M.V. (2015). Centralised evaluation practices: an ethnographic account of continuous and comprehensive evaluation in a government residential school. *Contemporary Education Dialogue*, 12(1): 59–86.

Tyler, R. (1949). *Basic Principles of Curriculum and Instruction*. Chicago, IL: University of Chicago Press.

Willis, D. (1993). Learning and assessment: exposing the inconsistencies of theory and practice. *Oxford Review of Education*, 19(3): 383–402.

Part II
Curriculum and teaching

'Curriculum', the term, draws its meaning from the procedures characteristic of a system and the ethos that they create. The meaning, therefore, can differ considerably between national systems, although they all use the term in a routine manner. In the Indian context, a major factor that shapes the meaning of 'curriculum' is the vastly differentiated economic and social clientele that is involved in institutionalised education. Mass or public examination, on the basis of a confidentially set paper, has served as the axis of equality in such a variegated system, and the curriculum has been tied to the examination process. Stability of examinable knowledge and fixed ways of teaching are understandably common. No matter what subject or discipline we look at, certain basic features of the examining and teaching processes govern the curriculum. Change is limited and difficult to initiate and manage even if the body of knowledge in the discipline loudly warrants it.

The study of curriculum and attempts to reform it are necessary for making sense of the larger picture of institutionalised education in India. Each area of the curriculum presents its own challenges for such a study because the nature of knowledge in each area poses distinct problems for efforts to reform the curriculum. In school education, the drafting of the National Curriculum Framework (NCF) 2005 marks a major attempt to take a comprehensive view of syllabus, textbook, and pedagogy in each area of knowledge. Though vast and ambitious, this exercise could not influence the examination system. Moreover, no parallel exercise was initiated in higher education. Both of these limitations can be explained with reference to institutional or organisational structures that govern the system. The reader will find a reflection of these factors in the chapters included in this section. They focus on science and the social sciences. The area of language education is covered by a chapter that brings into focus a peculiarity of the role that language plays in the Indian social system as a 'medium'.

This part has five chapters dealing with the general issues pertaining to curriculum and pedagogy in Indian schools and universities. In the first chapter, Chaise LaDousa discusses a theme relevant to the entire system of education in India, namely the language of teaching. In customary parlance, the term used is 'medium of instruction'. The chapter draws attention to the deeper, social meanings of this theme, referring to the stratification based on competence in the use of English. This stratification reflects the divisions that characterise the Indian education system between different kinds of schools. They also relate to different markets in which their products seek employment. The division of schools on the basis of the 'medium' or language used for teaching is fully embedded in the everyday discourse of education, hence its implications for the knowledge and learning are altogether ignored. All that receives attention is the 'quality' of learning that the English-medium school is supposedly able to deliver because it is privately run. The 'medium' thus serves as an ideological label for a deeper division between types of schools and the social classes they serve or mobilise into existence by their service.

The other three chapters in this part are concerned with curricular problems and reforms in science, mathematics, and the social sciences, especially history. Shobhit Mahajan examines the difficulties that the teaching of science and mathematics has chronically faced in colleges and universities in India. Some of the difficulties have to do with infrastructure, especially for experimentation, but more substantial problems are rooted in traditional curriculum design, pedagogic practices, and the examination system. There are continuities between school and college, but as recent experience shows, school science has responded to reform efforts somewhat more readily than has college teaching of science.

Hari Vasudevan and Kumkum Roy are both historians, but their chapters have a wider focus. Vasudevan examines the trajectory of social science teaching in schools since the time it was called social studies. He places Indian developments in this area in the wider setting of international discourses of reform. The chapter also demonstrates the important role played by key institutions in higher education in giving substance to the curriculum reform effort at the school level in the recent past. In her chapter, Roy draws closer attention to the distinctive effort made in the post-NCF 2005 textbooks of the NCERT to apply a constructivist approach to the portrayal of historical events and processes. Roy's chapter also dwells on the disconcerting effect of the entrenched examination system on the attempt made to redefine the content and pedagogy in school history, and the parallel effort that a creatively inclined teacher might make. Her discussion helps us grasp the inner constraints that the system of education and its own habit-energy places upon the process of curricular reform. These constraints are further magnified when we take into account the federal character of India and its education, and the limited institutional resources available to pursue substantial changes in curriculum design, textbooks, and teaching.

The final chapter in this section concerns an experiment in rural education based on an innovative curriculum associated with a major historical legacy. Nidhi Gaur presents a glimpse of Anand Niketan, a school set up by Mahatma Gandhi to pursue his plan for basic or 'new education' as he called it. This institution has recently been revived and its new incarnation demonstrates how some of the most difficult questions related to India's educational choices can be addressed by pedagogic means.

5

Mind the (language-medium) gap

Chaise LaDousa

At every halt on Delhi's Metro rail service, with the announcement of the upcoming station, comes a warning for the deboarding passengers. The announcements in Hindi such as '*doori ka dhyan rakhein*' are soon followed by 'mind the gap' in English. Sometimes, even the pronunciation of the names of stations are different in the Hindi and English messages. The second item in 'Chawri Bazar' is rendered with equal length and stress in the Hindi version, but is pronounced with a shortened initial vowel and stress on the second syllable in the English version. But while two languages coexist on the Delhi Metro, one can argue that schools across North India are doubly implicated in the language difference. Schools resemble the Delhi Metro because more than one language can be found within them, but a school is – additionally – identifiable by what language it uses as a primary language of pedagogy. The word used to refer to this phenomenon is '*madhyam*' in Hindi and 'medium' in English.[1] It would be like having separate metros and finding the order of the sets of messages in each kind reversed, the Hindi one with Hindi and English and the English one with English and Hindi. This chapter outlines some of the underpinnings and consequences of the language-medium divide in North India. It traces some of the ways in which the language-medium divide has undergone a change in its articulation during the past 20 years that I have been studying it in Varanasi, and, more sporadically, in Delhi. Changes in the language-medium divide have articulated the changing relationships between metros and villages in the social life of education in India, specifically through the increasing salience of provincial or small cities, like Varanasi. Such cities provide the crossroads between metros and villages and offer places where people struggle in various ways with the inequalities, tensions, and contradictions embedded in ties between language and education.

The language-medium opposition among multiple school types

There are various ways in which the federal, state, and municipal governments play a part in differentiating schools as types, and there are additional ways, outside of official administrative and funding structures in which people recognise schools to belong to types. Furthermore, the various governmental entities have occasionally been involved with the launching of education schemes, often with the intent of providing schooling to the poor and previously excluded. In the 1960s, a system of Kendriya Vidyalayas, often called Central Schools, was established all over the country to serve the children of government officials who faced transfer from time to time. Since the 1980s in the government of Prime Minister Rajiv Gandhi, a system of Sarvodaya Schools has been created nationwide to offer quality schooling, including instruction in English, to those children who would lack access to such schooling because of their rural residence or lower-class family origins (Vaish 2008; Viswanathan 1992). States, in turn, have the choice of whether to approve curricular materials created by the National Council for Educational Research and Training. Sometimes state governments have created their own curricular materials for use in schools (affiliated with the state's education board). Increasingly, the funding that some schools used to receive from the federal government in the form of grants-in-aid has been shifted to state educational administrative bodies (Jeffery *et al.* 2005). States are also the locus of administrative oversight of the massive network of Sarva Shiksha Abhiyan schools (Programme for Universalisation of Elementary Education) that is meant to provide the schooling necessary to fulfil the guarantee of universal education set in place by the Right of Children to Free and Compulsory Education Act (RTE), passed by Parliament in 2009. Municipal corporations, in turn, administer schools that were already teaching children from the poorest backgrounds when the Sarva Shiksha Abhiyan schools began to emerge.

Privately administered schools can receive grants-in-aid from the state or can function from the tuition, fees, and donations they receive. Schools can have religious affiliations. Convent schools have their origins in the colonial period and were often the schools for local elites desiring schooling in English for their children. Madrasas of various sectarian affiliations operate, as do schools with various Hindu reformist origins or more recent affiliations with the Hindu chauvinist Rashtriya Swayamsevak Sangh (National Volunteer Organisation). A huge number of schools in Varanasi have been founded for children who would not attend traditional institutions. Some of these have a building, but some operate from their founders' living rooms and rooftops. Some receive funding from non-governmental organisations (NGOs) and some operate because of volunteer efforts. Some have begun to pay teachers and have attained school administrative board affiliation. People also talk of schools for boys as well as girls, and sometimes remark that such schools obviate the need to police tensions brought on by puberty that is necessary in coeducational institutions (N. Kumar 2007).

One of the most common ways in which people talk about schools as belonging to types in Varanasi and Delhi, as well as in locations throughout the massive Hindi belt of Bihar, Chhattisgarh, Haryana, Himachal Pradesh, Jharkhand, Madhya Pradesh, Rajasthan, Uttar Pradesh, and Uttarakhand, is to refer to the medium of instruction. The array of school types reviewed above only partly touches on the issue of language medium. For example, while it is true that convent schools always derived part of their identity and prestige from their teaching in English, most of the schools that people now refer to as English medium are not convent schools. Furthermore, the government of India has long had policy measures that address the intersection of language and education, but the mandated teaching of three languages in schools developed by the Kothari Commission in the 1960s for national multilingual integration remains unknown to most people in Varanasi and Delhi (see also Aggarwal 1988; Brass 1990; Gupta *et al.* 1995; Khubchandani 2003; Pattanayak 1981; Srivastava 1990). This is despite the fact that their schooling has been structured by the policy. I have argued elsewhere that the Kothari Commission's three-language formula is not reflected in – and is subverted by – reflections on schooling that are configured by language-medium distinctions (LaDousa 2014). While the three-language formula advocates for the teaching of a language outside the language region to which one belongs, configured by the salience of the divide between Indo-Aryan and Dravidian languages, reflections on language-medium schooling focus on which of two languages, perceived to be available locally, a certain school claims.[2]

Language ideology and language-medium schooling

When people talk of schools in Varanasi, Delhi, and other locations in the Hindi belt, they inevitably draw on a juxtaposition of two types, Hindi and English. One of the reasons for which the distinction gives evidence that language ideology – ideas that people have about language, including its forms, social locations, and speakers – helps to configure the ways that people reflect on the school system is that a single opposition serves to sort an enormously complex set of institutional types such that each instance belongs to one of two options, or is deemed irrelevant to the distinction (Silverstein 2000).

One of the frames for the ideological distinction between Hindi and English that informs people's ideas about Hindi- and English-medium schooling is the nation. People speak of Hindi as the *rashtrabhasha*, or national language, and English as the *antarrashtriyabhasha*, or international language.[3] Scholars have long noted that people in India (and elsewhere in South Asia) exhibit an immensely rich set of notions about the multiple languages they speak, describing them by area, quality, and domain of practice (Lelyveld 1993; Pattanayak 1981). For example, people in Varanasi often speak of Bhojpuri's importance to the city. Bhojpuri is a language associated with a large region in Uttar Pradesh and Bihar, and is spoken elsewhere in India and the world (Mesthrie 1991; Mohan 1978). People in Varanasi take pride that there is an eponymous variety of Bhojpuri, Banarsi Boli. They describe Bhojpuri generally as sweet and sometimes as rustic, and sometimes draw a contrast between it and Hindi (LaDousa 2004; Simon 1986, 1993, 2003). But the domain of schooling narrows the possibilities of metalinguistic reflection. In the domain of schooling, only Hindi stands as mother language. This is likely due to the fact that people often remark that Bhojpuri does not have a literate, standardised form, but also because Hindi, and not Bhojpuri, represents the national with respect to English in the domain of schooling. People told me that Bhojpuri is *ghar ki bhasha* (language of the house) and *gaon ki bhasha* (language of the village), but never, like Hindi, the school *ki bhasha* (language of the school), much less *desh ki bhasha* (language of the nation).[4] I often heard teachers lampoon the idea of offering Bhojpuri in school, much less conducting lessons in classrooms in Bhojpuri.

The fact that only standardised forms of language are used in curricular materials also serves to differentiate the language varieties thought to be appropriate for use in schools from what is called Hinglish (K. Kumar 1988). The salience of Hinglish has grown enormously, especially since the liberalisation of the Indian economy in the early 1990s and the subsequent rise of advertising activity and digital communication. Utterances like '*ticket liya hai*' (I got the ticket) are so common and have been for so long that they might not raise questions about the boundaries of Hindi and English (Snell and Kothari 2011; Trivedi 2011). In my own work, for example, I have noticed that classroom activity in Hindi-medium schools and in Hindi class in English-medium schools often includes such forms, and that when I ask teachers about their use of words like 'dance' and 'programme' in their lessons, they state that such words might as well be accepted as Hindi, given their commonness (LaDousa 2014). Pal and Mishra, however, note that Pepsi's Youngistaan concept used in advertising of its various products specifically invoked the label Hinglish and drew connections between it and 'youthfulness, living carefree, [and] never giving up' (2011: 173). They report:

> At MICA [Mudra Institute of Communications, Ahmedabad], a group of students called itself the Youngistaan Gang! These were new-age people, up to date with everything, always setting the bar for the 'cool' quotient, and also relating closely with Hinglish.... The notable point, however, is that these young people (and others who would qualify as the Youngistaan Gang members) all came from affluent families and were comfortable with the concept of 'commodity'.
>
> *(Pal and Mishra 2011: 174)*

The disjunction between salient invocations of Hinglish in advertising and in usages wherein aspects of identity are at play, on the one hand, and school invocations of Hindi as necessarily separate from English, on the other, has not been studied. Such a study is pressing, one might argue, because at least some invocations of Hinglish are associated with relatively elite youth, precisely those who are attending schools wherein language boundaries tend to be drawn particularly sharply.

With the permission of the principal and teachers, I distributed a questionnaire about language attitudes to classes at two schools in Varanasi during fieldwork in 1997. One was a private school serving grades 1 through 8 affiliated to the Uttar Pradesh State Board of Education, and the other was a school receiving funds from the state serving grades 9 through 12, also affiliated to the state's board. In each school, principals, teachers, and students describe the school to be Hindi medium. Responses to the question 'Why is Hindi important?' without exception included the notion of national language, and almost as often, included the notion that love for Hindi is tied to love for goddess Saraswati, the Hindu deity of music, poetry, and learning more generally. Sometimes, student responses explicitly contrasted the notion of Hindi as national language to English as international language. Responses to the question 'Why is English important?' consistently included a list of professions including doctor and scientist, and also consistently included the Hindi verb *ghoomna* (to roam). The use of the verb resonated with conversations I had with teachers, parents, and students at both Hindi- and English-medium schools. English, people claimed, was necessary if one was to leave the city and its environs to find work, especially if the area was located in a place where Hindi was not commonly spoken. Such reflections implicitly ignored the kind of migration that has been happening for decades, whereby people from Uttar Pradesh and Bihar travel to Delhi, Kolkata, and other metros to find work in manual labour and transportation. Thus, the notion of movement attached to English-medium schooling is itself marked in terms of intersections of labour and social class.

Years later, in 2007, my student, Patrick Hodgens, and I interviewed five Class X students at a private school in Varanasi. The school is part of a chain widely described to be English medium, and the students were picked by the principal because, as she explained, they were toppers and high scorers in exams.

PATRICK: So, what do you think about the English language?

PRIYA: It's a, that's a, it's a very bold language, means you can express your feelings very freely, I feel like. So I feel like everywhere English is required. I feel like it's an administrative language and you need it everywhere. I feel it's a good way of explaining your thoughts.

AMIT: I think it's a global language and we can communicate in English everywhere. We can continue in our business everywhere, and English is always essential for us to do any global activities. So, English is very important.

RAJ: Sir, English is a language which is everywhere in the world so we will not face problems surrounding anything. We can express our views regarding anything.

RAM: It is the backbone of industrialisation and all over the world people are communicating in English. Without English, a person cannot build up his personality.

ABHISHEK: Since English is universal it can be used everywhere in the world and so it is very easy to establish friendship with any person, I feel, in any part of the world.

(LaDousa 2014: 53)

The students stressed the connection between the global nature of English and the ability to conduct business elsewhere, but they also raise another consequence of language-medium schooling, the development of one's personality. The concept is specifically tied to English-medium schooling and is oriented to the confidence one is urged to feel on becoming an English-medium student.

When we asked the same group of students about Hindi, their answers were brief.

PATRICK: And when you think of Hindi what do you think of?
PRIYA: Hindi. Ah, Hindi has respect from me as well.
RAJ: It's our mother language.
AMIT: It's our mother language, so … it has so much importance.
PRIYA: Yeah, it's importance cannot be mentioned in words. In words … it is not possible.

(LaDousa 2014: 54–55)

Fieldwork in other schools confirmed that students at schools described as English medium use words like 'respect' to describe their mother language, but that their descriptions of Hindi are much briefer and less elaborate than those of their Hindi-medium counterparts. Furthermore, neither students at schools described as Hindi medium or English medium used Hindi as a vehicle for descriptions of personality development and confidence building.

The language 'complex'

The language ideology underpinning students' reflections on Hindi and English, and the organisation of that ideology by language-medium distinctions, hint at inequalities in the acquisition of what Pierre Bourdieu (1986) has called symbolic and cultural capital made possible by the notion of medium. The inequality in the acquisition of symbolic capital shaped by the dual-medium system becomes apparent at the university level, if not long before. This is because the university is the first place in which students from Hindi-medium schools and students from English-medium schools will necessarily meet in the classroom. Vaidehi Ramanathan explains:

> If the proficiency of students educated in the Vernacular is deemed insufficient at the end of the XII grade, which by and large is the case, they are denied access to these 'prestigious disciplines'. Furthermore, in instances when VM [vernacular-medium] students are admitted to EM [English-medium] colleges, they face the uphill task of not only taking classes with their EM counterparts but of having to make the same set of state-mandated examinations in English. In many cases, this proves to be insurmountable for many low-income VM students and many of them drop out of the education system during and after college.
>
> (Ramanathan 2005a: 6; see also Ramanathan 1999, 2005b)

The VM schools to which Ramanathan refers teach in Gujarati because Ramanathan conducted her fieldwork in Gujarat, but the situation that she describes applies to Hindi-medium students in the Hindi Belt as well.

Ramanathan's invocation of 'prestigious disciplines' provides further evidence of the ways in which language-medium schooling structures the uneven provision of symbolic capital to students in India. Students' progress in one of three 'lines' of study as they approach their high school and intercollege levels: arts, commerce, or science. In the 1990s, I met many parents who had decided by the time their child entered the first level that they should be able to opt for a science line later in their schooling. Since the mid-2000s, parents desiring a particularly prestigious and potentially prosperous line of study have begun to claim commerce as their child's future possibility. The rise of digital technology industries in India and their connections to undergraduate, graduate, and professional training in courses for which the commerce line serves as preparation explains the growing predominance of the line in school ambitions. What has remained stable is that parents who desire that their children might be able to study in such a line claim without equivocation that English will be necessary. Many point to future plans to study in a prestigious line as the motive for attendance at an English-medium school. In turn, I have met many students enrolled at Banaras Hindu University (BHU) who associated their prolonged schooling with having studied in the arts line. Some students argued that if one were to come to their classes at BHU, one would see a majority of students who had attended Hindi-medium schools, but that if one were to visit the Indian Institute of Technology at BHU, the majority of students there would have attended English-medium schools.

The notion of a 'complex' was one of the primary means of identifying the result of language-medium schooling in an individual's life. Many people I knew who had studied in either Hindi- or English-medium schools talked about the growth of a complex that emerges when a person from one of the language-medium 'backgrounds' comes into contact with a person from the other. Many people also explained that the complex can emerge at different times in a person's life depending on when he/she shifts to a school of the other language medium, but that the complex is all but inevitable at the university level. There, students from Hindi- and English-medium schools will find each other in class and the former can feel inferior to the latter. Most people who mentioned the emergence of a complex noted that students from a Hindi-medium background might fall silent as a result, and students from an English-medium background might be unwilling to take criticism. The notion of the complex sees the seat of the language-medium distinction in the individual, and seems to be a response to attempts to reckon with an extremely complex interweaving of language varieties, institutional types, and sociological positions (LaDousa 2014).[5]

The inequalities underpinning the notion of complex take on a political geographic dimension when one considers the postgraduates studying for government placement exams and the ways in which issues of language medium configure their reflections. On a visit to Varanasi in 2014, I had the opportunity to meet a number of college graduates studying at a coaching centre in preparation for taking the Union Public Service Commission examinations. All of them were studying for the exams in Hindi medium. Asked whether they were from Varanasi, they showed surprise. One of them quipped that had they been from Varanasi, they would have attended coaching classes in a yet larger city, probably Delhi. The branch manager later explained that their Varanasi branch did not have English-medium lessons simply because students preparing for the English-medium exam usually relocated to nearby Allahabad or more distant Delhi. In sum, that coaching classes in Varanasi were conducted in Hindi – at least in a branch of a larger coaching centre headquartered in Delhi – seemed like a foregone conclusion. Furthermore, that students were studying at a coaching centre in Varanasi seemed to imply that they were from rural outlying areas. There are many students from Varanasi who do study in coaching centres for all manner of professional graduate programmes and civil service examinations, but to the rural students to whom I was speaking, the chance to move to more central nodes in a chain made good sense.

The voice of language-medium discourse

When people reflect on the relationship between education and language, they enter a landscape that is bifurcated by institutional types. The relevance of medium in people's reflections on others lasts much longer than their time in school. Indeed, the language-medium distinction comes to enable people to attain what Bakhtin (1981) called a voice, a means structured by language and institutional difference of inhabiting time and space in specific ways. Varanasi is representative of the great many emerging cites in North India that provide English- and Hindi-medium schools, helping people imagine the relevance of their as well as others' origins and aspirations. The city has long been famous as a major Hindu pilgrimage and an international tourist destination, but it is important also because it provides educational institutional types similar to those in other smaller cities such as Allahabad, Gorakhpur, and Patna, as well as many others further away.

Sometimes people imagine their children's futures and distance themselves from the city by claiming its educational offerings are inadequate. For example, during initial fieldwork in the 1990s, everyone in our lower middle-class neighbourhood called a certain paying guest 'Bank-walla'. The reference, in part, recognised the man's supervisory position in several local branches of a national bank. He had been transferred to Varanasi from Delhi, and although he was very satisfied with his pay, he was not happy to live away from his wife and daughter. I asked Bank-walla why he chose to live in our neighbourhood when much nicer options were available, and he responded that he wanted to save as much money as he could for his wife and daughter's expenses in Delhi. When I asked him why he had not brought them with him to live in Vara-nasi, he asked me whether I had ever heard of the tutorial sessions that my landlord's daughter was engaged in during the afternoons. He took my look of surprise as a cue to explain that my landlord's daughter was not likely be able to speak in English without using some Hindi. I noted that there are English-medium schools in Varanasi, but Bankwalla scoffed and retorted that no school in Varanasi could teach English in the manner that his daughter was enjoying in Delhi. Proctor (2014) notes that some elites in Delhi do not value English for its international status, but rather see it as a national language, whereas students in government and non-elite private schools in Delhi reproduce the ideological underpinnings that Hindi and English education presented herein. Thus, reflections on the language-medium distinction in schooling can serve to mark distinctions between places seen as central versus those seen as peripheral, and can index the class status of the person reflecting on language.

By and large, however, people in Varanasi used the medium distinction to engage in a voice that considered the two language mediums as the sum total of educational possibility. The dispositions towards Hindi- and English-medium schools and those affiliated with them can vary, as illustrated by the cases presented herein. One's reflections on issues of caste, class, region, nation, and more or less cosmopolitan origins can be configured by the language-medium distinction. One can go so far as to claim that the distinction between Hindi- and English-medium schooling in North India has come to play an organising role in the voice by which one takes up a position in the world.

While I heard many varied perspectives on the benefits and drawbacks of one or the other medium school in Varanasi, only one person I have met managed to throw the medium distinction itself into question (LaDousa 2014). In 1997, I had the opportunity to interview a veteran government school teacher from Rewa, Madhya Pradesh who had come to visit her ailing sister, my landlady. In an interview, the teacher conveyed the voice of the present wherein Hindi- and English-medium schools are locked in a mutual opposition. But, the teacher also recalled the circumstances of her educational past wherein the boundaries of language medium were not so starkly defined. She noted that her textbooks contained a good deal of English and that the presence of English in a Hindi-medium school was hardly remarkable. A voice from her past allowed the teacher to bring to bear the possibility that language and language mediums used not to line up so neatly and present such a sharp contrast. However, her ability to problematise the notion of medium was singular in my experience, further lending weight to the argument that the voice of medium distinction has come to pervade the present.

Cost and board affiliation

A practice germane to people's understandings of schooling throughout Varanasi is the collection of fees. A large number of schools are considered to be extremely inexpensive by virtue of the grants-in-aid made to them by the state. The schools run by municipal corporations can be included in the group of schools that are considered to cost very little. Indeed, families sending their children to such schools have reported that expenses such as pens, pencils, copies, uniform material, and uniform tailoring are the most dear (PROBE Team 1999). When asked about fees at such schools, parents hesitated to report the extremely small amount, and often accompanied the amount with a descriptor like *sasta* (cheap) or, occasionally, using the English, free. Parents at such schools used the adjective *sarkari* (government) to explain the low fees charged (Saranga-pani 2003). Asked about fees at private schools, parents sending their children to government schools often guessed wildly exaggerated amounts, indicating that they did not know what such fees really are. Indeed, private school fees vary a great deal (Ganguly-Scrase and Scrase 2009; Majumdar and Mooij 2011). During the period of my initial fieldwork in 1996, fees at the most expensive schools in Varanasi were just over Rs. 300 per month. These have roughly tripled since. There were private schools in Varanasi charging Rs. 40 to Rs. 80 per month in 1996.

Parents of children at private schools continue to complain that fees constitute only part of the cost of schooling. Equally dear are the various charges for supplies, programmes, and outings that private school attendance regularly includes. Indeed, children attending expensive private schools can be identified by a large set of material items and practices that set them apart from others. Private schools often require students to buy several different uniform sets that correspond to seasons or special events. More recently, select private schools have come to advertise that their facilities are air-conditioned, and sometimes that their buses are too. Students display their awareness of popular media trends by the characters and celebrities donning their pencil cases, book covers, and the like.

When I asked principals, teachers, and parents about the relationship between the language medium of a school and the amount of fees it charges, many claimed that the two were distinct issues. People said something like, 'fees *aur* medium *alag alag baat hain*' (fees and medium are two separate issues) or, referring to one or the other topic, '*yahan to doosri baat hai*' (that's a different issue). At the same time, people treated as a foregone conclusion that the most expensive schools in Varanasi were English medium. In conversations in which I would talk about Hindi-medium schools and government schools, people would often interject that they are '*ek hi baat*' (the same thing). Indeed, there are many Hindi-medium schools in Varanasi that are private and take fees. These schools tend to be forgotten in reflections on fees because they do not belong to the extremes. They are not government schools, and yet they are not among the most expensive schools in town either. For example, people never refer to such schools using the label 'public', which denotes a private school that caters to people who want their children to be able to speak a form of English that is seen as legitimate, at least regionally. Thus, there is a polar opposition that people frequently invoke between cheap Hindi- and expensive English-medium schools by talking about the government versus the private.

Early on in my fieldwork, in 1996, I noticed that a select number of schools advertised, whether in the streets or in newspapers, that they were affiliated to the CBSE. Already in 1996, people apocryphally explained that '*ek ek gali mein angrezi medium school ban gaye hain*' (an English-medium school has been built in each and every lane). The intersection of language-medium schooling and board affiliation has become more complex since the mid-1990s. People were right that new English-medium schools were being built, but, in the mid-1990s schools made obvious their board affiliations in advertising. Since then, most elite English-medium schools have stopped advertising their board affiliation because, as principals explained to me, people have come to assume the prestige of the school. The fact of the matter is that board affiliation with the CBSE is not so rare as it used to be. Furthermore, schools that aspire to be affiliated with the board use the word 'pattern' in their advertisements, indicating that their syllabus is in keeping with the board. A massive number of English-medium schools have now been built in Varanasi, but also in surrounding areas too, weakening the relationship somewhat between rural education and Hindi-medium schooling. What is certain is that the field of English-medium schools has grown and that indications that once were overt markers of legitimacy and prestige (such as CBSE affiliation) are only now part of a much more varied set of English-medium schools (LaDousa 2007). Bhattacharya (2013), for example, has remarked that the increasingly complex field of EM schooling likely hurts its least advantaged aspirants, the rural poor, by seeming to offer a kind of prestige particularly poorly.

Language-medium schooling in public

Schools and, increasingly, coaching and tutorial centres, do not just offer students engagement with a syllabus, classroom instruction, and, along with board affiliation, access to a set of examinations; they also advertise vigorously (Bhatia 2007). During my initial fieldwork between 1996 and 1997, schools were among the most commonly advertised institutions, products, and services on the walls and in the streets of Varanasi. The advertisements were either painted directly onto surfaces or painted or printed on paper and cloth signs and banners. Since 1997, advertising by city schools has continued unabated, even increased now with new avenues such as Hindi or English newspapers. Advertising for coaching and tutorial services too has increased dramatically. With reduction in printing costs and cheaper availability of coloured paper, one finds entire wall and building surfaces pasted with advertisements, the same appearing many times at one spot. In tandem with this is the arrival of a new phenomenon since the mid-2000s – advertising by individual BHU students. Often handwritten, these advertisements are accompanied by a subject and a telephone number.

The ways in which the language-medium division articulates with issues of cost, board affiliation, and prestige in advertising is especially complex. This is because schools as well as coaching and tutorial services do not just use Hindi and English to advertise themselves. They also use two scripts: Devanagari and Roman.[6] Hindi can be represented in Devanagari and Roman script and English can be represented in Roman and Devanagari script. Thus, visual language includes a semiotic resource that complicates any direct correspondence between language and medium.

The combination of language and script combinations on signboards and advertisements for schools presents an especially obvious means for ascertaining that the prestige of schools depends on a complex interplay of cost and board affiliation (LaDousa 2002, 2014). In short, schools that advertise in English in Roman script and schools that advertise in Hindi and Devanagari script tend to represent a polar opposition of prestigious English-medium schools affiliated to the CBSE and Hindi-medium schools affiliated to the Uttar Pradesh Board (UPB). These are schools that, in turn, figure as representative instances of what people reflect on and recognise as relatively elite English-medium schools and government-affiliated Hindi-medium schools, respectively. 'Mixed' lexical and script combinations are typical of the relatively newly formed English-medium private schools or Hindi-medium schools that are often associated with a lack of legitimacy and prestige. Furthermore, a handful of schools that used to advertise their CBSE status have stopped doing so. One principal revealed that they did so because the school now had a 'reputation'. At the same time, newer schools are advertising their affiliations prominently.

In turn, some schools have begun to advertise that they are seeking UPB affiliation. Such schools often represent some English lexical items in Devanagari script.

An example of a school using English lexical items in Devanagari can be found in the signboard for a municipal corporation school depicted in Figure 5.1. The school signboard includes the elements of most schools, except for two: it is painted as if an individual were writing and the proper name of the school is left ambiguous. Its designation as a municipal corporation school is rendered in Hindi in Devanagari, but then its designation by grade level is rendered in English in Devanagari. While school is spelled correctly, 'primary' is not. Most school signboards identify the neighbourhood where they are located, thus making the locality a part of their name. Furthermore, the designation can be read as a clue as to why the word 'primary' might be misspelled. Part of the school's identification includes reference to the sweeper colony in which it is located, a Dalit neighbourhood.[7] Indeed, during the Bahujan Samaj Party (BSP) government in Uttar Pradesh (2007–12), a statue of Ambedkar was installed right in front of the school entrance. The signboard's representation of English in Devanagari script contrasts with signboards of English-medium schools affiliated to the CBSE (English in Roman) and Hindi-medium schools of some prestige affiliated to the UPB (Hindi in Devanagari, with a more stylised rendering).

Coaching and tutorial services exhibit somewhat lesser adherence to the polar oppositions of lexical affiliation and script rendering exhibited by schools. For example, the advertisement for the Career Point coaching service depicted in Figure 5.2 primarily uses English in (mostly

Figure 5.1 Varanasi municipal corporation school signboard.

Source: all photographs in this chapter are by the author.

Note
Transliteration: nagar nigam (municipal corporation) prāimalī skul safāi bastī durgā kuṇḍ (sweeper colony Durga Kund) vārāṇasī.

Figure 5.2 Career Point tutorial service advertisement.

capitalised) Roman script. Place names, curiously, are rendered in Hindi, suggesting – in the confines of this advertisement, at least – that references to local places are best rendered in Devanagari script. The English rendered in Roman script seems to coincide with the (CBSE and ICSE) Boards mentioned for the XI and XII intercollege levels. However, the advertisement first includes the names of more specific examinations for which the centre will prepare students. 'Bank' refers to a whole range of organisational bureaucracies that run examinations for posts, and 'SSC' refers to the Staff Selection Commission of the government of India that holds an examination for various posts. The catchy phrase between 'ADMIT TODAY' and 'CAREER POINT' includes an industry-specific register item, 'Super Prep', as well as the use of 'n' as an abbreviation for 'and'. Such language usages contrast with the school advertisements in Varanasi, but are similar to the mid-range private English-medium school advertisements in Delhi (LaDousa 2014).

Advertisements for coaching and tutorial services have proliferated on the city walls and buildings so much so that some public spaces in Varanasi are literally covered with them. Figure 5.3 includes a depiction of three different coaching and tutorial centres. On the left are two different centres that offer preparation for the entrance examination to the same institution: Institute of Engineering and Rural Technology. The institute is located in the nearby city of Allahabad, which goes unmentioned in the advertisements, and offers a BTech in several technical fields. The two signs exhibit many parallels. Both use all lexical and script combinations, except the representation of Hindi lexical items in Roman script. Both render their titles in English, '[Pandey's] Excellent Tutorials' and 'Career Mentors', but do so using the Devanagari script. Indicating just how early coaching and tutorial services can become relevant in students' lives, even for entrance examinations to a specific institution for undergraduate study, the first advertisement announces that students will be accepted after their XI year. Like the advertisement in Figure 5.2, Pandey's Excellent Tutorials and Career Mentors give their locations using Devanagari.

Figure 5.3 Three tutorial service advertisements.

Notes
Transliterations:
(upper left)
New Batch Start
pāliṭeknik IERT
saphaltā kā dusrā nām vigat 11 varṣõ se (success's second name – since 11 years)
Pandey's
Eksīlent ṭyūṭoriyals
dharmasãgh, durgākuṇḍ, vārāṇasī
(lower left)
pāliṭeknikal/IERT
kī taiyārī karẽ (prepare for)
kairiyar menṭars
ravidās geṭ, lankā vārāṇasī
(right)
SPOKEN
GD GRAMMAR BASIC
ENGLISH – SSC, BANK, NDA, CDS
ENGLISH mẽ kamzor STUDENTS ke liye viśeṣ baic (weak in … special batch for)
ENGLISH CLASSES by – JP SIR
ravidās geṭ (hindustān hoṭal ke bagal vālī galī mẽ) lankā

In contrast to the primary use of Devanagari in the advertisements on the left, the one on the right for English Classes by JP Sir appears predominantly in Roman script. Just what the abbreviation 'GD' stands for in the list of aspects of English to be covered at the centre is ambiguous. Otherwise, the fact that 'SPOKEN' English is mentioned first and rendered largest seems suggestive. Some of the same examinations are included as in the advertisement for Career Point, depicted in Figure 5.2. Indeed, these exams are themselves bifurcated by medium, and students can opt to take them and conduct subsequent interviews in either Hindi or English. This advertisement makes it apparent that weaker students in English should be addressed using Hindi and

English in Devanagari script, while holding out the lexical items 'ENGLISH' and 'STUDENTS' to identify what such students should aspire to be. The only words rendered in Devanagari that might be taken to be English are 'batch' and 'hotel'. The first is a commonly used word in the coaching and tutorial services industry and the second is a common reference to a hotel. Many people might claim such words to challenge the distinctions between Hindi and English.

What is certain is that when a nearby polytechnical institute is being advertised, many English lexical items will be germane to that institution. Translations of such words into Hindi would render what is being referred to unknown to most readers. The rendering in Devanagari seems to coincide with the polytechnical institute's location nearby, in a relatively non-cosmopolitan location in the Hindi Belt, but the use of English seems to render the names of the coaching and tutorial services catchy, and perhaps aligned to words like 'polytechnic' (N. Kumar 1998). When spoken English is one of the services on offer, contrastingly, Roman script comes to dominate the advertisement. Yet, English lexical items rendered in Roman script are not simply oriented to the offer of English. Those students weak in English are to be addressed in Hindi in Devanagari. The advertisement for English Classes by JP Sir renders in sharp relief the ways in which speaking in English – tied to notions about personality development introduced earlier herein – provides a coaching and tutorial niche aimed at differential histories of students who have attended Hindi- and English-medium schools – more specifically, schools that offer varieties of English seen as legitimate. Thus, although signboards and advertisements exhibit a great range of lexical and script combinations, schools continue to reproduce signs of polarity between relatively elite English-medium institutions and relatively legitimate Hindi-medium institutions, and coaching and tutorial services reproduce signs cued to a more varied set of educational services that nevertheless are calibrated to the distinction between Hindi and English and Hindi- and English-medium schooling.

Conclusion

With the massive proliferation of English-medium schools and the provision of universal schooling through the Sarva Shiksha Abhiyan system, the salience of the language medium of a school continues, though now it presupposes the class and caste backgrounds of students and their parents less straightforwardly than in the past. From the peripheral position where the English they desired was provided by some in more cosmopolitan locales, Varanasi and other small cities across North India have moved to a place where they are offering coaching and tutorial services to students from their neighbouring towns and villages. Some of these private educational ventures teach in Hindi, but others rely on the inadequacy of the city and its surrounds to provide adequate spoken ability in English through the school. Advertisements reveal that the indication of students as weak in English is best conveyed in Hindi. And just as people like Bankwalla desire an English for their children that the city cannot provide, the spoken English of the coaching centre is likely to be found wanting in the eyes of certain offerings in large metros. Language-medium distinctions thus remain salient despite the fact that they articulate with an increasingly complex set of inequalities.

Notes

1 When speaking in Hindi, people often pronounce 'medium' with a retroflex stop.
2 See Bate 2010; Cody 2013; Mitchell 2009; and Ramaswamy 1997 for overviews of the antagonism that people in South India felt as a result of the government's efforts towards Hindi serving as the national language and Hindi being taught in schools in the South.
3 Some of the scholarship on Hindi in India includes Dua 1994b; Fox 1990; K. Kumar 1991; Orsini

2002; Al. Rai 2001; Am. Rai 1984; Sonntag 1996. Some of the scholarship on English in India includes Aggarwal 1997; Agnihotri and Khanna 1997; Dasgupta 1993; Dua 1994a; Faust and Nagar 2001; Khubchandani 1983; Nadkarni 1994; Rajan 1992; Rubdy 2008; Sonntag 2000; Verma 1994.

4 For an example of how such medium distinctions play out in Maharashtra, see Benei (2008).
5 Sandhu (2014) notes the ways in which the medium divide can play an insidious role in reflections on romantic relationships and marriage.
6 A small number of schools use the nastaliq script to advertise their schools in their signboards, but they are largely left out of reflections on the divisions between Hindi- and English-medium schools (Ahmad 2011; King 1994).
7 Some schools use place names in their names, but tend to be elite. For example, Delhi Public School uses the name of the national capital in its name, along with the designation 'public'.

References

Aggarwal, K. 1988. 'English and India's Three-Language Formula: An Empirical Perspective', *World Englishes* 7(3): 289–298.
Aggarwal, K. 1997. 'What's Indian about Indian Plurilingualism?', *Language Problems and Language Planning* 21(1): 35–50.
Agnihotri, R. and A. Khanna. 1997. *Problematizing English in India*. New Delhi: Sage Publications.
Ahmad, R. 2011. 'Urdu in Devanagari: Shifting Orthographic Practices and Muslim Identity in Delhi', *Language in Society* 40: 259–284.
Bakhtin, M.M. 1981. 'Discourse and the Novel', in M. Holquist (ed.), C. Emerson and M. Holquist (trans), *The Dialogic Imagination: Four Essays*, pp. 259–422. Austin: University of Texas Press.
Bate, B. 2010. *Tamil Oratory and the Dravidian Aesthetic: Democratic Practice in South India*. New York: Columbia University Press.
Benei, V. 2008. *Schooling Passions: Nation, History, and Language in Contemporary Western India*. Stanford: Stanford University Press.
Bhatia, T. 2007. *Advertising and Marketing in Rural India: Language, Culture, and Communication*. Delhi: Macmillan Publishers.
Bhattacharya, U. 2013. 'Mediating Inequalities: Exploring English-Medium Instruction in a Suburban Indian Village School', *Current Issues in Language Planning*, 14(1): 164–184.
Bourdieu, P. 1986. 'The Forms of Capital', in John Richardson (ed.), *Handbook of Theory and Research for the Sociology of Education*, pp. 241–258. Westport: Greenwood Press.
Brass, P. 1990. *The New Cambridge History of India. Part 1: The Politics of India Since Independence, Vol. 4*. Cambridge: Cambridge University Press.
Cody, F. 2013. *The Light of Knowledge: Literary Activism and the Politics of Writing in South India*. Ithaca: Cornell University Press.
Dasgupta, P. 1993. *The Otherness of English: India's Auntie Tongue Syndrome*. New Delhi: Sage Publications.
Dua, H. 1994a. 'Hindi Language Spread Policy and Its Implementation: Achievements and Prospects', *International Journal of the Sociology of Language* 107: 115–143.
Dua, H. 1994b. *The Hegemony of English*. Jaipur: Yashoda.
Faust, D. and R. Nagar. 2001. 'English Medium Education, Social Fracturing, and the Politics of Development in Postcolonial India', *Economic and Political Weekly* 36: 2878–2883.
Fox, R. 1990. 'Hindu Nationalism in the Making, or the Rise of the Hindian', in Richard Fox (ed.), *Nationalist Ideologies and the Production of National Cultures*, pp. 63–80. Washington, DC: American Anthropological Association.
Ganguly-Scrase, R. and T. Scrase. 2009. *Globalisation and the Middle Classes in India: The Social and Cultural Impact of Neoliberal Reforms*. London: Routledge.
Gupta, R.S., Anvita Abbi, and Kailash Aggarwal (eds). 1995. *Language and the State: Perspectives on the Eighth Schedule*. New Delhi: Creative Books.
Jeffery, R., P. Jeffery, and C. Jeffery. 2005. 'Social Inequalities and the Privatisation of Secondary Schooling in North India', in Radhika Chopra and Patricia Jeffery (eds), *Educational Regimes in Contemporary India*, pp. 41–61. New Delhi: Sage Publications.
Khubchandani, L. 1983. *Plural Languages, Plural Cultures: Communication, Identity, and Sociopolitical Change in Contemporary India*. Honolulu: University of Hawaii Press.

Khubchandani, L. 2003. 'Defining Mother Tongue Education in Plurilingual Contexts', *Language Policy* 2: 239–254.

King, C. 1994. *One Language, Two Scripts: The Hindi Movement in Nineteenth Century North India.* Delhi: Oxford University Press.

Kumar, K. 1988. 'Origin of India's "Textbook Culture"', *Comparative Education Review* 32(4): 452–464.

Kumar, K. 1991. *Political Agenda of Education: A Study of Colonialist and Nationalist Ideas.* Delhi: Sage Publications.

Kumar, N. 1998. 'Lessons from Contemporary Schools', *Sociological Bulletin* 47(1): 33–49.

Kumar, N. 2007. *The Politics of Gender, Community, and Modernity: Essays on Education in India.* Delhi: Oxford University Press.

LaDousa, C. 2002. 'Advertising in the Periphery: Languages and Schools in a North Indian City', *Language in Society*, 31(2): 213–242.

LaDousa, C. 2004. 'In the Mouth but not on the Map: Visions of Language and Their Enactment in the Hindi Belt', *Journal of Pragmatics*, 36(4): 633–661.

LaDousa, C. 2007. 'Liberalisation, Privatisation, Modernisation and Schooling in India: An Interview with Krishna Kumar', *Globalisation, Societies and Education* 5(2): 137–152.

LaDousa, C. 2014. *Hindi is Our Ground, English is Our Sky: Education, Language, and Social Class in Contemporary India.* Delhi: Cambridge University Press.

Lelyveld, D. 1993. 'The Fate of Hindustani: Colonial Knowledge and the Project of a National Language', in Carol Breckenridge and Peter van der Veer (eds), *Orientalism and the Postcolonial Predicament: Perspectives on South Asia*, pp. 198–214. Philadelphia: University of Pennsylvania Press.

Majumdar, M. and J. Mooij. 2011. *Education and Inequality in India: A Classroom View.* New York: Routledge.

Mesthrie, R. 1991. *Language in Indenture: A Sociolinguistic History of Bhojpuri-Hindi in South Africa.* Johannesburg: Witwatersrand University Press.

Mitchell, L. 2009. *Language, Emotion, and Politics in South India: The Making of a Mother Tongue.* Bloomington: Indiana University Press.

Mohan, P. 1978. 'Trinidad Bhojpuri: A Morphological Study'. Unpublished PhD dissertation, University of Michigan.

Nadkarni, M. 1994. 'English in Mother Tongue Medium Education', in R.K. Agnihotri and A.L. Khanna (eds), *Second Language Acquisition: Socio-cultural and Linguistic Aspects of English in India*, pp. 130–142. New Delhi: Sage Publications.

Orsini, F. 2002. *The Hindi Public Sphere 1920–1940: Language and Literature in the Age of Nationalism.* Delhi: Oxford University Press.

Pal, S. and S. Mishra. 2011. 'Hinglish and Youth: A Campus Perspective', in Rita Kothari and Rupert Snell (eds), *Chutneyfying English: The Phenomenon of Hinglish*, pp. 161–175. New Delhi: Penguin Books.

Pattanayak, D.P. 1981. *Multilingualism and Mother-Tongue Education.* Delhi: Oxford University Press.

PROBE Team. 1999. *Public Report on Basic Education in India.* Delhi: Oxford University Press.

Proctor, L.M. 2014. 'English and Globalization in India: The Fractal Nature of Discourse', *Journal of Linguistic Anthropology*, 24(3): 294–314.

Rai, Al. 2001. *Hindi Nationalism.* Delhi: Orient Longman.

Rai, Am. 1984. *A House Divided: The Origin and Development of Hindi/Hindavi.* Delhi: Oxford University Press.

Rajan, R. 1992. 'Fixing English: Nation, Language, Subject', in Rajeswari Rajan (ed.), *The Lie of the Land: English Literary Studies in India*, pp. 7–28. Delhi: Oxford University Press.

Ramanathan, V. 1999. '"English is Here to Stay": A Critical Look at Institutional and Educational Practices in India', *TESOL Quarterly*, 33(2): 211–231.

Ramanathan, V. 2005a. *The English–Vernacular Divide: Postcolonial Language Politics and Practice.* Clevedon: Multilingual Matters.

Ramanathan, V. 2005b. 'Ambiguities about English: Ideologies and Critical Practice in Vernacular-Medium College Classrooms in Gujarat, India', *Journal of Language, Identity, and Education* 4: 45–65.

Ramaswamy, S. 1997. *Passions of the Tongue: Language Devotion in Tamil India, 1891–1970.* Berkeley: University of California Press.

Rubdy, R. 2008. 'English in India: The Privilege and Privileging of Social Class', in Peter Tan and Rani Rubdy (eds), *Language as Commodity: Global Structures: Local Marketplaces*, pp. 122–145. London: Continuum.

Sandhu, P. 2014. '"Who Does She Think She Is?" Vernacular Medium and Failed Romance', *Journal of Language, Identity, and Education*, 13(1): 16–33.

Sarangapani, P. 2003. *Constructing School Knowledge: An Ethnography of Learning in an Indian Village*. New Delhi: Sage Publications.

Silverstein, M. 2000. 'Whorfianism and the Linguistic Imagination of Nationality', in Paul Kroskrity (ed.), *Regimes of Language: Ideologies, Polities, and Identities*, pp. 85–138. Santa Fe: School of American Research Press.

Simon, B. 1986. 'Bilingualism and Language Maintenance in Banaras'. Unpublished PhD dissertation, University of Wisconsin, Madison.

Simon, B. 1993. 'Language Choice, Religion, and Identity in the Banarsi Community', in Bradley Hertel and Cynthia Ann Humes (eds), *Living Banaras: Hindu Religion in Cultural Context*, pp. 245–268. Albany: State University of New York Press.

Simon, B. 2003. 'Here We Do Not Speak Bhojpuri: A Semantics of Opposition', in Cris Toffolo (ed.), *Emancipating Cultural Pluralism*, pp. 147–162. Albany, NY: State University of New York Press.

Snell, R. and R. Kothari. 2011. 'Introduction', in R. Kothari and R. Snell (eds), *Chutneyfying English: The Phenomenon of Hinglish*, pp. xxvii–xxxix. New Delhi: Penguin Books.

Sonntag, S. 1996. 'The Political Saliency of Language in Bihar and Uttar Pradesh', *The Journal of Commonwealth and Comparative Politics* 34(2): 1–18.

Sonntag, S. 2000. 'Ideology and Policy in the Politics of the English Language in North India', in Thomas Ricento (ed.), *Ideology, Politics and Language Policies: Focus on English*, pp. 133–150. Amsterdam: John Benjamins.

Srivastava, A.K. 1990. 'Multilingualism and School Education in India: Special Features, Problems, and Prospects', in D.P. Pattanayak (ed.), *Multilingualism in India*, pp. 37–53. Clevedon: Multilingual Matters.

Trivedi, H. 2011. 'Foreword', in R. Kothari and R. Snell (eds), *Chutneyfying English: The Phenomenon of Hinglish*, pp. vii–xxvi. New Delhi: Penguin Books.

Vaish, V. 2008. *Biliteracy and Globalization: English Language Education in India*. Clevedon: Multilingual Matters.

Verma, M. 1994. 'English in Indian Education', in R.K. Agnihotri and A.L. Khanna (eds), *Second Language Acquisition: Socio-cultural and Linguistic Aspects of English in India*, pp. 105–129. New Delhi: Sage Publications.

Viswanathan, G. 1992. 'English in a Literate Society', in Rajeswari Rajan (ed.), *The Lie of the Land: English Literary Studies in India*, pp. 29–41. Delhi: Oxford University Press.

Further reading

Benei, V. 2008. *Schooling Passions: Nation, History, and Language in Contemporary Western India*. Stanford: Stanford University Press.

Cody, F. 2013. *The Light of Knowledge: Literary Activism and the Politics of Writing in South India*. Ithaca: Cornell University Press.

Kachru, B. and Y. Kachru (eds). 2008. *Language in South Asia*. Cambridge: Cambridge University Press.

Khubchandani, L. 1983. *Plural Languages, Plural Cultures: Communication, Identity, and Sociopolitical Change in Contemporary India*. Honolulu: University of Hawaii Press.

Kumar, K. 1991. *Political Agenda of Education: A Study of Colonialist and Nationalist Ideas*. Delhi: Sage Publications.

LaDousa, C. 2014. *Hindi is Our Ground, English is Our Sky: Education, Language, and Social Class in Contemporary India*. Delhi: Cambridge University Press.

Ramanathan, V. 2005. *The English–Vernacular Divide: Postcolonial Language Politics and Practice*. Clevedon: Multilingual Matters.

Vaish, V. 2008. *Biliteracy and Globalization: English Language Education in India*. Clevedon: Multilingual Matters.

6

Science and mathematics teaching in schools and colleges

Shobhit Mahajan

The dominating feature of the contemporary world is the intense cultivation of science on a large scale, and its application to meet a country's requirements. It is this, which, for the first time in man's history, has given to the common man in countries advanced in science, a standard of living and social and cultural amenities, which were once confined to a very small privileged minority of the population. Science has led to the growth and diffusion of culture to an extent never possible before. It has not only radically altered man's material environment, but, what is of still deeper significance, it has provided new tools of thought and has extended man's mental horizon. It has thus influenced even the basic values of life, and given to civilisation a new vitality and a new dynamism.

(Government of India 1958)

These words, written in 1958, sum up the attitude to science that prevailed in the early decades after India's Independence. This was the time when the policy-makers were convinced that science and technology (S&T) would be important in pulling up India from centuries of under-development. S&T were thought of not just as a panacea for our underdevelopment, they were also seen, as the Resolution above makes clear, as important in themselves for civilisation. Scientific temper, a term associated with Pt Jawaharlal Nehru (Nehru 1946: 512) though possibly influenced by Bertrand Russell (Arnold 2013: 360–367), was an important part of the making of a 'modern' India. The harnessing of S&T for development, as well as a rational outlook towards the world, was an essential part of the narrative of nation building in the first couple of decades of independent India.

The central role of S&T as envisaged by the policy-makers meant that a large infrastructure of research, training, and teaching would need to be created virtually from scratch. Thus, the early decades after Independence saw the establishment of laboratories, research institutes, universities, and technology institutions. The network of research laboratories, under the Council of Scientific & Industrial Research (CSIR) and the Indian Council for Agricultural Research (ICAR), as well as the Departments of Atomic Energy and Space, were set up not just as ivory towers engaged in scientific research but indeed to meet the challenges of rapid economic development.

The education sector too witnessed an unprecedented expansion in this period and indeed in the subsequent decades. The total expenditure on education, as a percentage of GDP, went up from a little over 0.6 per cent in 1950–51 to around 3.8 per cent in 2010–11 (University Grants Commission (UGC) 2013). Technical and professional institutions like the Indian Institutes of Technology (IITs) and engineering colleges were set up to provide human resources to the industrialising economy. The growth in the number of primary and second-ary schools, colleges, polytechnics, universities, and professional colleges has also been very impressive, though obviously from a very low base. Thus, for instance, the number of univer-sities has grown from 30 in 1950–51 to over 700 in 2012–13 (ibid.) The expansion was not just in higher education – the number of schools, including primary, upper primary, second-ary, and senior secondary schools went up from around 225,000 to more than 1,425,000 between 1950–51 and 2013–14 (Kumar *et al.* 2008; Ministry of Human Resource Develop-ment (MHRD) 2014).

Though the disaggregated data for the number of high schools or colleges where science is taught are not available, it is reasonable to assume that given the large numbers of institutions, there are a fairly large number (in absolute terms) of them where science is offered.

There is no doubt that we have made impressive quantitative gains, as the numbers above testify. It can, of course, be argued that there is still a lot of pent up demand for both schools and institutions of higher learning and we need to expand the sector at an ever-increasing pace. For instance, the National Knowledge Commission (NKC) recommended setting up at least 1,500 universities as well as 50 national universities in the country to 'provide education of the highest standard' (NKC 2006).

However, to look at education purely as a matter of providing more schools and colleges is missing the important issue of quality. Herein lies the problem as even the NKC, in a surpris-ingly forthright manner, has pointed out:

> [T]here is, in fact, a quiet crisis in higher education in India that runs deep. It is not yet discernible simply because there are pockets of excellence, an enormous reservoir of tal-ented young people, and an intense competition in the admissions process.
>
> *(Ibid.)*

The problem is not just limited to higher education, but is in fact much more serious in schools. The two are of course linked, as we shall examine below. As the Kothari Commission noted in 1966, 'Indian education needs a drastic reconstruction, almost a revolution' (Kothari Commis-sion 1966). Sadly, this is even truer today than half a century ago.

Statistics and numbers

The UGC was set up in 1945 as a result of the recommendations of the Sargent Report (Sargent Report 1945). However, it was only in 1956 that the UGC was established as a statutory body for coordination, determination, and maintenance of standards in university education. This regulatory body sits at the apex of the landscape for non-technical education and thus, *inter alia*, for higher education in the sciences. In addition, in an odd conflict of interest, the UGC is the regulator as well as the funding agency for all central universities.

The higher education sector comprises central universities, state universities (both private and public), deemed universities, Open universities, institutions of national importance, and finally the bedrock of the higher education system, undergraduate colleges. Their respective numbers are given in Table 6.1 (MHRD 2014). Table 6.2 (ibid.) gives the statistics for schools at different levels.

The massive increase in both institutions of higher learning and at the school level that has been mentioned already has led to impressive strides in the gross enrolment ratio (GER) at

Table 6.1 Number of institutions of higher education

Universities	Central university	42
	State public university	310
	Deemed university	127
	State private university	143
	Central Open university	1
	State Open university	13
	Institution of national importance	68
	Institutions under State Legislature Act	5
	Others	3
	Total	**712**
Colleges		**36,671**
Stand-alone institutions	Diploma level technical	3541
	PGDM	392
	Diploma level nursing	2674
	Diploma level teacher training	4706
	Institute under ministries	132
	Total	**11,445**

Source: MHRD 2014.

Table 6.2 Number of schools

Type	Number
Primary	790,640
Upper primary	401,079
Secondary	131,287
Senior secondary	102,558
Total	**1,425,564**

Source: MHRD 2014.

almost all levels. Table 6.3 (ibid.) shows the latest available statistics, while Figure 6.1 (UGC 2013) depicts the GER for higher education over time.

Though we see that higher education enrolment has increased substantially, the disaggregated figures for various disciplines shows that in 2011–12, the percentage of students in the sciences was around 13 per cent of the total, as shown in Table 6.4 (MHRD 2014). The figures might understate the total number of students in science and mathematics since in several universities mathematics is a separate faculty and the degrees given are bachelors or masters of arts.

The total enrolment numbers for higher education combines all levels – undergraduate, postgraduate, and research. If one looks at the disaggregated figures for the various courses, one finds that enrolment is the highest at the undergraduate levels and falls substantially as one goes up, though in the case of sciences this fall is not as sharp as in other disciplines.

Some figures are available for enrolment in various streams at the senior secondary level, though they are not very comprehensive. Thus, in 2002 the number of students appearing in economics in CBSE and ICSE Boards combined was 158,548, while those appearing in physics

Shobhit Mahajan

Table 6.3 Gross enrolment ratio at various levels

Level	All			Scheduled Castes			Scheduled Tribes		
	Boys	Girls	Total	Boys	Girls	Total	Boys	Girls	Total
Primary (I–V)	98.1	100.6	99.3	110.8	112.2	111.5	111.5	108.8	110.2
Upper primary (VI–VIII)	84.9	90.3	87.4	93.2	96.5	94.8	86.5	85.7	86.1
Elementary (I–VIII)	93.3	96.9	95.0	104.2	109.4	102.8	102.5	100.5	101.5
Secondary (IX–X)	73.5	73.7	73.6	76.0	76.2	76.1	67.5	66.7	67.1
I–X	89.4	92.4	90.8	98.6	103.0	97.6	95.9	94.2	95.1
Senior secondary (XI–XII)	49.1	49.1	49.1	48.1	49.7	48.8	35.5	33.2	34.4
I–XII	83.3	85.9	84.6	91.1	93.3	92.2	87.5	86.0	86.8
Higher Education	22.3	19.8	21.1	16	14.2	15.1	12.4	9.7	11

Source: MHRD 2014.

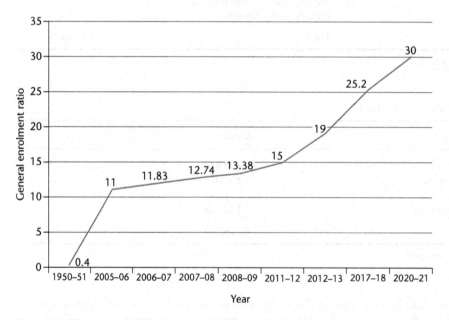

Figure 6.1 Change in GER for higher education with time.
Source: 'Higher Education in India at a Glance June, 2013', www.ugc.ac.in/pdfnews/6805988_HEglance2013.pdf.

was 162,175 and those in mathematics was 173,919. The numbers appearing in chemistry were similar to those in physics, while for biology the figure was 75,369 (Garg and Gupta 2003). These numbers, though suggestive, are obviously not very comprehensive since they leave out all the State Boards where the total enrolment is much higher. Nevertheless, taking these figures as representative of the overall trend, it seems clear that the fraction of students opting for science and mathematics at the senior secondary level is higher than those opting for these subjects at the undergraduate level.

Since the bulk of undergraduate training takes place at the college level, it seems obvious that for any meaningful analysis of higher education in science and mathematics, one has to consider

100

Table 6.4 Percentage enrolment in various courses

Programme	Male	Female	Total
BA – Bachelor of Arts	28.22	37.84	32.55
BCom – Bachelor of Commerce	11.51	11.30	11.42
BSc – Bachelor of Science	10.41	12.09	11.17
BTech – Bachelor of Technology	9.10	4.46	7.01
BE – Bachelor of Engineering	8.07	4.06	6.26
BEd – Bachelor of Education	1.34	2.84	2.01
LLB – Bachelor of Law or Laws	0.86	0.48	0.69
MA – Master of Arts	3.45	5.42	4.34
MSc – Master of Science	1.59	2.31	1.91
MBA – Master of Business	2.25	1.44	1.88
MCom – Master of Commerce	0.77	1.16	0.94
MCA – Master of Computer Applications	0.92	0.75	0.84
MBBS – Bachelor of Medicine and Bachelor of Surgery	0.46	0.52	0.49
MTech – Master of Technology	0.61	0.39	0.51
ME – Master of Engineering	0.25	0.22	0.24
Other	20.20	14.72	17.73

Source: MHRD 2014.

the undergraduate college as the unit of analysis. Of course, since only a handful of colleges are degree-granting institutions, the linkages of the colleges to the degree-awarding universities will also need to be considered. Furthermore, in matters academic as well as administrative, there is almost no autonomy for the colleges and so it is imperative to look at the functioning of the universities too, to gain any insight into the state of education at the undergraduate level.

While undergraduate colleges may be the loci for teaching science, research is almost always a preserve of universities in India. This complete separation of research and teaching at the undergraduate and to an extent at the postgraduate level has profound implications for the teaching of science, as we shall see.

Issues and analysis

The various issues which impact education in the specific cases of undergraduate and postgraduate education in general and in science in particular include the curriculum, the assessment or examination system, human resources, infrastructure, and access. We shall consider each of these in the following.

However, to look at science and mathematics education at the undergraduate level, it is important to have some understanding of how science teaching is done at the secondary level in schools. This is crucial because to a large extent, the pedagogical issues faced at the undergraduate level are a result of the quality of school teaching. And this is particularly true in the sciences.

However, there is a problem when we try to analyse the teaching of science in schools – and it stems from the enormous heterogeneity in the school system in the country. For instance, 25 per cent of all schools in India are private schools, while 54 per cent are managed by central/ state governments and 21 per cent by local bodies. Again, 96 per cent of schools are affiliated to their respective state boards and 1 per cent to the CBSE (E&Y 2014). Non-uniformity is, of course, also a feature of undergraduate education, though to a lesser extent. Thus, though the differences between teaching in a well-funded college of a central university and a small *moffusil* college affiliated to a state university might be large, a great number of colleges do populate the middle of the distribution. For schools, this problem is more severe.

Nevertheless, we can still try to find commonalities in pedagogy across schools which transcend the differences. First, a large majority of the schools still have poor infrastructure. Physical infrastructure in terms of laboratories, libraries, and computers, as well as broadband connectivity, is nowhere near what is required for efficient and effective teaching of science. In fact, a survey of over 240,000 secondary and senior secondary schools conducted by the Unified District Information System on Education (UDISE) and data analysed by the Delhi-based National University for Educational Administration and Planning (NUEPA) found that around 75 per cent of them lacked fully equipped and functional science laboratories (*Times of India* 2014). Even this dismal statistic hides wide divergences – thus, for instance, even in a relatively prosperous state like Karnataka, only 6 per cent of the schools have fully equipped labs at the senior secondary level (ibid.).

The paucity or poor quality of infrastructure extends to human resources as well; the teachers, who might technically be qualified to teach science, are in general not terribly inclined to communicate the excitement of doing science. The lack of good, inspiring, and effective teachers proves to be a major stumbling block in the students' engagement with the subject.

The indifferent quality of teaching is, of course, not restricted to the sciences, but it certainly does result in a large number of students being put off the subject for the rest of their lives – whereas an exposure to the sciences, if done in an engaging and exciting way, can prove to be of immense help in shaping a general culture of science and scientific temper. Invariably, the lack of good teaching makes students apprehensive of the subject. The same is true, even more acutely so, for mathematics. A majority of the population with school and college education still suffer from a phobia of mathematics due to uninspired teaching at the school level. In fact, there are now websites claiming to assist schools to overcome this (MB 2016)!

There is also the issue of the curriculum and its stress on a passive dissemination of facts. Despite numerous attempts to make science interesting, relevant, and ultimately a joy to learn, the actual situation is that it is usually taught as a collection of facts and theories that need to be memorised. In fact, the National Focus Group on Teaching of Science brings out the issues very clearly: 'science education, even at its best, develops competence but does not encourage inventiveness and creativity' (NCERT 2006).

Teaching science in a way in which learning is done primarily by doing and supplemented by constructing theories and hypotheses is significantly more challenging for teachers and hence is usually neglected. In fact, an important lacuna in the curriculum and its implementation is the almost complete neglect of experimentation. And this is not just because a majority of the schools lack the resources and infrastructure – the same is also true for the so-called elite schools which are otherwise very well equipped.

The issue of curriculum in schools is an important one – it is an important link in the development of scientific literacy.

> From the beginning of modern science in the 1600s, there has been an interest in how to link academic science with the life world of the student. This requires a lived curriculum and a range of thinking skills related to the proper utilisation of science/technology information. The extent to which students acquire these cognitive competencies determines whether or not they are scientifically literate. The supporting science curriculum must be culturally-based and in harmony with the contemporary ethos and practice of science.
>
> *(Hurd 1997: 407–416)*

There have been several experiments in various parts of the country to change the way science is taught. The Hoshangabad Science Teaching Programme is an example of a well-designed and competently implemented programme to address the above issues. Learning by doing, keeping the quantum of 'facts' to a minimum, extensive teacher training, and a commitment by the state were some of the key elements responsible for its success. However, the replication of this and similar experiments across the country has not been very successful (Eklavya 2007).

The National Focus Group on Teaching of Science seized on the importance of the problem and recommended

> that science education in India must undergo a paradigm shift. Rote learning should be discouraged. Inquiry skills should be supported and strengthened by language, design and quantitative skills. Schools should give much greater emphasis on co-curricular and extra-curricular elements aimed at stimulating investigative ability, inventiveness and creativity.
>
> *(NCERT 2006)*

The nature of assessment, as we shall also see later, has a major impact on the quality and quantity of science teaching at the school level. In fact, the above-mentioned position paper of the National Focus Group on Teaching of Science recognises this and adds that 'the overpowering examination system is basic to most, if not all, the fundamental problems of science education' (ibid.). The recommendations of the National Focus Group on Teaching of Science are radical: 'we recommend nothing short of declaring examination reform as a National Mission (like other critical missions of the country), supported by funding and high quality human resources that such a mission demands' (ibid.).

Coming to higher education, the basic institution for imparting science education at the tertiary level is the undergraduate, affiliated college. A typical university might have affiliated to it tens of colleges spread over a large geographical area. This situation, which might have been appropriate when it was introduced more than 50 years ago, is now one of the major impediments in improving the quality of science education.

Typically, the affiliated or constituent college has no academic autonomy. The curriculum, the academic calendar, and the examinations are all centralised with the affiliating university. Colleges just happen to be the locations for teaching. The disjunction of the actual site of learning and that of decision making has proved to be disastrous. We will look at each of the issues mentioned above in some detail now.

Curriculum

The undergraduate science curriculum of most universities is decided by the science departments in the university. Though there are various institutional mechanisms whereby the college teachers, the people who actually have to teach, are consulted, in practice curriculum framing becomes an exercise carried out almost exclusively by the faculty members of the affiliating university.

This is unfortunate since the college teacher is the fulcrum around which science education at the tertiary level revolves. This is not only because she is the person most informed about the actual reality on the ground, but also because she is the only person who has the potential to excite her students about the subject. Having had no say in the framing of the curriculum has a major impact on the quality of teaching since there is no sense of ownership.

The curricula themselves are mostly outdated, uninspiring, and usually err on the side of including too much. Even where syllabus revision takes place frequently, there is little connection with reality in terms of capabilities of teachers to teach the syllabus, the infrastructure required to teach, and, most importantly, the level of the students. For instance, introducing new experiments in laboratories without adequate preparation in terms of equipment and personnel makes it imposs-ible for the colleges to actually undertake them. Or, introducing new subjects (like microproces-sors, computer programming, genetic engineering etc.) without training the faculty members (who may not be familiar with them) leads to their teaching becoming a farce.

The curriculum is mostly designed in such a way that it encourages passive reception of knowledge. The need for the student to investigate, develop problem-solving abilities, and work in teams is neither required nor encouraged. This has the effect of science being taught in a way that is contrary to its basic principles – discovery, comprehension, and application to dif-ferent situations.

Laboratory work, which is seen as integral to any serious scientific teaching, is mostly done as a matter of routine. It is important for students to be aware of experimental techniques, data processing, and analysis, as well as to be familiar with the equipment used. Most institutions lack the infrastructure to effectively carry out this exercise. The laboratory curriculum itself consists of experiments that are outdated and have little pedagogical value. In short, there is nothing in the laboratory that could inspire or excite the student.

Frequently, there is also a project component in the curriculum. The spirit behind this is admir-able, but the actual implementation has destroyed it. The project is supposed to train the student to formulate a problem, investigate it, collect data, and prepare a detailed report. This would be useful in developing skills in a variety of areas like literature search, technical writing, data analysis, and experimental techniques. However, in most cases, what actually happens is that the project is bought off-the-shelf – there being shops which specialise in preparing projects!

Research seems to confirm what has been known to science educators for some time – stu-dents who are given more freedom to think and less instruction in laboratory classes seem to perform much better than those who are given a 'cookbook' approach to the class (*The Hindu* 22 February 2007). Unfortunately, the laboratory curriculum in our colleges and universities is a classic example of the cookbook approach in which students are provided step-by-step instruc-tions to carry out the experiments, resulting in almost no innovation or understanding.

Thus we see that both at the school and college level, the curriculum and the methodology of teaching leads to science being taught as a collection of facts that need to be memorised. Lack of infrastructure and demotivated teachers also contribute to the student not experiencing science as an exciting method to learn about and analyse the world around her. An important factor which reinforces this malaise is the assessment system.

Assessment

The examination or assessment system prevalent in most undergraduate institutions is highly centralised, where no distinction is made between the immense variations among the colleges. It is a system which is not conducive to innovation or initiative.

The nature of the examinations is detrimental to any assessment of genuine learning. Most examinations do not test anything more than memory. This is very damaging in all subjects, particularly the sciences, where no training is given for problem-solving or application of con-cepts. Commenting on the dismal state of the examination system, the Knowledge Commission has noted that:

> The nature of annual examinations at universities in India often stifles the teaching–learning process because they reward selective and uncritical learning. There is an acute need to

reform this examination system so that it tests understanding rather than memory. Analytical abilities and creative thinking should be at a premium. Learning by rote should be at a discount. Such reform would become more feasible with decentralised examination and smaller universities.

(NKC 2006)

All this is disastrous for science education – not just because the marks obtained at the end of the course are no indicator of the quality of the student, but more importantly because it has a negative feedback effect on the teaching per se. There is no incentive for the teacher to be innovative in the class. The student also takes the path of least resistance and is not interested in doing anything more than what is required for getting good grades in the examinations.

Decentralisation of the examination system will certainly help since motivated teachers could devise ways and means to encourage students to develop critical skills. One way to do this would be to incorporate some form of an Internal Assessment system which allows continuous assessment rather than an end-of-year assessment. This will also have the advantage of the teacher who is teaching the course being able to frame an assessment method which is suitable to the course and the students.

A common objection against decentralised assessment is grade inflation. While this is undoubtedly true to an extent, there can be several solutions to this. Thus, for instance, one can think of a relative grading where a student is only placed relative to his/her peers in the class rather than across institutions. Then the assessment will gauge a student's true ranking in his/her class. The relative placement of students across institutions can be done by standardised tests at some point.

In the sciences, there is also an additional examination for laboratory work. This by and large is a farce, since the methodology of testing the students does not test their experimental abilities or skills. And since here, too, everyone gets good grades, this examination serves no purpose as an assessment since it does not differentiate.

Human resources

The most important element in any educational system is the teacher. Competent, qualified, and motivated teachers are essential in maintaining the quality of education.

Contrary to popular perception, teaching is not very high on the list of attractive professions for good students. Even among teachers, teaching science is not a preferred option for many students. There are of course many reasons why science as a career is not high on the priority list. The job opportunities for professional degree holders are better and there is a lot of parental and peer pressure to secure a good future by becoming a professional. But one of the main reasons for a lot of students getting turned away from science is the dismal state of teaching at the school level.

Science teaching in even the best and most well-endowed schools does not inspire the student. As noted earlier, the syllabus and the pattern of assessment at the secondary level are such that most students are turned off. The whole philosophy behind science, one of discovery, problem-solving, and critical questioning, is discouraged and rote learning is encouraged and rewarded.

The quality of teachers is also poor, given that the best students opt for other careers and it is those who are left with no option that pursue a career in school teaching. Thus a typical student who enters college is already disillusioned with science, having never experienced the joy of learning and discovery. This is not just a problem in India – declining interest in science among school students has been noticed globally. The reasons given are many, though an important one is that 'students reject a school science that is disconnected from their own lives, a depersonalised science, where there is no space for themselves and their ideas' (UNESCO 2010).

The lack of motivation on the part of the students has a negative feedback effect on the teaching process, with the teacher not delivering her best to a class of disinterested students. This is a very serious problem and though no numbers are available, anecdotal evidence suggests that in the University of Delhi, even in good colleges, the percentage of students who want to pursue a degree in science out of choice is no more than 15 per cent.

The teaching profession has little charm for a bright and motivated student. This has disastrous consequences for science education since it creates a vicious circle. Students who go through their course with bad teachers lose interest and become demotivated teachers themselves, producing disinterested students, and so on.

This problem has been highlighted eloquently by the Indian Academy of Sciences *Report on Higher Education, 1994*. Bemoaning the lack of interest in science as a career, the report points out,

> In contrast to the situation a few decades ago, students, parents and indeed society as a whole do not presently view a career in science as rewarding or challenging, or even as offering a satisfying professional life. Career opportunities in science are perceived as limited, and as being not at all comparable materially with other professions. Intimately related to these negative impressions is the fact that faculty positions in colleges and universities appear lacking in prestige and respect.
>
> *(IAS 1994)*

The issue is not just one of quality, but also of quantity. The number of teachers with the requisite qualifications and competence is woefully inadequate, especially in the sciences. This is evident in the number of vacant teaching positions in most institutions, including the new ones (IITs, Indian Institutes of Science Engineering and Research, central universities). The administrators of these institutions have repeatedly pointed out that the paucity of qualified and competent teachers is their biggest challenge (*Economic Times* 2015).

Physical infrastructure

We have already indicated the dismal state of physical infrastructure for science teaching in secondary schools. Many schools operate from makeshift buildings and without the bare minimum of facilities in the classroom. Libraries are mostly defunct or barely functional; laboratories, which are anyway skeletally equipped, are not used for most of the year and opened only at the time of the Board examination. It is a dismal state of affairs that in seven states more than 80 per cent of the schools are without toilets (*The Indian Express* 2015).

The situation at the undergraduate level is hardly any better. Barring a few extremely well-funded institutions (the IITs and the recently established IISERs), the physical infrastructure in most of our higher education institutions is simply not good enough. Physical infrastructure includes classrooms with at least elementary teaching aids, tutorial rooms, and rooms for faculty members, well-stocked libraries, computers, internet connectivity, and laboratories, as well as recreational areas, toilets, etc.

In most colleges, there is a paucity of classrooms and tutorial rooms for discussions. Classrooms are in most cases non-functional. This environment is certainly not conducive to learning and exploration. In a situation where even functional blackboards are hard to find, there is little point in talking about high-technology teaching aids like projectors and display screens.

A well-stocked library with ample sitting space is an essential part of any educational institution. Unfortunately, most colleges have libraries that are not functional in any real sense. The maintenance is shambolic and there is little budget for increasing the holdings or even maintaining subscriptions in view of the ever-increasing costs of journals and books. This is disastrous since, given the high cost of books, the majority of students are dependent on the libraries for access to them.

Information technology can play a very important and enabling role in education. However, a majority of the colleges in the country have limited resources to provide computers for student use. There is also a lack of infrastructure in terms of uninterrupted power supply in most colleges; therefore, laboratories and computer resource centres function sub-optimally, leading to tremendous loss of time and efficiency.

Undergraduate teaching laboratories are in a pathetic state. The rising cost of equipment and spare parts has meant that the measly resources available for the laboratories are grossly insufficient to even maintain the labs, leave alone introduce new experiments.

Surprisingly, the Education Commission in 1948 had similar observations on the state of teaching laboratories:

> There is no doubt that modern teaching and research in scientific subjects require adequate and even costly equipment. Modern scientific research is largely a matter of evolving new techniques, the apparatus for which is costly and can only be provided by making adequate capital and recurring grants.
>
> *(Education Commission 1948)*

The gross neglect of undergraduate teaching laboratories has disastrous consequences for science education. As one commentator has noted:

> A major area of investment in Chinese universities is the upgrading of undergraduate teaching labs. We spend almost nothing on this front even as we stuff up a few 'prestige' institutes with costly equipment. But there will be a real pay-off only if we invest in training young people in the universities well. This is where China is correctly placing its money, and this is where we are totally off track.
>
> *(Desiraju 2007)*

Equality of access

J.P. Naik, in a seminal article, spoke of equality, quantity, and quality comprising the elusive triangle in Indian education (Naik 1979). This is the aspect of education which, though critical, is usually not considered in most discussions on education. Access, defined in a very broad way, implies real opportunities for everyone for a high-quality, meaningful education at affordable rates.

The first and the most obvious fact is that there are simply not enough vacancies for all the interested school-leaving students to get into colleges. Even though our GER for higher education is now a fairly respectable 20 per cent or so, it is clear that there is still a large unmet demand for education. This is evident from the large number of applicants for the limited number of college seats across the country. For instance, in 2015 Delhi University received around 320,000 applications for 54,000 seats (*India Today* 2016).

For those who do manage to secure a position at a college or a university, there are several barriers to a meaningful education. These barriers range from language skills, lack of textbooks and reference material in their native language, and a very heterogeneous school education leading to a huge gap in informational and conceptual training, etc.

In many parts of the country, the medium of instruction at the college level, especially in the sciences, is English. This automatically places a large number of students who have had their school education in vernacular languages at a disadvantage. The challenge of understanding the language has to be first overcome before even attempting to meaningfully engage with the subject.

The availability of high-quality and affordable books is another problem faced by most students. Even in English, the number of locally produced books which are of good quality is very small. The books that are normally used in most universities are of very poor quality, since in most institutions books written by foreign authors are either not prescribed or not used in practice by the students. The reasons are many – the cost of these good-quality, though foreign, books is much higher; the engagement demanded on the part of the student while using the book is much higher than locally produced books; and finally, the language used is frequently difficult for students who are not comfortable with it. Instead, what we get are locally written clones of these standard books, which in trying to make the subject and language more accessible, often end up being glorified guidebooks. It is ironic that with the third or maybe fourth largest manpower base in S&T in the world, one cannot point to more than a handful of good textbooks written in India which are of a global standard. Unlike, say, China or the post-revolution Soviet Union, where the best scientists wrote textbooks, some of which became classics in their subjects, our scientists don't seem to be inclined towards this enterprise (Wikipedia 2016).

A related issue is obviously the availability of books in languages other than English. In the sciences, there are almost no good-quality textbooks available in any of our languages at the college level. The non-existence of good reading material in the vernacular was recognised by the NKC, which recommended the setting up of a Translation Mission to translate material into Indian languages (NKC 2006).

Finally, we have a huge gap in what we expect our undergraduates to know and the skills that they ought to possess and what the reality is. The entering student is supposed to possess skills and have a level of awareness and information which is presumed to have been acquired either at home or at the secondary level. However, because of the huge variation in the standards of secondary education which exists in our country, there is a concomitant range of capabilities of the students entering the tertiary level.

Furthermore, the policies of affirmative action and reservation have resulted in a number of students from less-privileged backgrounds entering colleges and universities. In fact, some of them are first-generation learners. However, it would be a fallacy to think that lack of preparation to handle the rigours of college education is restricted to those who have gained access owing to reservations. It is far more general and widespread.

The solution, of course, is not to dilute the academic standards and thereby make a mockery of the whole system, but rather to provide the deficient students opportunities to catch up. After all, how does one expect them to cope with the huge demands that our system puts on their comprehension and informational capabilities given their deficient training? Is it fair on the students to be admitted (because of reservation or otherwise) and then be left to their own devices to compete in this harsh, alien ecosystem? Or should there be institutional mechanisms to empower and train these students? These could range from remedial classes in the afternoon or evenings, extensive preparatory classes during vacations, or some other methods to bring the ill-equipped students up to speed.

University of Delhi: a case study

We can consider the case of a large central university like the University of Delhi (DU) as illustrative of the above-mentioned malaise. DU is one of the largest institutions of higher education in the country. There are more than 80 constituent colleges where undergraduate teaching takes place. Postgraduate teaching is almost entirely done in the 80-odd departments of the DU, which are grouped into 14 faculties. The total student enrolment, including the distance education programme, is upwards of 500,000 (DU 2016).

The science subjects are aggregated into two faculties – science and interdisciplinary sciences – while mathematics has a separate faculty. Undergraduate teaching shifted to the colleges at various times in the past; for instance, in the case of physics it was only in 1971 that undergraduate honours course teaching moved to some of the colleges. Prior to this, all teaching was in the Department of Physics.

There have been several curriculum revisions in the sciences course over the last few decades. Let us focus on the Honours course in physics.

The Honours course in physics underwent at least three revisions prior to 2010. The process of curriculum revision, though in principle a fairly democratic one, in practice has some of the teachers in the postgraduate department in consultation with a small cohort of undergraduate teachers deciding what is to be taught and when. Genuine widespread consultations are not the norm and even if they take place, the suggestions are often overlooked.

Nevertheless, it must be said that the curriculum in the physics Honours course has, until recently, always been more or less comparable to the best in the world. Thus, for instance, what is usually considered the core for an undergraduate degree in physics – namely mechanics, electricity and magnetism, heat and thermodynamics, modern physics, and waves and oscillations – were all covered in some detail in the course. The topics covered in these subjects were comprehensive and essentially followed the standard treatment of these subjects as in well-known textbooks. In addition, one of the notable features of the physics Honours course was its stress on training in mathematical physics. This emphasis on mathematical physics, with one paper in each year, was something that was not practised in most universities in India or even abroad. A strong grounding in mathematics, the language of physics, means the student is given ample training in the techniques of problem-solving, at least at the theoretical level.

The course, as we noted, was extremely well designed and of high quality. Nevertheless, the quality and quantity of what is supposed to be taught is crucially dependent on how it is taught. Here the problems of centralisation of decision making in curriculum framing becomes obvious – the colleges in the DU are very uneven in terms of human and physical infrastructure. Thus, for instance, there are colleges where there are not enough teachers to teach all the subjects in the curriculum. The colleges then have to engage guest lecturers who, because of their limited engagement, are of limited efficacy. Even in colleges which are adequately staffed, the absence of any meaningful training and refresher courses means that most of the teachers are not equipped to teach some of the newer subjects. For instance, in the 1990s, when the Honours curriculum was revised for physics, several new subjects like microprocessors and digital electronics were introduced. Most teachers had never been exposed to these subjects and were therefore unable to teach them effectively. Furthermore, most of the colleges did not have proper equipment for the laboratory courses that went with these subjects. In such a scenario, the high quality of the curriculum itself becomes meaningless.

The curriculum, though otherwise of very high quality, has always had a major lacuna in terms of laboratory work. The choice of experiments and the structure of the lab courses is woefully inadequate to prepare the undergraduate student to develop any appreciation, let alone training of experimental physics. This is further exacerbated by the extremely poor infrastructure available in most colleges and even the postgraduate department. The funding available to the laboratories is pitiful. For instance, the total capital expense on laboratories in physics in 2012–13 at a premier college in the DU was around Rs. 16,000 – not even enough to buy a decent oscilloscope, an essential piece of equipment nowadays. It is pertinent to note that the number of students using the labs would be upwards of a couple of hundred (Ramjas 2013).

All this changed with the latest set of changes in the DU. In the last five years, the poor undergraduate has had to get used to the introduction of the semester system, then an abortive attempt to introduce a four-year undergraduate programme (FYUP), and finally a new avatar of the FYUP, the current Choice-Based Credit System (CBCS).

Whatever the theoretical merits and demerits of these revolutionary changes introduced in a blitzkrieg fashion (and with no discussion or debate), their effect on the curriculum has been disastrous. The changes in the curriculum to fit the new models have made a mockery of a perfectly good course of study. How else can one characterise the process through which the annual course of study was simply arbitrarily cut into two to fit the semester mode? In some of the subjects, this meant the load on the students increased since it was not possible to distribute the content evenly over two semesters. Worse, sometimes the two halves of the course were not even taught in successive semesters thereby making it all the more difficult for the teacher and the taught to maintain continuity in the development of the subject.

The mayhem caused by the FYUP and its new mutation, the CBCS, was even worse. Now we had the discipline courses slashed to make room for the so-called minors and foundation courses. This may not be such a bad idea per se, had it been done in the proper way with widespread discussion and adequate preparation. However, what actually happened was that the curriculum and structure of the foundation and minor courses made a mess of any meaningful pedagogy. The foundation courses, in particular, were designed it seems by someone like Rip Van Winkle – someone who had missed the developments of the last few years. How else does one explain a compulsory course for all undergraduates which in this day and age teaches students how to send an email or how to search for something on the internet (Mahajan 2013)?

Even though the curriculum till recently, with all the limitations of its implementation, remained of high quality, the assessment system was not conducive to any meaningful pedagogy. Examinations were held at the end of the year and assessment was centralised without any distinction between the hugely disparate academic standards of the colleges. Furthermore, the examinations tested nothing more than the ability to recall. In a subject like physics, an assessment that totally ignores the problem-solving abilities of the students and instead rewards memory recall of standard textbook material is disastrous. This, of course, had a feedback effect on the teaching, with both the student and the teacher adopting a path of least resistance towards attaining high grades, irrespective of any real understanding. The situation in the laboratories, where, as we have seen, even the curriculum was outdated, was worse since there was no real assessment. Almost everyone got very high grades with or without any experiments being performed.

Things changed somewhat around 2003, when a system of partial internal assessment was introduced (University of Delhi 2003). Some percentage of the overall mark was assigned to internal assessment done by the teacher running the course. This at least meant that there was some element of continuity as well as decentralisation in assessment. However, this was a chimera – the propensity of the teachers to inflate grades and the fetish of 'objectivity' in grading led the university to adopt a 'moderation' of the grades which made the whole exercise meaningless. Worse, the moderation process was shrouded in secrecy and could not be subjected to elementary tests of fairness or rigour.

The introduction of the semester system and the subsequent changes also had a dramatic effect on the quality of assessment. The DU, in an attempt to make the hugely unpopular system more likeable, resorted to large-scale grade inflation in some subjects. Thus, while previously it was rare for even the best students to achieve marks of more than 85 per cent in the physics honours course, scores in the 90+ per cent range were now common. It was not just the highest marks which were inflated – the median score also jumped to an unprecedented level (Mahajan 2012).

In terms of human resources, the situation is extremely bleak. There are more than 4,000 vacant teaching positions in the DU. Although the number of these positions in the sciences is not available, if one takes the number of students as an indicator of the number of positions and assumes the vacant positions are evenly distributed across subjects, the estimate for the sciences would be close to 1,000. This is alarming to say the least (Mahajan 2016a).

The situation is actually much worse – governance issues in the DU, especially in the last few years, have meant that these vacant positions are actually staffed by 'ad hoc' teachers. These contractual teachers have no security of tenure, are made to take a disproportionately high teaching load and are therefore a demotivated lot. It would be too much to expect such a demotivated teacher to actually inspire students towards the subject.

The quality issues in teaching are also something that need to be addressed – with changes in curriculum and the introduction of new subjects, the teachers need to be offered high-quality in-service training and refresher courses. No systematic policy has been framed to address this crucial issue.

The DU is one of the best funded universities in the country. And yet, the physical infrastructure of most colleges as well as large parts of the campus leave a lot to be desired. Laboratories with outdated or, worse, non-functioning equipment, libraries which serve as little more than a lending library for textbooks and examination guides, and a paucity of classrooms and recreational spaces are common across the university. Poor maintenance of existing infrastructure, a fairly widespread malaise in our nation, is also evident.

Of course, lack of resources is the primary reason for this situation. Resource allocation has not kept pace with the increase in enrolment. However, there is certainly an element of misguided priorities where libraries, classrooms and laboratories always seem to have a lower priority in a resource-scarce environment.

Finally, the issue of equality of access has recently become of great importance even in the DU. For a long time, the university has attracted students from across the country and thus the student body has always been fairly heterogeneous. However, despite this heterogeneity, there were only a very small percentage of students in the sciences who had not had their school education in English.

With the recent increase in enrolment due to a constitutional amendment which also mandated a reservation for certain classes of students, a fair number of students from disadvantaged backgrounds are now entering the university.

These students, many of them from rural backgrounds, have not had the opportunities that their urban, middle-class fellow classmates have had. The schools they have gone to were poor quality and, worse, their exposure to English as a medium of instruction is nil. Indeed, some of them are the first in their families to reach college. Thus, for instance, in the entering class for MSc in physics in 2015, more than 40 per cent of students' parents had never studied beyond Class XII (Mahajan 2016b).

This is a huge problem especially in the sciences, since all the instruction in the DU is in English. Thus, these students from modest backgrounds face a double whammy – a deficit in their exposure to the subject as well as the medium of instruction. It doesn't help that there are no appropriate textbooks available at the undergraduate level in the vernacular. This huge disadvantage was brought home to me when a postgraduate student of mine asked me for some clarifications in a textbook that I had written. When he showed me the relevant page, I noticed that the margins were filled with translations of the sentences in Hindi. When I asked him about it, he sheepishly confessed that he didn't follow the language and so had asked a friend to translate it into Hindi, which he had transcribed.

This is not to argue that these students are inherently any worse than others. It is just that the opportunities that they have had have been limited and therefore for their university education to be truly meaningful, they require a degree of assistance. Sadly, neither the administrators in the DU, nor the policy-makers in the government are interested in this matter.

Although the scenario we have discussed is for a particular course in a particular subject, the situation in all the other science subjects in the DU is fairly similar. It is indeed noteworthy that this is the situation in an old, well-known, and well-funded institution like the DU. One can only imagine the state of poorly funded state universities and *moffusil* colleges where sometimes even a proper building is missing.

Conclusions and outlook

Science education at all levels is not in a particularly good shape as things stand. Although our enrolment ratios have increased dramatically because of an enormous increase in public expenditure on education, the results have not been very encouraging.

At the school level the situation is more alarming than at the higher levels. This is because to a large extent, the fundamental approach to learning gets imbibed by the student at that formative stage. Poor infrastructure, lack of qualified and, more importantly, inspiring teachers, and standardisation imposed across states and the country leads to dismal results. Grade inflation, which is rampant in almost all school boards, masks the actual state of affairs, with a large number of students scoring in the high 90+ per cent range and a majority of them scoring reasonably well. That such a kind of assessment loses its meaning as assessment is, of course, a cause for concern, but possibly more important is the impact on the actual learning by the student.

Learning science for a vast majority of the students becomes basically a question of memorising some facts and information without processing it. Problem-solving, analytical thinking, and working out what-if scenarios, which are the hallmarks of training in science, are completely ignored.

The situation in higher education is not much different. Although we might be producing a fairly large number of graduates and postgraduates in the sciences (see Table 6.3), it is now widely acknowledged that these graduates do not possess the requisite skills. A good measure of how our science training compares with others is the research output. Leaving aside the advanced industrialised economies, our research output in the sciences is lagging behind similar countries. Thus, for instance, China was lagging behind India in the number of scientific publications and citations till 1996, when it outpaced India and is now far ahead in both the quantity and quality of research (Kademani et al. 2014).

In this dismal landscape, there are several initiatives which are laudable and could produce positive results over time. Several schemes to encourage students to take up science have been initiated in the last several years. These include the Innovation in Science Pursuit for Inspired Research (INSPIRE) programme and the Kishore Vaigyanik Protsahan Yojana (KVPY), which aim to identify bright students with an aptitude for science at a young age and then provide them with scholarships (DST 2015). The INSPIRE programme also has a component of various scientists visiting schools and colleges to deliver talks and seminars. The impact on the students, especially in schools in rural and remote areas, of this exposure to the excitement of science should not be underestimated. The Homi Bhabha Centre for Science Education has been organising programmes based on the Science and Mathematics Olympiads across the nation, and these have certainly inspired some of the brighter school students. The Indian Academy of Science has a summer programme in which interested students get assigned to a mentor for a summer project (IAS 2015).

The Rashtriya Avishkar Abhiyan (RAA), another initiative of the MHRD, 'while emphasising the primacy of the schools and classroom transactions, aims to leverage the potential for Science, Mathematics and Technology learning in non-classroom settings' (RAA 2015). This too should yield positive results in the quality of learning outcomes for school students over time.

For improving the quality of human resources in our institutions, there are several in-service refresher courses which are mandatory for promotions. This requirement has unfortunately made these courses somewhat unattractive. Nevertheless, these courses can provide a valuable resource for teachers to get up to speed with some of the latest developments in the subject as well as in pedagogical methods.

In all of the above, we have not discussed the role of research, and have focused on teaching at the universities and colleges. This is because for a majority of our college faculty, continuing with research is an almost impossible task. Lack of facilities, paucity of time, and the overall inertia make it almost impossible for anyone but the most motivated teacher to continue with research. This, of course, has major consequences for teaching since it has been widely acknowledged that research work actually leads to an improvement in teaching quality (Prince *et al.* 2007: 283–294).

The infrastructure needed for scientific research, namely laboratories and access to journals, etc., is an area where some welcome steps have been taken in the last few decades. The development of central facilities by the UGC is a very welcome step. These inter-university centres cater to the college teachers who can avail of them, especially during vacation time. This provides teachers with an opportunity to use expensive and hard-to-obtain equipment to facilitate their research. Similarly, the expansion of initiatives like INFLIBNET will provide electronic access to journals to colleges, thus improving access to information and research for students and teachers there.

Both the school and higher education system in the country need a drastic and urgent overhaul. At the school level, there is an urgent need to rethink and experiment with new curricula, as well as pedagogical tools, while improving the physical infrastructure. For higher education, a massive expansion and qualitative improvement is required in such institutions to improve their access to all our citizens. This is imperative if we want to compete in an increasingly globalised world where knowledge plays a role as important as capital, labour, and natural resources.

Of course, improving the quality of and access to schools and universities requires enormous resources. But one should be careful in recognising that though this might be a necessary condition, it is by no means a sufficient one. What are really needed are a judicious use of resources, change in mindsets, improved systems of governance, and a proper use of incentives and disincentives. We must also realise that given our tremendous diversity, there is no single magic formula which will guarantee success.

Finally, apart from the institutional framework, it is also important to consider the broader social milieu if one wants to understand the issues facing science education in the country. Science as a vocation has been hugely downgraded in our society. This is a big change from the situation prevailing in the 1950s and 1960s, when science was seen as the career of choice for the best and brightest. People like Vikram Sarabhai and Homi Bhabha, the pioneers of scientific institution building in post-Independence India, were idolised by a generation of students. In the decade of the 1970s and 1980s, this changed drastically. Research and/or teaching as a profession was downgraded and presumed as unattractive for students. It was not just about monetary rewards of alternative careers – social recognition started playing a major part in career choices.

Education is not just about increasing the enrolment numbers by fiat. It is about providing genuine opportunities to students from diverse backgrounds to enlarge their mental and cognitive capabilities. Of course, there are challenges – financial, institutional, and human-resource related. These challenges are especially acute in the sciences because of the nature of the disciplines. However, education is such an important area of human activity – an enabler not just in the economic sense but also in a civilisational one – that the challenges are worth taking up.

References

Arnold, David. 2013. 'Nehruvian Science and Postcolonial India', *ISIS*, 104(2): 360–370.

Desiraju, Gautam. 2007. 'China shows the way in science education'. *The Hindu*, 19 February.

DST. 2015. 'INSPIRE'. www.inspire-dst.gov.in; www.kvpy.org.in/main (accessed on 23 March 2015).

DU. 2016. 'Academics'. http://du.ac.in/du/index.php?page=study (accessed on 12 June 2016).

E&Y. 2014. 'Private sector's contribution to K-12 education in India: current impact, challenges & way forward'. www.ey.com/IN/en/Industries/India-sectors/Education/EY-role-of-private-sector-on-K-12-education-in-India.

Economic Times, 2015. 'IITs facing faculty shortage by up to 40%; beefing up compensation packages to attract talents'. http://economictimes.indiatimes.com/jobs/iits-facing-faculty-shortage-by-up-to-40-beefing-up-compensation-packages-to-attract-talents/articleshow/47636795.cms (accessed on 10 June 2016).

Education Commission. 1948. *Report of the Education Commission, 1948*. www.teindia.nic.in (accessed on 20 March 2015).

Eklavya. 2007. 'Thirty years of Hoshangabad Science Teaching Programme: 1972–2002: a review'. www.eklavya.in/pdfs/HSTP/HSTP%2030%20years%20Review%201-3-2007.pdf (accessed on 23 March 2015).

Garg, K.C. and Gupta, B.M. 2003. 'Decline in science education in India: a case study of +2 and undergraduate level', *Current Science*, 84(9): 1198–1201.

Government of India. 1958. *Science Policy Resolution*. http://dst.gov.in/stsysindia/spr1958.htm (accessed on 23 March 2015).

The Hindu. 2007. 'Scientific literacy among students'. *The Hindu*, 22 February. www.thehindu.com/todays-paper/tp-features/tp-sci-tech-and-agri/scientific-literacy-among-students/article2267358.ece (accessed on 23 March 2015).

Hurd, P.D. 1997. 'Scientific literacy: new minds for a changing world', *Science Education*, 82: 407–416.

IAS (Indian Academy of Sciences). 1994. 'Report on higher education'. www.ias.ac.in/initiat/sci_ed/report.html (accessed on 20 March 2015).

IAS. 2015. 'Indian Academy of Science'. www.ias.ac.in/index.html (accessed on 23 March 2015).

India Today. 2016. 'Delhi University admissions 2016: over 1 lakh applications received in two days'. http://indiatoday.intoday.in/education/story/delhi-university-admission-process-began-2016/1/683174.html (accessed on 8 June 2016).

The Indian Express. 2015. 'Modi promised total sanitation in schools, but it might be difficult to achieve. Here is why'. 24 February.

Kademani, B.S., Sagar, Anil, and Kumar, Vijai. 2014. 'Indian science & technology research: a scientometric mapping based on Science Citation Index'. http://eprints.rclis.org/8398 (accessed on 15 March 2015).

Kothari Commission. 1966. *Report of the Education Commission 1964–1966*. Delhi: Government of India Press.

Kumar, N., Kumar, Vipan, and Kumar, Neelam. 2008. 'Educational infrastructure in India'. In *India S&T Report, 2008* (pp. 13–15). New Delhi: National Institute of Science, Technology and Development Studies (NISTADS).

Mahajan, S. 2012. 'Compounding the error – marks inflation at Delhi University'. https://kafila.org/2012/02/08/compounding-the-error-marks-inflation-at-delhi-university-shobhit-mahajan.

Mahajan, S. 2013. 'Weak foundations'. *Social Scientist*, 41(7/8): 35–38.

Mahajan, S. 2016a. 'Things to DU'. *The Indian Express*, 20 February 2016.

Mahajan, S. 2016b. 'Survey of M.Sc. (Physics) students at Delhi University'. Unpublished.

MB. 2016. 'Eradicate math phobia in schools'. www.slideshare.net/MathBuster/eradicate-math-phobia-in-schools (accessed on 9 June 2016).

MHRD (Ministry of Human Resource Development). 2014. *Educational Statistics at a Glance*. New Delhi: MHRD.

Naik, J.P. 1979. 'Equality, quantity and quality: the elusive triangle in Indian education', *International Review of Education*, 25(2–3): 167–185.

NCERT. 2006. 'Position paper: National Focus Group on Teaching of Science'. https://ideas.repec.org/s/ess/wpaper.html.

Nehru, Jawaharlal. 1946. *The Discovery of India*. Oxford: Oxford University Press.

NKC (National Knowledge Commission). 2006. 'Report to the Nation'. http://knowledgecommission-archive.nic.in/reports/report09.asp.

Prince M.J., Felder R.M., and Brent R. 2007. 'Does faculty research improve undergraduate teaching? An analysis of existing and potential synergies', *Journal of Engineering Education*, 96(4): 283–294.

RAA. 2015. 'Order of RAA guidelines'. http://mhrd.gov.in/rashtriya-avishkar-abhiyan (accessed on 10 June 2016).

Ramjas. 2013. 'Balance sheet as on 31st March 2013'. http://ramjascollege.edu/pdf/141095338473398661183.pdf (accessed on 13 June 2016).

Sargent Report. 1945. *Sargent Report on Education, 1944*. www.kkhsou.in/main/education/sargent_report.html (accessed on 25 February 2015).

Times of India. 2014. '75% of schools lack decent science labs'. *Times of India*, 19 August.

UGC (University Grants Commission). 2013. 'Higher education in India at a glance, June, 2013'. www.ugc.ac.in/pdfnews/6805988_HEglance2013.pdf (accessed on 10 March 2015).

UNESCO. 2010. 'Current challenges in basic science education'. http://unesdoc.unesco.org/images/0019/001914/191425e.pdf (accessed on 13 June 2016).

University of Delhi. 2003. Ordinance. http://dcac.du.ac.in/documents/ordinance.pdf.

Wikipedia. 2016. 'Course of theoretical physics'. https://en.wikipedia.org/wiki/Course_of_Theoretical_Physics.

7

The teaching of social sciences in schools and colleges in India

Hari Vasudevan

This brief chapter examines the teaching in India of a range of subjects associated with the social sciences – history, geography, political science, sociology, and economics. It focuses on their teaching in schools and at the first degree level, in universities (Jamia Millia, Jadavpur, etc.), or colleges affiliated to universities (Calcutta, Madras, Bombay, Delhi, etc.), locating developments against an international background beginning with India's late colonial experiences. The chapter traces the limited sense of the social sciences as an integrated domain of study at the time of India's Independence and its slow evolution towards the 1960s. In school and college/early university, though, the child/young person did not find reference to the composite space in any meaningful manner. The domain was often used as a descriptive category well into the mid-1990s, with substantial value inflection loading its treatment at the school level. Initiatives took shape in the mid-2000s in India's National Council for Education Research and Training (NCERT) moving in new directions. These did not find any serious uptake in universities, where training in the categories and information necessary for research orientation were standard until recently. The chapter ends with a short evaluation of later developments associated with the Right to Education Act (RTE) and the onset of privatisation in school and university education.

The chapter reviews the standard literature on Indian education, including government committee and commission reports.[1] An important part of the argument will be that the position of 'social science' in the Indian educationist's imagination has often differed from the way the domain has been represented abroad, where stress falls on the significance of the domain for a 'modern' society and the practical value of the subjects for such a society. In India, orientation towards values at school, and research at university, has been standardised, without flexibility in aims and processes. Social science education receives a more 'holistic' and practical inflection in special institutes that are concerned with specific goals, giving these a special role in the Indian educational system; but in these institutions, the larger aspects of the subjects are not considered worthy of attention.

India's encounters with social sciences: the global background of the early/mid-twentieth century

Global 'social sciences' education and significance for India: the British example

India's engagement with social science teaching came through educational initiatives taken during the late colonial period (i.e. from the late nineteenth century to the early twentieth century) in Indian schools and colleges.[2] The initiatives were given a different direction and shape after Independence in 1947.

In the disciplines making up the social sciences, Indian inputs and networks took shape in the inter-war period. In history, these centred on the Asiatic societies, the Archaeological Survey of India, and independent scholarship among groups in growing universities and their constituent colleges. An inter-war generation of lead scholars included figures such as Nilakanta Shastri and Jadunath Sarkar in history. In geography, the Survey of India exercised a prominent hold. In economics, the Indian Economic Association stimulated diverse research, while in sociology, the works of G.S. Ghurye, Nirmal Bose, and others had established a trend. In political science, constitutions and administration attracted scholars. The subjects were associated with a self-conscious 'nationalist' scholarship that touched the study of language and literature as well, and developed the agenda for education in science and technology.

This was a domain of discipline-specific research. In the education system, the work suggested itself for attention at universities, for higher degrees (a two-year MA or PhD), or at colleges for lower degrees (a three-year BA Honours and two-year Pass course). In preparation for this, research-based literature was included in intermediate or pre-university courses that followed nine or ten years of school. In practice, degree education came down to teaching of individual subjects at various depths, where focus fell on a cardinal subject or subjects and the teaching was based on research literature.

At school, history and geography were taught through the equivalent of upper primary and secondary stages, with some attention to civics, where administration, constitutions, and good public habits were the stock in trade. Education rose to its higher levels with a firm disciplinary orientation (focused on language, mathematics, general science, history, geography, and forms of civics). In so far as social sciences were recognised here, they meant history, geography, and civics. Competence was graded according to depth in terms of information as well as a general awareness of the terms and categories of analysis.

This approach to teaching the subjects of the social sciences had its reference point in the British system of education. Here, education at school and university level in two subjects of the social sciences – history and geography[3] – was well established, although economics came to attract attention by the 1920s. A composite space of social science education was seldom involved, though interactions across disciplines did occur, while the academic acknowledgement of this as a domain of study was evident (Seligman and Johnson 1938). History and geography were primarily taught as subjects that contributed to identity and as guides to appropriate social behaviour and basic practical wisdom.

After 1945, social sciences as subjects for study and research developed vigorously in universities. Acknowledgement of this domain for school instruction gained visibility. Economics and sociology were seen as subjects that aided policy – a status that political economy had acquired in the nineteenth century, assisted by inputs from history and geography. The subjects associated with the social sciences were registered as crucial to the development of 'modern man' (Institut de l'UNESCO de l'education 1962). The legacy, however, of different disciplines, exercised its own influence.

Global 'social sciences' education and significance for India

Much of what took place in Britain followed from ideas concerning education and the skills essential for policy. These ideas have taken on new forms, and the last half-century has seen the assertion in the UK, Australasia, Western Europe, and the USA of a programme for social sciences teaching at the school level in preparation for an integrated approach to the disciplines in higher education. This coincides with a quest for a 'holistic' approach to education at both levels. It also recognises the coincidence of many questions that attract economics, political science, sociology, history, and geography. How social sciences as a unified branch of knowledge may address such common ground is still in doubt, though, since the dimensions of such a 'grouping' have not attracted consensus.

Persistent imbalances have remained.[4] Questions concerning pedagogy, and the way in which school education may blend into higher education, have been posed in dealing with the treatment of subjects pertaining to the social sciences in education (Institut de l'UNESCO de l'education 1962). In Europe, there is no uniformity of approach to school curricula as a consequence of such questions and diverse legacies. But the Bologna Process has attempted to create a degree of conformity. These perspectives have been communicated to India and other sections of the developing world directly, through bilateral interaction, or through UNESCO.

Indian institutions of school and university education and the social sciences I: from Independence to 2004

General

After 1947, roughly three phases are discernible in Indian programmes that have evolved for teaching subjects pertaining to the social sciences in schools and, at the graduate level, at university or affiliated colleges. The first phase ran into the 1960s, and involved the emergence of social sciences beyond basic history and geography as a necessary focus of attention; the second phase involved important changes of the late 1960s and 1970s, initially understating the value of social science teaching in the quest to promote education, acknowledging that value with time, but uniformly involving a top-down approach to pedagogy. This approach was consolidated in the 1980s and faced challenges in the 1990s. The most recent phase involves the initiatives of the 2000s and after.

A variety of notions shaped these trends. At the time of Independence, existing school and university education in its prevailing form was associated with the colonial establishment: but subjects taught were considered fit to serve the goals of a new nation once content was altered in the direction of a 'nationalist' bent, and the process of education was reoriented. In the language that framed what was to be done, the conceptual focus was on how 'Eastern' or 'Western' this policy was or how 'colonial' the past had been. Such issues made up a nationalist discourse on education before Independence and came to influence later policy (see Basu 1974; Nurullah and Naik 1943; also Ministry of Education 1963: 29). Nationalist perspectives in general were varied. They ranged from 'official', 'Gandhian', and socialist positions concerning the best path for a goal of 'development' (Zachariah 2006) to a celebration of the practices and ideas of ancient India and piecemeal perspectives that centred on the practices of different communities.

Throughout, the importance of promotion of values was highlighted in social debate, and attracted attention in overall policy documents, but remained understated within the scope of the discipline-centred education system. Hence affirmative action, equality, and the meaning of 'secularism' were called into question at the school level through watch words, but with no clarity as to where the social sciences stood in the promotion of such values. With time, coping with social programmes was associated with adjustment of numbers in schools, in universities, etc., and the professionalisation of teachers in a material sense. This habit of the mind was reflected in the text of the Kothari Commission's report (1965).

Beyond this, subjects pertaining to the social sciences were called on to deal with challenges that were specific to each subject. History, which had been shot through with implications concerning the superior nature of British rule as a path to a just and 'modern' society, was met with questions from nationalist historiography that had developed a strong professional ethos by 1947. Geography was oriented towards physical geography in line with the needs of the Survey of India and the colonial government; the subject was required to change focus. Economics evolved strong nationalist and developmental dimensions by 1947, though the subject had been shaped overall by debates prevalent in the UK. Hence, the 1950s were marked by tinkering with instruction in subjects pertaining to the social sciences – projecting nationalist preference and thinking in history, economics and sociology, and the new approach to geography symbolised by the National Atlas over the Survey of India.

To crown this edifice of a national orientation and inspire modern research, the Delhi School of Economics was established by V.K.R.V. Rao as a special social science research institution in 1949. This would set goals oriented differently from those of mere nationalist enterprise, associated with the Calcutta University project to encourage research, following the institution of the postgraduate departments in 1912.

From Independence until the formation of the NCERT and the UGC

In 1947, substantial variety marked the framework within which schools and universities existed. They differed in institutional make-up and teaching in the various directly ruled provinces of British India (Bengal, Bombay, Madras, etc.) and the princely states. Nationalist enterprise in education also varied regionally. These variations continued after 1947, during the period of integration of the princely states and the first moves towards the formation of linguistic states (completed in 1956). Institutions sought to introduce a degree of uniformity through the Central Advisory Board on Education (CABE) and the Inter-University Board. But their range was limited. According to the Constitution, education was on a state list – i.e. the state governments had the major responsibilities and rights in this area. Religious and private education added to the list. The result was a large variation in the education system over the years following Independence, even if the Union government attempted to set the tenor of what was to be done via commissions and committees and the Ministry of Education.

Social science teaching varied in accordance with this set-up. In schools it was strictly non-constructivist. No allowance was made in the textbook material or the method of teaching for received ideas and means to engage with them. Education was seen as an interactive process only in so far as it tested whether the student had absorbed the lesson or lecture and wished to raise questions concerning this. The approach was evident in the didactic textbooks. Illustrations were used as back-up rather than as starting points for a discussion; questions set out to examine absorption of the material provided. The classroom test, or the terminal or annual examination, were the means of evaluation.

Evaluation in higher education came in the annual examination. Instruction in universities and affiliated colleges centred teaching through lectures, with a short reading list for follow-up. Syllabi reflected research in nationalist circles – often projected at discipline-centred congresses.

Immediately after 1947, the first Committee on Secondary Education (1948) focused on the language of school teaching – seeking to delimit the use of English and enhance the use of a 'federal language' to mark a departure from a colonial status; but teaching of specific subjects arose for comment almost immediately. Social science subjects were given importance and serious attention in the Radhakrishnan Committee on University Education of 1948–49:

> Everyone should know something of the society in which he lives, the great forces that mould contemporary civilisation. History, economics, politics, social psychology, anthropology belong to the group of social sciences. Whatever may be our specialised field, a general understanding of our social environment is essential.
>
> *(Ministry of Education 1962)*

A broad approach to nationalism in education and research at the university level was also stressed:

> We must give up the fatal obsession of the perfection of the past…. When we are hypnotised by our past achievements … we become fetish worshippers…. All that man has done is very little compared with what he is destined to achieve.

The Lakshmanaswami Mudaliar Commission on Secondary Education (1952–53) also showed a major interest in the area (Ministry of Education 1953). It stressed that an awareness of 'social studies' was important for citizenship. This coincided with contemporary debates on social studies in international circles. The upshot of these suggestions, during the late 1950s, was that while subjects pertaining to the social sciences continued to be pursued separately at school, they came to be seen as part of the domain of social studies, and were projected together as a source of social values. The Commission's ideas were unexceptionable:

> Social Studies is meant to cover the ground traditionally associated with History, Geography, Economics, Civics, etc. If the teaching of these separate subjects only imparts miscellaneous and unrelated information and does not throw any light on or provide insight into social conditions and problems or create the desire to improve the existing state of things, their educative significance will be negligible.

In its section on methods of education, its final report emphasised the significance of habits of cultivation of thought and the complex relationship between teacher and student:

> Any method, good or bad, links up the teacher and his pupils into an organic relationship with constant mutual interaction: it reacts not only on the mind of the students but on their entire personality, their standards of work and judgment, their intellectual and emotional equipment, their attitudes and values.
>
> *(Ibid.: 88ff)*

From this, the Commission worked towards recommendations for education based on activities, and projects as much as on lectures and examination. Taking up the problem of poor textbooks in circulation, the Commission also set the foundation for the production of national textbooks (ibid.: 79ff).

Much of this concurred with the general notions that were the focus of the UNESCO members in Delhi in 1954. But it differed from these notions in that the 'social studies' mentioned here did not wholly overlap with the idea of 'social sciences' that was projected for the UNESCO focus – political science, economics, sociology, and social anthropology. These disciplines were judged to be those that 'made a scientific analysis of social systems', with history and human geography important outsiders (Marshal 1954). The Mudaliar Commission involved these subjects in a wider association with values education.

As a consequence of the Commission's injunctions, when it came to schools, training of teachers noted social studies as the category to which history, geography, economics, and sociology belonged, and devoted a degree of importance to them accordingly. States were to teach the subjects individually, but grouped them together and found a place for them in the curriculum. Official sources were clear that these commitments were intended to '(i) develop a broad human interest in the progress of mankind and of India in particular (ii) to develop a proper understanding of the social and geographical environment and awaken an urge to improve it and (iii) to develop a sense of citizenship'.[5]

Initially, a challenge to these ideas came from an important source. The scope and aims of social studies were mainly defined by universities. The research orientation of the universities determined the fate of social science teaching in schools. The secondary school stage involved preparation for the university course and mirrored the concerns of the universities, which set up the requirements for the school-leaving or matriculation examinations. They were also responsible for the pre-university or intermediate courses that preceded the degree courses. Unusual projects existed: the Shantiniketan Project, the Jamia project, the Krishnamurthi Foundation Schools, etc. But the regular approach to the social sciences was that set by the dominant university school course systems of Madras, Bombay, Calcutta, Punjab, and 20 or so other universities that came after them.

Responding to nationalist awareness, both before and after Independence, a 'national' orientation in the syllabi was evident in the large involvement of Bengali, Assamese, Hindi, and Urdu textbooks among those recommended, for instance, for the Calcutta University matriculation examination. This was in addition to the standard books oriented towards physical geography and 'school' history in English (University of Calcutta 1960). The random, often contradictory, mixture demonstrated the scant attention to what was being taught and how.

This teaching would lead to a firmer academic orientation at the next level, where the intermediate or pre-university course was set by the university with a stress on groups. The syllabi and curricula at this level were oriented to university syllabi and were deeply discipline-centred, with little cross-referencing, except in so far as a subject combination required it. Hence, in Calcutta University in 1960, the pre-university syllabus included a paper on 'Elements of Economics and Civics'. This had two distinct domains, even if they referred to each other. One section of the syllabus included an outline of economics as a discipline and routine disciplinary discussions of the nature of money, the character of demand, the determination of wages, and so on; a second section dealt with constitutional government, law and liberty, party systems, and so on – a common area in discussions of the economic functions of government and the character of the planned economy.

At the level of the first degree, these subjects were firmly bifurcated and there was little or no discussion of government and its significance in the economics course. It was noticeable that the pre-university course in history was general; the subjects were general history, Indo-Islamic and world history, Islamic history and culture, and ancient history. Even though economic history was acknowledged as a subject, it was only taught in the economics syllabus (Ministry of Education 1953: 1ff, 25ff).

There were variations in other universities. But the bottom line here was that academic orientation at the school/early college level was directed, in the case of what may be termed social science (primarily history and geography), towards a university orientation. A determination to move away from this had been expressed in government commissions; but little had occurred that was of substance.

In higher education, meanwhile, the value of the subjects that made up the social sciences had been recognised. How they were to be taught was linked to the research agenda of a small but increasing number of universities. The Delhi School of Economics set a model, but given the variety on the nationalist agenda, this was not invoked, even in the central universities outside Delhi – Visva Bharati, Benaras Hindu University, and Aligarh Muslim University. The existence of private colleges added to the variety of what was being taught.

After the formation of the UGC and NCERT

Many of these approaches continued to thrive under the planned economy after the Second Plan (1956–61), but the profile altered structurally and conceptually. Structurally, the universities ceased to determine the way school education would be shaped. State Boards of Secondary Education (BSEs) were established as new states came into existence or shortly afterwards. These provided the space for public evaluation of the work of the host of public and private schools that the planned economy sponsored directly and indirectly.

Attempts were made to regulate and assist institutions through professional means. School instruction as a domain of its own came to be projected nationally with the formation of the University Grants Commission (UGC) in 1956, NCERT (1961) and its spin-off in 1973, the National Council for Teacher Education (NCTE), as well as NCERT affiliates in the states (SCERTs).

Approaches to social sciences in schools during the 1960s and 1970s

In the course of the 1960s, two contradictory trends were discernible as far as social science school education was concerned. An overwhelming focus on industrial development focused on technology and science and pushed for an increase in their reach numerically and socially within the education system, even as the social sciences came to be regarded by policy-makers as 'also rans'. Science and technology subjects were promoted with vigour at the cost of the social sciences. The spirit of the time was expressed in the Kothari Commission Report (1964–66), which said little concerning non-technical education, except in a rhetorical manner (Ministry of Education 1970). The Report also reflected a greater concern with teachers' salaries and professional requirements than education – partly the result of the Union government's direct responsibility for schools in the new Kendriya Vidyalaya Sangathan or Central Schools Network established in 1963, and a concern with increasing enrolment in central universities.

NCERT, however, took a keen interest in social sciences teaching, publishing model textbooks from the end of the 1960s and generating debates in the newly founded *Journal of Indian Education*. Programmes for school education set out here were substantially followed by the Central Board of Secondary Education (CBSE), giving NCERT and its output a national reach that no other institution had. NCERT books were preferred when they finally appeared. Programmes were run by a number of State BSEs, but a number used the CBSE as a reference point. The main Board that had authority equal to that of the CBSE was the Indian School Certificate Board (ISCB) that worked with textbooks produced privately, but its range was narrower than the CBSE and State Boards.

Wariness concerning books produced by private presses and approved by the mass of public and private schools was partly the reason for this turn of events. The K.G. Saidayain Committee on textbooks pointed out major problems with a host of standard books – and their handling of history and religious and minority issues (Ministry of Education 1969). Officials became concerned about this situation and found in the NCERT books a means of dealing with the problem.

In these circumstances, despite the marginal role played by social science education in projections of education policy at the time, a spate of textbook writing was generated within NCERT and important books for history and geography were produced, as well as for economics and sociology (the latter being taught from the 1970s at the higher secondary level). Social sciences here, though, came down to a descriptive grouping. The term had no analytical or pedagogic force. The subjects were variously described as 'environmental studies' or 'social studies' in different states.

Textbook production, especially in history, involved major figures of the universities: Romila Thapar, Bipan Chandra, R.S. Sharma, and Satish Chandra, the chairman of the UGC. The output gave significance and weight to subjects that had acquired weight at the university level, and where academics felt they had achieved merit stripped of colonial dependency – a status that made their work worthy of dissemination (UNESCO 1974). The textbooks began to appear from 1968, most coming in the late 1970s.[6] Significantly, the new books claimed to be scientifically accurate: arguing for a place on par with the hard sciences and technology. They built firmly on the nationalist narrative, but with a degree of social content.[7] Each discipline – history, geography, political science, economics, and sociology – followed its university paradigm. There was no attempt to address questions that were of mutual importance in any manner that suggested interaction, although each subject was considered to be part of a larger family of social science, whose importance was stressed by S. Nurul Hasan as Education Minister in 1973, and was mirrored in the country's commitment to the Asia-wide phenomenon of founding Councils for Social Science Research (Hasan 1977).

The university provided the main writers of these textbooks. The books also became guided by a strong nationalist ideology that was seen to be 'left-oriented'. History provided capsules of information on the nationalist movements of the nineteenth and twentieth centuries, with discussions not only on the social but also political agenda. The power of religion as a motive force in policy was understated. The whole mix was framed within a single compelling chronology that could not be questioned. In political science and sociology, the importance of nationalist thinkers was stressed; in economics it was the planned economy, as well as aspects of theory and the use of statistics.

At the college level, these themes were filled out. Many colleges in fact used the Class XI and Class XII textbooks as an introduction to the course, as the pre-university course became rare in the 1970s. The importance of this approach became greater with the arrival of education on a concurrent list, where both central and state governments had responsibilities.

National Educational Policies, which were elaborated from 1968,[8] receiving new formulations in 1986 and 1992, had little impact on these issues. But the practice also began of formulation of curriculum, with the first National Curriculum Framework (NCF) announced in 1975 (Yadav 2011). This gave little place to social sciences in the school, and was followed up by debate and a revised NCF in 1988[9] that had a more elaborate discussion of social science teaching. During the 1980s, the Union government's National Educational Mission attempted to use technology to extend the range of education, with television drafted in for the purpose, and programmes devised to supplement the range of the classroom. Other measures gave orientation to teachers to follow pedagogy specified by NCERT – through DIETs (District Institutes of Education and Training) and RIEs (Regional Institutes of Education). Teacher education outside these institutions was monitored by the NCTE, established as an independent institution in 1993.

Approaches to social sciences in universities and colleges during the 1960s and 1970s

In the degree colleges and in the universities, meanwhile, a pattern was established that would continue. In social science teaching, in political science and sociology, basic categories associated with analysis, as well as classics of thought were the methodological inputs, followed by themes that affected Indian politics and society ('Indian society', 'The Indian Constitution', etc.). International relations and additional subjects relating to public administration were items that were also an important part of syllabi. In history, a focus on Indian history, with stray subjects from European history, was the norm. In geography, division into physical and social geography components and subdivisions according to 'region' was characteristic, with a 'scientific' component added by way of acquaintance with surveying methods. Anthropology remained almost wholly physical anthropology.

This thematic pattern was revised in terms of the books taught, with the main presses supplying summaries of international work or Indian research. The overall structure was not reworked. The training was intended to be the basis for competition for civil service examinations, and other public service positions. An expanding public sector recruited its managers from such backgrounds. Broader acquaintance with such a sector was limited, most instruction being concerned with legislation. More appropriate training would come after selection – in the Indian Institution of Public Administration, or training in Hyderabad and elsewhere. Encapsulated versions of the research agenda of the university and the scholarly community were seen to be important. Awareness of disciplines across boundaries came through instruction in multiple subjects at BA (Pass) or through additional Pass subjects at the more specialised BA Honours level.

The Jawaharlal Nehru University model and its relevance for undergraduate education

It was partly to galvanise teaching at the undergraduate level, as well as to promote research, that the Jawaharlal Nehru University (JNU) model took shape in 1966. Like the DSE, the JNU had an orientation towards social sciences in its School of Social Sciences, as well as in sister schools, the School of International Studies and the School of Languages. But it had a social agenda, drawing for its MA programme from the country as a whole, making allowances for the underprivileged. Interdisciplinary study was promoted, and many took their perspectives to the states from which they came. The model was replicated in the Central University of Hyderabad and the North Eastern Hill University. In the 1970s, the authority enjoyed by JNU faculty in the UGC helped promote the syllabi of the JNU in the states and in central universities.

The preparation of college and university teachers through new methods set an interdisciplinary approach to education as the norm of higher education. In doing so it set out to restructure the national paradigm of teaching in subjects pertaining to the social sciences. It also took its lead from the left-wing values that were to be seen in the restructuring of school teaching.

Through the stress on research, the aims of the experiment failed to address the problem of application of social science education – even if such application were to be restricted to a refined training in values and the way techniques may be used as a measure of important issues. The departure also failed to address the problem of numbers in higher education. The number of colleges was substantially larger than at Independence, as was the intake into colleges – in the early 1970s ten times what it had been in 1950. The bulk of enrolment was for the 'Arts' (Ministry of Human Resources Development 2005: 7–9) – which required some attention to methods of teaching and application of disciplines. The JNU experiment could not address this adequately.

The Indira Gandhi National Open University (IGNOU), with its close links with those who directed the JNU experiment, was intended to deal with the problem of numbers. Its activities, though, failed to affect the large number of colleges and small universities that had set their own benchmarks.

Finally, future teachers trained in the JNU MA programmes in social science were trained to place a premium on independent research and writing. But given the stress at the NCERT on 'correct' scientific approaches, and a harum-scarum approach to teaching elsewhere, the students were hardly prepared for the departure. Products of the new university, meanwhile, had to face traditional discipline-oriented syllabi in the colleges; and their influence would be limited in the long-term. Where such influence would be considerable, it would reinforce the research orientation of undergraduate education rather than diversify its character.

'Crisis' in education and teaching of social sciences

In this process, if the social sciences had acquired a premium owing to the 'scientific' edge they had received with new textbook development and the JNU model, the educational system had come to be identified with a numerical achievement on the one hand and an exclusivity on the other. J.P. Naik identified a 'crisis' as a consequence, where at the level of the underprivileged, education was seen to be exclusive by the end of the 1970s (Naik 1979a). Meanwhile, various groups concerned with educational and pedagogic reform – such as the Ekalavya[10] group, founded in Madhya Pradesh in 1982 – placed part of the reason for the 'crisis' not on the failure to draw a larger tier of groups into the education system, but the system of teaching itself, which failed to appeal to a large contingent of students, losing the underprivileged and their concerns on the way.

In university education, the consequences of increased numbers in colleges for the nature of research preparation were not ignored. Awareness led to the creation of a system to evaluate quality – the National Assessment and Accreditation Council – in 1994. The new body's ratings were to be important for access to grants and other subventions. As was to be expected, though, a basis of evaluation that would apply effectively to various institutions was difficult to establish; and the rush for ratings meant, with time, a hastily assembled process whose value was suspect.

The government of 1999–2004 responded to the overall situation in two ways. In 2002, it made education a Fundamental Right and paved the way for a legislation that might solve the problem of numbers in the education system. To give this shape, it initiated the Sarva Shiksha Abhiyan to promote literacy and basic education. In the NCF of 2000, the government evaluated the onus for the limitations of the content of school education.[11] The NCF firmly placed the blame on the lead school subject of the social sciences – the one that shared space with geography throughout the upper primary and secondary stages, i.e. history. The failure of education to cultivate national pride and citizenship was associated with the prevailing teaching of this subject. NCERT books, in the period after 2000, attempted to create a composite social science syllabus and textbook that downplayed the role of history teaching and introduced a focus on 'heritage' (National Curriculum Framework 2000a,b). The latter mirrored a trend elsewhere, outside India, to view the past as a mere gloss on the present – a source of information on monuments and buildings.

Indian institutions of school and college education and the social sciences II: the NCERT initiative of the mid-2000s, the NCF 2005, and the broader context in the school–college system

These departures in schools' curricula and the reorientation of school textbooks in the process came in for immediate scrutiny (see CABE Committee 2005) following the advent of a new government in May 2004. The NCF 2005 was developed and a new approach to social sciences evolved at the school level in the CBSE system that followed NCERT syllabi and textbooks.

Developing a social sciences initiative at NCERT

The development of the NCF 2005[12] had, as part of its agenda, the task of dealing with the limitations of the attempt to take subjects pertaining to the social sciences in a direction where greater integration was achieved. Earlier syllabi and books (i.e. post-1968 and post-2000) had failed to articulate how they had understood the term 'social sciences' and how the approach to the disciplines that made up the social sciences varied from the approach that had been in vogue until the mid-twentieth century. Discussions regarding the task before schools also stressed that the previous books had dealt inadequately with the importance of marginal social groups and women in the development of social science perspectives.

The context of higher education

No initiative was taken at this time to reorient the UGC perspectives on social sciences and to stimulate a fresh agenda for colleges and universities. Ideas were presented concerning the school–college link with the development of a National Coordinating Committee from 2007 to draw in perspectives from those who were not involved in the processes set in motion by the NCF 2005. Discussions paid no attention to pedagogy at the college level, the importance of different phases of college education, or its overall position in the education system as a whole.

Development of a new school-level approach to 'social science': the Focus Group on Social Sciences

As NCF 2005 was taking its final shape, a Focus Group on the Social Sciences was constituted by NCERT. The group's main suggestions were to act as the point of reference for syllabus committees and textbook development committees that took shape thereafter. On the crucial issue of the integration of subjects that had been attempted under the previous framework, the group suggested a disciplinary focus. Hence, while a sense of the subjects as contributing to social science awareness was important, it was considered equally important that this was to be achieved through a heightened sensitivity to space, time, and institutions.

The group suggested the development of a phased pattern of social science awareness that would start in the period before upper primary (Classes VI, VII, and VIII), when 'environmental studies' was the standard subject taught outside basic language and mathematics; the 'environmental studies' here having science and non-science components. A point of major importance was that the nature of value discussion in the textbooks should be shaped within the disciplinary discussion. This was allied to the suggestion that the subject of 'civics' through which social values and political norms had hitherto been discussed in the upper primary level and early secondary level of school should be revised. Content traditionally involved discussions of the political structures of India as framed by the Constitution and a series of problems of public values (cleanliness, awareness, etc.). This could be handled through integration into disciplines.

The Focus Group also drew attention to the issue of principles of pedagogy that some of these suggestions led into. Constructivist perspectives were preferred. A full engagement was required, it was argued, with the environment where social science questions were raised if teaching was to be meaningful. Hence the 'lesson' should open the way to references to experience and drawing from experience, both in discussion as well as in project work. Pointing to the lacunae that had frequently become the reference of NCF discussions, the Focus Group emphasised the importance of attention to marginal communities and women in the model syllabi and textbooks that NCERT would establish.

Syllabus committees and textbooks

The Focus Group's suggestions were taken up in developing syllabi and textbooks after the publication of NCF 2005. The development of textbooks brought together a range of expertise as the work on syllabi had done. A draft conceived by one individual was subject to a rigorous process of editing and re-editing, with major inputs from illustrators who had their own opinions on what was most effective as pedagogy. Project work attempted to go beyond fixing the lesson in the reader's mind – the goal of the past. Pains were taken to address social issues that were neglected in the past, in all the subjects. Project-oriented work was recommended and attempts made to draw in the child's/young person's experiences. Legal cases were used to illustrate the points raised in the subject of social and political life that replaced civics in Classes VI to VIII. Archival material and visual material was used to raise questions in history rather than illustrate a point. The process of textbook development was completed by 2009. As they came out, textbooks were made available on the internet. A Curriculum Group of the NCERT was created to promote discussions with State Boards that did not automatically use NCERT as their main point of reference.

Beyond NCF 2005

Schools

Pedagogy in subjects pertaining to the social sciences faced a larger list of problems once the textbook work was complete. Initiatives under NCF 2005 were touching on larger problems. Attention to the teaching of social sciences did not solve the immediate issue of the comparatively limited numbers in school – which no policy could ignore. Problems concerning effective pedagogy itself could not be ignored – those regarding communication and evaluation. These problems attracted attention through the pursuit of the Sarva Shiksha Abhiyan and the Right to Education (RTE) Act of 2010, and the follow-up. In order to ensure that the latter had some effect, the MHRD allowed the establishment of private schools with public fund assistance providing that a minimum intake was guaranteed to underprivileged groups. The Ministry also organised task forces to look into how policy associated with the Act was given effect.

Steps were taken to address problems of pedagogy arising from measures taken under NCF 2005. Some of these problems could be solved by using Regional Institutes of Education (RIEs) and District Institutes of Education and Training (DIETs) to convey ideas. Model methods of 'continuous and comprehensive evaluation', framed by NCERT and implemented in a framework of only one major public examination, were considered a viable solution. A rising demand for teachers that would follow from the RTE initiatives posed problems. Standards could not be maintained by existing government organisations such as RIEs; nor could the promotion of CCE (continuous and comprehensive evaluation) methods be ensured. Rather, the task required attention from the institutions concerned with teacher preparation itself. Action was required, in fact, from the National Council for Teacher Education, the Teachers Training Colleges (TTCs) they approved and University and College Education Departments. The government turned its attention to this issue. The measures undertaken to solve crucial problems generated a sphere of private enterprise in school education, where perspectives framed in NCF 2005 for the school would be maintained uneasily.

Colleges/universities

The link between the university and the school was also weakening, owing to little or no reform in approach in universities as a whole until the late 2000s. Serious response was lacking all round to NCERT initiatives and ideas and their implications for higher education, albeit not for want of suggestions. The National Knowledge Commission made a series of suggestions in 2009 for overhaul of the education system without looking closely at education and its process in depth. These changes, though, it tied firmly to involvement of private investment and the creation of a new regulatory body for higher education to replace the UGC (National Knowledge Commission 2009). The UGC itself trod a conservative course and saw merit in greater autonomy to educational institutions, adherence to the yardsticks set by the National Assessment and Accreditation Council (NAAC), and extension of the number of central universities (CABE Committee 2005).

The 2009 recommendations of the Yash Pal Committee (Government of India 2009)[13] to establish a National Council for Higher Education and Research were more far-reaching and involved a deep examination of the system of higher education. Among its suggestions, a number addressed some of the problems that affected teaching of the social sciences – including academic and non-academic orientation and interdisciplinary access. The Committee argued for new approaches to undergraduate education, a 'holistic' approach to knowledge, and changes in undergraduate education that would involve close practical experience. Both the Knowledge Commission and the Yash Pal Committee, however, appear to have argued for initiatives that were too far-reaching and out of key with the prevailing system; their suggestions were hardly implemented before 2014. Equally, it has been clear that in the case of the preferred path of the UGC, the system of accreditation was deeply flawed and the grant of autonomy often ran against problems of how to evaluate institutional capability and competence.

In the circumstances, a combination of financial stringency, inflation, and limited but necessary expansion of infrastructure have led to stagnation of existing colleges and universities and the gradual development of a private sector in the area. Suggestions for a 'liberal arts' profile on the lines of the US model (involving subjects pertaining to the social sciences) has been suggested for some of these institutions, while others remain solidly technology- and medicine-oriented, where social sciences are support subjects attracting minimal attention. While the 'liberal arts' paradigm may involve international equivalence of a type for some institutions, it makes them far from fit to play any meaningful role in India's future, since their planning only provides a broad 'liberal education' that only raises questions about what is 'liberal' and what the 'education' is for, but fails to offer any answers on how these can be made relevant or meaningful.

Postscript

The current situation in education has been the result of these developments – a situation arousing concern and confusion. A somewhat ramshackle system of education where clear knowledge of purpose is at a premium. Wild variations in the way social sciences are taught and received has been part of this scenario. The inclination towards private education and accreditation is sometimes regarded as a trend towards democracy, pluralism, and a practical approach, since it decreases the burden of responsibility on the state, permitting it to focus on marginal groups and large initiatives in areas of professional training, scientific education, and the promotion of values' awareness. Whether the line of policy has been effectively gauged and adequately evaluated, in order for this to happen, however, remains a moot point.

In the case of the social sciences, competing systems of approach in a situation where professional awareness in the teaching community is at a premium presents a serious problem: a problem that leads to depreciation in the value of the subjects as well as a decline in their status. This occurs, regrettably, at a time when, through the education system, these very subjects look to achieve a more pointed direction and substance.

Notes

1 Kumar (1976–88) is the multivolume best source other than documents on the net.
2 Ideas that are associated with social science may be traced in various forms of knowledge developed in India's history outside the school or college classroom (in the madrasa or in the *toll*, for instance). But, pending research, it must be assumed, this area of awareness was the sketchy remnant of socially limited institutions of the past. See Naik (1979b). For an alternate view see Khasnavis (1983).
3 The Oxford and Cambridge Examinations Syndicate did not consider Economics worthy of attention until the 1950s. See www.oua.ox.ac.uk/holdings/Oxford%20&%20Cambridge%20OC.pdf (last accessed 19 August 2015). But both economics and economic history were popular in schools, as noted by the *Economic History Review* during 1927–34.
4 See 'Re-inventing the social sciences' at www.oecd.org/science/sci-tech/33695704.pdf.
5 Pires (1970) deals with the diversity of interpretation of 'social studies' in India as well as in other countries. Indian institutions picked up the debates in the West on the subject. They also generated a literature of their own, as indicated by Khasnavis (1983).
6 Romila Thapar's text book for Class VIII, *Medieval India* is a good example. For secondary school textbooks this included Arjun Dev's *The Story of Civilisation* (2 vols., Class IX and Class X), R.S. Sharma's *Ancient India*, Satish Chandra's *Medieval India* (2 vols), and Bipan Chandra's *Modern India*.
7 For interviews with textbook writers and interpretation of the books, see Guichard (2011).
8 http://mhrd.gov.in/sites/upload_files/mhrd/files/document-reports/NPE-1968.pdf and (for 1986 and 1992) www.ncert.nic.in/oth_anoun/npe86.pdf (last accessed 19 August 2015).
9 http://eledu.net/rrcusrn_data/National%20Curriculum%20Framework-1988.pdf (last accessed 19 August 2015).
10 For information on Ekalavya and assessments of their work, see www.srtt.org/institutional_grants/pdf/educational_titles.pdf and www.eklavya.in (last accessed 19 August 2015).
11 www.eledu.net/rrcusrn_data/NCF-2000.pdf (last accessed 19 August 2015).
12 www.ncert.nic.in/rightside/links/pdf/framework/english/nf2005.pdf (last accessed 19 August 2015).
13 The Committee suggested 'Universities to establish live relationship with the real world outside and develop capacities to challenges faced by rural and urban economies and culture' (p. 66). In its 'Agenda for action' it pointed to the necessity for a more broadness of interaction between disciplines at the undergraduate level and interaction between the domains of vocational education and university education (p. 64).

References

Basu, Aparna, *The Growth of Education and Political Development in India* (Oxford University Press, 1974).
CABE Committee, *Regulatory Mechanisms for Textbooks and Parallel Textbooks Taught in Schools Outside the Government System: A Report* (CABE Committee, 2005).
Government of India, *Report of the Committee to Advise on the Rejuvenation and Renovation of Higher Education* (Government of India 2009), http://mhrd.gov.in/sites/upload_files/mhrd/files/document-reports/YPC-Report.pdf, last accessed 19 August 2015.
Guichard, Sylvie, *The Construction of History and Nationalism in India* (RKP, 2011).
Hasan, Nurul, 'Social science in Asia: speech at the 1st Asian Conference on Teaching and Research in Social Sciences, Simla 1973', in Nurul Hasan, *Challenges in Education, Culture and Social Welfare*.(Allied Publishers, 1977).
Institut de l'unesco de l'education, *L'enseignement des Sciences Sociales au niveau pre-universitaire* (Institut de l'unesco de l'education, 1962).
Khasnavis, P.K., *Teaching Social Studies in India* (Abhinav Publications, 1983).
Kumar, Virendra (ed.) *Committees and Commissions of India 1947–1973* (Concept Publishing Company, 1976–88).

Marshal, T.H., United Nations Educational Scientific and Cultural Organization. Working Paper for the Round Table Conference on Social Science Teaching, Delhi, 15–20 February 1954.

Ministry of Education, *Report of the Secondary Education Commission. Mudaliar Commission Report. October 1952 to June 1953* (Ministry of Education, Government of India, 1953).

Ministry of Education, *The Report of the University Education Commission, December 1948–August 1949* (Ministry of Education, Government of India, 1962), www.teindia.nic.in/files/reports/ccr/Report%20of%20the%20University%20Education%20Commission.pdf (accessed 23 August 2015).

Ministry of Education, *UNESCO Projects in India* (Ministry of Education, Government of India, 1963).

Ministry of Education, *Report of the Education Commission 1964–66* (NCERT, 1970).

Ministry of Education and Youth Services, *Report of the Committee on School Textbooks* (Ministry of Education and Youth Services, 1969).

Ministry of Human Resources Development, *Report of the Central Advisory Board of Education on Autonomy for Higher Education Institutions* (Ministry of Human Resources Development, Department of Secondary and Higher Education, Government of India, 2005).

Naik, J.P. 'Equality, quantity and quality: the elusive triangle in Indian education' *International Review of Education*, 1979a, 25 (2–3): 167–185.

Naik, J.P., *The Education Commission and After* (APH Publishing House, 1979b).

National Curriculum Framework 2000. *Guidelines and Syllabus for the Secondary Stage* (NCERT, 2000a)

National Curriculum Framework 2000. *Guidelines and Syllabus for the Higher Secondary Stage* (NCERT, 2000b).

National Knowledge Commission. *Report to the Nation 2006–2009* (National Knowledge Commission, Government of India, 2009).

Nurullah, Syed and J.P. Naik, *History Education in India, during the British Period.* (Macmillan, 1943).

Pires, Edward A., *The Teaching of Social Studies in Primary Teacher Training Institutions in Asia* (UNESCO Regional Office for Education in Asia, 1970).

Seligman, E.R.A. and Johnson, A.S. *Encyclopaedia of the Social Sciences* (Macmillan, 1938).

United Nations Educational Scientific and Cultural Organisation. *Symposium on Social Science Research Development in Asia, Jakarta, Indonesia, 18–22 February 1974. A Review of Social Science Research Activities, in Asia prepared by the UNESCO Secretariat* (UNESCO, 1974).

University of Calcutta. *Syllabi in Different Subjects for the Pre-Degree Course and Three Year Course* (University of Calcutta, 1960).

Yadav, S.K., *National Study on Ten Year School Curriculum Implementation* (NCERT, 2011).

Zachariah, Benjamin, *Developing India: An Intellectual and Social History c. 1930–1950* (Oxford University Press, 2006).

8

The uses and teaching of history

Kumkum Roy

History occupies a rather unique space within the urban, literate, upper-caste/middle-class imagination in India at present. On the one hand, it is considered crucial for the formation and consolidation of identities, including a highly contested national identity; on the other hand, the actual pursuit of the study of history is viewed with an odd mixture of suspicion, disdain, and condescension. This is evident if one glances through the career guidance supplements of the daily newspapers, which typically list dozens of options such as becoming lawyers, managers, entering the hospitality and health 'industry', or making careers in interior design, the omnipresent information technology sector, fashion, the media, and tourism, to name a few. But the option of becoming a historian is virtually invisible.

Although impressionistic, conversations with those who have had systematic access to formal education, almost invariably middle class or aspiring to middle-class status, suggest that SST (the popular acronym for social studies) is low on the priority list of most students and parents. Within that schema, history often slips even further down the hierarchy of the social sciences, as it is perceived as irrelevant – about the past in a world that is hurtling towards the future at a breakneck pace. And yet, it remains critical for identity formation, for what a teacher described, with remarkable brevity and precision, in Hindi, as learning about '*acche acche cheezein*', literally, 'the good things'.

To cite just one example: most educated laypersons, when asked whether they remember anything about ancient Indian history, are likely to cite the Harappan civilisation. If pressed a little further, features like town planning, centralisation, and the drainage system constitute the core of these memories. Obviously, when smart cities are the ideal, it is reassuring to know that these had spectacular precedents in the past.

And yet, even as we acknowledge these features, archaeologists have provided us with a far more complex understanding of the Harappan civilisation, which persuades us to contextualise and problematise these 'achievements' (e.g. Ratnagar 2001). What prevents us from engaging with these discussions, even when they are presented in an accessible mode, shorn of academic jargon?

Part of the answer lies, I would suggest, in the training we impart in schools. This is evident if we explore the way in which material that is potentially open and creates space for critical thinking is circumscribed through the examination system and the 'assessment' it provides. I will illustrate this by discussing the way in which the French Revolution has been treated in a textbook (*India and the Contemporary World vol. I* (2006: 3–24); henceforth ICW) and compare this with a book *Golden Social Science* (n.d.: A: 2–32), meant to master the same theme in order to crack the examination. I will then move on to possible alternatives.

At one level, the examples I choose may seem somewhat far removed from the questions around which heated 'controversies' are frequently generated. These include the Aryan question, with almost interminable debates on whether the Aryans were indigenous or not, and whether the Aryans can be regarded as the authors of the Harappan civilisation or not (for a brief discussion, see Roy 2013: 35–50). The resilience of these controversies is at once remarkable and sterile. If we are to account for their persistence beyond conspiracy theories, we may wish to turn towards ways in which history is learned. Within the present context, the focus is on formal modes of learning, which are, inevitably, only the tip of the iceberg. And yet, these provide us with an opportunity and a space to develop skills (a much abused word) of critical thinking, of acquiring a sense of the ways in which historians work, and an ability to assess different positions and arguments. How we use this space, then, becomes a challenge.

Before going on to the specifics, it may be useful to bear in mind that history itself has had a long and chequered past (e.g. Arnold 2000; Bhattacharya, n.d.: 4–38). While the relevance of history in an immediate utilitarian sense has often been called into question, historians and others have almost invariably turned to history (among other things) in order to make sense of or find meaning in the worlds they inhabit.

It is also worth clarifying that while history is based on evidence, what is considered as evidence is by no means self-evident. Over a period of time, historians have cast their net wide – to include all kinds of traces of the past – written documents, inscriptions, remains of material culture, visual archives, and oral traditions, to name a few. Many of these explorations of sources have emerged as the concerns of ordinary people have attracted attention, as the focus of history has shifted, somewhat, from grand narratives about kings and queens to the less exalted lives of the vast majority. But there are other issues as well. These include the transformative potential of history. As Arnold (2000: 13–14) observes:

> And if the evidence that existed always spoke plainly, truthfully and clearly to us, not only would historians have no work to do, we would have no opportunity to argue with each other. History is above all else an *argument*. It is an argument between different historians; and, perhaps, an argument between the past and the present, an argument between what actually happened, and what is going to happen next. Arguments are important; they create the possibility of changing things.... Part of thinking about 'history' is to think about what – or who – history is *for* [emphases in the original].

Traces of the past can be both tantalisingly elusive as well as overwhelmingly present. By and large, histories have tended to be dominated by accounts of the powerful, who often both create and preserve written and visual records. Thus, we may find it difficult to reconstruct the histories of poor, non-literate populations. On the other hand, archives maintained by government and religious institutions, for instance, may be very carefully preserved. Sifting through and evaluating these vast quantities of data poses a different kind of challenge.

Arnold (2000: 56–57) draws attention to another set of issues as well – revolving around the professionalisation of history, traceable through the last two centuries or so. National agendas and a level of economic prosperity often constituted the context of professionalisation. Professionalisation has meant that historians are now paid for their work; it has also often widened the gulf between the historian and laypersons; and it underlies divisions among historians in terms of specialisation and perspectives, rendering a single, omnipresent 'true' history impossible. This often poses a challenge to teachers and learners who long for the comfort of certitude.

With these preliminaries complete, let me now turn to the specific examples to illustrate the potentials, problems, and excitement of teaching, learning, and presenting history.

The textbook as a pedagogical tool

ICW contains several interesting preliminary statements. It was part of an endeavour to bridge the 'gap between the school, home and community' (*ICW* 2006: iii), and to 'discourage rote learning' (ibid.). Underlying this attempt was a more radical shift – an attempt to 'treat children as participants in learning, not as receivers of a fixed body of knowledge' (ibid.). The preliminary pages included the preamble of the Constitution of India (ibid.: viii), which was particularly apposite, given that the very first chapter of the book dealt with the French Revolution and discussed ideas such as liberty, equality, and fraternity, among others.

The structure of the chapter (as indeed of many of the other chapters in this book) is at once rich, complex, and challenging. I will just highlight some of the elements. In terms of running text, the chapter contains an introductory page (ibid.: 3). The rest of the chapter is organised as shown in Table 8.1.

The sectional and subsectional heads give us a sense of the contents and focus of the text, the connections envisaged between society, economy, and political change, and the concern with relatively marginalised groups such as women and slaves.

Apart from running text, the chapter contains 17 visuals (see Appendix 1 for details), each of which carries a caption, and many of which are accompanied by thought-provoking questions. These visuals include reproductions of prints, sketches, paintings, charts, and maps, focusing both on the spectacular as well as on the everyday. The chapter also has a box spread over two pages, discussing the symbols commonly used by artists during the period (ibid.: 12–13). Additionally, there are representations of Marat, Robespierre, and Olympe de Gouges (ibid.: 11, 16, 19, respectively).

The third structural element of the chapter consists of boxes, set in the margin, dealing with relatively unfamiliar terms and concepts, inserted close to where they occur in the text. These include, for instance, eighteenth-century French terms for taxes (ibid.: 4). Intended to facilitate

Table 8.1 Details of sections in chapter 1 of *India and the Contemporary World*, part 1

Sections	Subsections	Pages
French society during the late eighteenth century	The struggle to survive	
How a subsistence crisis happens		
A growing middle class envisages an end to privileges		4–7
The outbreak of revolution	France becomes a constitutional monarchy	8–13
France abolishes monarchy and becomes a republic	The Reign of Terror	
A directory rules France		14–17
Did women have a revolution?		18–20
The abolition of slavery		21
The revolution and everyday life		22
Conclusion		23–24

Source: all tables in the chapter have been compiled by the author.

reading and understanding of the text, they are particularly useful in the spatial context within which they are placed, enabling the reader to shift from the text to the margin and back.

Far more challenging, and potentially exciting, are the boxes containing activities. Apart from two activities listed at the end, there are 12 activities located within the main body of the chapter. Many of these pertain to the visuals, inviting learners to explore the material, analyse it, and form and express an opinion about what they see. Some are fairly obvious: for instance, having to explain why the peasant is compared to a fly and the nobleman to a spider (ibid.: 5) may not be particularly demanding for the learner. Other questions, such as those posed on the print depicting ordinary women going to Versailles, and reconstructing the attitude of the artist towards them, have space for more than one answer, and create an opportunity for discussion and debate.

Other challenging activities include those inviting the learner to compare different view-points – such as those of Robespierre and Desmoulin on liberty and tyranny (ibid.: 16) or between the Declaration of the Rights of Man and Citizen, and the manifesto of Olympe de Gouges (ibid.: 20), advocating the rights of woman. These push the learner towards contextualising categories that have often been reduced to slogans, and to appreciate the grey areas within apparently transformative historical moments. They create space for moving beyond a simple classification of the 'event' of the French Revolution as either good or bad. In other words, they allow for and even encourage, if not necessitate, an argument.

There is a single box titled 'Some important dates' (ibid.: 8), containing a total of six entries. While other dates are mentioned in the text, it is evident that those who developed the chapter did not wish to foreground these dates, which lend themselves very easily to rote learning.

Another set of seven boxes contains extracts from written sources, accompanied by activities/questions. These include excerpts from contemporary accounts of the pre-revolutionary situation, from the writing of the revolutionary journalist Marat, from the Declaration of the Rights of Man and Citizen, the views of Desmoulin and Robespierre, and those in favour of as well as against women's rights. These convey a sense of the immediacy and intensity of the concerns and conflicts that shaped the Revolution. A single illustration of this rich material must suffice for the moment. This is from the writing of Camille Desmoulins, who opposed Robespierre. He asked:

> Would it be possible to bring a single person to the scaffold without making ten more enemies amongst his relations and friends?
>
> *(ibid.: 16)*

The chapter ends with a set of longer questions. As these, and other questions, are answered in the *Golden Social Science*, we will turn to it next. But before doing so, it might be useful to remind ourselves that the chapter compels us, time and again, to ask: from whose perspective are we seeing things or understanding them? In other words, it pushes us to move away from the comfort zone of mining history for 'good things' or achievements, to a more unsettling engagement with a complex world.

Comforting certainties: converting the chapter

The preliminary pages of the *Golden Social Science* emerge from a different but far more immediate milieu as far as the learners are concerned. The reader who can distinguish a fake from a genuine copy of the book is assured of a reward of Rs. 1000 (GSS, n.d.: ii). There are several other assurances as well:

A WORK OF WISDOM YOU SHOULD HEED THE GOLDEN GUIDES YOU SHOULD READ
The *Golden* Books contain all that is required in the examinations
The *Golden* Books are written in sweet, simple but idiomatic language.
…

The *Golden* Books contain all the Expected Questions likely to be set in the Examinations.
…

The *Golden* Books suit all the pockets and serve the triple purpose of Textbooks, Help-books and Examination Papers, just *All-in-One*.

(*ibid.: xv, original formatting retained*)

Running into 31 pages, with only a single visual (ibid.: A 23), the chapter is structured rather differently from that in *ICW*. Organised in seven sections, the chapter provides the reader with a relentless torrent of accurate information.

The first section, titled 'TECHNICAL TERMS' (ibid.: A 2–A 3), includes virtually all the words glossed along the margins of *ICW*, often adopted verbatim. The difference is that here each is a standalone term, deprived of the context in which it is used. This lends itself to being converted into a decontextualised item to be committed to memory. Given that a total of 29 terms are listed, studying the French Revolution can become an intimidating task.

The second section is titled 'NCERT TEXTBOOK QUESTIONS' (ibid.: A 3–A 6) and provides answers to all six questions posed at the end of the chapter in *ICW*. The largest number of questions is in the next section: 'VERY SHORT ANSWER TYPE QUESTIONS' (ibid: A 6–A 10). As many as 55 questions are included in this section. This is followed by 'SHORT ANSWER TYPE QUESTIONS' (ibid.: A 10–A 15), containing 19 questions, and 'LONG ANSWER TYPE QUESTIONS' (ibid.: A 15–A 22), with 18 questions. The next section, titled 'NCERT TEXTBOOK ACTIVITIES' (ibid.: A 23–A 27), is devoted to providing 'answers' to most of the activities suggested in *ICW*. Finally, 'MULTIPLE CHOICE QUES-TIONS' (ibid.: A 27–A 32) provides 48 questions.

There are three features that are noteworthy. First, all the questions are answered, and answered accurately. So there is nothing left for the learner to do but to memorise the 'correct' answers. Second, the chapter is converted into 140 questions. If we add the ten activities and the six questions from *ICW*, we arrive at 156 answers to be learned. Third, and implicit in the above, the structure of the chapter as developed in *ICW* is dismantled, and the information provided is reassembled. This follows certain principles.

The first strategy is to arrange the questions in an order that does not correspond to that of the chapter in *ICW*. While this is obvious in all the sections, I will illustrate this from the section titled 'LONG ANSWER TYPE QUESTIONS'. Consisting of 18 questions, it is at once inter-esting and disturbing to see how the questions zig-zag through the sequence of sections laid out in the chapter in *ICW* (Table 8.2)

If the sequencing of questions disrupts the logic of the chapter in *ICW*, the other strategy that renders the chapter skewed, if not redundant, is the weighting given to various sections. This is evident from the distribution of questions: there are five questions based on section 1, three based on section 2, one based on section 3, none on section 4, which poses and addresses the question 'Did women have a revolution?', one based on section 5, one based on section 6 and two based on the brief reference to Napoleon in one of the concluding paragraphs in the chapter in *ICW*.

It is also evident that some of the questions are repetitive. Compare, for instance, questions 1, 9, and 17, based on section 1. As such, the space devoted to them is not used to develop any fresh understanding, but simply to reiterate much of what has already been stated.

Table 8.2 Distribution of long answer type questions from *Golden Social Science*

Sequence	Question	Corresponding section in ICW
Q 1	Briefly discuss the condition of France before the French Revolution.	Section 1
Q 2	Give any five accomplishments of the National Assembly of France from 1789 to 1791.	Section 2
Q 3	Briefly discuss the role of the philosophers in the French Revolution.	Section 1
Q 4	How did the Revolution affect the everyday life of the French people? Discuss.	Section 6
Q 5	What was the impact of the events in France on Europe, especially the neighbouring countries such as Prussia, Austria-Hungary and Spain?	Section 6 [brief reference]
Q 6	*The teachings of Rousseau laid the foundation of democracy.* Give any four arguments to justify the statement.	Section 1
Q 7	What was the impact of the French Revolution on France?	Addressed in several sections
Q 8	Explain any five features of the French Constitution of 1791. *Or How did the new political system of constitutional monarchy work in France? Explain.*	Section 2
Q 9	Describe the social causes leading to the French Revolution. *Or Explain the organization of the French society during the late 18th century.*	Section 1
Q 10	Explain the achievements of Napoleon.	Conclusion [brief discussion]
Q 11	Mention any five political symbols which came up during the French Revolution and explain their significance.	Section 2
Q 12	What is the subsistence crisis? Mention any four factors responsible for this in France.	Section 1
Q 13	How did France become a Constitutional Monarchy? Why were women disappointed by the Constitution of 1791 in France?	Section 2
Q 14	Who were the Jacobins? Who was their leader? Who came to be known as *sans-culottes*? *Or* Explain the role of the Jacobins in the French Revolution. *Or* What was the Jacobin Club? Describe their activities.	Section 3
Q 15	What is meant by the Triangular Slave Trade? How was slavery abolished in France?	Section 5
Q 16	In which year did Napoleon become Emperor of France? What did he do as a modernizer of Europe? When and where was he defeated?	Brief mention in the conclusion
Q 17	What was the financial position of France at the time of Louis XVI? In which three estates was French society divided during this period? Write one main feature of each.	Section 1
Q 18	Explain the impact of abolition of censorship in France.	Section 6

Also, and expectedly, there is an overwhelming emphasis on rote learning. While this is apparent in all the sections, it is most striking in the section on 'MULTIPLE CHOICE QUESTIONS'. Here, as many as 38 of the 48 questions are based entirely on information recall.

Some of the information recall requires a degree of processing. For instance, No. 37 (ibid.: A 31) asks:

> *Which of these did not belong to the Jacobin Club?*
> (a) Printers (b) Servants
> (c) Daily wage earners (d) Nobles

But most are far more mechanical, as for instance No. 41 (ibid.):

Austrian princess Marie Antoinette was queen of which of the following French rulers?
(a) Louis XIII   (b) Louis XIV
(c) Louis XV   (d) Louis XVI

There are ongoing debates among educationists about the efficacy or otherwise of multiple choice questions as a mode of assessment. Without entering into these, I would like to share two examples of alternative ways in which multiple choice questions can be framed, to challenge learners to think through their answers. These were generated by a team working within the existing framework, and are not published:

1   The French Revolution is significant because
     a   France granted independence to all its colonies
     b   It led to several decades of peace in Europe
     c   It led to the Declaration of Rights of Man
     d   It was followed by an increase in agricultural production

2   Women were
     a   Active participants in the French Revolution
     b   Joined the army in large numbers during the French Revolution
     c   Employed in major industries during the French Revolution
     d   Granted equal political rights with men in the French Revolution

At another level, the *Golden Social Science* introduces fresh content. This in itself would have been unexceptionable, if not desirable – elaborating on some of the ideas touched on in the chapter in *ICW* would have enriched it and rendered it more accessible. What happens, instead, however, is that these insertions of 'fresh' material almost invariably cluster around a set of historical figures who lend themselves to being classified as 'good' or 'bad', or as winners or losers. So Louis XVI and Napoleon receive considerable attention.

The information on Louis XVI, reiterated through all the other sections in abbreviated forms, is encapsulated in the first SHORT ANSWER TYPE QUESTION (ibid.: A 10):

What role did Louis XVI play in bringing about the revolution?
Ans. Louis XVI played a significant role in bringing about the revolution.

(i)   Louis XVI was a pleasure loving, extravagant ruler who believed in the Divine Right of Kings.
(ii)   He was ignorant and indifferent to the conditions of the poor.
(iii) His wife Marie Antoinette constantly interfered in the administration.
(iv)   He squandered money and drove France into useless wars bringing the country to the verge of bankruptcy.

There are two things about this response: each of the statements is reasonably accurate. At the same time, the way in which this 'correct' answer is framed leaves no space for considering the other contexts of the Revolution, which gave Louis XVI's personal proclivities a unique significance. In other words, possibilities of engaging with any kind of complexity, and contingency, are erased through these formulations.

What is also interesting, and sad, is that the *Golden Social Science* simply omits addressing some of the more challenging activities suggested in *ICW*. The latter has an activity on page 20 which could have opened up possibilities of a lively and possibly contentious debate on 'women's nature'. Addressing this, or converting it into suitably digested 'points' was probably somewhat uncomfortable for the authors of the *Golden Social Science*.

I will conclude this section with just one more illustration, this from the list of technical terms inserted at the outset in the *Golden Social Science* (ibid.: A 3):

> **Revolution:** A recognized momentous change in any situation. A revolution may result in sudden overthrow of an established government or system by force and bloodshed, *e.g.*, the French Revolution. It can also be a great change that comes slowly and peacefully *e.g.*, the Industrial Revolution.

ICW does not attempt to circumscribe or define a revolution. In fact, once revolution is reduced to a definition, there is a compulsion to delimit it. More specifically, whether the Industrial Revolution, which involved impoverishment, displacement, and dislocation for vast numbers of people, can be classified as peaceful is a question that is not even raised. Nor is it possible to raise such questions once we are faced with such a categorical definition. So, at the very outset of the text we are provided with an authoritative definition, distinguishing neatly and conveniently between a violent political revolution and a peaceful economic one. Given the use of the rhetoric of *ahimsa* in Indian political discourse, this distinction acquires a certain significance.

It is likely that the majority of students and teachers, for whom the examination is a hurdle to be crossed, and for whom the social sciences are a low priority in any case, will pay far more attention to the *Golden Social Science* and its equivalents, and ignore or at best refer occasionally to *ICW*. While this may be an effective strategy of survival, it means that most learners with access to formal education will end up considering history as an assortment of facts, more or less easily recalled, and more or less relevant. The challenge of thinking through the past, of engaging in a dialogue between past and present, is virtually erased. Also lost is the potential for argument, debate, discussion, for evaluating and assessing historical writing, and the blurred and constantly shifting lines between history and myth/fiction. Are these losses significant? And are there ways of recovery? I will touch on both of these issues by looking at two recent works in the next two sections.

The attraction of the Sapt Sindhu

The *Scion of Ikshvaku*, Book I of the Rama Chandra Series by Amish (Amish 2015) is among the current bestsellers, and is likely to remain so for a variety of reasons. The book is set in India of 3400 BCE, and a map is provided on the inside back cover and referred to in the preliminary pages (ibid.: xv). The date chosen is significant; pre-dating the Harappan civilisation by several centuries. The work itself is a heady blend of past and present: we have echoes of the Nirbhaya case (ibid.: ch. 12–14),[1] even as all the central figures almost invariably wear dhotis and *angavastrams* (ibid.: 1). The book makes few demands on the reader, except for a reasonably high level of tolerance for recurrent, graphic descriptions of violence (ibid.: 147–150). It also slides effortlessly between times, contexts, and spaces. While this might trouble some historians, it may be of little or no consequence to the average reader. What I will attempt here is not to measure the text against the yardsticks of fact and fiction. Instead, I will highlight the handling of four interrelated themes – the ways in which spaces have been named, the treatment of caste and gender, and the ideal polity that is projected.

The naming of the kingdom of Dashrath (and by extension that of the Ikhvakus as the Satp Sindhu (ibid.: 8) is an interesting strategy. It extends the geographical reach of Kosala, traditionally located on the Sarayu, a tributary of the Ganga in present-day Uttar Pradesh, to the Indus and its tributaries, and thus to the river from which the name India is derived. It also stakes an implicit claim to the heartland of the Harappan civilisation, a claim that is reiterated, nonverbally, through the use of a set of symbols based on the Harappan script, accompanied by a solar symbol, which serve to mark breaks in chapters (ibid.: 10, 11, 15).

Curiously, for a work that abounds in contemporary allusions, including weapons of mass destruction (ibid.: 267), the representation of caste resonates with the concerns of nineteenth-century upper-caste social reformers. Brahmanical and kshatriya identities remain unchallenged and intact, the former best exemplified by Vashishta, the family priest and preceptor of Ram, and the latter by Ram and his siblings. At the same time, there are occasional placatory platitudes thrown in: '*A person becomes a brahmin by karma, not by birth*' (ibid.: 253; emphasis original).

At first glance, representations of gender seem to be radically transformed – unlike the Sita of the Valmiki *Ramayana*, Amish's Sita is a capable administrator and has martial skills. At the same time, at crucial junctures, both she and her polity require the intervention of men for protection. Thus, Vishwamitra ensures the safety of Mithila by deploying the *Asuraastra*, which has an uncanny resemblance to an atom bomb (ibid.: 278–283), and when Sita seems to be hunting a wild boar fairly successfully, she has to be ultimately saved by Rama (ibid.: 330). What is more, in Amish's version the sexually charged Shurpanakha mutilates herself, thus absolving Lakshman of all responsibility. These are just examples of the ways in which gender relations are reworked, and hierarchies are gently reinforced, in a setting of near timeless antiquity.

It may come as no surprise that Amish's ideal polity is what can at best be described as a benevolent despotism – run by a king who follows the *shastras*, whose chronological order, complexity, and contradictions are erased by assimilating them to the Vedas located in a virtually timeless past (ibid.: 116). In this neat scenario, the messiness of democracy is irrelevant.

From the Malayaputras to Mizoram

At several points in the narrative, Amish introduces the reader to the Malayaputras, literally the sons (and daughters) of the hills. There are explicit references to tribal traditions (ibid.: 75), including norms governing gender relations, which are represented as different from those of settled populations. The relationship with the Malayaputras is represented as one of wary support (ibid.: 327), and as one where, ideally, control must be retained by Ram.

We learn that Amish is 'IIM [Indian Institute of Management] Kolkata educated, boring banker turned happy author' (ibid.: i). One has to be highly competitive and very well trained in order to gain admission to management institutions. This often involves blocking out other academic pursuits completely. Would Amish have written differently if he had been trained in the far less prestigious and lucrative discipline of history, instead, in any one of the institutions of higher education that still survives in the country?

Perhaps. I will conclude this discussion by illustrating the immense possibilities of writing rich, complex histories of some of the people Amish would classify as Malayaputras, drawing on a recent volume by Joy L.K. Pachuau and Willem van Schendel (Pachuau and Schendel 2015).

Organised around four broad themes, Pachuau and Schendel use over 400 visuals, mainly photographs, drawn from an archive of over 17,000 images, to reconstruct a history of Mizoram, one of the smallest states in India, ranging from the late nineteenth century to the early twenty-first century. Pachuau and Schendel carefully and systematically unpack stereotypes of 'primitivism, exoticism and stagnation' (ibid.: 3) and compel the reader to engage with 'the remarkable trans-formations and multiple forms of modernity that have flourished here' (ibid.: 4).

Pachuau and Schendel persuade us to engage with the everyday as well as with the spectacu-lar, more familiar mainstream processes. So there are discussions on the many ways in which the visual record was constituted, clothing and its significance, music, and the ways in which it was used, intertwined with responses to Western education, Christianity, and the colonial state. Moreover, complexities and conflicts are acknowledged rather than erased – so the engagement with Christianity, for instance, emerges as a dialogue, with diverse strands and possibilities.

The encounter with colonialism is reconstructed in painstaking detail, focusing on how the landscape was transformed, modes of communication changed, and negotiations with the market economy undertaken. Links with the outside world, including mobilisation during the World Wars, are also demonstrated through a rich array of visuals and texts.

The post-colonial world, with all its tensions and conflicts, is discussed with remarkable, often understated precision. Consider the following:

> Within India, Mizoram is the region with the highest proportion of 'tribals' (or 'scheduled tribes'). This makes Mizoram the 'tribal' state par excellence.
>
> Mizoram is also amongst the most highly educated regions in India, and its inhabitants think of themselves as more modern and better connected to the wider world than many of their compatriots. In other words, to them being card-carrying 'tribals' has nothing to do with 'primitive traits, distinctive culture, geographical isolation, shyness of contact with the community at large, and backwardness', which is how India's Ministry of Tribal Affairs defines tribes. It is an ill-fitting and external ascription that provides certain economic advantages but also comes with an unwelcome burden of prejudice, disdain and racism.
>
> Living under a paternalistic state that classifies you in this way affects how you represent yourself to it – and how you look at yourself. State officials and the Indian public at large found it helpful if 'tribals' were seen to be tribal. They should perform their identity. As a result, much emphasis was put on display by means of costume and artistic presentation.
>
> *(ibid.: 266)*

Pachuau and Schendel also document one of the most turbulent periods in recent Mizo history, a period of famine and revolt, which were handled with an unprecedented display of force, with quiet sensitivity:

> The Troubles would last from 1966 to 1986, a period during which violent and less violent periods alternated. This was a very dark time in Mizoram – and, at a different level, also for its visual history. More than four-fifths of the population were uprooted and shifted to new settlements, poverty and fear increased and armed confrontations were frequent. In these circumstances, many people lost their family possessions, including photographs, and few were in a position to document the distress that the Troubles caused in their lives.
>
> *(ibid.: 314)*

At the same time, they draw attention to unsettling issues of minorities within Mizoram, within territorial boundaries that have hardened over the decades (ibid.: p. 374). In doing so, they alert us to the possibilities of and the need to negotiate through contentious issues which refuse to be resolved through the reiteration of platitudes.

Does history have a future?

As a historian, one would like to answer the question in a quick, confident, affirmative. Yet, in order to make the affirmation effective, there is clearly much that needs to be done. More important, the political will to do so is an urgent and inevitable prerequisite.

Returning to our starting point, history can perhaps flourish if we constantly ask who our histories are meant for, and how we can shift the focus from the powerful to other social categories, to engage in a democratisation of processes of constructing and sharing knowledge in all its complexity. This is a challenge that is only beginning to be addressed. If Pachuau and Schendel's (2015) work reveals the immense possibilities of such strategies, the far more popular and accessible work of Amish (2015) is a reminder that we are contending with a dominant understanding that is far less demanding of the reader, and provides a scaffolding for existing socio-political and -economic hierarchies, of reassuring certainties in a rapidly changing world.

At another, more pragmatic level, are there ways of changing the system of evaluation, which at present allows, if not encourages, converting almost all learning material into a rote learning activity? Clearly, this is an enormous challenge. And yet, if it is not addressed, the pedagogical potential of history will remain largely unrealised. While rote learning may be common to several other disciplines, including the sciences, those at least are accompanied by the lure of potentially profitable job opportunities.

At yet another level, we need to understand and engage with the shrinking academic spaces available for formal training. Several central universities, set up recently, have no provision for teaching history – in yet others, such as the Guru Ghasidas University of Bilaspur, Chhattisgarh, a three-member faculty transacts courses ranging from the undergraduate, through the postgraduate and research programmes (information from www.ggu.ac.in, accessed 10 February 2015). And while a handful of high-profile private universities have created spaces for the teaching of history, the vast majority of private institutions simply find the discipline unprofitable.

History, as indeed many of the other social sciences/liberal arts subjects, seems to be poised at a critical juncture, demanding that practitioners revisit their academic concerns and work out ways and means of connecting the past and the present in ways that can be meaningful to those who have been excluded from these processes. At the same time, the paradox of supposed irrelevance combined with mining the past for sustaining and constructing a range of identities needs to be understood and addressed. Whether this enormous challenge can be met or not remains to be seen.

Appendix 1: list of visuals in chapter 1, *India and the Contemporary World*

Notes

1 I owe many of the ideas in this section to a stimulating discussion with Naina Dayal.
2 Abbreviated caption, provided by me.

References

Amish, T. *Scion of Ikshvaku*, Westland Ltd, Chennai, 2015.
Arnold, John H. *History: A Very Short Introduction*, Oxford, Oxford University Press, 2000.
Bhattacharya, Neeladri, 'History: Discipline, Craft and Narratives' in *Accessing the Past: Dialogues on History and Education*, Proceedings of the 11th Wipro Partners Forum, n.d., pp. 4–38.
Golden Social Science, New Delhi, New Age International (P) Limited, n.d.
India and the Contemporary World – vol. I, Textbook in History for Class IX, New Delhi, National Council of Educational Research and Training, 2006, ch. 1, pp. 3–24.
NCERT (2008) *History and a Changing World*; Director's Foreward (New Delhi: NCERT).
Pachuau, Joy L.K. and Willem van Schendel, *The Camera as Witness: A Social History of Mizoram, Northeast India*, Delhi, Cambridge University Press, 2015.
Ratnagar, Shereen, *Understanding Harappa: Civilisation in the Greater Indus Valley*, New Delhi, Tulika, 2001.
Roy, Kumkum, 'The Many Meanings of Aryan', in Shankar Goyal (ed.), *Investigating Indian Society: Essays in Honour of Professor S.R. Goyal*, Jodhpur, Kusumanjali Book World, 2013, pp. 35–50.

9

An experiment in rural education

The revival of Anand Niketan

Nidhi Gaur

After 68 years of independence, India is struggling to mark its presence in the 'developed' world. A majority of our population still lives in villages; the agricultural sector still contributes significantly to the country's gross domestic product (GDP); we still consistently miss deadlines for achieving 100 per cent literacy; and our prime minister still has to make emotional pleas for civic responsibility while burdening the citizens with cleanliness tax. These are a few indicators that we are far from our goal of modernisation.

Touraine (1998), while arguing for the importance of intercultural communication through comparative studies, differentiates between modernity and modernisation, which helps us in understanding the probable causes and resolution of the aforementioned issues. He defines modernisation as 'a movement, something willed, a mobilisation at the head of which is in any case the state, whatever the social forces on which it depends' (Touraine 1998: 451). For a country with a colonial legacy, modernisation through state machinery presents itself as a safe and quicker way of development because of the belief that 'developed' countries have gone through the same path. This implies state initiative and responsibility for setting up industries, expansion of cities, and other agents of modernisation. In other countries, the bourgeoisie/capitalist class performed this task while the state kept checks through taxation. In India, the state chose to partner with this class to speed up modernisation.

Touraine argues that 'modernisation through state machinery' is a misconception, for the 'developed' countries went through a process of modernity, which is an individual-centric process. He defines modernity 'as a set of attributes of social organisation'. This implies that modernity is not just a process of industrialisation but also a process of social upheaval leading to the discrediting of the older order and developing a new social order.

Ursula Franklin (1999), in her authoritative work *The Real World of Technology*, explains how social re-structuring paved the way for the Industrial Revolution. Franklin quotes Foucault's influential work *Discipline and Punish* to illustrate changes in the social structure in the seventeenth and the eighteenth century, particularly in French schools, hospitals, military institutions, and prisons. Application of discipline accompanied with detailed hierarchical structures, drill, surveillance, and record-keeping were applied to all these organisations. In the 1740s, La Mettrie wrote *L'Homme-machine*, that is, man-the-machine. In this book he described how the human body was 'an intricate machine, a machine that could be understood, controlled, and used'

(Franklin 1999: 53). Foucault illustrates how this idea of a human body led to the training of the human body into compliance, which was translated into organisations such as schools, hospitals, military institutions, and prisons. This, Franklin says, was the social setting prior to the Industrial Revolution. It was this blueprint of the society that factories took and through machines made more controlled, stringent, and invasive. 'The new patterns, with their breakdown of processes into small prescriptive steps, extended quickly from manufacturing into commercial, administrative, and political areas…. Planning thrived as an activity closely and intimately associated with the exercise of control' (Franklin 1999: 55). So, a social structure that rendered itself readily to the control and management of the human body evolved.

> In turn, the change in the structure of society and the nature and organisation of work and production during the Industrial Revolution became a pattern onto which our real world of technology with its much more extended and sophisticated restructuring is grafted.
>
> *(Franklin 1999: 56)*

India encountered industrial revolution partially during its struggle for freedom. The already established culture of compliance was more deeply ingrained in Indian society through colonial rule. But conflicts of caste, religion, and language added layers of complication. The process of state-run industrialisation that began after Independence rested on this social setting. Machines, as was true in Europe, did not bring about social change. But they strengthened the centralisation of power and control, which was already established by the British through the system of inspection and bureaucracy. Machines helped in making this control more invasive and stringent through their application and development of technology in administration and governance. This industrialisation required a compliant workforce to thrive on and a replica of Western education with its emphasis on training, drill, examination, and timetabling was established – the kind of schools that Foucault critiqued most convincingly.

This industrialisation was the modernisation of India. The process of becoming modern necessitates popular reorganisation of the society. Thus, making it a discontinuous process wherein older social structures have to be replaced by new ones. It has to be individual-centric and has to move from the bottom reaching the top, changing the entire structure in between. Taylor (1991) explains this change as a shift from honour to dignity; from ascribed status to achieved status. In the Indian context, it would mean questioning the caste structure and discrediting it. However, it is a gradual process, which the 'developed' countries went through to pave the way for a democratic and liberal society. It included the process of colonisation of India and other countries.

India's journey on this road began only after Independence. Our nationalist leaders understood the importance of social change in the whole modernisation process, but they believed that industrialisation would gradually modernise the society. India definitely converted some towns into cities. But even in cities, which were to become the face of modernity, we achieved it only in material terms. Socially, we are still traditional. Caste and religious fanaticism are still going strong, if not thriving. Modernisation has only added to our problems with over-populated cities, pollution, and violence. The government is forced to levy a cleanliness tax on its citizens to develop their civic sense in order to stop them from dirtying and destroying public infrastructure and keeping the streets clean. This is a clear sign of our lack of belongingness and ownership of our own country. While we are dealing with these issues and looking for possible solutions, it would be worthwhile to look at the alternative to modernisation, that is, modernity, and if it could present a means of social reorganisation.

In 1909, Mahatma Gandhi presented an alternative to Western civilisation in his classic work *Hind Swaraj*. He defined '*swaraj*' as living fearlessly. He interpreted it as '*swa-par-raj*', that is, rule over oneself. It rests on three pillars – self-awareness (truth), self-reliance (productive labour), and self-discipline (11 vows). Being truthful for Gandhi meant searching for one's truth and following it with absolute conviction. Disciplining one's mind and body through the practice of 11 vows and productive manual labour gives individual inner strength. Creating objects of everyday utility not only makes an individual self-reliant but is also rewarding for his/her mind and soul.

Modern scholar Charles Taylor (1991), in his influential work *The Three Malaises of Modernity*, perceives authenticity in an individual as a sign of modernity. He notes that this ideal of authenticity demands a definition of self in relation to others. Therefore, an authentic self can only be actualised through dialogue with the significant other. Gandhi also saw *swaraj* as a lived experience of an individual in the context of a community. Here, education plays a vital role. It can initiate the process of *swaraj* at an early age within a community. But what kind of education can create a conducive environment for the development of mind, body, and spirit as is required to experience *swaraj*?

Gandhi hinted at this kind of education in *Hind Swaraj*, in which he critiqued Western education as a mere learning of letters that would alienate the rural Indian child, developing in him an attraction or need for the city. This alienation would lead to an ambiguous personality because of conflicting values of the school and home. He quoted Thomas Huxley to present his ideal of education:

> That man I think had a liberal education who has been so trained in youth that his body is the ready servant of his will and does with ease and pleasure all the work that as a mechanism it is capable of; whose intellect is a clear, cold, logic engine with all its parts of equal strength and in smooth working order ... whose mind is stored with a knowledge of the fundamental truths of nature ... whose passions are trained to come to heel by vigorous will, the servant of a tender conscience ... who has learnt to hate all vileness and to respect other as himself. Such a one and no other, I conceive, has had a liberal education, for he is in harmony with nature. He will make the best of her and she of him.
>
> *(Parel 2009: 99)*

Gandhi found such potential in the teaching of crafts. The next section illustrates this point through classroom observations of some crafts taught in Anand Niketan. In this paragraph a brief explanation of this scheme is presented. Gandhi believed that a process of education centred around crafts could create a meaningful context for the learning of letters. It could become a bridge between the school and the home environment of a child since the practice of crafts facilitates development of the body, mind, and spirit. He advocated the mother tongue to be the medium of instruction.

Mahatma Gandhi called it 'Rural National Education through village handicrafts' in the foreword of the curriculum of the scheme that Dr Zakir Husain termed 'Basic National Education' (Gandhi 1938). By calling it rural, perhaps he wanted to differentiate it from English education, and with the addition of 'through village handicrafts' stressed the rural context of a school in which a teacher will live, as well as a selection of crafts from among the varieties being practised in that village. In other words, he wanted to stress the decentralisation of village education with little interference from the government. This was a vital part of his vision of a self-sustaining village society.

By self-sustaining village society, he did not mean an absolute self-sustaining, closed rural society. This needs to be interpreted in the context of the more popular idea of modernisation. What he meant was a self-reliant but interdependent rural society, and one that needs to be juxtaposed to the present state of the village to the city, wherein the former is an unequal/inferior partner of the latter. Its population is considered backward and a burden when it migrates to the city. Examining the relationship between rurality, modernity, and education, Krishna Kumar (2014), in an important paper, illustrated how the village has lost its relevance in modern times even in the construction of knowledge. It is the binary opposite of the city, which is modern and so, 'For the village, there is just one way to liberate itself from this binding relationship, and that is to develop into a town according to the agenda of evolutionist modernity' (Kumar 2014: 40).

In Gandhian vision, the village retains its dignity and its self-reliance and becomes an equal partner to the city. It also has something to offer to the city in lieu of its demands. The village can negotiate and survive with its dignity intact. He strongly believed that the progress of independent India is through the wellbeing of its villages. Hence the focus should be on strengthening the village community. He saw the core of Indian culture in the live tradition of crafts, which was the key to their self-reliance and creative self-expression. It was fundamental to their experience of *swaraj*. Critics of Gandhi see this as his legitimisation of casteism and untouchability. However, he took steps to reform the village society through constructive programmes. A craft-centred education aided in that reform by drawing out crafts from their rigid caste boundaries. These were taught to children from all castes without any bias. In this manner, he imagined mobilising a large mass of India's rural population for social reorganisation with the spread of modernity. After all if encouraging girls to play alongside boys and take up careers and become professionals is expected to create a more equitable society, encouraging children from all castes to learn all kinds of crafts should also de-stigmatise craftwork. Craft-centred education was to play a vital role here by questioning and diluting the structures of caste through separation of caste and occupation.

Another important aspect of modernity is the application of science and technology. Here, one can say that learning from the experience of the West, Gandhi strongly advocated the role of science but warned against an over-reliance on technology. He was suspicious of technology that would replace workers, leading to their deskilling and reducing them to appendages of machines. Some of these issues were raised in the British Parliament also through questions such as: 'Was it morally right that, in the name of trade, prosperity and efficiency, the mode of work could change so drastically that many people became uprooted and deprived of their livelihood?' (Franklin 1999: 58). Gandhi warned about the use of that kind of technology.

Displacement of the rural population by making the village, where a majority of Indians live, irrelevant in modern society has led to a situation of crisis. It has stripped villagers of their right to livelihood and a dignified life by compelling them to migrate to cities and labour as domestic workers and live in urban slums. It has also created problems of overcrowding, seething competition, pollution, and violence in urban India. Also, the present nature of the application of science and technology rooted in exploitation and control over nature has led to a range of environmental issues, such as global warming.

These glaring issues compel us to look for viable alternatives for a better future. Gandhi's vision of an alternative Indian civilisation based on *swaraj* presented one such possibility. Craft-centred education, specially designed for rural children, was an integral part of this vision. In the light of the present circumstances, a re-examination of craft-centred education will help in four ways. First, it will be able to provide quality education to rural children who are the future of the country. Second, it can help in the socialisation of children. Gaur (2016), in her doctoral thesis, argues for the potential of craft-centred education in dealing with gender issues through socialisation of children. Third, as Srinivasan's (2015) recent doctoral thesis brings to the fore, the hollowness of higher education in India can also be addressed by listening to Gandhi. Fourth, science in craft-centred education facilitates a harmonious relationship with nature, as presented in the following section.

Gandhi's emphasis on science is inherent in the practice of crafts. It comes in the use and repair of tools and implements, modifications of existing tools and implements as per requirements, developing an understanding of raw materials used through their careful observation and manipulation, and exploring the process of making through creating the desired object. Students applied this understanding/knowledge of science in informal activities too. This became the thread for dialogue between home and school spun by children themselves. This was a subtler but lasting form of reform that Gandhi tried to initiate through schools, when children started understanding the world around them through minute observations of processes and their questions and reflections on these processes. A glimpse of this is presented in the following section on Anand Niketan.

Revival of Anand Niketan

Anand Niketan was a village school founded by Mahatma Gandhi in 1938 in the Sevagram ashram premises. It was part of his ideal vision of a self-sustaining village, complete with a village school where crafts practised in the village were taught not as hereditary occupations but as educative work that would facilitate the development of mind, body, and spirit. Teachers lived in the school or ashram premises and in some cases the classroom was an extension of the teacher's house. For example, the art room at Anand Niketan was in front of the cottage of the art teacher, celebrated artist Devi Prasad, who also designed it. The two rooms were so close that at night when children put their clay objects in the kiln, they would use their teacher's kitchen to make tea and pakoras while waiting. Similarly, the music teacher's cottage was next to the music room.

The school was shut down in the 1970s and was reopened in 2005 by some Gandhians with the help of the Jamnalal Bajaj family. Now it functions from 9.30 a.m. to 5.30 p.m. in summer and from 10 a.m. to 5 p.m. in winter. Gardening, spinning, embroidery, stitching, and weaving are some of the crafts taught in the school. Some classroom observations are described in the following paragraphs.

The school appears to be a vast, open space dotted with trees and cottages. The vastness of the sky is just as overwhelming as the feeling of sand under one's feet. The quiet and serene surroundings and the chirping of the birds is welcoming. On the porch of a cottage on a rainy day I saw a group of Class V girls sitting and talking. Since it was lunch, I thought they were eating but I found them with small bowls of water cleaning a transparent paste. They had scratched some 'dink' sap from the bark of the neem trees around. The dirty sap was being cleaned to make gum. First, two girls cleaned it with their hands. Two other girls then gave it a rinse with water and kept the clean 'dink' on a piece of white paper. A chain was thus formed. They stored it in a bottle with water. In some time, it would get mixed with water, they said. This was not a learned technique but a childhood instinct. They were aware of their surroundings and thought of an activity around them. They broke the activity into smaller tasks, divided the work among themselves, and executed it well. There are two points to note here. First, the ethos of the school provided the children with an opportunity where they could devise such plans and work on them without fear. They lived among trees, birds, and animals and had developed an intimate relationship with them. Second, they were attentive and observant and comfortable in trying out their instincts. They knew the creative process and could confidently pull it off.

Gardening

In a gardening class, a teacher was helping a student prepare soil with a large fork. The girl followed his instructions but found it difficult to push the fork because she was not applying enough pressure at the right point. The teacher stood by her side watching and waiting patiently for her to look up and ask for help. He would then repeat the instruction. While this was going on, another student was handling the fork on his own. I asked him what he was doing. He explained that he was preparing the plot for sowing. I asked him about the seeds he would sow. He said he was still thinking. 'Spinach takes more time to grow than fenugreek, but then its produce is better and sells more. Last time, I planted spinach', he said. A student was taking out spinach, another was measuring his produce, and some others were watering their plots.

I observed a group of students plucking fenugreek from a plot. They were busy talking when I joined them. One of them was talking about the recent appearance of berries on the shrubs near the ashram farms. They were all planning to go there after helping their friend harvest fenugreek from her plot. Then one of the girls got up to get a rope to tie the produce. Another one ran to the school and ashram to inform people about the produce, so that interested buyers could come and buy. A third stood in a queue to weigh the produce. The other two were still plucking. As soon as the rope was brought, they took the produce to the weighing scale. Two of them weighed while the third jotted down the weight in a notebook, after which the produce was tied up. Soon, a group of teachers arrived to buy fenugreek. Details of the sale and purchase were diligently noted. Once the job was done, the girls ran to the other side of the garden to pluck the berries. At this point, I noticed a small rocky gate-like structure on one of the plots. I went and asked about it. A student told me that it was the grave of a frog that was killed in the process of preparing the plot.

After the initial set of instructions on how to use a fork to prepare a plot of land and different kinds of seeds and their needs, children worked independently on their plots. But things like speed and keeping up with others did not appear to be a concern for anyone. They decided on everything from the choice of seeds to the processes of sowing, watering, and harvesting. There was no right answer or the right way of doing it. They learned by doing. They learned from their failure. Helping each other and working with each other came naturally and it was neither encouraged nor discouraged by their gardening teacher. Not even once did the teacher ask the children to work silently or to focus on their own plots or to do their work. The students took responsibility for the task at hand and did it on their own.

Each plot looked different not only because of the variety of crops, but also because each child had embellished his/her plot with their choice of materials. The thought of making a grave for an animal that died during working reflects a student's relationship with nature, which developed from his gardening experience. The instinct to decorate their plots and to give them an identity also reflects their sense of ownership.

Science

It was 11.45 a.m. and the sun was warming up the winter noon, making the Class V classroom comparatively colder than outside. So when the bell rang, the science teacher entered the room and suggested holding the class on the porch, provided they shifted there quickly with their mats and bags. The teacher brought her chair outside to sit. The next few paragraphs describe this science period and analyses the classroom interaction as well as its content. Since the Maharashtra State Board of Education (MSBE) teaches all its subjects in the Marathi medium, an attempt has been made to translate the discussion in English as accurately as possible.

The teacher opened a science textbook provided by the MSBE and announced that this was an introductory class on a chapter titled 'The Chemical Properties of Plastics' that they would be dealing with in the next few classes. She did not ask the students to open their textbooks, but some of them opened them anyway. After speaking for about ten minutes on the properties of plastics described in the book, she asked if the students had any questions. Many hands went up immediately. The discussion that followed is given below:

STUDENT 1: What if we bury a plastic bag in soil for a long time? Would it stay there as it is?
TEACHER: Yes, it would.
STUDENT 2: How does plastic decompose? How much time does it take?
[There was complete silence in the audience as the students appeared eager to hear their teacher's response.]
TEACHER: It does not decompose at all.
[The students expressed shock on hearing this with some repeating her words. A minute later, a third student told the class that Kurkure, a spicy snack brand, was said to contain plastic. She then asked, 'What happens to plastic when it enters our body and is not digested?']
TEACHER: I know everyone likes to eat Kurkure because of its taste, but it is harmful and we must avoid eating it.
STUDENT 4: What happens to plastic, if it does not decompose?
STUDENT 5: I have seen big machines on Discovery channel. Maybe they destroy it.
[Just then the bell rang, and the teacher left, but the students took a little longer to get back into the class. They were still talking about plastic among themselves.]

Two kinds of classroom interaction could be observed in this description. One, the teacher used Ausubel's technique of an advance organiser to acquaint the students with the concepts of the new chapter so that they were able to assimilate new information. Here she was the actor and her students were listeners. The equation changed completely when the floor was opened for questions. The students who had been listening so far were now actively asking questions while the teacher answered them. The kids could also respond to each other's questions. Together the group was actively engaging with the newly acquired information in accordance with the knowledge they already possessed.

The focus of this active engagement was the fact that plastic is a non-biodegradable substance. The children had learned from their intimate engagement with the environment (including gardening) about nature's law – anything that is born will die. Their experience of composting was a major source of the counter-questions they asked. However, personal experiences and information acquired at home was also used effectively when a girl talked about Kurkure. She was talking about a rumour that Kurkure contains plastic in some form. However, its manufacturer, PepsiCo, rubbished these rumours.

The practice of gardening facilitated experiential learning among the children and showed that experience is more pervasive and deep-rooted, and has strong roots in a person's affective domain. This was evident in the questions asked, which were rooted in both cognitive and affective domains of learning. At one level, they were drawing inference from nature and its law that whatever is born must die after its due time. At another level, on realising that manmade objects are disturbing the law of nature, they became concerned about their implications for their surroundings. This concern for the environment was facilitated by their experience.

Spinning and weaving

In the spinning room, the weaving teacher was struggling to set up a handloom for Class VII. During the summer vacations, two teachers had gone to Guwahati for ten days to learn weaving. They planned to introduce weaving in Class VII in January. By the end of the semester, the students were expected to weave at least one mat – and, if possible, a mat for Class I students too. Two looms were to be set up in the spinning room and students were to learn it as and when they got time.

Working on a handloom requires a strong body since the loom is attached to the weaver's back for support. But the excitement that the sight of the loom generated among the students who were spinning was far more than any worry about their frames. Some of them who had completed spinning gathered around the teacher to observe her weaving. They started asking her questions about the loom and what she was doing. They wanted to know the product they would get after the process and also when they would be allowed to work on it, and so on. The teacher explained to them the terms 'tana' (warp) and 'bana' (weft). The loom then had threads in two colours, one used as 'tana' and the other as 'bana'. They quizzed her about the eventual design and the colour that would be prominent. They then started discussing which two colours would look good together. The teacher let them help her out.

The students' questions about the colour and design of the final product reflected the degree to which they could imagine it even in the early stages of weaving. They could already tell which one of the colours would dominate the pattern, as they had noticed that the bana went through the tana only once, which meant addition of a single thread. In her design, however, while moving the bana from one end of the tana to the other, the teacher was using double threads of the tana together. This 2:1 ratio of tana to bana meant that the colour of the tana would dominate the pattern. The teacher explained that since the yellow thread wasn't enough for use as tana and the white thread also looked dull, she had decided upon using yellow as bana to add colour to the mat. Crafting products leads to an early understanding of breaking down a task into smaller ones to create a desired final product. This question–answer session indicates that the natural urge to observe and ask about something new was given due space in a class of students who may not be weaving for another two years.

Conclusion

This chapter began by distinguishing between modernity and modernisation. The distinction between the two is essential to realise their deep-rooted implications for our everyday lives. Modernisation is state-imposed development resting on the use of technology. Modernity is an individual-centric approach resting upon the growth of the individual leading to the progress society. India chose to modernise itself, with Nehru referring to dams as the temples of modern India. However, Gandhi presented another alternative based on the principles of modernity, but it ran into controversies even before its trial. This was his alternative to Western civilisation and was explained in *Hind Swaraj*. From this alternative concept derived the scheme of education he proposed, also called craft-centred education.

Gandhi's scheme of education was a rare experiment in education for several reasons. One, it was not an isolated scheme but an integral part of his alternative to Western civilisation. Two, the village was the foundation of this alternative as it presented itself as the site of modernity. Three, it was rooted in modernity and the concept of individual freedom, but unlike Western civilisation it aimed to develop direct ties with neighbours through self-reliance and interdependence. It saw modernity as an individual experience and aimed at strengthening the individual to strengthen community. Thus, modernity was a popular struggle and not a top-down approach, and it translated in the same way at the national level, depending on the demography and its strength and then building on it. It would have helped the nation develop an identity and stand on its own.

Gandhi saw the potential of craft-centred education in countering caste by diluting it through its separation from occupation. School would then have become an agency to introduce children from across classes and castes to learn crafts, which were given an inferior status in society. This would have separated caste from occupation, and learning it in school would have brought out the science of crafting. This would have not only dignified craftwork but also brought out its inherent scientific approach that was passed on over generations. It would have created a social awareness of the value of crafts. This separation from craft and caste would have diluted the hierarchical structure of caste through a healthy exchange of crafts across castes. It would have given other academic opportunities to lower-caste children who then had a fair choice to choose a field and have a career in it. This field could be any craft or any academic discipline. Similarly, it would have given an upper-caste child the choice of a variety of activities to make a career in. In this manner, the community would have interacted in many other constructive ways than just traditional castes. This separation would have been the first step towards change – a change that dignified the strength of the human hand and mind and its potential to create a civilisation.

Social change is a slow and gradual process. The first section of this chapter explained how even the developed world took nearly two centuries of social reorganisation to lay the foundation for the Industrial Revolution. Feminists and social activists are aware of how this change occurred from generation to generation. Therefore, this separation would have certainly paved the way for an initiation of the gradual process of social change.

We have already mentioned the understanding and application of science in the first two sections. Science in craft-centred education is seen 'as an approach to knowledge' (Kumar 1996: 2368). This education facilitates the development of scientific temper. The school also upholds this view of science. Students are observing, hypothesising, experimenting, reflecting, comparing, analysing, and manipulating objects not just in the class but in routine activities too. All the above examples show how students are taking responsibility for their learning and are actively engaging in various classroom situations. They come up with activities, break it into smaller tasks, divide these tasks among themselves, and do them. They are operating on the environment and looking for tools and materials from the environment that can help them complete their task. They are active and independent. They are taking decisions and going forward with those. Science is applied here for strengthening the individual worker/craftsperson. It retains the labour-intensive model. Implications of this alternative would have affected rural–urban relations and our relationship with technology and our concept of time and efficiency that are intimately connected to technology.

The idea appears convincing, but the desired growth is slow and its path is unknown as it remains uncharted. It unfolds as we grow. This has two kinds of problems. First, we have the impatience to catch up with the world, so we are always worried about our speed. Second, we fear that the idea may not unfold as it is envisioned, and since we don't have any examples we find ourselves ill-equipped to deal with the problems that may be presented during the process. But still it presents a worthy alternative that needs to be given a fair trial.

References

Franklin, U.M. 1999. *The Real World of Technology*. Ontario: Anansi.

Gandhi, M. 1938. *Hind Swaraj or Indian Home Rule*. Ahmedabad: Navjivan Publishing House.

Gaur, N. 2016. 'Gender and Craftwork in Rural Society: Role of Education'. Unpublished doctoral thesis, New Delhi.

Nidhi Gaur

Kumar, K. 1996. 'Agricultural Modernisation and Education: Contours of a Point of Departure'. *The Economic and Political Weekly*, 31 (35–37): 2367–2373.
Kumar, K. 2014. 'Rurality, Modernity and Education'. *The Economic and Political Weekly*, 49(22): 38–43.
Parel, A.J. 2009. *'Hind Swaraj' and Other Writings*. New Delhi: Cambridge University Press.
Srinivasan, S. 2015. 'Locations of Knowledge: The University, Liberal Education and the Case of India'. PhD, Manipal University.
Taylor, C. 1991. *The Malaise of Modernity*. Ontario: Anansi.
Touraine, A. 1998. 'Modernity and Cultural Specificities'. *International Social Science Journal*, 118: 443–457.

Part III

Training for professions

In this part, the readers will find three chapters that discuss professional training in three different fields. These three are hardly representative of the vast area of higher professional education in India. All they do is introduce you to the nature of the development that has taken place in this sector of higher education and also the nature of the problems and challenges that professional education faces. Although each field of professional education faces challenges that are specific to it, the three chapters included in this section might give a glimpse of some general or theoretical problems. These have to do with knowledge and its active application in the course of a professional career or life. A professional career implies specialised learning, which is used for a public purpose. The training for such a career involves learning of a kind that might include the experience of using it. Thus, professional education can be distinguished from higher education of a general kind which aims at imparting knowledge without necessarily focusing on the skill or a set of skills required to use such knowledge for a career devoted to providing a service based on such skill.

Professional education in law, engineering, and medicine started during the colonial period. The first chapter in this section concerns engineering, and it demonstrates the importance of taking into account colonisation as a factor for shaping the character of engineering education and its problems or challenges. We are not talking about the colonial legacy, a frequently used term in the context of education, but rather a wider inheritance that shapes the perception of knowledge and the role its application might play in addressing the problems of human life. In his chapter, Milind Sohoni first explains the development of engineering education in the West, especially the USA, in order to argue that the idea and image of a professionally qualified engineer there is embedded in socio-economic needs and expectations. He contrasts this case with that of India, where the engineer learns advanced knowledge in order to receive a high qualification, not in order to respond to or address any real and immediate needs. Thus, the engineering curriculum, even of apex institutions, fails to equip the young engineer to notice the problems that his knowledge and skill might solve in the Indian milieu, urban or rural. These characteristics of engineering education may be similar to other areas of professional education. A general point can be made about the social status that education leading to a medical, engineering, or architecture degree offers to its recipient. If Sohoni's analysis is extended, we can say that the status associated with professional qualification in an area like engineering may be the driving force behind the continued popularity of these courses, rather than the knowledge and skill they impart. A wider phenomenon of the 'commonisation' of the engineering degree over the recent period may also be linked to this. This phenomenon has resulted in a glut of private institutions and a decline of enrolment in pure science courses at higher levels, noticed by Shobhit Mahajan earlier in this volume.

Training of teachers is another area of professional education examined in this part. Concern for the quality of teaching has been a consistent theme in public documents and scholarly literature on education, and the expression of this concern has become shriller over recent years, with the recent expansion of the system and an increase in the number of children enrolled at all levels. Demand for trained teachers has mounted, and the state has responded to this demand by encouraging private initiatives in establishing and running teacher-training institutions. Over 80 per cent of all institutions offering training degrees today are private. The apex regulatory body, the National Council of Teacher Education (NCTE) has recently launched a series of reforms in various courses, including the Bachelor of Education (BEd) course that qualifies a teacher to be appointed at a secondary school. In her chapter in this section, Latika Gupta examines the established structure of the BEd curriculum, focusing on the division between 'theory' and 'practice'. She also presents an analytical description of the ethos of a teacher-training institution. An obsessive emphasis on methods of teaching, coupled with the inability to link educational theory with subject knowledge, is identified in this chapter as a key weakness of the BEd curriculum. The ethos accentuates the absence of academic depth of the course, reinforcing the influence of an unreformed school education system on the new generation of teachers.

Unlike engineering and teacher education, management education has no historical legacy as such. It is a relatively new area of professional education and it does not seem to suffer from financial constraints. Pankaj Chandra examines the growth of management education in India and the role it has played in providing specialised personnel to the expanding industrial establishment. This chapter brings out the strengths that institutional responsiveness to the needs of industry has imparted to the curriculum in apex institutions. It also points out how the state's attempt to regulate the sector has made it vulnerable to problems similar to other areas of professional education.

10

The making of India as an engineering society

Milind Sohoni

Education, especially higher education, is perhaps the most direct intervention that a society may make in changing itself, and thus its design offers an effective formal tool for social transformation. Within that, engineering education is certainly privileged, since its very objective is to prepare agents of material change. The training of an engineer within a society offers a unique insight into what the society attributes as important as well as amenable to scientific or technological analysis, the nature of accumulation and transmission of material knowledge, and finally the effectiveness of the society in delivering material wellbeing to itself. It is within this broader connection with the material society that we explore engineering and scientific education.

Hence, it is important that we examine the massive problems of inequity and development in our society, at least partly as problems of design and conduct of higher education. In this chapter I look at the profession of engineering and of applied physical sciences in India and the system of training and research that supports it. The objective is to tease out its structural features, its social and cultural embedding, and, increasingly important, its linkages with global knowledge. In the first three section, I will (1) describe a mechanism of knowledge formation and delivery, (2) narrate a history of the evolution of this mechanism in the West, and (3) use the above two constructions to analyse the Indian system of engineering education, post-Independence, and its outcomes. I use the West as a reference, since it is one which is closest to us in organisation, and which has served as a role model, and yet which is antipodal in initial conditions and conduct. In a later section, I collect together various strands from the earlier parts and point out the central role of culture and of rigour in the trajectory of an engineering or scientific society. We will also look at the emerging global knowledge system and its key axioms as an example of a scarce and (culturally) hegemonic science. Finally, we propose a science and engineering system that is more likely to deliver development. In the final section I conclude by embedding the outcomes of our analysis into the broader question of the design of higher education, its political economy, and the role of the social sciences.

The meaning of a profession

Professional education, as opposed to a 'liberal education' such as in the humanities, social sciences, or the pure physical sciences, is by nature instrumental and embedded in society. It aims to produce agents (1) who satisfy an expressed demand for a particular service or social value and expect to be rewarded in money or in kind, and (2) who access a body of professional knowledge and yet tailor it to suit a particular situation. Inherent in the notion of a profession is an association or group of professionals, their body of professional knowledge, and, finally, a charter, i.e. a social recognition of the profession and the above transaction. The profession is then a mechanism organised as (1) a *paired vocabulary*: an external or social vocabulary in which problems or demands are specified, and an internal professional vocabulary in which knowledge is expressed and solutions are designed; (2) *a professional knowledge* and a system of translation which is *sound*, i.e. which is successful in meeting posed demands; (3) *a method of accumulation*, i.e. an epistemology which is *rigorous* – which maintains soundness and expands the profession. The translation from the external to the internal vocabulary may well be called analysis and design, while the reverse may be termed as synthesis or implementation.[1]

A simple example of a profession is football coaching, where, for example, the social vocabulary would be of scoring goals and executing popular manoeuvres, while the internal vocabulary may have theories of physical fitness and technique. The social charter of the profession is achieved through certification exams aligned with national and international sports associations. Note that the internal vocabulary of the professional may well be an interdisciplinary combination, e.g. in this case, of human physiology, ergonomics, and strategy.

Engineering is largely the profession of bringing about change in the material wellbeing of a society. It is concerned with the building of bridges and buses, shampoos and phones, various other gadgets, of provisioning services such as water supply and electricity, and also of goods and services sought by other industries, such as steel and shipping. As a profession, engineering is as old as history itself. Early engineers included shipbuilders, blacksmiths and smelters, lens-makers, and masons and other craftsmen and artisans. Their knowledge was largely situated within guilds and their practices, and entry into these guilds was frequently difficult. The modern engineer, however, is typically a university graduate and has access to a public body of professional knowledge.

Engineering in the West

Let us now quickly review the recent history of engineering in the West in terms of the mechanism that we have outlined above. It will serve to illustrate the various strands that have contributed to the evolution of the mechanism and also set up a framework for analysing Indian engineering.

Phase 1

Early organisation and transmission of engineering knowledge in the West was largely through two mechanisms, namely the guilds and the state machinery. Guilds were professional bodies of craftsmen organised around commercial production and services, e.g. for printing and stationery, leather-work, carriage-building, and apothecary. Entry into the guilds was managed through an elaborate apprenticeship protocol that was partly cultural and partly technical. The social embedding was frequently achieved by obtaining a royal charter, i.e. a monopoly on standards, regulation, and training of the particular activity within the royal domain. This charter was essential in maintaining the profession.

The second organisation of knowledge came from the engineering needs of the state; for example, in public works such as bridges and roads, in military engineering, and shipbuilding. This was organised around state departments, key contractors and companies, and their institutions of training. Civil engineering (i.e. the non-military part of the state agenda) was the first to achieve the public-access structure that is known today. The Institute of Civil Engineers was formed in England in 1818 and was itself preceded by the Society of Civil Engineers, founded in 1778. The institute began as a body of professional engineers and heads of building companies, which met regularly. It then transformed into a professional body with its own library and publications. By the late nineteenth century, it had evolved a curriculum and was also conducting certification examinations that were widely recognised. In fact, the Indian university is based on this tradition of certification on a recognised curriculum.

In France, the early 1800s saw the founding of the *grandes écoles* in various areas such as military engineering, shipbuilding, and bridges and roads. Similar progress was made in Germany as well as in the USA. The first degree/certificate in engineering in the USA was in civil engineering and was awarded in 1835 by the Rensselaer Polytechnic Institute, which was also the first purely technical university in the country. The need for professionals to run India's colonial administration led to the formation of the Thomason College at Rourkee in India in 1847. Though open to the public, it had separate programmes for Englishmen and for natives and its graduates were absorbed into the public works department of the colonial state.

There was a third knowledge tradition – the university. However, till the early eighteenth century, the European university was largely denominational and its training was in the classical traditions of metaphysics, philosophy, history, jurisprudence, and medicine. It was only in the eighteenth century that science entered the old university as a part of the philosophy of nature. Recognition of experimentation and theorisation as a method of science and engineering came much later.

Phase 2

The Industrial Revolution led to many innovations in engineering, and much of this happened outside the universities. In fact, one of the tasks of the scientific societies in Europe was to document and codify these inventions. With the advent of factories, and the capitalist mode of production, the producer no longer owned the means of production. Whence, the earlier role of the craftsman bifurcated into two distinct roles, namely the workman or tradesperson, and the professional engineer. The workman was to perform a fixed role of operating certain machines, while the engineer was to keep the machines and the factory in good order, and perhaps invent or adapt existing machines. In this connection, two important examples are the Mechanics Institute at Manchester, England, founded in 1824 jointly by the city and local industrialists, which later became the University of Manchester Institute of Science and Technology, and the Technical University at Dresden, Germany, in 1828. Both were non-denominational, open to the public, and were started to train existing workers in applied science and thus help them transcend their class and become engineer-inventors. This model of the technical university to prepare the engineer-inventor, as distinct from the workman, was replicated across Europe and led to many private and state-funded technical institutions.

In the USA, an important experiment in engineering education was the public land-grant university, which was funded and managed by individual states. These were large multidisciplinary public institutions founded around the 1860s, with the explicit agenda of knowledge provisioning for regional needs and preparing human resources for regional development. Agriculture, its mechanisation, management of natural resources, and urban and rural planning were important areas of applied research and training. Thus, these combined the cultural agenda of the older universities and yet provided for the 'extension' requirements of society. To this day, the Universities of Illinois, California, Minnesota, and others are important knowledge instruments in the hands of the states within the USA. In fact, the popularity of the American scientific fairs and other formal and informal extension activities led Oxford University to start its own version in the 1830s, called 'Continuing Education'. This was implemented as an outreach programme of public lectures in small towns on all aspects of knowledge and culture. American professional bodies started in the 1850s, with the American Society of Civil Engineering (ASCE) in 1850 and the American Society of Mechanical Engineers in 1880. These bodies devoted much energy to journals, standards, and curricula.

There was still much engineering and experimentation outside the university, and an active patent regime to protect inventions. A typical thread is the development of the external combustion engines, i.e. the steam engine of James Watt in 1788, the Stirling engine in 1818, and later the internal combustion engine of the 1860s, which eventually led to the modern car engine.

By this time, the scientific societies and the classical university had joined hands in the furtherance of the 'natural sciences'. This contributed many fresh ideas to engineering and to the economy. An important example is the discovery of electricity in scientific circles, and its uses in industry, e.g. in electroplating and telegraphy. The founding of the Institution of Electrical Engineers in 1871 in England marked the absorption of electricity and magnetism into professional academia as well as industry.

An important philosophical thread which emerged in this phase was the exploration into the role of science in the design of society, pioneered by Bacon and then later by Rosseau and Comte (see Scharf and Dusek 2014). Economic models of society, such as the fictional dog-and-goat island of Townsend, actually motivated Darwin to look for such islands in the natural world (Polanyi 1944). Many philosophers, such as Marx and Weber, and later Heidegger and Foucault (again see Scharf and Dusek 2014), have commented on the influence of technology on society, such as disenchantment, 'enframing' of nature and society by technology, and the creeping governmentality of personal and social interactions.

Phase 3

By the 1900s there was an effective convergence between the old university, the new technical university, industry, and the state. This was exemplified by the formation of the Imperial College of Science and Technology in London in 1907. Both science and technology entered into a new partnership, and so did theory and practice. Professional bodies had matured and served as a bridge between academia, industry, and state. They did this by publishing journals, through certification, curriculum design, and maintaining state-supported industrial standards, and therefore the charter. Research was conducted both in industry as well as at the research universities. For example, in Germany the Max Planck Institutes were founded in 1911 to extend the Humboldtian vision of the research university. This network of research institutions rested on the foundations of a large state-sponsored university system. As the civic infrastructure was put in place, the traditional 'civil' requirement of the state for engineers slowly declined, and by the 1960s it was the industry and the professional firms that hired the engineer and set the curricula. In 1958, MIT did away with the Sanitary Engineering Department and now, in 2017, the word 'sewage' does not appear in the *body of knowledge* document of the ASCE (ASCE 2008).

The engineer was now typically trained in a large, public, multidisciplinary university and his/her training was complemented by a 'liberal education' in the social sciences, humanities, and the physical sciences. The university was largely residential and provided a unique cultural experience and a common social understanding.

There also emerged two paradigms of research. Foundational and disciplinary research in both the sciences and engineering was done by the university and this was largely in the public domain. On the other hand, industrial laboratories of large companies, which had now emerged, did proprietary research in applied areas. Much of the research in these laboratories was done by interdisciplinary teams of professionals from all disciplines of engineering, sciences, economics, and other social sciences. This eventually grew to what is now called Mode-II research, i.e. highly technological and fundamental research, with large investments and long gestation periods, and yet proprietary and profitable. This intruded upon the earlier Mode-I university-driven research of the early 1900s, which was publicly supported, in the public domain, and moderated and critiqued by peer groups (Nowotny *et al.* 2001).

Today, in the West, there is a clear and dominant paradigm of 'scientific engineering' in the modern engineering curricula and that is a belief in abstract models of phenomena and the use of mathematical techniques for analysis. This highly disciplinary and specialised approach was pioneered by American colleges in the 1960s and now dominates engineering curricula world-wide, right from the design of core subjects for first-year undergraduate students. It is also insti-tutionalised by the way research is evaluated, and in the sites for applied research. Perhaps this viewpoint arose from the great success of 'deep science', e.g. theoretical physics in the early 1900s, and its connection with actual technological devices, e.g. relativity translating into nuclear energy, quantum mechanics into the transistor and other semiconductor devices.

Behind the disciplinary curriculum is also a corporatist belief that (1) the society is well served by the corporation; (2) it is also the correct location to operate and reward the interdisciplinary vocabulary of the engineering profession; and finally (3) the corporation is again the correct location to absorb the deeper disciplinary knowledge of the employee scientist-engineer and convert it into something useful. Thus, it is the corporation that generates social value and shares it with its employees.

This viewpoint has been challenged on two fronts. The first, which is still corporatist, views the modern engineer as a member of various interacting and interoperational teams who will design and test large engineering systems such as an aircraft engine. The disciplinary training fails to imbue in the student various interfacial skills of working within deadlines, designing around legacy black-box systems, the role of testing and standards, and the overall value of good prac-tices. All of this, it is argued, must find a place in the training of the modern engineer.[2] The second criticism comes from the outside and points to the missing societal interface in profes-sional training, and wants it unmediated by the corporation. This viewpoint, as followed by, e.g. Olin College, USA, sees designing for concrete users such as an urban cyclist as essential to its pedagogy. This is the entry point to teaching innovation as well as to framing broader normative concerns such as sustainability and global development.

On the whole, the progression in the profession of the engineer first as a guildsman, then as a state engineer, later as an engineer-inventor, and finally as a deep-science employee-engineer (i.e. 'the geek') has been an important ingredient in the social and material processes in the West. Moreover, the evolution of engineering into a curriculum within a public-access univer-sity was the amalgamation of several historical and cultural strands. This included the social churn arising from 'enlightenment' and the Industrial Revolution, and also numerous experi-ments in the definition of the university, e.g. the extension role or the technical university and the training of workmen. It was also shaped by a wide range of socio-economic and political agents, and a broad understanding within society on the role of science and technology in its transformation. Finally, the de-socialisation of the modern engineer in the West is a culmination of its current economic processes, and is not without its critics from within and without science and engineering.

The outcomes

Let us connect this with the socio-economic and cultural trajectory of the West. Life expectancy increased from about 50 in 1830 to about 65 in 1940, and is now close to 80 (Roser 2015). Better engineering has contributed as much to this increase as the 'governmental' role of gathering data and putting it to use. Remarkably, having a theory for the price of prevention, i.e. the counter-factual, is a hallmark of the West and this led to many investments and innovations in engineering and medicine. In fact, these empirical systems also led to the emergence of the 'rational' bureaucrat and a revolution in governance. The basic needs of water, food, etc., and energy in the form of electricity, have long been met. Professional bodies remain strong and peer groups define the conduct of science and technology all over the world. Culturally, too, the university continues to be a strong influence on the conduct of the state and the market. It has contributed to a common social appreciation of the sciences and the arts and a social comprehension of the state. People of Western societies are remarkable in their broad understanding of a common rigour and causality, which in turn allows collective action and a view of the future as amenable to a shared design. Science and engineering in the West, behind its material facade of gadgets and factories, 'natural' theories, and 'physico-mathematical' laws of causality and conservation, remains a deeply cultural tradition.

Given our colonial past, and the material successes of the West, it is only natural that Western traditions of science and technology should serve as a role model for us in India.

Engineering in India

Let us now turn to India and take a brief look at its evolution as an engineering and scientific society. Persistence of medieval socio-economic and cultural arrangements alongside cultural and material upheaval caused by years of colonial rule was the backdrop against which India gained Independence. The 150 years prior to 1900 was also a period in which the country suffered major de-industrialisation and a significant loss in wages and numbers. The number of industrial workers, largely in cottage industries, came down by half to about 8 per cent of the population. In the second half of the period significant land was devoted to cash crops, namely cotton and indigo, which were used by the British as tribute. India was wracked by many famines, including the great famines of 1896 and 1943, which wiped out five million people each. The life expectancy actually fell from about 26 in the 1800s to 24 in 1900, and then rose to about 32 in 1947 (Roser 2015).

At the time of Independence it was clear that engineering was to play an important role in India's development, and naturally so. India had begun as a poor country with few material resources and fewer means of their production. Steel, for example, was added at roughly 4 kg per capita per year, i.e. barely enough for a *pucca* house for a miniscule fraction of the population, or an even smaller investment in infrastructure. Agricultural yields, e.g. at 1,000 kg of wheat per hectare, were already low and falling. In most of the Deccan plateau and South India, agriculture was largely rain-fed and prone to failure. Ambedkar, in his analysis of small agricultural holdings, was a strong advocate of industrialisation, which would serve two objectives: reduce the pressure on land and produce much-needed material goods.

There was already existing in India a tradition of the engineering college, albeit in the idiom of the colonial project and its instrumental needs. Historically, the earliest engineering colleges in India were the Thomason College (1847) at Rourkee, Colleges of Engineering at Pune and Shibpur, near Kolkata (both in 1856) and at Guindy (1858). All were started by the regional colonial administration, and their charter was to satisfy the demand for engineers and designers of public works. An eminent alumnus of Pune (in 1888) was Sir Visvesvaraya, who went on to design several important irrigation projects in the states of Hyderabad and Mysore. Many later graduates went on to lead industry houses. The next batch of colleges arose in the period 1910–47, which included the Dhanbad School of Mines, colleges at Jadhavpur, Benaras, Patna, the Indian Institute of Science at Bangalore, and others. Many of these colleges had begun as polytechnics with a shorter course, called the 'licentiate' or the 'diploma'. This course was usually for preparing manpower for operational positions and did not include design. All told, at Independence, India had about 38 engineering colleges that were graduating roughly 2,500 engineers, and about 50 polytechnics graduating about 4,000 students, every year. Two eminent private colleges were the Businayana Mukundadas Sreenivasaiah College at Bangalore and the Birla College at Pilani.

The development of science in India is more complicated, linked as it is with the colonial experience of early Indian scientists and the role of culture in the conduct of science (see, for example, Kumar 1995). But it was also more influential in the formulation of policy and institutions of engineering education. Perhaps, the country saw its first *professional* or *salaried* scientists and engineers in those who came with the colonial administration to survey, document, and exploit the resources of the colonies. These scientists and engineers were first-class scientists in the European scientific tradition and yet created extraordinary value for the colonial state. Moreover, Indian intellectuals were also familiar with the scientific methods of the West by actually having visited their universities. This led to the formation of Indian science as a conflation of big science – i.e. science as a salary-paying institution of the state – with high science – i.e. science of the well-funded laboratories – and the dream of moulding it to serve the Indian poor. This vision influenced the Indian elite in their conception of the role and methods of science and technology in India and their own agency. This vision was present in the first planning exercise of 1936 of Sir Visveswaraya, and took more concrete shape in subsequent national plans. These plans eventually led to the establishment of the National Chemical Laboratory, the National Physical Laboratory, and other centrally sponsored laboratories as the first national investment in science. Following that, they led to the formation of the centrally sponsored Indian Institutes of Technology (IITs) and then to the Regional Engineering Colleges (RECs, now called the National Institutes of Technology, or NITs) as the first investments in technology. This network of institutions now constitutes the core of the scientific bureaucracy in India.

This vision was also reflected in the holding of the portfolio of science and technology (S&T) by the highest executive office in the country, the Prime Minister, and a nominal role for provincial governments in S&T policy. This centralisation of conduct of S&T persisted till the 1970s, when the first few state commissions were formed. The centralisation of expenditure continues to this day. It is also instructive that in many speeches by Pt Jawaharlal Nehru, especially those at the launch of the various central institutions, we find both a reference to the 'autonomy' of S&T and yet an exhortation for it to work for the deliverance of the common Indian from the 'grinding poverty' that traps him. But there were very few concrete mechanisms proposed or any concrete accountability that would bring these institutions close to the day-to-day problems faced by the provincial governments in bringing development to their poor citizens. The top-down view also missed the rather important role that small inventors, artisans, and amateurs had played in the development of Western science. It also missed the historical continuity and the deep civil society processes that had supported and shaped it.

Coming back to engineering, at Independence there were three central (overlapping) expectations from engineering as an institution. These were articulated by the Sarkar Committee report[3] of 1946 as the manpower and research needs for (1) management and development of key resources such as water and energy; (2) development of basic infrastructure and heavy industry; and finally (3) the supply of trained engineers for industrial production of material goods in the private sector. One may add to this the constitutional vision of a modern Indian people equipped with a scientific temper, who have risen above caste and superstition. Given the enormity of the problems, it was felt that the existing institutions were not adequate and a national investment was required.

We will divide the post-Independence growth of engineering education into three broad phases marked by three key policy choices. Each is remarkable in its own way and had important consequences for the conduct of engineering in India.

Phase I: the foundations

The Sarkar Committee report led to the first visible investments by independent India in engineering education, namely the setting up of the centrally funded and autonomous IITs. Soon after this, a recommendation by the Planning Commission led to the founding of 20 RECs. The RECs were also autonomous and founded by the Centre, but the running costs were shared with the states. While the IITs were to focus on excellence in research and the 'scientific' development of engineering, the RECs were to satisfy the demand for engineers in regional development projects.

The design of the first IITs was carefully done. In the Sarkar Committee report itself was the mention that the IITs must be modelled after the Massachusetts Institute of Technology (MIT) or the Manchester Institute. Correspondingly, an abstract disciplinary scientific engineering curriculum, as opposed to the practice-based curriculum of existing colleges, was carefully drafted and generous capital as well as running expenditures were requested and approved. A faculty nurture-and-mentoring programme was set up to prepare teachers of this scarce and special knowledge. IIT Kanpur was mentored by the USA, and IIT Bombay by the then USSR. Proximity to the West, complete autonomy in academic matters, an exclusive curriculum, a large budget outlay, a monastic residential campus for each IIT, and a nationwide competitive admission exam pushed the IITs into the national imagination. They were an immediate success with the middle and upper classes. However, right from the first year, many IIT graduates chose to migrate and the phrase 'brain drain' came into the popular lexicon (Sukhatme and Mahadevan 2004).

The IIT system had several important socio-political features: (1) it was the first indigenous elitisation, i.e. a systematic construction of elite agents and a belief in their ability to transform;[4] (2) it was supported by a belief in the excellence of a text-based analytic S&T which was visibly linked to elite institutions of the West, and not to field experience of existing institutions or agencies; and finally (3) a *physical separation* of science into the elite and the common, and a physical removal of the elite from their social milieu. The elitisation was implemented by creating a national system of 'merit' to be measured through nationwide competitive exams and a cloistered system of centrally funded institutions, removed from the hurly-burly of the regional universities. *Thus an elite, scarce, and transcendental knowledge system was created.* Remarkably, all of these features – elite agency, abstraction, scarcity, selection, and separation – have spread to other disciplines and continue to be the pillars of Indian higher education. The separation of engineering students, both from society and from the social sciences and arts, in curriculum as well as in location, persists to this date.

Next, the old colleges, the IITs and RECs, were further complemented by a system of government engineering colleges (GECs) within each state. Most of the GECs were not autonomous, but affiliated to various regional universities. The IIT and REC system first sat in parallel to the older premier colleges of Rourkee, Pune, or Benaras, and specialised institutions such as the Department of Chemical Technology at Mumbai (UDCT) and the Dhanbad college. Eventually, however, these older institutions were eclipsed by the new institutions, largely because of greater financial outlays, administrative autonomy, a more competitive student body and better outcomes for its graduates *outside* Indian engineering. Ironically, the possibility of exactly this outcome was pointed out by two dissenting notes in the Sarkar Committee report. Surprisingly, the RECs were not modelled after the land-grant universities of the USA, with their strong regional connection. In fact, most of the RECs have no academic programmes of regional relevance. This was further cemented in 2007 by the Centre renaming the RECs as NITs and taking over full control. Thus, an important bridge for the states to connect with the Centre and to organise their engineering system was lost to the Centre.

Phase II: growth and decoupling

The number of engineers graduating every year grew steadily so that in 1987 there were about 30,000 graduates from about 300 institutions, most of which were state-funded. The output of the IITs were about 1,500, i.e. about 5 per cent of the total. However, in the late 1980s, the IT boom began and this led to a proliferation of the private engineering college. The All India Council for Technical Education (AICTE), though formed as an advisory body in 1945, was empowered in 1987 to regulate the entry of new colleges and to ensure that student interests were protected. These colleges were required to demonstrate adequate finances, equipment, space, and qualified faculty members, for example, to meet AICTE requirements,[5] and site visits by AICTE inspectors were dreaded events. Most private colleges would still affiliate themselves to state universities for their curricula and examinations, and that was generally found acceptable by the AICTE.

The numbers of graduates and institutions rose rapidly to 120,000 and 400 institutions in 1997, 187,000 in 2000, and 550,000 and 1,600 institutions in 2006. By 2014 there were over 1,000,000 students graduating from about 3,000 institutions.[6]

The sheer enormity of these numbers is without parallel around the world. For example, about 110,000 engineers every year from about 400 engineering colleges suffice for the USA. What these numbers do not show is a severe loss of quality and distortion of engineering education in India. This increase was largely because of the boom in the IT sector, which grew from 240,000 employees in 1999 to 690,000 employees in 2005, to about 13,000,000 employees in 2009, and used engineering colleges as recruiting grounds. While the colleges responded by expanding their seats in the IT-related streams such as IT and CS/CSE, IT firms would gladly poach from other streams of engineering as well. This practice continues today. For example, in 2012, the IT sector hired 65 per cent of the graduating batch of 440 at GEC Thrissur, most of whom were not from the CS/IT branch. At IIT Bombay, too, in 2013 the IT sector hired about 24 per cent of the graduating enrolment, of which only about half came from the CSE stream.

Thus, the IT boom effectively converted the engineering college into an *aspirational* marketplace for English-speaking and well-paying, intermediate economy service sector jobs. This caused many distortions within and without college. Core engineering companies found it difficult to find fresh engineers at reasonable salaries. IT and CS departments faced a faculty shortage, while core engineering departments faced a lack of student interest. This was visible in macroeconomic indicators as well: it was service sector employment, especially in IT and communication services, that grew the most and best rewarded tertiary education. This decoupling of engineering jobs from engineering education was one important outcome of this phase. Ironically, an important impetus to this 'de-industrialisation' was provided by the World Bank project IMPACT (1989–1993), which trained faculty members of engineering colleges to teach an IT/CS/EE curriculum.

The IT boom was a precursor to the overall service sector boom for fresh engineers and was again led by the IITs. By this time, given the number of engineering graduates, the IITs were graduating about 1 per cent of the total number of graduates. These elite found jobs in the financial and consulting companies, and global IT majors, as more rewarding and better paying, than engineering companies catering to domestic needs such as cement or construction companies.[7] The high salaries of a few IIT graduates fed into a thriving coaching class industry of several hundred billion.[8] This led to the second decoupling of the actual aspirations and trajectories of IIT students from the stated charter of the IITs as an institution. All the same, its reputation as a global merit-based technological institute was crucial for the branding of the IIT graduate.

It also marked the emergence of 'brand IIT', of the smart and well-marketed institute, a national example of global values of knowledge and merit, iconic jobs for a few graduates, and yet an underbelly of a huge coaching industry and inordinate media attention. This emergence was driven by several factors. First, the IITs had long ago exempted themselves from the AICTE and its bureaucracy. Second, they are far less accountable to regional demands and budgets, and their students better connected and more adept at industry relations and brand-building. As compared to state colleges, they also receive far more funds from the MHRD directly, and from S&T funding agencies that are typically situated at the centre. Third, and most importantly, the IITs are the high-priests of engineering education since they administer both the iconic JEE (Advanced), which defines 'scientific' prowess at the high-school level, and the GATE exam, an entrance examination for engineering graduates for postgraduate study within the IITs, which has now become the de facto standard for engineering education.

Thus, the end of this phase was marked by decoupling of engineering institutions from engineering jobs, a consolidation of the definition of engineering, and, paradoxically, elite branding and deployment of the elite engineer into global service.

Phase III: the global alignment

In 2003, the MHRD and the World Bank launched the 'Technical Education Quality Improvement Programme' (TEQIP), a Centre-sponsored scheme of Rs. 13 billion that sought to improve the overall quality of select engineering colleges across the country. Not surprisingly and without offering any analysis, the project documentation began by installing the IITs as role models and offered a roadmap for the selected 127 colleges (henceforth, TEQIP colleges) to become like the IITs. These colleges were largely government colleges, i.e. the NITs, the GECs, and a few well-performing private ones. The programme was rolled out in two phases. In phase I, participating colleges were to '(i) develop academic excellence, (ii) network with selected institutions for the benefit of faculty and students, (iii) provide service to community and economy, (iv) develop management capacity'.[9] The words 'excellence' and 'global quality' appear about 100 times in the project documentation. The roll-out of TEQIP was accompanied by (1) the formation of the National Board of Accreditation (NBA), under the AICTE, and (2) movement towards signing the Washington Protocol (which was accomplished in 2014), which committed India to a global definition and certification of engineering education.

The objectives of TEQIP translated into requiring TEQIP colleges to (1) improve academic and management processes (but not to review the curricula) leading to academic autonomy; (2) improve infrastructure; (3) accredit their programmes to the NBA; and (4) incentivise faculty members to do research and report it in national and international journals. Though provision of service to the community was an objective, there was very little design in the programme to actually effect it or to measure outcomes, and it largely did not happen. Shockingly, the NBA points to the American accreditation agency, ABET, as one of the references, thus in effect pushing the TEQIP colleges to accredit to ABET – i.e. to a curriculum that does not have 'sewage' as an area of study.

Phase II selected 160 colleges, largely covered by phase I, and cemented these 'global' outcomes in existing TEQIP colleges by sponsoring 'Centres of Excellence' and by initiating graduate programmes.

The outcomes of TEQIP were as designed. The number of research publications shot up and new and mysterious fields of research were discovered.[10] Actual student outcomes and their participation in the Indian engineering industry were not measured. Most TEQIP colleges adopted accreditation, which further consolidated the power of the NBA. Accreditation is now mandatory for new programmes or increasing the strength of old programmes in all colleges, new or old, public or private, *except for the IITs and the NITs*.

Requiring accreditation severely limits the space for new initiatives in engineering education, for either these must find a place within ABET or must be led by the IITs and NITs. More importantly, the TEQIP reform missed an important opportunity to respond to the inherent needs of the state agencies for new knowledge and new partnerships. It also failed to acknowledge small and medium enterprises as legitimate partners in engineering. These small producers have little access to quality control, standardisation and certification, packaging, and branding – i.e. areas where regional institutions would have helped. Thus, TEQIP failed to step outside the corporatised straitjacket of the disciplinary curriculum. Even today, most engineering graduates, including those from the IITs, have not seen any of the following as a part of the curriculum: a factory, small or medium enterprise, a public system (such as a railway station or an urban water supply system), an ordinary drinking water well, or a *chulha*. Thus, the final phase established an alignment of the top tier of engineering colleges with the global definition of engineering and also put in place a global research metric for faculty performance.

On the vocational side, the polytechnics of the early years bifurcated into the Diploma-granting polytechnics governed by the state ministries of education and the Industrial Training Institutes (ITIs), which offered training in 'trades'. The Diploma has been slowly decaying until recently. The ITIs were roughly 11,000 in number in 2014, of which about 2,500 are state-funded and the remaining are private institutions. These train roughly 1.2–1.6 million students each year. Besides this, there are the fewer Industrial Training Centres, which are integrated within large companies. Typically there is at least one state-funded ITI in a block, and perhaps several in industrial towns and cities. These are governed by the Directorate of Vocational Education, an agency of each state's ministry of industry, and receive funding and attention based on its priorities. The objectives, curricula, and pedagogy are, of course, quite different from a typical institute under the state's higher education department. Each ITI teaches several 'trades' in variable-duration programmes, but the typical course is between one and two years long. However, most courses prepare students for trades in the formal sector, which has traditionally employed a small fraction of all workers. It was only recently that several new trades – e.g. food processing – have been added which actually cater to the self-employed or the informal worker.

The input to the ITI is usually secondary or pre-secondary, and instruction is in an informal mixture of vernacular and English. A work-week is typically of 40 hours, of which more than 20 will be spent in the workshop where students work on standard machines and are trained to measure, quantify, draw, and manufacture standard jobs. Lectures supplement this material and cover aspects such as costing and safety. The ITI training is capped by an apprenticeship under the Apprentice Act (and its amendment) and aims to place these graduates within a suitable company for another year. The ITI has been an important avenue for rural youth to find industrial employment, but performance has differed greatly across states. While in Maharashtra the ITI graduate commands a substantial premium, it is only moderate in Tamil Nadu and even less in some other states. As mentioned earlier, it is only recently that small and medium enterprises composed of rural and cottage industries and informal enterprises have been able to articulate their training needs and also their technical and research needs – e.g. in standards, pollution control, and process modernisation – and bring these to the attention of the ITIs and broader engineering education and research.

One must mention the professional bodies in India. The Institute of Engineers (IEI) was founded in 1920 and has about 0.3–0.4 million members. It has administered a certification exam (AMIE) for the past several decades and many government bodies recognise the AMIE as being equivalent to a BE/BTech. Its recognition by private companies or other universities is doubtful. The IEI also publishes a journal that is popular with regional colleges. The Institute of Electronics and Telecommunications Engineers (IETE) is a sister body of the IEI. The 'official' Indian National Academy of Engineers, a government-supported body, started only in 1987, and does not publish a journal.

The outcomes

The most alarming outcome is the hollowing out of the engineering academia. Elite institutions have chosen to preserve their 'autonomy' and remain subservient to the global research culture. And they have arranged their incentive structures accordingly (Sohoni 2012). Barely one-third of their graduates work in Indian engineering, and barely one-fifth of their research funding comes from the industry. As a result, they have very little practical knowledge to offer to its graduates, the industry, or the state. Research on real-world problems, i.e. on 'provincial' issues remains largely non-existent. There are barely a handful of Indian journals of any repute. For institutions lower down, the projection of the IITs and their curricula as role models, the forces of 'global knowledge', and the bureaucracy of TEQIP and the AICTE have made them feeble players.

The obvious corollary of this is a uniformly poor quality of education and a job market which is completely driven by brands and perception. For example, in the JEE (Advanced), the entrance exam for the IITs, close to 90(!) of the top 100 students choose to study either at IIT Bombay or IIT Delhi. This is hardly indicative of the quality of education that these provide or other IITs fail to provide. It has more to do with a vicious cycle of multinational service sector companies offering multi-million 'packages' to graduates from these institutions, which acts as the magnet for 'the best'. This sets up the *aspirational dysfunction* in the engineering profession: a few globalised jobs of high wages, a redefinition of the practice of engineering, and a well-marketed system of merit, i.e. the JEE. The JEE is based, presumably, on the autonomy and excellence of science, but whose principal function is to offer a 'fair' argument to reject the 98 per cent, perpetuate elite agency and its global linkages, and bolster the legitimacy of the Indian elite knowledge bureaucracy. As before, provincial governments and their colleges are unable to play this aspirational game or to contest this notion of science. Nor can they fight this usurpation of a regional curricula which, if designed well and without this severe distraction, may offer local relevance, and a system of smaller rewards, but for a large number of graduates, at lower costs and substantially better odds.

So is this competitive science and engineering competent enough, i.e. does it have a body of knowledge and is it effective? These two questions strike at the essence of engineering as a profession, namely expertise and agency. The instinctive answer is of course, a guarded YES. Are we not building tunnels and bridges? Do we not have mobile coverage over most of India? Are we not one of the biggest manufacturers of steel? However, it is instructive to look deeper into each of these engineering activities. Consider, for example, the standard workhorse of Indian Railways, the diesel locomotive engine WDM2 of 1962 to the current WDP4 introduced in 2001. Both are imported designs which were re-engineered here in India. The plan for the new 6,000 hp engine is also to import the technology and re-engineer and not to develop it in-house.

If we look at the wellbeing of our people, our life expectancy at 65 is the lowest among all our neighbours, and lower by a full ten years than those of China and South Korea, which had comparable numbers in 1947. Next, in the basic engineering services of drinking water and cooking energy, about 70 per cent of our rural households still use biomass in *chulhas* as an energy source. Year-round access to drinking water has actually fallen.[11] This is largely a result of the failure of the state in managing knowledge and practice. For example, do we know how much water flows in our rivers to implement a reservoir control regime? Why do water supply schemes fail? Or how does sugarcane in Pune district affect drinking water availability in Marathwada? More generally, what is the traffic on Indian railways and optimal schedules for them? Or how to build network routers and manage watersheds? Unfortunately, the answer to all of these questions is 'No'. There is no systematic knowledge *and* agency in any of these areas. The Indian state remains woefully short on scientific processes, analysis, and training, and must work without any support from its research institutions. And this is aggravating core development outcomes such as drinking water, cooking energy, and public transport.

Looking at the private sector, consumption of engineering goods has increased, but so have imports and charges for intellectual property. Multinational companies have ramped up their royalty payments while spending large amounts on marketing and brand-creation (Varman 2014). They are spending less than 1 per cent of their revenues on R&D. Investments in research by domestic companies remains tepid and their linkages with research institutions remain weak. The import bill on electronic equipment is now close to what is spent on importing hydrocarbons. The fraction of India's GDP contributed by the engineering industry has steadily decreased. Salaried jobs in manufacturing have decreased and casualisation has increased. Agriculture remains the largest employer by far. Small enterprises with low productivity, poor quality, and absent branding remain the backbone of employment in manufacturing. And these have been unable to penetrate the more profitable urban middle-class markets, thereby allowing rent extraction by large branded companies.

India remains a poorly engineered society. Many state agencies are in a downward spiral so that we now hear of 'minimum government, maximum governance'. The development agenda, i.e. reduction in poverty through better knowledge in the core sectors, resource management, and industry, the very basis of our investments in engineering education, remains well outside the training and research of the engineering system.

Finally, has the culture of science or the access to it changed? Has science and engineering helped the common man understand and manipulate his material world, or comprehend the activities of the state or the market? Do we have a collective understanding of how to face repeated droughts? Is there a civil society to apprehend or comprehend on his or her behalf? Unfortunately, again, the answer is a resounding 'NO'. The public imagination of science remains in elite capture as it has been for the last 50 years. It is now managed by the IITs, IISc, IISERs, and their funding agencies, as the singular pursuit of a high science for an eventual greater common good, and of a global race which we will, *nay must*, win. For students, it is thus limited to the 'fair' *merit* to locate the top 2 per cent in national exams. Repeatedly, through various programmes (such as the Kishore Vaigyanik Protsahan Yojana), national agencies identify the same set of 'gifted' students and reward them and reaffirm their faith in elite agency. Excluded from it (statistically) are the poor, the rural and the vernacular, girls, and students from State Boards.[12]

Curiously, this competitive 'science' of the 2 per cent may have the vocabulary of refractive indices, aldehydes, and ketones, or the *latus rectum*, but there are no people in it and no events. It has no biographies and no role models, e.g. of the illustrious chief engineer, the neighbourhood factory or rice-mill owner, the local blacksmith, or the girls on their machines in the village handloom. It has no measurements, no theorising, and no comprehension. Nor does it have the design of experiments or of arguments. It does not measure, e.g. the efficiency of *chulhas* in a village, or argue for better bus routes. It has no case studies, no piecemeal social engineering, no memory of repeated droughts, and no accounting of the long trips to fetch firewood. It has no agency, nor a theory of causation and no outcomes for the bottom 98 per cent. *In fact, it is a bureaucracy which will never have the idioms and dialects necessary for a true science to emerge.* No, Indian science and engineering does not answer 'Why am I poor?' or 'Why did my child die?'

Where do we go from here?

This is a difficult question but let us begin with some observations.

Four observations

One, much of science and engineering for a society are closely aligned and operate on a common mechanism. This cyclic mechanism is of a paired system of vocabularies, one which is external, e.g. natural or social, and the other which is internal or conceptual and a feedback loop. The loop is composed of cultural skills of (1) translation, i.e. of theorising and validation, or in engineering, of design and implementation; (2) a theory of outcomes and of soundness; and (3) a rigour, i.e. a process of accumulation of knowledge. A system of rigour may well be empirical, i.e. borne out of experience, or may seek tight mathematical relations between the two vocabularies or a combination of the two. Each of these is a social and cultural choice, and also depends on prevalent ideologies or *schools of thought* for repairing faulty theories. Thus, a science for a society is determined by various material as well as cultural realities. A potter, a theoretical physicist, an urban planner, and a professional violinist from within a society will each have a different science, and the tapestry of such sciences is the *scientific culture* of that society.

Two, what is claimed as global science and technology is actually such a tapestry of cultural outcomes of the pursuit of the West for its own material and cultural wellbeing. This science has been developed by both amateur and professional scientists, by political agents, and shaped and chiselled by the many scholarly and popular critiques of *cultural* and *philosophical* agents. Its libraries and journals, the Ivy League, Fermat's Theorem, the Bunsen burners, and round-bottom flasks are artefacts of this pursuit. None of these are predestined to be on the trajectory of every culture in its hunt for its science and engineering. Many of the West's programmes, such as anthropometry in the past, or neoclassical economics and genetic biotechnology of the present, are fraught with danger. Moreover, the West itself is going through a crisis of elite capture, but more on that later.

Three, there is a great reliance of elite Indian institutions on the borrowed rigour of Western science and engineering and its artefacts such as journals, universities, and institutions, and therefore on its external and internal vocabulary of describing society. Much of this reliance is hard-wired into professional curricula and career advancement within academia and also within large national and multinational corporations. This is accompanied by an insistence on the apparent 'autonomy' of this borrowed science as being its true nature. There is also a great confusion regarding the very nature of rigour and whether Indian problems are actually amenable to rigorous articulation and solution in the chosen vocabularies. The answer to this last question is, of course, 'No'. The claim of universality of Western science by a few agents of the West or our elite must be viewed as arising from this confusion, or as the purely strategic objective of rent-seeking, or finally as the intellectual laziness in constructing the required vocabularies and systems of rigour and soundness. The water sector, or for that matter computer science and engineering, in India presents us with examples of all of the above.

Finally, Western science has now been superseded by a modern *global science*, an agency of the global economy. This is a coalition of iconic researchers spanning all disciplines of knowledge, multilateral agencies, and elite institutions which seeks to propagate and consolidate elite agency. It does this by insisting on (1) an idea of a 'rational' behaviour which is natural, i.e. without culture or politics; (2) an idea of a scarce and rarified science of breathtaking power and global reach, i.e. an overarching explanation for all phenomena, regional or global; (3) an insistence on 'gold standards' for evidence, thereby controlling the legitimacy of regional studies by regional agents and restricting its impact on the conduct of science; and finally (4) appropriation of words such as Development Economics or Development Engineering[13] to deal with the 'irrational' world, and to put their usage under expert supervision. It obviously sees a useful client in Indian elite science.

The way ahead

The way ahead is to set aside the hegemony of a scarce and transcendental science and build the empirical foundations for a broader and more democratic knowledge formation. This new science should move away from the purely disciplinary and industrial employee-engineer to a model of the engineer-scientist as a social agent. It should prepare our youth for a more direct role in probing their material reality and to try to change it. The exact design of such a science and engineering must be done carefully for it must slowly disentangle itself from the 2 per cent outcome game of elite science and its aspirational ladder. On the other hand, it must engage with the small and medium enterprises, the core sectors of agriculture, water, energy, and environment, and local agencies and state departments. The state should, in turn, see these social agents as essential collaborators if it must ride over the severe environmental stresses which lie ahead.

This must begin with hundreds of rigorous case studies that students can execute and which formalise the problems in their vicinity and thus set them up for discussion and eventual solution. These may be, e.g. templates for government programmes such as the watershed programme, or energy and technology audits of neighbourhood enterprises, or computer models of urban water supply systems. Over the years, these case studies will develop into a body of knowledge and of practitioners who will deliver engineering value to the community. It will define a new and innovative profession – the *vernacular engineer* – as one who is well-versed with the interdisciplinarity of everyday life, the normative concerns of community development, and who can access various disciplinary skills to deliver solutions. It will define a rigour of its own, which is sound, which has agency, and yet which is accessible to the community to contest and refine. The faculty member is then a community consultant as well as a role model, and the institution the regional knowledge resource. Such an approach will restore science and engineering as the cultural pursuits they really should be.[14]

Broadly speaking, a cultural and convivial society and a matching science and engineering is the only path that will avoid the 'rational' traps of modern *global science*. Perhaps, more importantly, it will empower us as a society to understand that the contours of the state and the market, and even of science, depend on the *consumption* choices that we make. Ultimately our consumption, and what attributes we choose to discern in it, will decide the modes of production and the knowledge of that society to produce it. If we must have branded and world-class (but mass-produced) goods offered by a few iconic companies, then science must locate the 'top' 2 per cent to manage such companies, and shove a lot of wealth and power into their hands. If we must live longer at any cost, and track every courier package online, then our science will create cocoons of managed environments for a few of us, while the rest of us, and our co-habitants on this planet, must stay in a largely degraded and unstable biosphere. It is this *cultural* choice of consumption that will underpin the viability of the vernacular engineer and the sustainability of our diverse society and its environs. Perhaps it is the only path to ensure that the beauty and bounty of the seasons and a teeming multitude of cultures and organisms remain on this earth.

Conclusions

How does all this connect with the broader contours of higher education in India? First, the focus on numeric and universal targets of access, equity, and quality hides an essential confusion about the destination society for which the design of higher education is needed. Only after this confusion is resolved can the objectives of higher education be stated and the choice of a curriculum and pedagogy, of rewards and recognitions, be made.

The heart of this confusion actually lies in the theory and practice of Indian social science. It comes from the inability of elite Indian social science to see vernacular life and the vicinity as subjects of common study and vernacular practices as possible instruments of change. Or perhaps from its fear of an unreconciled past placing unforeseen obstacles in forging a culture for the future. In engineering, it appears simply as an unsaid commitment to a corporatist society as a matrix in which culture may be expressed, and a devotion of the state's energy and treasure to train employees for this future society. It ignores, as we have argued, the agency of cultural agents and the historical antecedents of Western corporate societies, our role models, and their

Table 10.1 Starting jobs by sectors for IIT Bombay graduates in 2013

Placements IIT Bombay 2013				
Sector	Engineering	Finance	Consulting	IT
Super-GG	25 (2.77)	10 (3.5)	7 (5.4)	42 (5.13)
GG	116 (0.79)	82 (1.17)	110 (0.96)	102 (1)
IG	54 (0.65)	19 (0.72)	11 (0.58)	28 (0.72)
GI	24 (0.93)	10 (1.42)	10 (0.52)	5 (0.93)
II	64 (0.65)	13 (0.95)	8 (0.58)	22 (0.79)

Source: All tables in the chapter are compiled by the author; prepared by the author from data provided by the Placement Office, IIT Bombay.

GG refers to a global company serving a global market (e.g. Bank America or General Electric), while II refers to an Indian company serving the Indian market (e.g. Ambuja Cement or Tata Motors). IG and GI are similarly explained (e.g. Infosys and Hindustan Unilever respectively). Super-GG are placements abroad. The number, e.g. 116 (0.79) indicates the number placed and the average annual salary in rupees (million).

Table 10.2 Average household spending on education by families having one studying member

		Andhra Pradesh Urban	Andhra Pradesh Rural	Rajasthan Urban	Rajasthan Rural	Odisha Urban	Odisha Rural	Tamil Nadu Urban	Tamil Nadu Rural
Households with one studying male	Mean (Rs.)	9,919	5,706	19,096	4,362	5,765	1,787	11,046	8,493
	Number of samples	365	373	235	263	143	291	373	293
	Gini	0.61	0.58	0.56	0.64	0.65	0.70	0.64	0.67
Households with one studying female	Mean (Rs.)	9,233	3,752	9,369	3,431	4,278	2,292	12,653	6,949
	Number of samples	281	245	98	126	94	191	321	259
	Gini	0.61	0.55	0.60	0.56	0.82	0.76	0.65	0.69

Source: the author's analysis of 68th round data, NSSO, 2012.

Milind Sohoni

Table 10.3 Number of papers published with at least one Indian author, by word appearing in title of the paper: novel areas of research

Topic (Phrase)	All years preceding 2003	2003–09 (TEQIP I)	2010 onwards (TEQIP II)
Neural network	692	1,818	2,467
Fuzzy logic	110	327	759
Wavelets	96	905	1,846
Genetic algorithms	262	989	1,373

Source: prepared by the author from data obtained from Scopus, an online catalogue of scientific publications.

Table 10.4 Number of papers published with at least one Indian author, by word appearing in title of the paper: research in engineering services

Topic (phrase)	All years preceding 2003	2003–09 (TEQIP I)	2010 onwards (TEQIP II)
Water supply	84	74	87
Sanitation	30	51	63
Groundwater models	11	29	70
Public transport	5	15	25
Power grid	12	56	288

Source: prepared by the author from data obtained from Scopus, an online catalogue of scientific publications.

Table 10.5 Statistics of students appearing for and qualifying for entrance to the IITs by gender

	JEE 2012			JEE (Advanced) 2013		
	Appeared	Qualified	Pass (%)	Appeared	Qualified	Pass (%)
Boys	337,916	21,226	6.28	103,660	18,468	17.8
Girls	168,568	2,886	1.71	23,089	2,366	10.2
Percentage girls	33.2	11.9	–	18.2	11.4	–

Source: prepared by the author from various publicly available sources.

Table 10.6 Statistics of students appearing for and qualifying for entrance to the IITs by place of passing the XII standard (%)

	JEE 2011		JEE 2012		JEE (Advanced) 2014	
Cohort	Registered	Qualified	Regsitered	Qualified	Registered	Qualified
Village	19	10	19	11	13	10
Town	29	25	29	26	19	14
City	52	65	52	63	68	76

Source: prepared by the author from various publicly available sources.

science and engineering. As a corollary, it pays scant attention to the knowledge needs of the vast number of non-corporate entities – the small enterprises, the district administrations, the elected representatives – who serve an increasing fraction of our population. It also ignores the incomprehension of the vernacular student who must look at her own immediate material environment with great detachment, become 'globally competitive' and yet not be assured of such a job. It ignores that the skills of *manipulation, articulation, description and argumentation* are essential to any science and that the vicinity is the real laboratory.

How will this change? Indian science lacks both an *external* as well as an internal critique. The internal non-elite critic has been delegitimised by elite capture. The absence of a systematic external critique is more remarkable, for it is the dog that did not bark. It perhaps hides vested interests within other areas of our academe or a true confusion about where our society is headed. For the social sciences, elite or vernacular, this constitutes an important responsibility which they must squarely face. They must design alternative worlds for a diverse society such as ours and inform us on our choices. They must tell us what is amenable to science and engineering and what is not. They must tell our vernacular youth *what is worth learning and who are their role models.* Must we chase mirages of global jobs or resign ourselves to 'skilling' for mundane temporary jobs? Is there anything in my decrepit world which is beautiful which I must learn to describe? Is culture malleable? How do I articulate and argue for a different social reality and bring it into existence? Can both knowledge and agency exist within me? Can I and my community forge a common future? *Or is escape for the few the only solution?*

Notes

1 A broader discussion by this author, of engineering and society and the creation of value, is available as *Knowledge and Practice for India as a Developing Country*, at www.cse.iitb.ac.in/~sohoni/kpidc.pdf (accessed on 12 October 2015). A shorter version was published in *Seminar* in February 2014.
2 See, for example, the agenda of the Institute for Complex Engineered Systems at the Carnegie Mellon University.
3 The Viceroy's office set up the Sarkar Committee in 1946 to consider the setting up of new institutions for the industrial development of India. An online version is available at: www.iitsystem.ac.in/admin/SarkarCommitteeReport.pdf (accessed on 12 October 2015).
4 By an elite class, we mean (1) a class which has inordinate influence as compared to its size, and (2) an acceptance of this influence as being reasonable. See, e.g. Gramsci's writings on cultural hegemony.
5 *AICTE Approval Process Handbook*, published every year by the AICTE, India.
6 See statistics available at AICTE website. Also see Banerjee and Muley (2007).
7 See Table 10.1, taken from author's submission to the AICTE, available at www.cse.iitb.ac.in/~sohoni/commentsAICTE.pdf, and which is to appear in the *Current Science* journal. It illustrates that much of the IIT Bombay goes into the global services sector, that which is left is pressed into engineering services for a global society.
8 The NSSO data also reveal that households are spending huge amounts on education and that there is great inequality in this spending across states, across genders, and across rural and urban households. See, for example, Table 10.2.
9 TEQIP phase I and II documents are available with the National Project Implementation Unit of MHRD. They are also available online at: www.npiu.nic.in/archives.htm (Phase I) and www.npiu.nic.in/ongngprj.htm (Phase II) (accessed on 12 October 2015).
10 Research areas such as 'Wavelets, Simulated Annealing' and 'Genetic Algorithms' have thousands of papers published by Indian researchers (see Tables 10.3 and 10.4). Thus, we see a proliferation of areas of research with little practical relevance, and very little research on our basic engineering systems such as groundwater or electricity.
11 This is seen from various rounds of the NSSO survey on basic amenities or by the census data of 2001 and 2011.
12 See Tables 10.5 and 10.6. Girls constitute only about 11 per cent of the total student strength in the IITs. This is in stark contrast to the fact that about 30 per cent of engineering students are now girls.

Moreover, in the less competitive CBSE XII exam, girls excel at all levels. Similarly, about 11 per cent of IIT students come from rural backgrounds. More than 70 per cent come from cities (as opposed to towns). More than 50 per cent of students who succeeded in the JEE (Advanced) 2014 were from the CBSE.

13 See, for example, the composition of the editorial board of the highly regarded journal *Development Economics*, or the new journal *Development Engineering*. Also see the scope of these journals and their notion of rigour.

14 One step in this direction was taken in October 2014 by the launch of the *Unnat Bharat Abhiyan* (http://unnat.iitd.ac.in) by MHRD, which mandates the IITs to (1) build an understanding of the development agenda as an academic pursuit; (2) to bring interdisciplinarity, stakeholders, outcomes, and fieldwork into the curricula; (3) to work as a regional knowledge resource by consulting with local bodies; (4) to improve development outcomes by collaborating with state agencies; and finally (5) to foster a broader dialogue on science, society, and environment. It also requires each institution to form an *empowered* cell to execute the programme. The mandate thus requires the IITs to recast their incentive structures. Moreover, the *abhiyan* offers a unique window of opportunity for state governments to reclaim the science and engineering agenda and use elite institutions as a part of their regional knowledge infrastructure. Most importantly, through provision (3) it makes the elite institutions accountable to the common person for his or her knowledge needs. In principle, by citing the *abhiyan*, a *gram panchayat* may approach an IIT to analyse their water supply problems. The programme does not come with attached funding; this must be found within each state's governance processes. Locating such processes (which are ample) and aligning them with the *abhiyan* should be an agenda for civil society organisations to pursue with their state governments. In January 2015, the state of Maharashtra launched the Unnat Maharashtra Abhiyan (see www.dtemaharashtra.gov.in/teqip/CMS/Content_Static. aspx?did=325 or www.ctara.iitb.ac.in/tdsc/uma, the mirror site hosted by CTARA).

References

ACSE. 2008. *Civil Engineering Body of Knowledge for the 21st Century*, 2nd, edn. American Society of Civil Engineers.

Banerjee, R., and Muley, V.P. 2007. *Engineering Education in India*. Observer Research Foundation.

Kumar, Deepak. 1995. *Science and the Raj:1857–1904*. Oxford University Press.

Nowotny, Helga, Scott, Peter, and Gibbons, Michael. 2001. *Re-Thinking Science: Knowledge and the Public in an Age of Uncertainty*. Polity Press.

Polanyi, Karl. 1944. *The Great Transformation: The Political and Economic Origins of our Time*. Beacon Press.

Roser, Max. 2015. 'Our World in Data'. http://ourworldindata.org (accessed on 12 October 2015).

Scharf, Robert and Dusek, Val (eds). 2014. *Philosophy of Technology: An Anthology*, 2nd edn. Wiley Blackwell.

Sohoni, M. 2012. 'Engineering Teaching and Research at the IITs and its Impact on India', *Current Science*, 102(11): 1502.

Sukhatme, S.P. and Mahadevan, I. 2004. 'Brain Drain and the IIT Graduate'. *The Economic and Political Weekly*, 39(2): 285–293.

Varman, R. 2014. 'Royal Treatment of Foreign Investors'. *Aspects of Indian Economy*, 56. http://rupe-india.org/56/royalties.html (accessed on 12 October 2015).

11

Discourse of teacher education in India

Latika Gupta

The context

This chapter focuses on the Bachelor of Education (BEd), i.e. training programme for secondary-
and senior-secondary-level teachers offered by Indian universities in their departments of education and in affiliated colleges. In the last three decades, beginning since the mid-1980s, there
have been widespread efforts to reform elementary education in India. However, the secondary
and senior secondary stages of school escaped with sketchy efforts to reform. The only significant effort relevant for these stages has been the identification of priorities in the National
Curriculum Framework (NCF) 2005 (NCERT 2006) and the development of textbooks under
its aegis. The NCF 2005 based textbooks are not used by all states and systems of school education. The training of the teachers to teach in secondary and senior secondary schools remained
largely unreformed and impervious to the growing demand for an overhaul throughout the
entire country. In the last three decades, winds of discontent blew over different institutions
related to education, and dissatisfaction was expressed over established curriculums of teacher
training (TT) institutions. Despite increasing criticism, universities had failed to innovate and
make the BEd more attuned to the developments in the field of educational theory.

In December 2014, major changes were notified by the National Council for Teacher
Education (NCTE) in the *Gazette of India* in teacher training programmes for all stages of school
education. The background to this notification lay in the appointment of a commission by the
Supreme Court in response to a public interest litigation (PIL) seeking judicial intervention in
matters pertaining to the recognition of private teacher education institutions. Chaired by the
late Justice J.S. Verma, this commission gave wide-ranging recommendations for reforms in this
sector, including remodelling in the BEd and other programmes, and in the functioning of the
NCTE, an apex regulatory body with statutory powers. The duration of the BEd programme
was increased from one to two years and its curriculum was changed at the behest of the NCTE.
The two-year BEd programme is different from its antecedent not just in terms of duration but
also in the emphasis it attaches to certain practicum and theoretical courses. The first batch of
the revised BEd programme has been admitted in all the universities and colleges of India in
2015 and its nuances are unfolding at different places in different ways. This marks an opportune
moment to interpret some of the key features of the discourse on BEd. Here, it is important to

remember that the demand for a reform neither came from the schools nor from the institutions of TTs. This prompts many critics to wonder whether this change in norms and standards will succeed in transforming the way candidates are trained to be secondary- and senior-secondary-level teachers in India and whether such teachers can bring fresh energy into school education.

Bachelor of Education (BEd): a description and reflection

The BEd programme is composed mainly of three kinds of engagement. In the first category are the foundation courses that familiarise students with the theoretical postulates of education, its philosophy, psychology, sociology, and political science. Conventionally, the foundation courses have been: (1) philosophy of education, (2) psychology of education, and (3) contemporary concerns and trends in education. As the titles suggest, these courses offer perspectives formulated in other disciplines but relevant to education. In some universities, the first course had a more grounded title, i.e. issues in educational theory or similar. However, even in those universities, students and teachers referred to this course as a philosophy paper – Delhi University being a case in point.

The second category of engagement in BEd belongs to the realm of practical work, with an idea of giving some experience and exposure to the functioning of a school and a teacher's work-life. As a regulatory body, the NCTE had prescribed a norm that trainee teachers must 'transact' 40 lessons for two subjects during their school placement. This implied that a trainee teacher taught topics of two subjects over 40 school periods. Faculty members were associated with every school group for monitoring and mentoring the trainee teachers during their school experience. The supervisors, irrespective of their area of research and interest, observed all the trainees in one school while teaching their subjects in different classes, and gave feedback about pedagogy, classroom management, relationship with the students, language skills, and so on. This involved a lot of negotiation with the schools. The supervisors had to constantly spend time and effort in convincing the principals to allow the trainees to carry on teaching in regular periods and not only give games or music periods to BEd trainees. There was a great deal of variation across universities in this dimension of BEd. The students of several colleges affiliated to the Delhi government universities never got more than a week to ten days to teach. They had to make do with whichever class was available, whenever it was possible.

The school experience programme was operationalised in a learning–trying–learning sense. The students went to school on Tuesdays, Thursdays, and Saturdays to teach and came to the department on the remaining days of the week from September to January every week. In the remaining months, they attended theory classes on a regular basis. This arrangement of one day in the department and the next day in the school provided a specific character to TT institutions. Everybody was seen to be running around chasing a goal. The students were occupied in getting their lesson-plans checked so they could use them on the following day, and the faculty members were caught up in giving feedback to every student and counting the number of remaining lessons to be observed for every student. Everybody was anxious and nervous.

In addition to direct school experience, there was a component of community outreach in BEd. The students were expected to do voluntary work in orphanages, old-age homes, or other such institutions. The idea that a teacher was essentially a community developer originated in educational circles immediately after Independence and seeped into the structure of TT programmes as well. J.K. Shukla (1970) has identified two trends in the professional preparation of teachers in India. First, 'increased emphasis on social understanding and social service'; and second, 'increasing emphasis on direct experience through participation, visits, organising community service camps and so on' (p. 30). The idea of the teacher as a community developer has its roots in the colonial history of India and found a place in the discourse and practice of teacher education. The examination-centred character of the Indian education system (Kumar 2014) ensured that this aspect of social service was assessed by the teacher educators when allocating marks. This component has been dispensed with in the reformed structure by the NCTE. However, it is necessary to take note of this component as it kept the notion alive that a teacher-in-the-making needed personality traits and acumen for social service more than professional knowledge and excitement for ideas. For more than 50 years, teachers-in-the-making donated clothes to poor people and got marks for it.

The third category of engagement is of pedagogy courses in which the focus area is how to teach a particular subject to students of different levels. The word pedagogy is a new entry in this context. The term in vogue has been methodology or methods. Conventionally, pedagogy courses have been of two levels. In level one courses, students learned the strategies of teaching one subject to secondary-level students, i.e. Grade VI–X. In level two courses, students learned teaching strategies of the same subject to Grade XI and XII students. These levels were termed as level A and B or 1 and 2. The students who enrolled in a BEd programme after completing a master's degree in their subject were allowed to opt for level B/2 methodology courses. The students who enrolled in BEd after their graduation were allowed to take two methods courses from related or sometimes unrelated disciplines. This often resulted in strange combinations of subjects that students took, and had no consistency with the demands that the school system posed. For instance, the subject combinations that students got were: English and mathematics, English and Hindi, chemistry and English, and so on. In the reformed BEd structure, the level distinction in pedagogy courses has been removed, but in implementation it remains a grey area. The belief that teaching children in upper-primary grades is absolutely different from teaching students in senior secondary grades is so firmly entrenched in the system that the implementation of the reformed perspective on pedagogy is currently facing considerable resistance.

The popular notion has been that the candidates preparing to be teachers need to acquire a collection of strategies or techniques in order to make the transmission of the body of knowledge appealing to the learner. Writing more than 45 years ago, Shukla drew a conclusion that 'the programme for the preparation of teachers, in order to be effective, should provide scope for continuing increase in subject-knowledge and the necessary skills and techniques needed for imparting that knowledge in a classroom situation' (1970: 39). As we can see, a teacher is perceived as a skilful transmitter of knowledge – *read:* information – given in the prescribed textbooks. Figure 11.1 presents the essential components of the curriculum of teacher education programmes.

Minor differences crept into the organisation of the three components across universities because of specific influences. For instance, a course in gender was a part of the elective courses in BEd in some universities, whereas in others students completed their programme without hearing the word 'gender'. Across universities and a time span of several decades, the basic structure of the BEd programme remained largely the same, comprising the three categories shown in Figure 11.1. This was observed by the National Focus Group (NCERT 2007) that was set up to discuss teacher education in India:

> A quick glance through surveys of educational research in India conducted periodically over the years 1974–1998 substantiates the point that teacher education programmes have remained unchanged in terms of their substance, experiences offered and modalities adopted.
>
> *(ibid.: 3)*

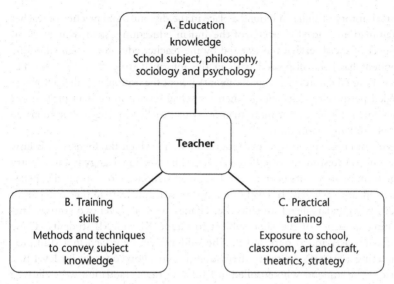

Figure 11.1 Three curricular components of teacher education programmes.

Source: all figures in the chapter are drawn by the author.

The knowledge of an uncanny uniformity in BEd across time and geographical location became accessible to me in personal settings as well. My identity in the neighbourhood and the kinship is that of a BEd teacher. Often, I faced questions from acquaintances, strangers, and relatives: I am doing BEd, please tell me how should I prepare for the final exams? What are the important topics? I faced these questions in diverse social gatherings such as birthday parties, wedding ceremonies, and funerals, in hospitals, markets, and in tailor shops across several towns of north India and in southern states too. The confidence with which so many diverse questioners asked it revealed to me the general perception and the reality of BEd. They did not perceive BEd any differently from graduate and postgraduate programmes in which high scores in the final examinations constituted the most important dimension. The examinations are conducted in the form of a one-time 2–3-hour written test. The questions are based on select topics and are direct in nature, requiring reproduction of learned information. The questioners were aware that a BEd programme did not require any different kind of engagement from liberal arts and science programmes, even though there was a provision of 10–15 per cent internal assessment in every course and the practicum was evaluated without an exam. The requirement was to rote memorise the answers to potential questions which would be asked in the examinations and score highly. Hence, the candidates could imagine a sacrosanct uniformity and saw me as a source of information about important topics and expected questions in the final examinations.

The BEd programme attracted severe criticism in the reports of all the major commissions set up to study school education over the last 50 years. The recognition of the problem of ill-prepared teachers led to the creation of several NGOs that tried to improve teacher quality by providing in-service training. However, the basic organising principle of TT wasn't altered. 'A whole century has gone by without the instrumentalist character of teacher training being challenged or reformed' (Kumar 2008: 38). Batra (2009) has identified six factors responsible for the stagnation in this discipline, out of which two have a direct bearing on the daily experiences of students and teachers in a BEd programme.

The first factor is the popularity of belief in a discourse that unlinks 'theoretical reflection' from effective educational practice. Borrowing from Carr (2003), she draws implications of the belief that teaching is envisaged as a matter of practical tricks which doesn't require any theoretical support. I often heard an allegory in policy discussions which reflected this discourse: A teacher is like a driver who should know how to work with a steering wheel, gears, and brakes in order to drive. A driver doesn't need to understand the machinery, functioning of the engine, or larger issues of vehicular pollution.

Batra's second factor is that in TT no attempt is made to 'develop a grounded understanding of children's thinking and learning processes, curricular and pedagogic studies within the Indian socio-political context' (Batra 2009: 128). The integration of theory into practice is either not attempted or is over-simplified to certain behaviouristic notions. The mechanised theories of education, borrowed from late nineteenth-century Europe, have found a permanent settlement in the BEd programme. The over-simplified link between theory and practice is the result of this settlement. An attempt has been made in this chapter to capture the nuances of the experiences of a student in a BEd programme, which can enable us to assess the extent to which the recently brought about policy-level changes will alter the discourse of BEd. For this assessment, we will review three points. The first one is teacher-educators.

Teacher-educators

Russell (1925) identified certain problems of departments of education in England; he discussed the teacher-educator as one of these. The job of teacher-educators is to organise students' learning in three categories. These three cornerstones of teacher preparation have become so sacrosanct in the Indian system that they define the identity of teacher-educators and categorise them into distinct leagues. The first constituent creates the identity of foundation course teachers; the second creates pedagogues; and the third leads to the role-identity of an expert supervisor who could be from either of the first two categories. This distinction of *specialisation* among teacher-educators gets further classified into subcategories. The subcategory of the first constituent is expert in psychological foundations or philosophical or sociological or contemporary thinker in education (alluding to all the policies and concerns).

The second constituent created the identity of pedagogues of different school subjects. The teachers of foundation courses are considered ineligible to teach a pedagogy course and pedagogues are not expected to teach foundation courses. The criteria for deciding who would fall within which constituent category is based on the subject that the person has studied for his/her postgraduate degree. If the postgraduate programme was in any of the three core disciplines, then the teacher-educator becomes a foundation course teacher. If the postgraduate degree was in any of the school subjects, then the teacher-educator becomes a pedagogue. Rarely is this rule flouted. These identities are so fixed in BEd that they create impervious boundaries for any exchange of ideas. And, it is within these impenetrable boundaries that the learning of students takes place. Physically, the students permeate through the boundaries because they interact with teachers in all the 'identity' groups, but cognitively the osmosis through which the teachings of different teachers mingle and coalesce only takes place in a student's mind. The teachers do not aim for any cohesion between different theoretical viewpoints.

The interaction between the teachers of different foundation courses – at the level of syllabus formulation and teaching – is completely uncalled for or is unwarranted because, after all, they stem from three distinct disciplines, i.e. psychology, philosophy, and sociology. As a result of a hermetic conceptualisation of these courses, students do not get a chance to engage with their full complexity and do not develop the ability to understand children in totality by drawing on ideas from different fields. For instance, students are expected to engage with the criticism of behaviourism as a framework to understand learning in one foundation course and explore its alternatives. This engagement has the potential to introduce them to the development in the field of cognitive theory in which the progressive perspectives on learning moved beyond the idea of behavioural change almost 50 years ago (Bruner 2004). However, in a different foundation course, students learn the theory of behaviourism as a source of ideas to ensure learning. BEd students do learn about structuralism and constructivism, but without acquiring a developmental perspective required to appreciate the shifts in the theoretical world. One doesn't need a genius to guess what happens as a result of this gap. The students do not get inspired by theoretical ideas to function as a teacher in most cases. They start viewing behaviourism and constructivism as equally relevant and efficient theories. As a result, when they teach they end up interacting with children with the instincts that they imbibe in the socio-cultural ethos of Indian society in which adults interact with children by hitting and scolding them regularly (Kumar 2011).

Lesson-plan

A specific kind of hiatus exists between foundation and pedagogy courses. It is important to point out here that though the students get theoretical perspectives from several teachers, their pedagogical perspective comes only from one teacher, who is the method master.[1] The students learn in foundation courses that teaching is not 'telling'. The real meaning of teaching is to create opportunities in which learners arrive at an understanding in the same manner in which that knowledge was developed in a specific field. They also engage with epistemological issues that knowledge is not a compilation of topics and sub-topics. It involves grasping of fundamental principles, development of basic attitudes and hunches for a discipline, and excitement for its applicability. However, in pedagogy courses, this understanding does not get related to the specifics of a discipline and its constituent school subject. This epistemological nuance does not acquire a specific discipline-based flavour in the pedagogy course. The discourse of the pedagogy course is largely shaped by the terms shown in Figure 11.2.

The use of the word 'method' can be easily found in the syllabus of pedagogy courses across Indian universities. Kumaravadivelu (2001) states that in the 1990s congruence was achieved in teacher education between the two mutually informing currents of thought in America. One argued for the need to go beyond the limitations of the concept of method and another emphasised the need to go beyond the limitations of the transmission model of teacher education. These currents of thought reflect a long-felt dissatisfaction with the concept of method as the organising principle of teacher education. However, departments of education in Indian universities remained ignorant of such ideas and maintained the watertight distinction between theory and method. Furlong has analysed this distinction as 'one of the most abiding dilemmas in the UK' (2013: 69). According to him, four broad discourses about what it means to know as a teacher have been identified so far in the UK. They are: liberal education, propositional knowledge, practical knowledge, and moral knowledge. The dilemma remains how much time should be devoted to each of these and in what manner. In the Indian context, this distinction continues to escape any sense of scrutiny, and faculty members teach without any quandary. There is no common will to recognise this distinction as a challenge and to work around addressing it. To this, the flavour of India's socio-cultural hierarchy gets added and the introduction of any ideas becomes a personalised battle. 'My idea is better than your idea' or 'I do not like your idea' are the general reactions to the feeble attempts made to raise issues such as softening of the boundaries between foundation and pedagogy courses.

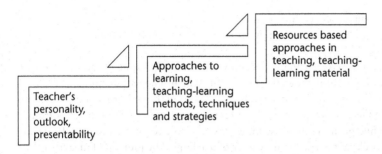

Figure 11.2 Discourse of pedagogy courses.

As a result of this, pedagogy and foundation courses carry on as several parallel streams in the lives of students. In the foundation courses they think about future learners' caste, age, developmental stage, identity, and so on; in the pedagogy courses they think about school subjects. The imagined learners' (to be taught by BEd students in schools later) caste, religion, and adolescence cease to be important factors. The imagined learner in school becomes a recipient of the knowledge offered by political science or chemistry or English in isolation. In this method model, it falls outside the realm of political science how a young person conceptualises the idea of choice and decision making in school when she is facing an identity crisis in adolescence as theorised by Erikson (1959). For instance, the pedagogy course in mathematics does not engage with the challenges that students face in Grade VI and VII, when they are 12–13 years old and the capacity for formal operational thought begins to develop (Elkind 1981). The units of algebra and arithmetic acquire a different kind of pedagogic challenge if the teachers-in-training realise that the learners in school may not have reached the stage of formal operational thought. This requires a convergence between knowledge that psychology offers and the nuances of mathematical concepts.

This example helps us to identify the two distinct worlds that BEd students inhabit when they sit in the classes of foundation and pedagogy courses. The aims of education (discussed in the foundation courses) never get synchronised with the purpose of teaching chemistry or geography or any other school subject. The criticism of behaviourism never finds an extension in pedagogy courses. Thus, students make Thermocol[2] models of polling booths, election symbols of political parties, atoms, animal cells, bulbs, telephones, and equilateral triangles, and so on. Environmentalism is a concern that all the disciplines address and students develop notice boards and organise events to draw attention to these environmental concerns. However, even while making their own models, the students do not exhibit any sensitivity towards the environment. No pedagogy course trains them to use disciplinary knowledge to take decisions about their own conduct. The culmination of pedagogic discourse is in the form of lesson plans that students make to teach certain topics during their school placement (the erstwhile term is 'practice teaching'; now in vogue is 'school experience'). A lesson plan includes a topic to be taught, specific and general objectives, children's previous knowledge (as expected by the trainee), materials to be used, questions to be asked and answers to be expected, and finally, recapitulation and homework. One important dimension of lesson-planning is that of questions to be asked by the teacher *as well as* the expected answers that children would give. BEd students read Socratic dialogues and Buber's (1958) construction of dialogue, but in their lesson-plans they perceive a teacher's main job as that of posing questions. Ideas like child-centred education and constructivist teaching remain confined to the theory courses and are not reflected in lesson-plans. Often, students recognise the tension, but carry on with the flow of ritualised, mechanised teaching that their lesson-plans reflect. Sinha observed that 'they are depressingly similar to the usual teaching that goes on. Nothing strikes new in terms of the conceptualisation of classroom transactions' (2002: 19).

There is a sharp contrast between the expectation from the BEd students and the reality. They are taught to become critical about the manner in which schools function and teachers teach. They learn about the importance of critical engagement with the learner and the subject matter when they study Dewey, Krishnamurti, and Freire, but they do not get the opportunity to apply this learning while planning their teaching activities. As a result, within their BEd programme span, they fall back on the ritualised manner of teaching. The journey of ideas that they pursue in foundation courses does not carry on in pedagogy courses. 'The lesson-plan culture perpetuates a "product" model of pedagogic work' (Kumar 2002: 12). In this culture, the teacher's job is to create products that give a structure to their work and which become evidence of their work. The lesson-plan has become established as the most important product. In this dichotomy, ideas do not inform their practice. What informs their practice is the stuff about transmission given in pedagogy courses. This degree of desynchronisation between ideas expressed in different courses certainly creates cognitive dissonance (Festinger 1957).

Raina and Raina conducted a study to determine what concepts teacher-educators in India have of the ideal student in terms of characteristics to be encouraged, as well those to be discouraged. Out of 62 characteristics, the chosen top six were: (1) industrious, (2) considerate of others, (3) receptive of others, (4) obedient, (5) courteous, and (6) does work on time. Indian teacher-educators assigned less importance to asking questions, independent thinking, and unwillingness to accept things without examining the evidence. The authors speculated that 'the emphasis on industriousness is perhaps associated with the concerns of the teacher's colleges to equip prospective teachers with all the "tricks of the trade" during a short span of one session extending to 200 working days' (Raina and Raina 1971: 305).

The desire for an industrious student is prevalent even now and, in that, lesson-plans play a big role. Students spend a lot of time in writing the same objectives repeatedly because they make a couple of plans to use one textbook chapter. BEd students work hard to make a sketch of the blackboard in their lesson-plan files to convey its final appearance when they have written everything on it, as planned. They paste black paper in their files and write on it with a silver pen to give the impression of the final look of the blackboard. In addition, students decorate lesson-plans with colours, strings, ornamental strips, sparkles, glitter, ribbons, and colourful paper. I will always remember a student who had written his lesson plans on sheets of letterhead paper, not plain. It had hearts drawn in several colours, with sparkles on the cupid. The decorative presentation of lesson-plans reveals that it is not perceived as an intellectual exercise that involves knowledge and cognitive dimensions. Rather, it is seen as a product that has to be presented to somebody. The emphasis on industriousness meets the lesson-plan-making skill component in the life of BEd students and creates a solid bond. The presentation of information becomes an end in itself and occupies the student's time and energy fully. It isn't for nothing that students miss classes to make their lesson-plans and get them checked by their respective method masters. There is no room for serendipity in the life of BEd students as they end up becoming tricksters rather than rationally independent professionals. The distinction between the roles played by teacher-educators contributes to this end.

Material of instruction

The general understanding has been that a BEd student learns to make lesson-plans; to execute those plans, one needs some material. Mellan (1936) prepared a key of educational material patented by various people in the USA since 1790. The key is divided into a couple of sections based on the title under which the material was patented. The titles were: invention, apparatus, device, means, appliance, instrument, and machine. The entries in the key are reminiscent of experimental psychology in which the current of thought was to train animals to prove various points about learning. According to Mellan, after World War II, active steps were taken in the USA to equip a large number of classrooms with appropriate apparatus to demonstrate the role that planning plays in the pursuit of efficient teaching methods. At that time, the most widely discussed educational problem was 'classroom procedure known as the instruction by mechanical devices' (Mellan 1936: 291). According to Bruner, this kind of psychology conceived of learning as essentially an individual process in which the individual's mind acquired neutral and objective knowledge with the help of related or unrelated material (Bruner 2004).

Searching for teaching-learning material (TLM) or making such material themselves is a major activity that BEd students engage in while making lesson-plans. They practice instruction with mechanical devices. That learning takes place when the work done in the classroom is aided by concrete material has become the most accepted stance. BEd students spend more time on the task of collecting 'appropriate' material compared to philosophical reflection on ideas and theories about learning and the specific nature of knowledge in different fields. Mannheim and Stewart's deconstruction of the use of the word 'training' is consistent with what BEd students experience in Indian universities. Referring to the word *training*, they postulated that

> it [training] is associated with the tricks of the trade, with dependent attitudes and with a limited understanding of the purposes of any activity.... It has to do with technique and it is for this kind of reason that 'training' has often helped to confuse some of the principal issues in education.
>
> *(Mannheim and Stewart 1970: 13)*

The dominance of the idea that a teacher must acquire all the 'tricks of the trade' leads to a fixed routine, a procedural orientation to teaching, and views the child as somebody who needs textbook content in easily graspable and attractive forms. Dewey warned us against seeing education as an enterprise of routine application. Dewey's progressive education required teachers to be prepared in a way that they would become self-reliant in setting new aims and accordingly fresh ways of teaching, and not become accustomed to the plans and material. He was anguished with teachers colleges in America during the middle of the previous century, for in them the ideas and principles were converted into a 'fixed subject matter of ready-made rules, to be taught and memorised according to certain standardised procedures and to be applied to educational problems eternally' (Dewey 1952: 132). The departments of education in India work in this manner. The BEd students pick up some rules and procedures, and become familiar with certain problems that they are taught to expect later when they start teaching in schools.

The relationship between ideas about children, learning, knowledge, society, and aims of education acquire a distant location in the minds of BEd students, while material acquires immediacy. They are seen mostly in the open grounds making charts and models, and rarely in the library with books. The need to read classics in education, the latest and old research, commentaries and other kinds of books, acquires the status of a not-so-necessary intellectual activity. For them, teaching does not become an 'interaction of the minds of teacher and the taught' (Mannheim and Stewart 1970: 14), and influencing the younger generation's knowledge and attitudes; it rather becomes an activity of passing on information in an appealing way. Describing the character of the TT institution, Zaidi put it succinctly:

> It is not an uncommon though only a tacitly-owned belief in the Training College circles that 'method is the thing', that a student teacher who is initiated in the mystic lore of method will, by some mysterious process, be transformed into a paragon of pedagogical virtues. A mystique of method 'has come into being, which is handed down to successive generations of teachers with the fond hope that it will somehow more than compensate for their utter ignorance of the relevant subjects.
>
> *(Zaidi 1971: 160)*

The inordinate importance of method keeps alive the out-of-proportion significance of the need for teaching-learning material. What student-teachers lack is the wide knowledge, enthusiasm for ideas, and a genuine ability to engage young people with the basic structure of any discipline (Bruner 1960). According to Kumar (2009), NCF 2005 (NCERT 2006) described two facets of a desired teacher. One was the social facet that posed the challenge of overcoming the social hierarchies in the classroom; the other was the facet where the teacher recognised multiple curricular sites and the plurality of resources. To have such a teacher, it is important to develop the capabilities of reflection. However, what we end up developing is the capacity to arrange or make material to play better tricks on children. This keeps BEd students restricted to viewing children as – similar to Pavlov's dogs and Watson's rats – capable of responding only when stimulated and reinforced with the help of some material.

Ethos of BEd institutions: cultural and celebratory

A BEd institution has a distinct ethos that arises from the daily institutional circumstances of students and faculty members. The combination of regularly conducted activities, timetable, and faculty members' and students' way of conducting themselves create an ethos which acquires relative stability and provides a unique character to the institution. According to Mills (1959), it is important to understand the different ethos that people access if we want to understand the rise of individuals in them. Using this construct, an attempt has been made here to grasp the ethos of BEd institutions to comprehend the rise of the teacher in BEd students.

When the programme starts every year, students undergo a week-long orientation which sets the tone of the experiences to come in the course. The students get introduced to the practice of a compulsory morning assembly and weekly cultural activities as an important component of life in a department of education. There are fixed slots in the timetable for cultural activities. These activities include singing songs, dancing, debates, extempore speeches, and certain games for building team-spirit. A working day begins with a morning assembly in which the students sing the national anthem and discuss an issue of contemporary or universal relevance. Sometimes, this discussion takes place in the form of debates or poetry reading sessions. The discussion and singing is followed by announcements with regard to their classes and other activities. A morning assembly, involving religious prayers and a few activities of public speaking, in TT institutions is a country-wide phenomenon. A faculty member is designated as in-charge of the assembly, whose work is to supervise and communicate the need for regularity, punctuality, and active participation in the assembly. In Delhi University, till recently, participation in morning assembly carried scores in the form of a larger exercise that involved cultural activities and was equivalent to some of the theory and pedagogic courses in terms of their weighting. The new curriculum notified by the NCTE has done away with such a provision, but the singing and dancing fervour continues unabated and its related weekly and annual events are being held, the same as earlier.

BEd students spend their first half-hour in the morning in exactly the same manner as children do in schools. The insistence on participation in the morning assembly and in the cultural activities of the BEd programme establishes an acute similarity with the lives of schools in India, and it enables us to understand the desired personality of a teacher-in-the-making. The insistence takes us back to the 'trick master' model of a school teacher. The premise of this model is that a teacher needs to perform tricks from morning to afternoon every day, and thus she or he must learn to conduct assembly and organise cultural activities by doing so on a daily basis. This has reflections of the earlier popular apprenticeship model in professional programmes that implied that the learner learns by engaging in exactly the same activities that she or he will do in the future. This echoes an inherently mechanical view of learning and the sense is that all teachers are required to be 'cultural beings' who must have the wherewithal to organise outside-the-classroom activities. It is true that this dimension has a rather direct connection with school life. To begin with, there are several such activities for which an average Indian school suspends teaching for days altogether; the number of these has increased considerably in the last few years. The bureaucracy, central and local governments, and boards of examination issue orders on a regular basis to mark and observe week-long activities such as hand-washing week, neighbourhood cleanliness week, good governance day, plantation week, and celebrating our heritage week, and so on. So far, a critical view has not been taken of this aspect of Indian schools in TT institutions. In fact, there has been a sense of conformity to this and thus the organisation of such exercises emerges as one of the major enterprises in BEd.

The students are divided into groups and faculty members are designated as being in charge. Their responsibility is to ensure that there are students willing to dance, sing, and debate. The students often miss classes on the pretext of preparing for such activities, with a sense of legitimacy. It also gives them a sense of being industrious because they run around to decorate, arrange various things such as furniture, an audio system, dresses, refreshment, etc. Such activities are organised regularly and give rise to a celebratory ethos consistent with that of families in India when they celebrate big or small festivals and weddings. During cultural activities, BEd students and faculty members engage on matters which have no bearing on their academic interaction. They talk about food, dress, films, dance, relationships, and so on. In this celebratory ethos, faculty members shed their academic personas and emerge as cultural beings similar to BEd students. This is how Indian schools function. While organising such activities almost every week, teachers end up in situations in which their engagement with children in schools does not revolve around any field of knowledge. Its epicentre remains a non-academic activity. We can, therefore, notice that this situational teacher–student interaction is identical in TT institutions and in schools.

The school-like fervour carries on in other aspects of general conduct. One indicator is the ardour with which students wish 'good morning', 'good afternoon', and so on to their teachers as many times as they cross them. As a practice, BEd students stand up to issue such a greeting when a teacher enters the classroom, just like children do in schools. The verbal wish is accompanied by a slight bow that Indians acquire at school, and which also has a feudal heritage. The students pay respect to the professional authority of the teacher (Freire 1970) by repeating this gesture mechanically.

The necessity of this wishing is internalised so deeply that they wish even while talking on their mobile phones and holding animated conversations, while stepping in and out of the toilets, while noting down announcements, and even while the teacher is engaged in a serious conversation with somebody. This is indeed a common sight in a large number of academic institutions of higher education in India, but in a department of education it acquires significance because the BEd students are expected to appreciate the role of a teacher as somebody who thinks critically about real life (ibid.). In the real life of a BEd programme, the intellectual inspiration of Gandhi and Tagore and the rituals to mark teachers' authority go in parallel. They never intersect and create contradictions in the minds of the BEd students. They do not become even slightly critical about this ritual, that their act of repeated wishing may disturb the teacher's flow of conversation or that it's not needed so many times in a day. Mostly, students call themselves *bachche* (children), and also behave like them. A large number of students remain casual, playful, and insouciant. It seems as if they just pass their time and fill their institutional life with sporadic activities.

At a very young age, learners in India internalise that missing school often is not a big deal; this concept becomes rock solid as they progress up the educational ladder. BEd students also miss classes quite regularly. Under the NCTE's mandatory provision, a minimum of 85 per cent (earlier 75 per cent) attendance throughout the year is required. The implication of this provision is that every class either starts or ends with attendance-taking activity by calling out the name of every student. The attendance record of every student needs to be maintained by faculty members and submitted to the authorities at least twice every academic year. It is an interesting eventuality of the attendance regime that a few students remain absolutely regular and some remain highly irregular throughout the academic year. However, the bulk constitutes what can be called the floating population of BEd students. They attend a few classes and miss a few as a practice. During winter, one finds students basking in the sun and sipping tea/coffee rather than being in class.

The reasons for missing classes are wide-ranging and deserve a full-length discussion. However, a brief reflection is needed here. The reason for missing a class is often covered by a few common excuses: I (or a family member) wasn't well; I had to attend a wedding or festival celebration in the family; I had an exam; and so on.

On average, BEd students are 21–26 years old. Many of them pursue the programme along with several other professional options such as jobs in banks, lower and higher bureaucracy in the state and central governments, and so on. With their minds busy with a wide range of professional options and dealing with the reality of family and kinship responsibilities, characteristic of social life in India, there is little room left for unobstructed commitment to the choice of becoming a teacher. This results in a sketchy understanding of issues or ideas. For instance, a student comes to the class in which the discussion on Gandhi's ideas on education starts, and then she misses the next four classes for a relative's wedding. Gandhi's ideas become a casualty in such a case, and this is a fairly common phenomenon. One knows very well that the student will not make any effort to engage with Gandhi's ideas on her own.

The fervency born out of cultural activities, students' irregular presence in the classes, and their conduct altogether give rise to an ethos in which the students' enrolment in a BEd programme does not become a distinct purpose. They carry a fluid perception of institutional academic spaces and their function. Their minds do not become 'disciplined' in the structure of the discipline of education. At best, they acquire the sense of teaching activity that encompasses several kinds of performances. Smith (2003) has applied the construct of habitus (Bourdieu 1990) to organisations. His argument is that an educational institution's ethos is continually constructed under the influence of individual students' habituses and that of institutions in the external environment. In TT institutions, school is the external environment. A school's life remains a model for how students and faculty members structure their behaviour while being members of a BEd programme. The TT institution's habitus is not marked by the nuances of the discipline of education. It is largely shaped by India's socio-cultural fabric, which comes in the form of students' and faculty members' habituses and by a school's shadow.

Every year, BEd programmes set out to prepare teachers who will be able to reform a senior-secondary school. In its processes and activities it replicates school most of the time and treats school as a frozen entity in time and behaviours. At the end, the programme produces teachers who do not take long to fit into the structures of schooling. The secondary and senior-secondary schools in India have not received substantial policy attention for their reform, except a minor scheme of the central government, Rashtriya Madhyamik Shiksha Abhiyan (RMSA), which hasn't been implemented with great energy or zeal. The unreformed school becomes the demand agency for which BEd has been supplying trained teachers. So far, there has been no major conflict between the two. If by chance one or two BEd students pick up critical insights and ideas and try to practise them in schools when they get jobs, in no time the school's daily circumstances will dampen their spirits and so they adjust to the prevailing system. They cannot carry on the project of bringing fresh energy into that school. The biggest challenge ahead of the reformed structure of the BEd programme is the narrowness of the discourse of teacher training in India.

Notes

1 It is a commonly used term in the Indian context for those teacher-educators who teach pedagogy courses.
2 Thermocol is a commercial name of polystyrene, a synthetic petroleum product. Polystyrene is one of the most widely used plastics. Uses include protective packaging in packing peanuts and CD and DVD cases, clamshells, lids, bottles, trays, tumblers, and disposable cutlery. In India, Thermocol has found its biggest use in making models of various concepts that children study in different school subjects.

References

Batra, P. 2009. 'Teacher Empowerment: The Education Entitlement–Social Transformation Traverse'. *Contemporary Education Dialogue* 6(2): 121–156.
Bourdieu, P. 1990. *The Logic of Practice*, trans R. Nice. Cambridge: Polity Press.
Bruner, J. 1960. *The Process of Education*. London: Vintage.
Bruner, J. 2004. 'A Short History of Psychological Theories of Learning'. *Daedalus* 133(1): 13–20.
Buber, M. 1958. *I and Thou*. New York: Charles Scribner's Sons.
Carr, D. 2003. *Making Sense of Education: An Introduction to the Philosophy and Theory of Education and Teaching*. New York: Routledge Farmer.
Dewey, J. 1952. *Dewey on Education: Selections with an Introduction and Notes by Martin S. Dworkin*. New York: Teachers College Press.
Elkind, David. 1981. *Children and Adolescents*. New York: Oxford University Press.
Erikson, Erik. H. 1959. *Childhood and Society*. New York: W.W. Norton.
Festinger, L. 1957. *A Theory of Cognitive Dissonance*. Stanford: Stanford University Press.
Freire, P. 1970. *Pedagogy of the Oppressed*. London: Penguin.
Furlong, J. 2013. *Education: An Anatomy of the Discipline – Rescuing the University Project?* Routledge: London and New York.
Kumar, K. 2002. 'Planned Lessons and Other Problems of Teacher Training', in M.S. Bawa, Geeta Sahni, and B.M. Nagpal (eds) *Reflections on Lesson Planning*. Delhi: IASE, University of Delhi.
Kumar, K. 2008. *A Pedagogue's Romance: Reflections on Schooling*. New Delhi: Oxford University Press.
Kumar, K. 2011. *Banning is Just the Beginning in Eliminating Corporal Punishment in Schools*. New Delhi: NCPCR.
Kumar, K. 2014. *Politics of Education in Colonial India*. Delhi: Routledge.
Kumaravadivelu, B. 2001. 'Toward a Post-method Pedagogy'. *TESOL Quarterly* 35(4): 537–560.
Mannheim, K. and Stewart, W.A.C. 1970. *An Introduction to the Sociology of Education*. London: Routledge and Kegan Paul.
Mellan, I. 1936. 'Teaching and Educational Inventions'. *The Journal of Experimental Education* 4(3): 291–300.
Mills, C.W. 1959. *The Sociological Imagination*. New York: Oxford University Press.
NCERT. 2006. *National Curriculum Framework 2005*. New Delhi: NCERT.
NCERT. 2007. *The National Focus Group Paper on Teacher Education*. New Delhi: NCERT.
Raina, T.N. and Raina, M.K. 1971. 'Perception of Teacher-Educators in India about the Ideal Pupil'. *The Journal of Educational Research* 64(7): 303–306.

Russel, J.E. 1925. 'Problems of the School of Education'. *Journal of Education* 101(12;2522):331.

Shukla, J.K. 1970. 'Professional Preparation of School Teachers in India: Changing Trends'. In S.P. Ruhela (ed.) *Sociology of the Teaching Profession in India*. New Delhi: NCERT.

Sinha, S. 2002. 'Lesson Plan: Examining the Underlying Assumptions'. In M.S. Bawa, Geeta Sahni, and B.M. Nagpal (eds) *Reflections on Lesson Planning*. Delhi: IASE, University of Delhi.

Smith, Edwin. 2003. 'Ethos, Habitus and Situation for Learning: An Ecology'. *British Journal of Sociology of Education* 24(4): 463–470.

Zaidi, K. Sabira. 1971. *Education and Humanism: A Collection of Essays*. Simla: Indian Institute of Advanced Study.

12
Management education in India
How far have we come?

Pankaj Chandra

The idea of management is to develop perspectives, processes, and values that drive growth of innovative ideas, products, and services in order to give meaning to human endeavour and provide improvements in quality of life. It is also about effectiveness and efficiency in delivery of goods and services in society. Education in the world of management was about learning to manage organisations and individuals therein in the realisation of their own potential and aspirations. In that, many different drivers have defined the pathways to growth of organisations and, more importantly, their role and impact on societies. Globally, institutions of management education have led the changes in the world of business and industry through their graduates and their thinking.

Today, competing principles of management are readily seen driving business and industry as they do social organisations and political institutions like governments. Strategies of focus and differentiation, financial ideas of leverage and risk, policies on pricing and consumer insights, integration of supply chains, and the operations of execution, to name very few, are now common influencers in such disparate fields as law and security, judiciary and governance, infrastructure and environment, etc. The reach of managerial thinking is widening and its principles and logic are seen as complementing the philosophy, economics, and sociology behind the functioning of any society. The question, however, remains as to how well the practitioners of management are able to grow their knowledge and consequently influence in helping make society better. And, as a corollary, how well the institutions of education in management are performing in their job towards preparing such managers who understand the organisations of the society as well as they may do in business in order to truly become agents of social change. For, business has the strongest potential for achieving the same.

This chapter is about the promise of management education in India and its journey into the future. In that, it is closely linked to the transformation of the global economy and the accompanying changes in the world of business in India. But here, the story of Indian management education takes a path that makes its sojourn a bit more interesting than those of many other nations. In this chapter we track the big changes, comment on its journey, engage with the discipline(s), explore the challenges, and identify aspects that render the current project of management incomplete.

Formal management education in India can be euphemistically called the child of the newly independent nation, as the new nation had the need to build for itself enduring factories, roads, power plants, financial system, etc., not only to run a nation but also to lay the foundation of its industrial future. It has come quite some way since then. Structurally, it is estimated that India has around 3,900 institutions that offer management degrees and postgraduate diplomas, and that enrol about 0.35 million students. The postgraduate students in management (and management education in India has largely been a postgraduate affair) comprise about 16.5 per cent of all postgraduate students in India across all disciplines, only second to the social sciences that comprise 20.6 per cent of the total population of postgraduate students (Government of India-MHRD 2014).

The promise of management education

The promise of management was a structured understanding of organisations and all that they stood for and undertook. To understand what has happened to management education, one has to recall briefly the evolution of industries in India and their different managerial systems and styles. At Independence, the country struggled to reconcile the contrasting managerial systems and styles of the mill owners of western India, the sugar barons of the north, the jute mills and the tea plantation owners of the east, and the big spice growers and merchants of the south. In between there were traders from India who carried goods to East Asia, Arabia, and Africa, the small producers of engineering and consumer durables all over the country, and road contractors who became the early infrastructure developers (along with the accompanying raw material providers). There were some dissimilarities in how they conducted their business. The big distinction in managerial form, however, came from firms with British origins (mostly out of Calcutta and sometimes Chennai) – at the most trivial level, it was suit-and-tie-wearing managers versus the dhoti-clad agency firms of western India; at a higher level of managerial sophistication was the 'parta' system of accounting as practised by the Marwari traders and producers versus those working towards the annual royalty payments to the owners in England that was used by the British companies in India! Their managerial systems were different. But the real breakthrough in managerial form and structure came through the management of public sector enterprises, with their largely technical manpower that subsequently became the bedrock of Indian management until the liberalisation of the Indian economy in 1991. These contrasting forms have influenced significantly how education on organisations evolved over time.

For a long time, until the early 1950s, people learned on the job (a rare few were educated abroad formally in management). They came with a variety of graduate degrees – largely arts and social sciences. Entry into private firms was often through an introduction and connections. You climbed the ladder and if you stayed long enough you would have learned most of the managerial traits – the engineers, however, managed the plants, and the chartered accountants handled finance; production was people management and the rest was largely implementation of standard technology. The salespeople were considered articulate and worldly wise – they were the ones who would travel and see the 'world'. Finance functions were kept close to the family or the trusted. The people management function or 'personnel' took care of industrial relations, managed housing colonies, and looked after their welfare. The promise of a private industry job was better remuneration, a style of working and living, and sometimes travelling to larger cities. They were distinct from government jobs. Much of the thinking in the organisation was driven by the owner's perception of the opportunities and his connections. The bureaucracy, however, had full control over what organisations did and both benefited from this relationship.

With Independence came the public sector units (PSUs) – enterprises established by the government in a variety of domains – steel-making, machine tools, heavy engineering, large electrical motors and turbines, telecom, pharmaceuticals, etc. – all things that were required to service the public and their needs. With them also came service firms like banks and insurance and airlines, as well as the expansion of railways. All needed skilled manpower to manage these enterprises and help them increase their reach. These enterprises borrowed heavily from both – the rules and regulations from the government and a managerial form from the private – a truly hybrid form of organisation, though over time the former eclipsed the latter. While the government was the owner, it was a faceless owner and lived at a distance, at least in the perception of most employees of a public sector organisation. The PSUs became a strategy for developing underdeveloped regions of the country. They came with new facilities, often with the help of a friendly foreign government and expatriate managers, newer technology, planned townships, high-quality schools, and a sense of brotherhood and purpose – building the newly independent nation. They publicly recruited large amounts of technical and non-technical manpower. Industrial towns (other than the older private ones like Jamshedpur in Jharkhand, Nagda in Madhya Pradesh, Kirloskarwadi in Maharashtra, etc.) like Bhilai, Durgapur, Bangalore, and Dehradun started to grow post-Independence. To the list of industries from groups like Bajaj, Kirloskar, Tata, Birla, Dalmia, Lalbhai, Mafatlal, Godrej, Scindia, Walchand Hirachand, Thapar, Goenka, Bangur, Morarji Goculdas was added, first, the names of private firms (with British origins) like the Imperial Tobacco Company (today's ITC), Imperial Chemicals Industries (ICI), Metal Box, McNeil and Magor, Martin Burns, Jessop and Co., and then the PSUs like Steel Authority of India Limited (SAIL), Indian Telephone Industries (ITI), Hindustan Machine Tools (HMT), Bharat Heavy Electricals Limited (BHEL), Heavy Engineering Corporation (HEC), Coal India, Indian Space Research Organization, Life Insurance Corporation, State Bank of India, etc. Such was the diversified nature of the industrial base of India. For a detailed account of Indian business see Tripathy and Jumani (2013). This growth needed people with diverse skills (production, technical, human resources, sales, finance and accounts, industrial relations, organisational design and behavioural science, etc.), including people to manage facilities and townships, people to take products to potential consumers, and people to coordinate with the government. And equally important was the need to understand the various differences in the management systems across this spectrum of firm types. The need for management education had been established. The first task, however, was to understand: what did people do in organisations? Who did what? And why did they do things differently? Why did ownership matter in the way we did things? How could each be improved? These formed the early questions that became the basis of thinking of a management education curriculum.

Phases in management education

Early managers learned on the job and came from diverse backgrounds. Development of management education in India can be described through four phases. The first two phases of managerial education in India could easily be termed as the pre-Indian Institutes of Management (IIM) era (until 1960) and the coming of IIMs era (1960–2001), reflecting the overwhelming influence of the IIMs on the state of management education in India and the role of their graduates in business and industry. Subsequently, it has been influenced by the impact of liberalisation of the Indian economy, the expansion of IIMs, as well as the establishment of private institutions like ISB. The final phase reflects new directions post-2015.

Phase I: the pre-IIMs era (until 1960)

The first phase of managerial education was largely driven by the discipline of 'commerce'. Starting in the early 1950s, three institutions started to devise curriculum that were broader and

191

wider than the traditional commerce education that placed heavy emphasis on accounting, principles of finance and legal aspects of business, i.e. company law. This was found to be insufficient in managing affairs of the new enterprises. The early leaders of organisations often had such training. Education at these three institutions was mostly practice-driven and vocational in nature. These institutions were the Xavier Labour Relations Institute (XLRI) in Jamshedpur, the Indian Institute of Social Welfare and Business Management (IISWBM) in Calcutta, and the Faculty of Management Studies (FMS), University of Delhi. XLRI started by offering in 1949 courses for management and unions, and focused on industrial relations in organisations. It developed a close relationship with neighbouring Tata firms in Jamshedpur and later offered a master's degree. IISBM offered the first graduate-level programme (i.e. MBA) in management in India in 1953. Kolkata was the centre of business and industry (especially jute mills, textile mills, tea estates, and agency firms from British times), and this programme was affiliated to the University of Calcutta. At the same time, in Delhi (in 1953), the commerce department of the Delhi College of Engineering was closed down and the FMS of the University of Delhi was established in its place with a faculty member from the engineering college as its head. All these programmes were amalgamations of commerce education, some behavioural skills that involved understanding labour and unions, a sprinkling of topics that would provide skills in planning, an understanding of the economy, as well as some inputs on markets. These were pioneers in management education, but their way of looking at organisations was still quite traditional.

Phase II: the coming of IIMs (1960–2001)

The coming of the IIM in 1961 in Calcutta (a decision taken by the government in 1960 after the submission of the Robbins Report on setting up of IIMs) and at Ahmedabad in the same year with their contrasting circumstances, styles, and cultures announced the beginning of a new era in industrial management. They also started to produce managers in larger numbers and quickly made their presence felt with greater engagement with industry and government, as well as their commitment to quality teaching. Calcutta attracted stars of management education; Ahmedabad decided to go with younger academics. Calcutta was quantitatively driven; Ahmedabad was process driven. Calcutta chose a lecture-driven pedagogy; Ahmedabad adopted a case method of teaching. Calcutta became close to theory; Ahmedabad was close to practice. It showed careful experimentation by early adopters. Was it a replay of the urbane British-styled Calcutta and its rivalry with the pragmatism of entrepreneurs of western India? One was led by a lawyer and celebrated practising manager, K.T. Chandy (who had been a Director at Lever Brothers and rose to become the Chairman of the Food Corporation of India) and the other was conceived and nurtured by celebrated technocrat and entrepreneur Vikram Sarabhai. Both came with the academic support of two distinctive institutions of Boston – MIT and Harvard, respectively. The Indian Institute of Management Calcutta (IIMC) and Indian Institute of Management Ahmedabad (IIMA) were pioneer institutions. They did two things that innovators do – one, they educated the industry on the role of young managers in their organisations and the need for imparting structured learning of managerial principles to junior, middle, and senior managers of the companies (Anubhai 2011). This led to the tradition of executive education and the building of cadres of managerial talent. And two, they formalised the structure of management education in India (as distinct from 'commerce' education) as:

- understanding the individual and the collective in the context of an organisation and the setting of its goals;
- understanding the environment and the forces that define its constraints;

- understanding the nature of competition facing the industry and its sources; and
- building of skills to address managerial problems – structuring the problems and learning the art and science of problem-solving and decision making.

These two institutions laid the foundation of managerial education both within the company and outside. IIMA, with its unique case-based pedagogy, captured the imagination of organisations as well as institutions that were to follow them. It made them understand the issues of companies better. Hence, they were able to respond with managerial options. Like the ice-breaker ship, they did much of the heavy lifting and convincing of people in industry, government, and society at large of their value. They also established the structure of the managerial curriculum and provided a framework for functional learning from both a strategic perspective as well as a discipline of execution.

IIM Bangalore (IIMB) came about a decade or so later (in 1972) with a distinctive focus on the public sector; it started to prepare graduates for these government-run enterprises. Its graduates, in addition to learning about general management, focused on health, energy and environment, transport, etc. It was also established indigenously without any external support. Over the years, IIMB gave up its public sector focus as its graduates looked towards private enterprises for employment. New IIMs subsequently came up at Lucknow, Kozhikode, and Indore. Liberalisation of the economy in 1991 changed the demand for managerial education and a large number of institutions in the private sector started to establish management schools and provide the postgraduate diploma in management, the same as the IIMs.

Phase III: ISB and the newer IIMs

By the end of the 1990s, graduates of the two older IIMs (IIMC and IIMA) were leading national organisations both in the public and private sectors. A few had started to head global organisations. Their graduates, fresh out of college (though largely engineers by now), were getting hired by Indian and multinational firms, both for their national and global operations. The placement of these institutions, unfortunately, became the focus of media attention. The institutions had, however, changed – from having a scholarship and learning-oriented ethos to becoming platforms for placement of young people. This created a new kind of hierarchy among undergraduates, with management institutions leading the preferences.

Two events changed managerial education once again in the decade of the 2000s: one was the establishment of the Indian School of Business (ISB) in Hyderabad, with immense corporate support and a one-year graduate programme in management (until then all programmes were two years in duration) and the second was the decision of the central government to blanket the country with more IIMs. By 2013, there were 13 IIMs operating while six more were announced in 2014–15. Suddenly, the nature of the relationship of the IIMs with society at large (and the government, in particular) had changed – the students, faculty, governance, curriculum, placement – were all struggling to adjust not only to the new global economic reality, but also to the new regulatory stance of the government. The old IIMs were starting to consolidate their programmes, especially their research, while the new ones were struggling to get themselves going. After some time there were several IIMs (i.e. the new ones) that were not as reputable as their private counterparts. Society did not know how to benchmark an IIM! Perhaps a new PSU structure with its 'navratnas' was emerging. This period saw an unprecedented growth in private management institutions, many with poor infrastructure – both physical and intellectual. The private institutions were very dependent on people outside academia for teaching. The government institutions were getting more and more structured by the whimsical thinking of agencies like the AICTE. The ISB, on the other hand, started to seek students with work experience, something that has always been debated at an IIM but never received support internally; it expanded quickly and forced the entrenched IIMs to react with their own strategy. They also centred on research, something that government institutions like IIMs refused to do as self-preservation.

It must be mentioned that the private institutions have been struggling at the hands of the government. For most of the 1990s and early 2000s, it allowed private Postgraduate Diploma in Management (PGDM) programmes to grow; it never cared where they were established – whether they were close to centres of business and industry or far from them, thereby cutting off important sources of learning. The government has never known how to handle the private institutions and their programmes.

Phase IV: post-2015 and new directions

Globally, management education is being restructured. Programmes are becoming more flexible, more global, have more content from emerging economies, and are aimed at creating enterprises and new jobs rather than seeking jobs. Research in management has become more interdisciplinary and it cuts across boundaries of disciplines outside management. Executive MBA programmes have grown tremendously. But none of the above appear to have taken root in Indian management institutions. Institutions have established incubators to support start-ups, but these remain at the periphery of the institutions and have not been integrated with their core strategy. Indian institutions look alike in their treatment of the curriculum, unlike their global counterparts that have experimented and created niches for themselves (Datar *et al.* 2010).

The government is struggling to restructure the PGDM programmes, but they lack vision and the institutions' deep capabilities. As a result, it might even attempt to control what they teach by affiliating these institutions to neighbouring public universities – a bad way of reforming institutions through those that are already below par. Worse still, it is once again attempting to control the destiny and the activities of IIMs (as it has done periodically in the past) by trying to pass an IIM Bill in Parliament that will circumscribe what IIMs can do. First, it expands the number of IIMs; now, under the disguise of needing to coordinate, the government is trying to standardise the activities in these institutions through a 'coordination council' that will comprise lots of politicians and bureaucrats and will be chaired by the Minister of Human Resource Development. Is it the end of a grand experiment in management education to become responsive to the market? Will the IIM Bill change the degree structure, make it difficult to experiment, impact their curriculum, governance, and future direction? At the same time, there are now at least 25–30 management schools that have had more than three decades of experience in delivering programmes and are perhaps ready to experiment with a new direction in management education. It is against this backdrop that we now look at what is happening to learning in management institutions and what may be needed today.

The changing external environment and its requirements

While the governments were reducing management education to vocational learning and making it trivial through attempts of the AICTE and UGC to control all aspects of its functioning – from teachers to the content – the context of management education changed dramatically. From the commanding heights of public sector development in the 1950s to private entrepreneurship post-liberalisation, from an agriculture- and manufacturing-driven economy to a service-driven one, from government running the firms in various sectors to government setting up regulators to govern industry behaviour, from large firms to small start-ups, from manual operations to digital production – the context of business became very different. The global business environment was also being revolutionised. With the coming of the WTO and bilateral free-trade agreements, the flow of manufactured products and services across borders grew manifold. The East Asian meltdown of the late 1990s, the dotcom bust of 2000, the financial crisis in the USA in 2008, falling oil prices, the slowdown in China, and the recent problems of Greece, as well as the upcoming exit of the UK from the EU have all led to restrained growth in economies and consequently managerial employment, a restructuring of economic leverage and consequently a slowdown in national wealth, and a search for new business paradigms for survival. At the same time, extreme poverty around the world is more visible today. These factors have all been responsible for changing emphasis in management schools.

Three phenomena have also had significant impacts on the world of business – growth of civil society (through non-governmental organisations) who would monitor the impact of business on society, the mandating of corporate social responsibility (CSR), and the influence of the digital world. The last two have made the former more effective. At the same time, CSR investments and the digital revolution and social media have ensured that civil society is held responsible for its actions. The internet and e-commerce have changed the way goods and services are procured and distributed. These have been accompanied by many innovations and changes in the way businesses operate. New forms of aggregating firms like Uber, Ola, or Airbnb are rapidly changing the structure of the industry, nature of employment, and even the locus of revenues and taxation. In the last two decades many skills have become obsolete and demand for several new ones has grown, especially with the expanding use of technology. Competition from across borders has been intensified, particularly from China, and Indian businesses have become vulnerable in many traditional areas of strength. On the labour market side, as skills started to become obsolete, young people started to change jobs more frequently – sometimes to extract the maximum returns from existing skills and sometimes to move into newer domains of expertise so as to remain current for longer periods. Managerial wages led by the IT industry kept going up and demand for management education, as a consequence, kept increasing – all this while existing skills remained current for shorter and shorter periods of time. This was an opportunity for academic institutions in the form of executive education, full-time as well as part-time. At the same time, new areas of industry and instruction were growing in the form of banking, finance, services, and insurance (BFSI), analytics, and digital – all related to the IT sector. New opportunities for managerial learning were also arising.

This led to three distinct requirements:

- service professions grew and became more formal – requirements to manage them grew as well;
- some sectors of industry started requiring technical manpower with greater managerial skills. For example, the telecom sector required people who could combine telecom technology knowledge with telecom strategy and related knowledge on pricing as well as spectrum allocation expertise;
- new sectors opened up for private and multinational corporation (MNC) participation – some were new to the country like biotech or arts and heritage management, while others were liberalised, i.e. moved from the government to the private sector, like health, energy, infrastructure, primary and secondary education, transport.

All of these created a new demand for managerial knowledge. For instance, organisations like Ranga Sankara that was set up to promote theatre and related commerce started looking for people who could help them develop strategic models of engagement and run the organisation as a business. Energy companies needed new skills to merge or acquire and grow or raise capital for infrastructure investments. The e-commerce and agglomeration models of Amazon, Flipkart, Ola, Uber, etc. required new ways of valuing and growing firms even when they were making revenue losses. Corporates were seeking new kinds of learning. The big and busy world of management had changed. How did the academic institutions and their offerings fare on these counts? Did the content and focus of learning change with the changing requirements of industry, i.e. what was fundamental to management learning that would withstand time and changes and what had to change with time?

Management education and institutional progress

Management draws on a variety of areas like humanities, social sciences, physical sciences, and engineering to define itself intellectually. Early academics came from mathematics and statistics (who taught quantitative and analytical skills), sociology and psychology (who studied organisations, labour, markets, and consumer choices), economics (who provided an understanding of the micro and macro environment, including assessing the impact of policy), and industrial engineering (who looked at the process of production and distribution of goods). Commerce graduates provided skills on accounting and finance. At the same time, a motley crew of quantitatively oriented as well as engineering graduates educated the rest in the use of information and technology for competitive advantage. It is interesting to note that the celebrated industrialist N.R. Narayana Murthy, cut his teeth setting up the computer systems and related learning environment at IIM Ahmedabad in the late 1960s and early 1970s. That is how the foundation of the supply side was laid.

Management education as it has evolved over the years grew its own applied disciplines like strategy, organisational behaviour and human resources, finance and accounting, marketing, and operations and technology management, reflecting broadly organisation of knowledge systems to manage functions in an organisation. It is interesting that management education grew graduate programmes first with a keen appreciation that one needed a basic grounding in a classical discipline of learning before seeking a professional degree (in an applied discipline) at the graduate level. The structure of management programmes also followed a similar philosophy – a two-year master's programme comprised teaching of core subjects that covered knowledge essential to understand various functions in an organisation and its strategic stances, followed by a series of electives reflecting choices in the curriculum to cater to varied interests of students in terms of functions of specialisation in their career. That was the MBA or the PGDM (at schools that were neither a university nor affiliated to one nor deemed to be a university). There was no difference in the two degrees – the latter simply provided operational flexibility to programmes and institutions. As the need for teachers grew, institutions created their own doctoral programmes (a PhD at a degree-granting university or a Fellow Programme in Management (FPM) at a non-degree-granting institution). The IIMs started the FPM with an underlying philosophy of producing a 'generalist specialist' rather than training specialists as in other parts of the world. They first trained their doctoral students in the fundamentals of management (the first year of the programme was the same as the postgraduate programme, i.e. PGP, students) and then in their respective disciplines. The doctoral programme was distinct from those at the universities – it comprised two years of coursework followed by a comprehensive examination to prove deep knowledge in the discipline and its methods before proceeding to work on a research problem. While the MBAs or PGPs largely admitted fresh graduates, schools were looking for people with experience to join their doctoral programmes. However, weak doctoral programmes of Indian institutions has been found to be a key determinant of poor research productivity at these institutions (Sahoo *et al.* 2017).

On the one hand, institutions provided training on advances in mainstream business and industry; they also focused on the management of under-managed sectors (like agriculture, energy and environment, health, etc.) quite early in their history. For instance, recognising the importance of agriculture to India, IIMA started the first programme in the country on agriculture management. Similarly, a special programme focusing on management of rural organisations came up in the form of the Institute for Rural Management Anand (IRMA). This made the evolution of management institutions in India different from others around the world and also more interesting. Understanding the role of the state and civil society in shaping business and industry and the concomitant development of society became an integral part of its programmes (it is interesting to note that most programmes globally started to address them quite late in their history – somewhere in the early 2000s).

But this came with immense challenges. Schools grew to meet industry requirements, but it happened largely through standalone institutions, i.e. outside the university system without the benefit of input of many disciplines that form a university. The management departments in universities unfortunately acted no differently – they protected their turf, and the university culture as well as its processes did not allow interdisciplinary teaching and learning, which is what management education is actually about. As the management knowledge system grew in academia, so did the isolation of management disciplines globally, and particularly in India. While this situation has started to thaw elsewhere in the world, instruction in Indian universities remains isolated. This has had another side effect – management at a large number of institutions started to get taught by people who came from the world of practice. Shortage of faculty also played into this situation. This set of instructors had practical knowledge but many did not know how to bring out deep conceptual learning from their own experiences. Management classes at many places were filled with war stories, and rigour was lost in the processes. The students quite often enjoy these practical insights as opposed to what they see as 'knowledge from books'. Lecturing as a pedagogy did not deliver cutting-edge applications, while case studies did not deliver rigour. It appeared that students were becoming adept at terminology and less at deep understanding of concepts and fundamentals. Management education in India was in utter chaos by the early 1990s. Great demand for graduates led to high variance in the preparation levels of graduates entering the workforce. For a long time this was one programme where the likelihood of getting a job was highest – and a well-paying one, too. Interestingly, growth in industry also led to growth in executive programmes that brought in more money to institutions as well as individual faculty – more than anyone else on a university campus. But education was suffering as the institutions had started to become complacent – less careful about what was being taught in the classroom and less focused on the rigour of the disciplines.

The requirements of the domain

Unlike most disciplines, students who come to do management at the graduate level (which is indeed the majority of students) come from disciplines other than management. As a consequence, the need for a set of foundation courses becomes imperative. The challenge, of course, is to decide what will comprise the foundation, given the changing environment and the diversity of roles that its students pursue (most schools, however, tend to choose functions of an organisation and some skills as their core). The bigger question to be asked is what, if the world of management is so disparate, should be the basis of its foundation – management, after all, comprises many disciplines. How should it then integrate the various disciplinary strands to create a coherent view of the discipline of management?

Management education is premised on deep understanding of industry sectors as well as those that require managerial intervention, like infrastructure, not-for-profits, government, etc. This requires both, a deep knowledge of the issues of the sector as well an understanding of theories and research in related disciplines outside management. There are only a few individuals and institutions that have cared to develop such a view on building deep expertise, even though that is the best and quickest way of developing a strong research focus for a management school. Consulting companies fill this vacuum somewhat. Useful as it may be, their work is not a substitute for a rigorous academic analysis of various issues, since their objectives are different and their work aimed at commercial clients rather than building new theories to unravel the workings of an issue or design of systems.

Management courses place special emphasis on analytical thinking (a bit more than reflective thinking), structuring of problems and problem-solving, observing and understanding, and developing a process view of execution and strategy. Of late, analytical methods for risk assessment have become prominent, while understanding of people, especially in groups, has become nuanced due to advances in our understanding of uncertainty and in behavioural neurosciences. At the same time, organising work, handling crises, negotiation, and persuasion have become more tactical and less strategic in their consideration in most curricula, much to the detriment of learning how to build harmonious organisations.

The choice of pedagogy, as noted earlier, also has a deep impact on building the processes of structuring, questioning, and learning, especially in professional educational settings. Three aspects of this choice needs highlighting. One relates to the nature of pedagogy – the common ones have been experiential learning (including a 'clinic' view of learning), case-based and Socratic learning, lectures and tutorial-based teaching, learning through field observations, and reflective learning. Different disciplines of management lend themselves to different approaches. Among them, the case-based pedagogy has taken root, though several experiments are underway to create a more meaningful yet rigorous experiential learning system. Those schools that have been established and operated by practitioners tend to bring more of a corporate-training style learning environment to their programmes. These tend to prepare students for the next job rather than providing them with deep education.

Executive education has become an integral part of management education and that segment has experimented greatly with experiential learning. Most of the premier institutions have elaborate executive education programmes for Indian companies, and some conduct programmes for MNCs and companies overseas. India has a lot of demand for management education, especially when it comes to executive education. As a result, foreign institutions also conduct programmes in India. Some, like Harvard, Chicago, and Cornell Universities, have established offices in India that write cases on Indian organisations and conduct programmes for them. This is an area that is waiting to grow exponentially once more institutions develop mature capabilities to develop innovative programmes for practising managers in the public and private domains. The nature of engagement is quite different from traditional MBA-style education.

Management research has all the requirements of any science – physical and social. It needs to understand real issues and phenomena by using robust methods to explain the phenomena, on the one hand, and finding innovative solutions to the problems embedded therein, on the other. For example, why do people behave differently in groups than they would if they were to make decisions individually? What mental heuristics are at play in making decisions regarding personal life versus product purchase versus decisions made on behalf of others, especially those that are less endowed? How do you design policies to price service exposures that provide intrinsic value? How do you organise production of goods and services that evoke certain technological preferences and buyer attitudes? How do you design contracts that are compliance proof? And so on. In fact, it is a discipline where physical and social sciences come together just as they do in any product or service organisation that management purports to study. Management research requires a wide set of perspectives and skills – practical knowledge via engagement with the domain of study, theoretical understanding of various fields of enquiry, deep methodological abilities, and a deep desire to influence decision making through implementation of one's research. The work of the best researchers in management spans all the above areas. However, we also find researchers who have built expertise in one or few of these areas. For instance, there are some who develop new methods of decision making. There are others who may be designing strategies for organizations, implementing them and measuring their effectiveness. The discipline of management, globally, has evolved into its own disciplinary culture comprising academic and industry conferences, journals and publications, granting systems, etc. The Indian management education community, unfortunately, has not been able to organise itself intellectually and consequently remains restricted to teaching and training using knowledge derived from elsewhere rather than developing its own markers of universal appeal. Indian academic institutions have systematically ignored and often opposed building such scholarly cultures that are premised on curiosity and rigour of their own research and subjecting them to peer review globally.

India, today, is a researcher's paradise as its context is one of a traditional society transiting through rapid changes in technology, urbanisation, and social systems, and aspiring to become an economic leader in the twenty-first century. It faces several serious challenges of social development as well as numerous opportunities linked to a large population of young people. Linking management of undermanaged sectors to technology and cutting-edge scientific developments while creating opportunities for innovation in organisations and new enterprises is the real challenge for Indian management. Can the Indian management educational system lead the change with its ideas and thinking? Will its research matter to India?

The India of tomorrow will have young people whose experiences are going to be very different from their parents' generation. They will have to develop their own tools and methods for understanding issues in this new India. Their success will depend on how they traverse the bridge between the past and the future. Do we have an understanding of what it will take for them to change India and succeed? Large Indian organisations are scaling through jobless growth. Automation and digital technologies in industry and especially in the services sector (e.g. IT) are leading to changes in job content. It appears that the youth of tomorrow will experience many more jobs than ever before, will change their skillsets several times in their working lives, will work for smaller firms and for themselves, and will work increasingly with people of varying backgrounds and abilities. Do we know what will be the impact of these changes on work productivity, family life, working with others, and on concepts of employment and even nationality? Understanding tomorrow's India and the organisations of the future will require intense imagination, dedication, and research. Are Indian institutions up to that challenge? Do we have faculty and institutional systems to attract and prepare scholars who will lead thinking on such changes and translate their impact for the society to understand? At the same time, can Indian institutions generate research that will have local application but global appeal?

Students of management will have to understand more intensely the society in which their organisations operate and where people work. This would mean engaging intellectually, and not anecdotally, with its changing values, with its motivations, and with its aspirations. It would require creating a more diverse learning environment and situating management learning as well as institutions amid other disciplines that could help unravel these mysteries for our organisations and the people of the world. Why would a college of arts and sciences of a university not become a centre of managerial learning? Do the numerous standalone institutions like the IIMs and XLRIs and ISBs stand a chance of contributing to the future of India and the world with their inherent deficiency of not being a part of an interactive university with schools like humanities, social sciences, and the sciences from who management education draws its knowledge and wisdom? The nature of contributions of numerous management programmes in all parts of the country that do not have the wherewithal to even draw from such an ecosystem will remain constrained and limited.

The unfinished agenda of management education

Management education, today, struggles to find a firm ground of rigour and relevance, despite its spectacular growth and the phenomenal demand. As the challenges before industry change and as society's priorities transform, their requirements of educational institutions will change as well. How will the managerial learning ecosystem cope with these requirements? There remain several challenges before management education can truly find its place as a strong area of scholarship and application in India. These include the following:

- Absence of academic rigour at a large number of management institutions and fast growth in demand. Consequently, institutions have allowed management education to become light and often frivolous (e.g. institutions are providing etiquette training as part of the curriculum) and war stories passed off as education. The rigour has not improved over the years. Whenever a government and its agencies define a curriculum it gets reduced to being a dead package, while education is about life and learning survives because individuals experiment.
- Management education, as practised, has contributed to building stereotypes and in the process it is destroying the precious individuality of employees and consequently creativity in organisations. It has also focused too much on preparing generalists at the cost of building deep expertise. The myth that management is all about strategy and social networks is being shattered. Most organisations paid less attention to execution and processes, which also got reflected in mindsets of graduates coming out of management schools. In fact, the most exciting work (read: innovation) was being done by organisations and individuals who picked up management perspectives and skills and went back to innovate in their prior domains of experience (especially in a technical field). They were building on their deep technical knowledge of their prior areas of work by applying management expertise in those domains as opposed to starting afresh in a newer domain of understanding and complexity.
- Related to this issue is the narrow range of skills that companies pick up from management institutions. Most students have an engineering background. This made the thinking of companies very homogeneous and narrow (i.e. structured around numbers and not people) in terms of backgrounds and prior perspectives. Companies in India, post growth of management institutions, did not consciously bring in people with other backgrounds like economics, history, sociology, design, sciences, etc. into their organisations. Many elite management programmes also started to do the same. It may have led to narrowing of the space for innovative ideas that is driven by diversity of educational and social experiences.
- As programmes grew, so did the need to teach executives with practical knowledge. This added a new flavour to management education and a rich application of their learning and knowledge systems. There were too many people, both academics and executives, who

forgot in the process that education was about preparing people for life and not for the next job. Classrooms have turned into structured sessions for gossiping with war stories. The need is to balance practical exposure with research and new ideas. Good theory always makes for good practice.

- Management education places too much of a premium on analysis and less on action or generation of new ideas. Management educationists have always wondered: what may be analogous to a clinic-based learning approach of medicine and the codified learning environment of cases in law for the world of management education? We believe it simply requires construction of a new learning and practising environment within the context of educational programmes.

- Management education also does not focus adequately on understanding, building, and modifying one's own and their organisation's sources of emotions, trust, integrity, and courage. It is amazing how many students will decry learning of organisational behaviour in classrooms while coming back a decade later to claim that these were the most essential elements of education that they use now in their working lives. It talks either of the poor structuring of organisational behaviour classroom processes and the inputs therein, or the students' own poor socialisation with the world of business before coming into these programmes. The world of exploration of the self is either mechanical or is increasingly becoming spiritual, but much less rational. Recognising that emotions can be part of the rational self is less appreciated. As a result, management education as practised in our institutions has become a collection of ideas, theories, and ways of thinking where the integration and execution is left to the imagination of the student.

An MBA carries a variety of valuable skills that range from assimilation of ideas from several independent disciplines to problem-solving to thinking strategically to execution, with varying levels of expertise. But most important, it is built on the foundation of a core discipline at the undergraduate level. Unfortunately, the bachelor's degree in management (BBA) in India has not been able to build such a foundation on which a robust learning-based career can be built. This programme has become more vocational and less foundational in terms of deep grounding in a discipline:

- The admissions process has become very narrow and does not judge any sort of managerial proclivity. Its intense quantitative nature (due to its focus on number-driven analytics) precludes a large majority of students in the humanities and social sciences and even some sciences from looking towards management education as a possible option. Having said that, there is also an underlying flaw in the undergraduate education of many students as well that assumes that quantitative techniques, science, and technology are for others, and that they can build a career in the twenty-first century without building any appreciation of them.

- Hiring from elite schools by bigger and prestigious organisations is nothing short of a scandal: alumni hiring current students is perpetuating the myth of the tyranny of the connected class. This is also unhealthy in a society that is very diverse in endowments, and leads to loss of skills and value in corporations that are also trustees of public confidence and wealth.

- Management has to engage much more deeply with disciplines in the humanities, social sciences, and the sciences in preparing leaders of tomorrow. For instance, a student who wants to work in the telecom sector should be able to take courses in execution and telecom strategy at the business school, pricing and spectrum allocation from the school of economics, related regulation from the law school, spectrum design and communications and transmission technology from the engineering school, and social impact of technology from the school of policy. Such a person will then contribute tremendously to any telecom organisation. This does not happen in India today.

Quality of teaching needs to become more sensitive to the long-term impact of education and hence become more rigorous. The same is true of research as well. First, Indian institutions need to develop stronger capabilities and engagement with problems facing the nation in their research. Second, they need to become rigorous in their research methods and subject themselves to peer review globally. Third, more institutions need to engage with research to build a larger pool of researchers in the country and for teaching to remain relevant.

- Most management programmes focus on producing general managers – generalists who move around different kinds of organisations producing different kinds of products and services and performing different tasks. This model is under intense pressure. It also requires very high levels of resources that only a few institutions carry. Many others have failed to develop sector-specific programmes or programmes that cater to regional needs and development. Institutions with limited resources, which is where most of our institutions will lie, would be served well by remaining focused and building deep capabilities in a limited area rather than being diversified as most larger institutions like IIMs are.
- Management education needs to put more emphasis on training of academics, particularly in research methods and in key pedagogies to ensure that the classroom experience is not frivolous, as it has implications for how organisations will perform in times to come.

The decade to come will test, much more than any period in the past, the resolve and capabilities of institutions to generate new knowledge and translate this into useful applications. There is less patience with organisations of all kinds and they will have to experiment dramatically to deliver value to society at large. Technology and global trade regimes, on the one hand, will ensure that global innovations reach all corners of the earth while the multitude of regulatory regimes, on the other hand, will ensure that goods and services crossing borders are impeccable in their construction, safety, and value. New technologies like 3D printing, synthetic and computational biology, and high-speed transport, as well as autonomous, personalised energy systems, consumer insight, and neuropsychology for delivering targeted value are expected to dramatically change the industry structure as well as organisations of tomorrow. The big opportunities will lie at the intersection of design, management, and technology and through entrepreneurial ventures. This would require new experiments and new thinking. Whether Indian management institutions can lead thinking within the nation and the world through their intellectual energy is the real question. The answer will decide their relevance and reach in times to come.

References

Anubhai, P. (2011). *The IIMA Story: The DNA of an Institution*. New Delhi: Random House India.
Datar, S.M, Garvin, D.A., and Cullen, P.G. (2010). *Rethinking the MBA: Business Education at a Crossroads*. Boston: Harvard Business Press.
Government of India-MHRD. (2014). *Educational Statistics at a Glance*. New Delhi: GOI.
Sahoo, B.K., Singh, R., Mishra, B., and Sankaran, K. (2017). Research Productivity in Management Schools of India During 1968–2015: A Directional Benefit-of-Doubt Model Analysis. *Omega*, 66 (Part A): 118–139. http://dx.doi.org/10.1016/j.omega.2016.02.004.
Tripathy, D. and Jumani, J. (2013). *The Oxford History of Contemporary Indian History*. New Delhi: Oxford University Press.

Part IV
Universities and society

The advent of universities in India is a major facet of modernity and institutionalised education. Universities are crucial to the modern occupational structure and forms of knowledge that arose under colonial conditions in India. Although universities existed in India, we do not have precise knowledge about how they functioned, and even less about their relationship with society. In any case, a vast chronological break – with obvious implications for society – separates those ancient institutions from India's present-day universities. The latter were formally set up to serve the emerging colonial state apparatus and the limited social needs this apparatus recognised in the mid-nineteenth century. This section opens with Philip Altbach's chapter on the development of universities in India since that time. For a while, universities performed mainly as examining and degree-granting roles; teaching was added later, and research later still. Thus, knowledge generation as an aspect of the higher education system has a relatively short history in modern India. The question Altbach focuses on is why excellence in this role continues to elude India despite its growing importance in the global economy. This chapter also draws the reader's attention to the institutional diversity that prevails in higher education (parallels with school education, discussed in Part I, are obvious). The policy-related matters this chapter discusses need to be considered in conjunction with conceptual issues raised in the context of curriculum design and the pedagogic and examining practices discussed in Part II. A larger theoretical perspective on knowledge and its generation is required to appreciate why so few universities in India meet the standards of quality that are commonly applied for international comparison.

The other three chapters included in this section explore the social base of higher education in India. This, by itself, can be regarded as a factor of quality in the experience of learning provided by institutions of higher education. However, that is not the way the debate on quality in higher education is normally looked at. Customarily, issues of access are considered different from issues of quality. This kind of separation permits the discussion of inclusivity as a moral goal. Apparently, the higher education sector in India has remained largely bereft of reflection and research on the role that pedagogic issues such as the social composition of the classroom or the medium of interaction play in determining the quality of teaching and learning. The Indian university has remained remarkably unchanged as far as its role as an examining body is concerned. In the matter of language, too, English has maintained its dominance. What has changed is the composition of the clientele, and the two main reasons to which this change is related are expansion of school education and the policy of reservation for the Scheduled Castes, the Scheduled Tribes, and the Other Backward Classes. In terms of their presence in the classroom, universities and colleges have become more inclusive. To an extent, the curriculum and syllabi in certain areas have accommodated larger social concerns, but this kind of change is restricted to a handful of institutions.

This bigger picture of an institutional set-up helps us grasp both the nature of the problem that higher education faces in India and also enables us to assess more objectively the relevance of new remedies such as online or distance education and private universities. These remedies bypass the core problem that has to do with the social base of universities and the manner in which the extant narrow base keeps the pedagogic environment stagnant.

The chapters included in this part are aimed at assisting the reader to assess the size of the social base and the change it has undergone in the recent past. The chapter by Karuna Chanana focuses on the participation of women in higher education. She looks at both the presence of women and the areas of knowledge in which it occurs. The chapter underscores the practice of associating certain areas of knowledge with men and others with women. The chapter by Satish Deshpande examines university enrolment and performance from the perspective of social justice. More specifically, this chapter examines the provision of caste quotas as a means of pursuing the Constitutional goal of equality with social justice in higher education. The other chapter on this theme in this part discusses the experience of tribal groups in obtaining higher education. Here, Virginius Xaxa examines the status of higher education among the Scheduled Tribes of India. Xaxa locates the problem in the meagre expansion of the sector. Owing to limited expansion, higher education has become a site of intense competition. Data show that tribal groups continue to be a victim of deprivation of opportunities for knowledge and mobility that higher education is supposed to provide to all sections of society on an equitable basis. In as much as inclusivity is a factor of quality of educational experience at any level, these chapters demonstrate how large a constraint is placed upon the quality of higher education by the inequitable distribution of higher education among women, lower caste strata, and tribes. Inequitable distribution is also an indicator of the limited role that universities and colleges have been able to play in building a democratic social order.

13

Indian higher education

Twenty-first-century challenges[1]

Philip G. Altbach

The saga of Indian higher education since the 1960s is complex, variegated, and reflects the country's development over time. The country's education development has, for much of this period, lagged behind economic and social development. Like India itself, higher education realities are contradictory. India, in 2015, has the world's second-largest higher education system in terms of student numbers, having recently overtaken the United States in enrolments, with 20 million students enrolled in post-secondary education, attending more than 35,500 colleges and 574 universities. It is estimated that more than half of the world's post-secondary institutions are located in India – many of the colleges are uneconomically small. Approximately 20 per cent of the 18–22-year-old age cohort is in post-secondary education – with a goal of enrolling 25 per cent by 2017 and 32 per cent by 2022 – an extremely ambitious target (Rashtriya Uchchtar Shiksha Abhiyan 2013). Dropout rates are high, with many of those who enter the system failing to complete a degree. Quality is generally poor – although there are significant islands of excellence, the system overall is a sea of mediocrity – and none of India's universities score well on any of the international higher education rankings (Altbach 2006).

India, like many developing countries, has been swamped by massification – the rapid expansion of higher education enrolments that is the result of an unstoppable demand by growing segments of the population for access. India's challenges have been magnified by increased demand for access, combined with overall population growth. In no country has rapid expansion been accompanied by improvement in overall quality, and in this respect India is no different than many other countries (Carnoy *et al.* 2013).

India had several advantages at the time of Independence in 1947, but was unable to capitalise on them. English was the near-universal medium of higher education, giving India immediate links to the outside world, access to scientific information, and textbooks. Although fairly small, India had developed a fairly mature higher education system, with several reputable universities and specialised institutions at the top, and a respectable number of undergraduate colleges, a few of which were of international standard. While access was limited to a small urban elite and most higher education institutions were located in metropolitan areas, colleges and universities could be found throughout India.

Though the system grew fairly rapidly throughout most of the post-Independence period, population growth and an expansion of primary and secondary education meant that higher education could not keep up with demand. In line with global thinking concerning education and development, emphasis was placed on primary education and not on higher education. In most developing countries, overall quality declined as enrolments increased.

Despite considerable rhetoric in the past few years about India's higher education 'takeoff' and the link between higher education and recent economic growth, there is little evidence that economic success has had much effect on improvements in higher education. Indeed, it is argued that if higher education is not improved, India may lose the advantage of its 'demographic dividend' of a large population of young people who could, if well educated, spearhead continuing economic growth (Altbach and Jayaram 2010).

It is worth examining some of the broad trends that characterise Indian higher education. These are presented in no special order of importance. They are, however, linked and constitute a pattern of development over time.

A challenging history

Like much of the developing world, India experienced a long period of colonialism. British rule over much of the subcontinent lasted for several centuries – longer than the colonial experience of most other countries. British-style higher education dates back to 1823, when several colleges were founded – significantly by Indian initiatives rather than by the colonial rulers. Universities were established in Bombay, Calcutta, and Madras in 1858 – around the same time that higher education was expanded beyond Oxford and Cambridge in England (Kaur 2003). When compared to most developing countries, India has had a longer history of modern higher education. For example, higher education was largely absent from sub-Saharan Africa until the 1960s (Ashby 1966).

While the British were in general not avid supporters of higher education in India, they did not prevent its establishment. After a laissez-faire period, higher education was organised as part of the colonial policy, ensuring that the language of instruction was English and that the organisation and structure of academic institutions conformed to British patterns and policy. The British were more supportive of higher education in India than they were in their colonial possessions in Africa (Ashby 1966). The colonial authorities spent few resources on higher education, and the impetus for the modest expansion of higher education in India during colonial rule was from Indians. Indeed, there were efforts to keep enrolments small in order to prevent the emergence of a subversive intelligentsia or unemployed graduates. Both of these goals were, at least in part, failures, since educated Indians spearheaded the Independence movement. The British sought to ensure that the graduates of the colleges and universities were suited to serve the needs of the colonial administration, rather than the emerging Indian society and industry.

At the time of Independence, there were 19 universities and 695 colleges, with an overall enrolment of fewer than 270,000 students. By the standards of newly independent developing countries in the mid-twentieth century, India was well situated. It had a relatively comprehensive array of higher education institutions, although few were vocationally or scientifically oriented. The quality of this small system was relatively high. While serving only a tiny proportion of the age cohort – well under 1 per cent – India had the basic structure of a higher education establishment to build.

The challenge of coping with the demands for expansion, combined with political and other pressures on higher education, meant that it was not possible to take advantage of existing strengths and to build for both quantity and quality. For example, the basic organisational structure of the higher education system inherited from the British and designed for a tiny elite remains largely in place in 2015.

Language: a continuing dilemma

At the time of Independence, the language of instruction in higher education throughout India was almost exclusively English. While there are no accurate statistics for English literacy in India, it was quite unlikely that even 5 per cent of Indians were literate in English in 1950. Thus, the huge majority of Indians did not have access to higher education. There were fundamental disagreements among the founders of modern India about language policy. Mahatma Gandhi argued strongly for the use of Hindi as the national language – and the medium of instruction in higher education. India's first prime minister, Pt Jawaharlal Nehru, was sympathetic to the continued use of English. Many political leaders in the south and in some other parts of the country were opposed to Hindi and, thus, favoured English as a 'link language' and some emphasised the use of regional languages in education, while others favoured English. India's federal constitution gave authority over education largely to the states, which had considerable power to decide on language issues. These post-Independence realities resulted in a hodgepodge of policies in different parts of the country.

Some of the states in the 'Hindi belt' in north India stressed the use of Hindi, and the central government made some efforts to produce and translate textbooks into Hindi for use in undergraduate education. Almost all of the universities and specialised research institutions, most sponsored by the central government, continued to use English as the language of instruction and scientific work. The states varied considerably in language policy. Most southern states continued English as the main language for higher education. Some permitted the use of regional languages. States in other parts of India varied in their policies. A few used a combination of English and the regional language. In some cases, specific universities preferred to retain instruction in English despite the state policy. Thus, language policy and practice in higher education was, and remains, varied throughout the country.

Without any reliable statistics, it is certainly the case that the use of the English language has increased in Indian higher education, especially in the more prestigious universities and colleges and in the highly selective institutions – such as the Indian Institutes of Technology and the Indian Institutes of Management. Much of the private higher education sector functions in English as well. The research sector is entirely dominated by English, and most scholarly communication in journals and on the internet takes place in English. While the language debate in Indian higher education has not entirely ended, English has emerged as the key language in Indian higher education. Its role, always strong, has increased in importance as globalisation has affected the higher education sector in the twenty-first century.

The traditional role of English has given India significant advantages in global higher education. Professors and students can communicate easily with peers in other countries, and mobility is enhanced. Indian universities can more easily enrol international students. Indians may contribute directly to the global knowledge network (Altbach 2007). Yet there are some disadvantages as well. English is not the mother tongue of Indians, and it remains to some extent a foreign language. A large majority of Indians do not speak and are not literate in English – thus they are at a significant disadvantage in the higher education sector and unable to gain access to the social and economic mobility that English medium conveys in India. While there seems to be no accurate estimate of the proportion of Indians who speak English, 10 per cent seems to be a realistic number. This constitutes more than 100 million English speakers – more than the populations of the United Kingdom, Australia, New Zealand, and Canada combined – but still a modest percentage of Indians.

Indian universities in a globalised world

Indian higher education has interacted gingerly with the rest of the world. The higher education sector, as the economy in general until recently, has been largely protectionist. While many Indians have gone abroad for postgraduate study – and many have contributed significantly to technological and economic development in, for example, Silicon Valley in California as well as in India – Indian higher education has been largely closed to the rest of the world. Non-citizens cannot normally be hired as permanent members of academic staff, and branch campuses and other foreign academic transplants have not been allowed.

In the past decade there has been a lively debate in India concerning how Indian higher education should engage with the rest of the world. Kapil Sibal, the minister for human resource development from 2009 to 2012, proposed to open India's education market to the world and asked Parliament to approve legislation for this purpose. However, the legislation was repeatedly delayed, and thus India remains largely closed to foreign universities and other education providers. Even if the law is passed, the conditions for establishing branch campuses and other initiatives are sufficiently unfavourable for attracting foreign institutions – despite considerable interest overseas in the Indian education 'market'. However, many less-formal arrangements have been put in place – including a number of joint-degree programmes, franchised arrangements, partnerships, and others. Thus, the door is perhaps half-open.

Some have argued that India is better off developing higher education on its own. Others favour an open door, and the idea that the rigours of the market would have a positive impact on Indian higher education. Clearly, India needs good ideas – and insulating the system from international concepts and practices is not helpful.

The sea of mediocrity

Indian higher education can be characterised by a sea of mediocrity, in which some islands of excellence can be found. A large majority of Indian students attend the 574 universities and the 35,500 colleges affiliated to them. While a few of the universities – most notably those without affiliated colleges, such as Jawaharlal Nehru University in New Delhi, several other universities sponsored directly by the central government, and some colleges offer high quality teaching – most provide mediocre to poor quality instruction. Most of the 286 public universities that are managed by state governments, 111 private universities, and 129 'deemed' universities provide poor to middling quality education. The vast majority of colleges, particularly newer private 'unaided' colleges that receive little or no government funding, are of quite low quality. A small number of well-established colleges managed by state authorities, some of those established by Christian and other religious organisations, and a small number of others are quite good – but these are a small percentage of the total. As with much in India, there are exceptions to these generalisations. For example, several new non-profit private universities established by wealthy philanthropists, such as the Azim Premji University, the Ashoka University, and the Shiv Nadar University, show much promise.

Graduate unemployment in many fields, especially in art and science subjects, is a perennial problem in India. This situation, in part, is due to too many graduates for available jobs in these fields and in part due to the low quality of many degree holders. Even in fields such as management and engineering, where there is a demand from employers, graduates from many colleges and universities are considered deficient in quality and poorly trained for the positions available. Employers indicate that they must retrain many of those they do hire.

To some extent, a decline in quality at the bottom tier of Indian higher education is an inevitable result of massification and can be found worldwide. Students with poorer academic qualifications are able to gain access to higher education. In India, the complex system of the reservations policy for disenfranchised groups has exacerbated this problem – while at the same time providing opportunities that did not exist before. The existing modest admissions standards are relaxed for these groups, while little extra help is provided for students without adequate secondary school achievement, thus contributing to high dropout rates. The reservation system identifies specific historically disadvantaged groups, such as lower caste populations, tribal groups, and 'other backward castes', and reserves a specific proportion of admissions place – and faculty slots – which can be filled only by these groups. The percentage that is reserved is often close to half of the total. This system also applies to faculty hiring in most fields, and contributes to a shortage of qualified teachers, since in many cases an insufficient number of applicants from the required groups seek employment.

Expansion has also brought many new types of institutions onto the post-secondary education landscape – mostly at the bottom of the system. Many of the 'deemed universities' are institutions of modest to poor quality – although some of the older ones are well established. New private universities present a similarly mixed picture, with most of lesser quality. Thousands of 'unfunded' undergraduate colleges in engineering, information technology, and other fields have emerged in the past several decades and are affiliated with universities and thus able to offer degrees. Again, the overall quality of these colleges is often quite poor, and many are quasi-for-profit institutions.

The traditional universities and their affiliated colleges have proved resistant to reform. In terms of their structure, role, and governance, these institutions have been virtually unchanged for half a century, despite widespread recognition of their problems. Some reforms have been put in place, such as permitting some of the best colleges to become independent of the universities and offer their own degrees, but implementation has been limited. The entrenched bureaucracy of the affiliating system remains the core of higher education; and until it is significantly improved or modified, essential improvement in Indian higher education will not be possible.

Islands of excellence

Despite the immense problems of the Indian higher education system, a small sector of globally competitive, high-quality post-secondary institutions exists. It is significant that all of them are outside the established university structure. Planners were unwilling to entrust new and innovative ideas to the traditional universities. The best known of these institutions are the Indian Institutes of Technology and Indian Institutes of Management. There are many others. These include the Indian Institute of Science, Bengaluru, the Tata Institute of Fundamental Research, and the Tata Institute of Social Sciences (both in Mumbai), the Indian Statistical Institute in Kolkata, and others. Several of the national universities supported by the central government, including Jawaharlal Nehru University in New Delhi, are also held in high regard.

These institutions share several attributes. They are all public and funded by the central government. All are relatively small and are outside of the structure of the traditional universities. These institutions have a significant degree of autonomy that is somewhat unique in the Indian higher education system. They are all initiatives of the central government, with little or no involvement by the states. While none of these successful institutions are lavishly funded – indeed, by international standards they are all underfunded – they have achieved considerable success.

All of these successful institutions were able to attract professors committed to high standards of teaching and innovation – without paying exceptionally high salaries – showing that some Indian academics are attracted by new ideas and high standards. However, it is sometimes difficult to attract top talent – and some of the Indian Institutes of Technology have experienced difficulties in recruiting. These top institutions also attract the best students in India – and indeed they and some of the others may be the most selective institutions in the world, accepting only a tiny fraction of the students who take the national entrance examinations for these schools.

The failure of planning

Indian higher education has not failed to create a 'world-class' system because of a lack of ideas. At least half a dozen high-level commissions have issued intelligent reports over the past 60 years, starting perhaps with the University Education Commission (Radhakrishnan Report) in 1948, and including the National Knowledge Commission Report in 2007 and the Committee to Advise on Renovation and Rejuvenation of Higher Education (Yashpal Committee) in 2009. The most recent effort, the 2013 Rashtriya Uchchtar Shiksha Abhiyan (National Higher Education Mission), is the latest well-documented and thoughtful analysis of current realities and recommendations for the future. These reports have recommended many ideas for thoughtful reform, development, and improvement. Over time, elements of some of these reports have been partly implemented, but in no case at all have any been comprehensively applied. The Planning Commission's five-year plans generally paid little attention to higher education, although occasionally initiatives were outlined and funds provided. The current 12th Plan for the first time gives some comprehensive focus to higher education. The Modi government's reorganising of the Planning Commission and new priorities at the central government level make it unlikely that the 12th Plan's recommendations will be implemented – joining the many other thoughtful suggestions on the shelf.

Although most of the funding and supervision of higher education is in the hands of the states, there is little evidence of planning or innovation at the state level. In general, the states have simply tried to keep up with the demand for expansion of higher education. A few have made some effort. Kerala has attempted to think systematically about higher education development, and Gujarat has recently focused on higher education as part of the state's development strategy in the 'Vibrant Gujarat' project.

The University Grants Commission – responsible at the national level for funding, innovation, and planning of higher education under the control of the central government – has developed some small-scale programmes in curriculum, teaching, and other areas, but by and large has not played an active role in large-scale innovation. The current proposal to establish a National Commission of Higher Education and Research will bring together a number of central government initiatives and provide a central focus for planning, research, and innovation.

As a result of divided control – lack of coordination among the different agencies with responsibility for higher education at the central and state levels, inadequate authority for implementation of change, and inadequate funding – it is fair to say that higher education planning has not been successful, despite a range of good proposals over the years.

The necessity of systems

Massification requires a higher education establishment, with institutions serving different purposes and missions that are organised logically to cater to different clientele and meet various demands. The best organised examples, such as the renowned California public higher education system, articulate different kinds of institutions so that students can move from one type of college to another. In California's case, the public system has community colleges, four-year and master's degree universities, and research universities – such as the University of California, Berkeley – that offer doctorates. Students may enter one type of school and, if the quality of their academic work permits, can transfer up to a different type of institution. Systems of this type hold costs at appropriate levels, provide access, and ensure that the various societal needs are met. Government authorities control the missions and budgets of the institutions at the various levels – deterring 'mission creep' and ensuring that institutions stay focused on their established mission.

India has never developed a clearly articulated academic system, at neither the central nor state levels, although informal systems have evolved over time. India is a federal system, with much of the responsibility for higher education in the hands of states and some authority with the central government. India's 35 states have little in common and range from Uttar Pradesh, with a population of 200 million, to small states with just a few million. All of India's universities have a research mission; some are better able to engage in research than others. Few universities at the state level receive adequate budgets for research, and few have a research-oriented academic staff. The rapid expansion of undergraduate arts and sciences and also professional colleges has also taken place largely without planning. The specialised high-quality institutions such as the IITs are treated separately from the mainstream colleges and universities.

The recent centrally supported initiative to establish state higher education councils is a move towards more rational higher policy and planning at the state level. However, only a small number of states, such as Kerala, have fully implemented councils and have appropriate coordinating bodies in place.

India requires, at both the state and central levels, higher education systems that are rationally organised and differentiated in order to ensure that the increasingly diverse needs of higher education can be rationally met.

Politics

Indian higher education, much to its detriment, is infused with politics at all levels. Colleges are often established by political leaders as a patronage machine and a way of providing access and jobs to supporters. The location of universities is sometimes influenced by state or local politics. Even the central universities have occasionally been enmeshed in politics.

University and college elections are frequently politicised. National, regional, and local political machines are frequently engaged in campus politics. Student unions are often politicised. Academic decisions are determined more by political than academic considerations. Political intrigue and infighting may infuse campus life. In extreme cases, campus politics can turn violent, and disruption of normal academic life is not uncommon. More often than not, the politics is not ideological but rather regional or caste-based.

Universities and colleges, which employ considerable numbers of staff and offer access to a highly sought-after commodity – an educational credential – are valuable political engines. Academic institutions are often local power centres and are clearly seen as valuable sources of patronage.

As long as political calculations enter into decisions about the location of universities, the appointment of vice-chancellors and other academic leaders, approval for establishing new colleges and other institutions, and other aspects of higher education, India will be unable to fulfil its goals of quality, access, and the creation of a world-class higher education system.

A pattern of inadequate investment

Higher education has never been adequately funded. In 2011–12 India spent a modest 1.22 per cent of its gross domestic product on post-secondary education – a more modest investment than some other rapidly expanding economies and below European levels of expenditure. From the beginning, emphasis was placed on meeting the demands of mass access and expansion rather than building up a meaningful high-quality university sector, and even financial support for mass access has been inadequate.

The divided responsibility for supporting higher education by the states and the central government was an additional detriment, since coordination was difficult. In any case, most of the responsibility fell to the states, many of which were unable to provide the needed support – and in any case were more concerned with basic literacy and primary and secondary education rather than higher education. Indeed, for much of India's post-Independence history, the concern of policy-makers at all levels was for literacy and basic education, rather than higher education.

In the twenty-first century, with the beginning of the Indian economic transformation, higher education has received greater priority. The National Knowledge Commission's (2007) reports stressed the significance of the universities and encouraged both expansion of access and improvement in quality. Little has been done to implement the recommendations. Without adequate funding, higher education can neither expand appropriately nor improve in quality.

The fall and rise of the guru

At the heart of any academic institution is the professor. By international and particularly developing country standards, the Indian academic profession is relatively well-off. While most Indian academics have full-time appointments, service conditions are poor in most private institutions, especially the private colleges. Academics typically have job security, although a formal tenure system does not exist. Salaries, when compared with other countries according to purchasing power parity measures, fall into the upper-middle ranks of a 2012 study of academic salaries in 28 countries (Altbach *et al.* 2012). While Indian academics will not become rich with their salaries, they can generally live in a middle-class style, at least outside of the major metropolitan centres. This is in sharp contrast to many other countries, including China, where academic salaries must be supplemented by additional income.

Yet, the academic profession faces some serious problems (Jayaram 2003). The differences in status, working conditions, and salaries are significant between the large majority of the academic professionals who teach in undergraduate colleges and the small minority who hold appointments in university departments and teach postgraduate students. Yet, even college teachers can in general live in a middle-class style, based on their academic salaries, due in large part to significant salary increases in the past few years.

The academic profession is characterised by high levels of bureaucracy and is bound by civil service regulations. Most colleges are hierarchical in structure and provide few opportunities for participation in college governance or decision making. College teachers, particularly, possess little autonomy and only modest control over what they teach, and teaching loads tend to be fairly high. It has been observed that college teachers have only a little more autonomy than high-school teachers (Altbach 1979). For the large majority of colleges that are affiliated to universities, control over many aspects of teaching, curriculum, and examinations is regulated by the university.

The small minority of academics with appointments in university departments is expected to produce research: they have modest teaching responsibilities and much greater autonomy. Indeed, almost all of the published research by Indian academics is produced by university-based academics and not by college teachers. Salaries are also more favourable. University staff also supervise postgraduate students and, thus, play a key role in educating the next generation of the academic profession. Many university departments work closely with the colleges to organise curricula, set and administer examinations, and carry out other responsibilities of the affiliating system.

Indian academics are seldom evaluated for their work. Their jobs depend mainly on longevity and rank. Few, if any, efforts evaluate productivity in teaching or research, and those whose performance is seen as marginal are allowed to continue. Salaries are also allocated by the length and rank of service for the most part, and there is no way of rewarding good performance or punishing inadequate work. Where top quality is the norm, such as in the Indian Institutes of Technology, it is more the culture and tradition of the institution than any reward system that is responsible.

The Indian academic profession is in a somewhat paradoxical situation (Patel 2012). Compared to academics in other developing countries, Indian post-secondary teachers are not badly off – either in terms of salary or working conditions. Yet, for the most part, the organisation of the higher education system does not encourage academics to do their best work. Further, well-qualified academics are in short supply. The Indian Institutes of Technology, for example, report that they are understaffed by approximately 25 per cent – indicating that the 'best and brightest' are not attracted to the academic profession.

An increasingly dominant private sector

India's higher education system has always been a curious, and perhaps internationally unique, combination of public and private institutions. Almost from the beginning, most undergraduate colleges were established by private interests and managed by private agencies such as philanthropic societies, religious groups, or others. Most of these private colleges received government funds and thus were 'aided' institutions. The universities were all public institutions, for the most part established by the states.

This situation has changed dramatically in recent years (Agarwal 2009). Most of the private colleges established in the past several decades are 'unaided' and thus fully responsible for their own funding, through tuition charges or other private sources of funds. Where tuition fees are capped, some institutions levy other capitation (a kind of required donation) fees and other charges. Similarly, many of the 'deemed' – this term refers to an arrangement for government recognition of some institutions as universities outside of the normal pattern – universities are also private institutions, receiving no government funds. Some of the unaided colleges and universities seem to be 'for profit', although management and governance is often not very transparent. Most, although not all, are in the lower ranks of the academic hierarchy. The unaided private colleges are affiliated to a university in their region; and it is increasingly difficult for the universities to effectively supervise the large numbers of colleges, particularly when the financial aspects of the institutions are not obvious.

As in many countries, massification has contributed to the rise of the private sector in higher education. The state has been unwilling or unable to provide funding for mass access, and the private sector has stepped into the void. Public control over the direction of the new private sector has often been lost, and quality has suffered as well. The Indian case is particularly complex, since the public sector universities that provide affiliation to the new unaided private colleges are directly involved in legitimising and supervising this new sector.

A new trend in private higher education is emerging as well. In the past several decades, a small number of civic-minded philanthropists have begun to invest in higher education, several of them creating non-profit universities with high standards and a social mission. The Azim Premji University, for example, focuses on the education system and is attempting to improve teacher education and research on education. These new institutions – if sustained, allowed sufficient autonomy, and endowed with innovative ideas as well as funds – may help to create world-class universities in India.

What has India done right?

If one were searching for international 'best practices' or 'top ideas' in higher education, there is little if anything from India that would spring to mind. As this chapter points out, India's contemporary higher education reality does not compare favourably with the most successful systems. When compared with two other BRIC nations, Brazil and China, India lags behind on most measures of higher education achievement.

At the same time, India has made significant progress in the context of post-Independence challenges. India's policy-makers stressed literacy and primary and secondary education in the first half-century of Independence and made significant progress in these areas, particularly taking into account continuing population growth. While post-secondary education did not receive the support it required, expansion was steady, and access has been steadily widened. Students from rural areas, disadvantaged groups, and especially young people from Dalit (formerly untouchable) communities have all gained greater access to higher education.

While the quality of Indian higher education has, overall, probably declined over the past half-century, it has not collapsed. The rigidities of the affiliating system and the bureaucratic arrangements have no doubt prevented the segment of the system from improving, but at the same time these systems have ensured stability in the context of continuing stress.

India has produced remarkable talent in the past half-century. The problem is that much of this talent left the country and is highly successful overseas. The statistics concerning graduates from the Indian Institutes of Technology are remarkable: a very high proportion of each graduating class leaves India and achieves remarkable accomplishments overseas. While a small number of graduates return to India, a somewhat larger group, based overseas, works with Indian colleagues and companies. Yet, it is fair to say that the 'brain drain' is still alive in the twenty-first century, although it is now combined with 'brain exchange' (Saxenian 2006).

A small but visible and impressive group of post-secondary institutions has flourished in the otherwise inhospitable soil of Indian higher education. Indian Institutes of Technology, Indian Institutes of Management, and a group of specialised teaching and research universities were built around the edges of the established academic system. Further, a small number among the thousands of colleges affiliated to India's universities have achieved high levels of excellence in undergraduate teaching. These examples clearly show that it is possible to build world-class higher education in India, if the conditions for their development are right.

There is no shortage of ideas for improving higher education in India. Various reports and commissions have pointed to a variety of ways forward. Small-scale experiments and innovative institutions have also proved successful. If these ideas and experiences could be used as templates for improvement, India may be able to move forward.

The challenges ahead

Given the realities of contemporary Indian higher education, it is not possible to be optimistic about a breakthrough in quality. It seems quite unlikely that any of India's existing universities will soon become world-class. Even if the Indian government identifies a dozen or so existing institutions for massive investment and upgrading, significant reforms in management, governance, and other areas would be required. It might be more successful to create entirely new institutions, without the constraints of existing universities. The establishment of the Indian Institutes of Technology shows that this can be successful, although in that case it was on a rather small scale. However, India does have the significant advantage of a diaspora that might be lured back for a worthy and realistic cause.

Due to the enormity of the challenges, the private sector will necessarily be a part of India's higher education future. But, so far, harnessing the private sector for the public good has been problematic. Yet, elements of solutions exist. Many of the traditional private non-profit colleges provide excellent undergraduate education, as do some private postgraduate professional colleges. A few of the new non-profit universities seem quite committed to their educational mission.

The greatest challenge, of course, is continued expansion of the system to provide access. In 2012, India enrolled approximately 20 per cent of the relevant age cohort – well under China's 26 per cent and below the other BRIC countries. Thus, India will need to devote resources and attention to continued expansion of post-secondary education. The National Knowledge Commission noted that 1,500 more universities will be needed. It has been estimated that China and India will account for more than half of the world's enrolment growth by 2050.

At the same time, India's increasingly sophisticated economy will need some colleges and universities of world-class standing – institutions that can compete with the best in the world – if manpower needs for the future are to be fulfilled. If India is to take advantage of its 'demographic dividend' and provide appropriate access and equity, the traditional universities and the thousands of colleges affiliated to them must be improved and reformed – this perhaps is the greatest challenge facing Indian higher education.

Note

1 An earlier version of this chapter entitled 'A World-Class Country without World-Class Higher Education: India's 21st Century Dilemma' appeared in Pawan Agarwal (ed.), *A Half-Century of Indian Higher Education* (New Delhi: Sage, 2012), pp. 78–83.

References

Agarwal, Pawan. 2009. *Indian Higher Education: Envisioning the Future*. New Delhi: Sage.

Altbach, Philip G. 1979. The Distorted Guru: The College Teacher in Bombay. In Suma Chitnis and Philip Altbach, eds, *The Indian Academic Profession*: 5–44. Delhi: Macmillan.

Altbach, Philip G. 2006. Tiny at the Top, *Wilson Quarterly* (Autumn, 2006): 49–51.

Altbach, Philip G. 2007. 'The Imperial Tongue: English as the Dominating Academic Language'. 2007. *The Economic and Political Weekly*. 42: 3608–3611.

Altbach, Philip G. and N. Jayaram. 2010. 'Can India Garner the Demographic Dividend?' *The Hindu*, 8 December.

Altbach, Philip G., Liz Reisberg, Maria Yudkevich, Gregory Androushchak, and Iván F. Pacheco, eds. 2012. *Paying the Professoriate: A Global Comparison of Compensation and Contracts*. New York: Routledge.

Ashby, Eric. 1966. *Universities: British, Indian, African: A Study in the Ecology of Higher Education*. Cambridge, MA: Harvard University Press.

Carnoy, Martin, Prashant Loyalka, Maria Dobryakova, Rafiq Dossani, Isak Froumin, Katherine Kuhns, Jandhyala B.G. Tilak, and Rong Wang. 2013. *University Expansion in a Changing Global Economy: Triumph of the BRICS?* Stanford, CA: Stanford University Press.

Jayaram, N. 2003. The Fall of the Guru: The Decline of the Academic Profession in India. In Philip Altbach, ed., *The Decline of the Guru: The Academic Profession in the Third World*: 199–230. New York: Palgrave.

Kaur, Kuldip. 2003. *Higher Education in India: 1781–2003*. New Delhi: University Grants Commission.

National Knowledge Commission. 2007. *Report to the Nation*. New Delhi: National Knowledge Commission.

Patel, Pravin J. 2012. Academic Underperformance of Indian Universities, Incompatible Academic Culture, and the Societal Context. *Social Change* 42: 9–29.

Rashtriya Uchchtar Shiksha Abhiyan (National Higher Education Mission). 2013. New Delhi: Ministry of Human Resource Development.

Saxenian, AnnaLee. 2006. *The New Argonauts: Regional Advantage in a Global Economy*. Cambridge, MA: Harvard University Press.

14

Gendered access and participation
Unequal subject choices in Indian higher education

Karuna Chanana[1]

Globalisation, privatisation, and higher education

What is central to globalisation is that the world has become increasingly interdependent and ever closer. Further, the direct nexus between the industry, corporate world, and higher education has brought a transformation in the skills needed for jobs. The most salient development is the rise of the for-profit private sector in higher education, which offers academic programmes and subjects in response to market demand. This explains the rise of private universities and colleges providing self-funded/self-financing education around the world and in India.

Simultaneously, the government or public universities are also increasingly expected to be financially self-sufficient, thereby forcing them to cut their costs and to think of ways and means to raise funds. The 'social compact' (Brennan and Naidoo 2006: 223) between the state and society to provide for education for all (Slaughter and Leslie 1997) has broken down. Slaughter and Leslie term this development as 'academic capitalism' (1997: 8), in which one of the easiest options is to ask students to finance their own education, giving rise to the phenomenon of self-funded education. Additionally, banks provide loans to students. And institutions introduce academic subjects with high market demand. This is a critical development in the nexus between the market demand for higher education and the proliferation of specific masculine subjects, namely, science, technology, engineering, and mathematics (STEM), management, etc., which have gendered outcomes.

While globalisation has increased opportunities and benefits, it also raises serious concerns about cultural identity, social justice, and equity. The higher education system has suffered a precipitous decline in state support, and the self-funded academic programmes have given rise to debt-ridden graduates and contingent faculty. How can women cope with these developments in a society where parents, by and large, are reluctant to invest in the education, especially higher education, of their daughters?

This point is discussed here by looking at the participation of women vis-à-vis their subject choices. This is done within a broader framework flowing from the questions: why do women in comparison to men choose different subjects and specialisations? Does higher education reinforce the difference or gender inequality in subject choices?

Gender and subject choice

This section looks at the reasons for the predominance of women students in arts and humanities and of men in physical sciences, engineering, and technology. In order to understand this phenomena, one has to understand the ideas of masculinity and femininity vis-à-vis their social construction. It is argued that students make the selection of subjects on the basis of qualities that these subjects are perceived to hold which, in turn, are related to the perceptions about masculinity and femininity (Thomas 1990).

Feminist educational researchers have written about the segregation of girls into arts and humanities and boys into science in schools. They argue that gendered socialisation,[2] which is related to traditional role ideology, impacts the subject choices of girls and their future roles. In fact, the binary opposition of masculinity and femininity is communicated at an early age to girls and boys through socialisation in the family and later on in educational institutions. In other words, similar ideologies underlie the socialisation processes at home and at school and its classroom processes, structure, and organisation (Chanana 2006: 269). The patriarchal imprint on the subject divide and choices, therefore, has received much attention (Acker 1994; Gautam 2015; Thomas 1990).

So far as the subject choices and resultant gendered segregation are concerned, it begins in school, especially at the secondary level. As well as gendered subject choices in school, this phenomenon in higher education has also received the attention of scholars (Acker 1994; Becher 1981; Harding 1986; Hudson 1972; Keller 1983; Thomas 1990). They went further and argued that the clustering of women in specific subjects narrows their occupational choices and leads to their occupational segregation (Deem 1978; Sharpe 1976; Wolpe 1978). Therefore, the subjects, when they are perceived as feminine and masculine, are social constructions in as much as masculinity and femininity are. According to Becher (1981), 'academic subjects are not neutral, they are cultures, each with its own way of perceiving and interpreting the world' (quoted in Thomas 1990: 7).

Harding (1986) says that the subject choices have to be understood in relation to women's place in society. Thomas (1990) goes further and argues that it is a reflection of the balance of power in society. Millett (1983) extends the argument further by saying that this assumption perpetuates male dominance in science. 'To both scientists and their public, scientific thought is male thought, in ways that painting and writing – also performed largely by men – never have been' (Keller 1983: 188).

According to Snow (1961), practitioners of science and of arts inhabit two distinct cultures. Arts and science are more than subject groupings, there are meanings attached to them (quoted in Thomas 1990: 24). More recently it is being argued that the concept of science and arts is a social construction. Further, subject specialisation reflects 'differences from' rather than 'communality with' (Thomas 1990: 24). Becher (1981) also looks at 'cultures' of various disciplines and talks of cultures across disciplines and also within disciplines, e.g. applied and theoretical physics, academic and practitioner lawyers (quoted in Thomas 1990: 24).

The *UNESCO World Atlas of Gender Equality in Education* 2012 underscores the point that 'it is essential to contextualise and ensure a nuanced understanding' of the phenomenon (2012: 77 quoted in David 2014: 31). It goes on to look at the significant differences in the fields of subjects selected by women and men.

Masculine/male and feminine/female subjects?

One of the major concerns in the context of subject choice and gender has been the low representation of girls and women in STEM. Research has been conducted abroad to answer the question: why are there fewer women in STEM?

Karuna Chanana

To answer this question, Kim Thomas looks at the relationship between subject and gender, between academic constructions of arts and science, and students' own sense of and perceptions about masculinity and femininity. According to her, masculinity/femininity and arts/science are both socially constructed oppositions. They make sense in relation to each other. Additionally, evaluation is inherent in this dual construction so that one is rated higher than the other. Further, gender has a cultural meaning because it is based on the differences between women and men. Moreover,

> the question of subject choice is not a neutral one and that individual school subjects can be seen to embody certain kinds of values. Further, the very notion that scholarship can be divided into two completely distinct areas, known as arts and science, in itself implies a value judgment. To choose to study arts rather than science is to make a statement about the values one considers important.
>
> *(Thomas 1990: 24)*

She observes that although education is expected to be the site for promoting equality, it also perpetuates inequality of opportunity (Thomas 1990: 2).

In her book she takes physics as an example of science and English as representing arts, and looks at the two cultures of these subjects. Throughout, her emphasis is on the social construction of the differences imputed to the subjects and perceived by the students who make the choices. She refers to the

> contrast, both implicit and explicit, that is made between the activity of studying science and the activity of studying the humanities. We discover that the contrast is based upon a particular set of values which science is believed to embody, and which is apparently lacking in humanities ... in describing physics, for example, as a particular kind of subject, students are also saying something about themselves, as people: the qualities ... which are central to their self-image.
>
> *(Thomas 1990: 38)*

She adds that the ideas about subjects and about gender, to a great extent, mutually reinforce each other (1990: 172). Further, students also perceive physics and physical science as objective and value-free, while English is subjective and uncertain (pp. 172–173). She argues further that 'these perceptions far from being simple or accidental, are intimately related to issues of authority and control, and the need to concentrate power in the hands of certain groups of people' (1990: 36).

Thomas goes on to argue that higher education does not actively discriminate against women, but by accepting certain beliefs and values about subjects and their appropriateness for women and men, 'it makes it difficult for women to succeed ... as a liberal social institution, women may be allowed to enter in good numbers in higher education yet by allowing gender divisions to be maintained it promotes "illusory liberalism"' (Thomas 1990: 179).

According to a recent study by Leslie *et al.*, certain qualities perceived to be innate in men, such as intellectual brilliance, and in women, such as hard work, are also ensuring that women do not pursue the professions of scientists and engineers. The practitioners believe that these professions require brilliance, which men have, rather than sheer hard work, which women are good at. Thus, the teachers reinforce this perception that these subjects require raw, innate talent and women are stereotyped as not having that quality, and so remain underrepresented in STEM subjects. In order to understand the gender imbalance in STEM subjects, a nationwide survey of 1,800 graduate students and university teachers from across 30 academic subjects was undertaken in the USA. It was found that a misconceived idea of brilliance is preventing women from taking subjects like physics, engineering, and mathematics. Instead, they take softer subjects such as humanities, languages, and social sciences. According to the authors, there is no evidence that women and men are intellectually different. The underrepresentation of women is due not to actual differences in intellectual ability but mainly to the perceived differences between women and men, termed by the authors as the 'field-specific ability beliefs hypothesis' (Leslie *et al.* 2015: 262).

The American Association of University Women (AAUW n.d.) has also been taking an interest in the problem of girls' underrepresentation in STEM subjects. Girls grow up thinking and believing they do not belong in science, engineering, mathematics, and technology. According to the AAUW, girls lose interest in the so-called male subjects by the seventh grade and few plan to pursue STEM subjects in college. In the *Huffington Post*, Robbie Couch (2015) writes about a Microsoft video ad which shows teenage girls who are good at science but who also believe that it 'is a boys' thing'. As a result, although seven out of ten are interested in pursuing STEM subjects, only two end up pursuing it. Couch also mentions another video ad by Verizon which focused on societal expectations that girls need not pursue science but be pretty. The ad goes on to say that it is time to tell girls that they are 'pretty brilliant'.

Penner (2015) addresses the question of underrepresentation of women in STEM fields or subjects and specialisations. He argues that one-size-fits-all does not work even though it is true that women are generally underrepresented in STEM subjects. For example, 'gender representation varies considerably both within STEM and within non-STEM fields'. He gives statistics from the paper of Leslie *et al.* to substantiate his point. 'As noted by Leslie *et al.*, in 2011 women received 54 per cent of US Ph.Ds in molecular biology, compared to 18 per cent in physics, 72 per cent in psychology, and 31 per cent in philosophy.' He explains this difference through Leslie's argument that there is a correlation between the perceived ability required of a field or subject and the representation of women and men in it. Therefore, while science is generally perceived as a 'male subject', some specialisations such as molecular biology are not. This is also true for some subfields within the arts, humanities, and social sciences. Therefore, physics and philosophy are perceived to require innate ability associated with boys and men, while effort, associated with girls and women, is considered important for success in molecular biology and psychology (Penner 2015).

Moreover, those girls and boys who do not choose stereotypical subjects have to face unequal treatment and discrimination because they are atypical (European Students' Union 2008). Those who do will be in a minority and may also find the classroom environment hostile. They will also enter a workforce which will not be friendly. 'Stereotypes, gender bias, and the climate of academic departments and workplaces continue to block women's participation and progress' (AAUW n.d.).

Do schools make a difference in the subject choices?

The segregation of boys and girls by subject starts at the school level (Deem 1978; Sharpe 1976; Thomas 1990) and continues in colleges and universities. It is not related to the achievement or performance of girls because they are doing well in school board examinations.

The type of schools make a difference. For example, girls who are enrolled in single-sex schools 'are more engaged and exude more competence and combativeness' (IFUW 2014, personal communication). In these schools, girls do better even in leadership roles because there is no male presence. In single-sex schools, girls are not discouraged from taking up one or the other subject, provided all are taught. This is discussed below.

There is also a difference between government or state and private schools which demonstrates that girls in state coeducational schools are much less likely than boys to study physics. This disparity is less visible in private schools. Of course, the students in these schools come from better-off homes wherein they may receive support to take unconventional subjects. Nonetheless, some state schools also bucked the trend. For example, the Institute of Physics, UK, undertook a statistical study to explore the links between gender and subject choice in schools (2013). The study was based on the National Pupil Database to look at the progression of students to a number of gendered A-level subjects from coeducational schools. It found that nearly half of core educational schools (49 per cent) that are state-funded are not encouraging girls to go for A-level physics, thereby making the gender imbalance worse. Only a small number (19 per cent) send relatively more girls to A-level physics. Therefore, there is a smaller gender imbalance in progression to other subjects in these schools. It concludes that the whole school environment is critical to the progression of girls to A-level physics.

Commenting on the report of the Institute of Physics, Donald (2013) says that the state schools 'not only don't do enough to counter prevailing gender stereotypes' but also reinforce the existing and prevalent ones, thereby narrowing the children's choice of subjects. Donald says that sexism is prevalent in the matter of subject choice in schools because they fail to 'encourage these in a gender-neutral way'. While boys are less likely to take stereotypically 'girls' subjects such as psychology and English, at A-level girls avoid physics or economics, stereotypically identified as 'for boys'. This is not good news. This is expected when teachers believe that 'boys can't do English' and 'may be girls don't like Physics'. So long as these are the prevalent attitudes of teachers and headteachers, gender stereotyping in subject choices will continue and girls will remain a majority in the English and boys in the physics classes (Donald 2013).

The same report also demonstrates that there are schools that are different and buck the trend. The state schools were compared with the non-state-maintained independent schools. There were 343 schools and these were equally divided into three groups: those that reinforced gender stereotyping, those that were neutral, and those that went against the trend (Donald 2013).

Quoting an earlier report, 'It's Different for Girls' of the Institute of Physics', Donald (2013) says that it 'demonstrated that essentially half of state coeducational schools did not see a single girl progress to A-level physics. By contrast, the likelihood of girls progressing from single sex schools were two-and-a-half times greater.' This difference in coeducational and single-sex schools shows that school ethos and teacher attitudes and expectations matter. It is not just a matter of girls or boys not liking a particular subject. Schools have a critical role to play in breaking down gender stereotypes and helping girls and boys achieve their full potential by making non-stereotypical choices. Donald concludes by saying that 'we should be able to construct school learning environments whereby teachers do not give out messages, subliminal or otherwise, that there are subjects that aren't for girls, or equally that aren't for boys.'

In India, science is a mandatory subject up to Class X since the 1986 New Education Policy made it compulsory for all students, including girls. Some schools, however, defy the national policy by not teaching science in Class XI and XII in single-sex schools for girls. This way the girls are denied access to science, presuming that it is not for them or that they would not want to study it. A recent study undertaken by the MacArthur Foundation in Rajasthan found very few government girls' schools or single-sex schools for girls, and they did not offer science and mathematics education at the senior secondary or +2 stage. Thus, the biggest problem here is access. First, because there are very few single-sex schools for girls. Second, because most coeducational schools teaching science are located in urban and peri-urban areas. Parents are reluctant to send their daughters to these. Similarly, Muslim girls were not sent to schools located beyond the boundaries of their Muslim neighbourhood. Therefore, the location of the school limits not only social access of girls to schooling, but also constrains their subject choices. Additionally, senior secondary schools that teach maths and science, although coeducational, are perceived as 'boys' schools' by parents and hence undesirable for their daughters. Thus, the parental perceptions deriving from socio-cultural traditions such as having to get married so they need not study maths and science denies girls access to science. Further, maths and science education may require extra financial input because of private tuition and laboratory expenses (Mukul 2015: 16).

Thus, researchers underline the fact that schools are critical in determining subject choices and that one needs to look at what happens to girls' choices therein because it has a long-term impact on their subject choices in college and university, and the job opportunities thereafter.

Why gender differences in subject choices?

Several factors can explain the gender differences in subject choices.

Most of the time the choice of subjects is determined by outdated gender stereotypes. Thus, traditional gender role ideology leads to gender inequalities in terms of subject preferences.

Socialisation at home and its link with stereotyped feminine social roles; peer group, the school, mass media, and consumerism; parental expectations from daughters' education; daughters' aspirations following from their socialisation – all these factors make for a complex situation.

Following from the above are the perceptions about subjects being masculine or feminine. Also there is the corresponding beliefs that there are gender differences in ability, and hence the inability of girls to pursue certain subjects such as mathematics and physics. These are social constructions.

The type of school also matters: whether it is state-maintained/government-run or private; and whether it is coeducational or single-sex.

Additionally, what matters is the school ethos consisting of classroom processes and teaching styles, the expectations of teachers and the headteacher, which encourage girls to take up arts and humanities while discouraging them from taking up mathematics and physics.

Equity and access: the contemporary situation

Social transformation or change through education presumes some fundamental changes in the political, social, and economic institutions of the society, with a positive impact on the relationships between social groups, genders, classes, or strata, and the distribution of wealth, power, and status. However, doubts have been expressed by leading scholars in the field of education. Brown et al. (2011: 3) say that 'the changing economic world evokes at once a sense of admiration and foreboding'. 'Clearly, globalisation has not made, and will not make, the world homogeneous' (McDonnelll 2008: 146). Bowles and Gintis express misgivings and scepticism about the impact of globalisation and the equation of knowledge as a commodity when they say: 'Today, no less than during the stormy days when Schooling in Capitalist America was written, schools express the conflicts and limitations, as well as the hopes of a heterogeneous and unequal society' (2002: 15).

According to McKinnon and Brooks (2001), the social movements that represent civil society have been questioning the dominance of technology in higher education. They also question the formulation of research agendas around the new technologies and at the marginalisation of social issues and the social policy research areas in which the disadvantaged groups, the marginalised, the minorities, and women academic staff and students, are generally dispro-portionately located.

Globalisation is also accompanied by an increased focus on techno sciences that have social and equity implications because the disadvantaged groups, the marginalised, the minorities, and women are less likely to be involved in those areas which are frontrunners in the new economy and the market; they are also likely to be at the lower levels; they may also be unable to adjust to the time-space compression that IT demands or fosters (Harvey 1993).

Moreover, the issue of compatibility between managerialism and equity (Sawer 1989; Yeatman 1990) has also been debated. It is argued that contemporary changes have an impact on pursuing equity issues within the universities because 'a commitment to equity and a com-mitment to cost-cutting' (Bacchi 2001: 120) may not go hand-in-hand. This situation is again a reminder that universities have always contained many contradictions that impact women (Brennan and Naidoo 2006: 226).

These contradictions can also be viewed as multiple roles which resist as well as draw on global and national forces that simultaneously push for change and also play a reproductive role. An important point is that at the systemic level, differentiation among higher education institutions has become common and is reflected in their academic programmes. For example, there are academic and vocational programmes, applied and market-driven professional subjects, and those in human-ities, social sciences, and pure sciences. Therefore, institutional and subject differentiation is hap-pening along with the diversification of the students in terms of their social composition. These two processes of institutional differentiation and diversification of students, 'allows higher educa-tion in the context of change to perform contradictory social functions, namely, helping maintain the status and position of social elites while providing some opportunities for social mobility' (Brennan and Naidoo 2006: 229). This is reminiscent of what was said long ago by Bourdieu (1977) when he expostulated the main contribution of education to the systemic reproduction with very limited contribution to change. In this context, let us look at the subject choices of Indian women to see whether they reflect the contradictory social functions of education.

Indian higher education system

In the Indian higher education system, most of the expansion since the early 1990s in the number of institutions and in professional subjects or the male-dominated subjects such as engi-neering, technology, ICT, management, etc., has been in the private sector. This development is also linked to the self-financing/self-funded subjects which are primarily market-driven pro-fessional ones and are offered mainly in private and public institutions. All subjects in private institutions are much more expensive than those in public HEIs. But both can deny access to students, especially, those from lower and middle strata due to high costs.

Additionally, market demand has impacted the stratification of disciplines or subjects, leading to the devaluation of arts, humanities, and social sciences. Traditionally, underprivileged stu-dents and women have entered arts, humanities, and social sciences, which is a continuing trend. How are the new developments in the market, its direct impact on the curriculum and higher tuition fees impacting the subject choices of women students?

Another development is the privatisation of public universities that have introduced market-oriented subjects on a self-funded basis in addition to those regulated by the government which are not expensive. It raises the question: which parents are able and willing to spend more on the education of their daughters in order to access the much-in-demand self-funded subjects? In the absence of a database, it is not possible to answer this but it deserves to be pursued through research.

In 2011–12 there were 624 universities of all kinds, out of which 195 were private while eight were exclusively for women. Out of 35,852 colleges, more than 71 per cent were private, mostly unaided (13,515) colleges, as per the report of the All India Survey of Higher Education (AISHE) (Government of India 2014: T9, table 5). However, private colleges enrol only 62 per cent of students. Simultaneously, the tuition fees are also increasing in the private as well as the state sector in the name of self-funded academic programmes and subjects. The women students have to compete for a few relatively inexpensive seats in a state-run system. Or their parents should be ready to shell out the high cost of private higher education. AISHE mentions that the enrolment of women students is low in private universities, which is anticipated to be due to high tuition fees (Government of India 2014: 36). There is no need to emphasise that high direct cost is a barrier to access, especially for women.

Women in higher education in India

Let us look at the access and participation of women in higher education in India. While access here means enrolment, participation refers to what happens after the students enter higher educational institutions. Do they transit to higher levels, i.e. from undergraduate to postgraduate level and to research? Which subjects and specialisations do they choose? There is a positive development so far as access is concerned since the numbers have increased generally. In this expansion, women have also gained. But then how do they fare when looked at separately and at the disaggregated level?

It is pertinent to mention that the private unaided colleges are self-funded and are not directly subsidised by the state government, while the private aided colleges receive substantial support and subsidy from the state government. Therefore, the individual cost of education in the latter colleges is as much as in the government colleges, while the private unaided colleges, referred to here as private colleges, are very expensive. This has gendered implications.

According to AISHE, in 2011–12, the total enrolment excluding the open universities was 29.2 million (Government of India 2014: 4), of which women formed 45 per cent (13 million). In addition, distance enrolment was 11.7 per cent of the total enrolment, of which 43.7 per cent were women (Government of India 2014: 7). The gross enrolment ratio (GER) for the 18–23 age group was very low at 20.8 per cent for all students: 22.1 per cent for men and 19.4 per cent for women (Government of India 2014: 4). Indications are that it is higher for women and men in states with private professional colleges.

The GER of Scheduled Caste (SC) women was 13.9 per cent and men 15.8 per cent; Scheduled Tribe (ST) women 9.7 per cent and men 12.4 per cent (Government of India 2014: 27). These figures substantiate the well-known fact that in spite of a very well formulated policy of positive discrimination, the representation of disadvantaged groups of SC and ST students is not adequate and the proportion of women from among them is negligible. Access is very limited for them as a whole, but more so for the women from these groups. For instance, SC and ST women comprised 11.0 and 4.3 per cent respectively of all women enrolled in 2010–11 (Government of India 2013: 4).

At the undergraduate level, there are 45.4 per cent women and 54.6 per cent men; at the postgraduate level, the proportion of women is 47.5 per cent as compared to 52.5 per cent of men; at the PhD level, their proportion falls to 39.6 per cent while men are 60.4 per cent. Women seem to dropout substantially between postgraduation and doctoral level research, where the leaky pipeline seems to be working effectively (Government of India 2014: 19). This is discussed below.

Let us look at the gender distribution by subjects at the undergraduate level (Table 14.1) to see if women's choices reflect a change away from the traditional feminine subjects while reflecting a gender divide. The maximum proportion of women (51.1 per cent) vis-à-vis men are still enrolled

Table 14.1 Subject enrolment of women and men at undergraduate level

Subject/discipline	Women	Men
Arts, humanities, social science	51.1	48.9
Science	48.8	51.2
Commerce	44.1	55.9
Education	60.5	39.5
Medical science	60.8	39.2
Computer science and computer application	40.2	59.8
Management	34.6	64.4
Law	32.0	68.0
Veterinary and animal science	30.8	69.2
Agriculture and allied sciences	24.6	75.4
Engineering and technology	28.5	71.5

Source: collated from Government of India 2014: T50–51.

in arts, humanities, and the social sciences, followed closely by sciences (48.8 per cent), in which their enrolment has been increasing due to the devaluation of pure sciences because it is no longer the first choice of men students (Chanana 2006). Again, there has been a gradual increase in women's enrolment in the traditionally male-dominated professional subjects such as commerce (44.1 per cent) and engineering and technology (28.5 per cent), yet they do not outnumber men in any of these fields except teacher education (60.5 per cent) and medical science (60.8 per cent). In management, which is a relatively new subject, their proportion has reached 34.6 per cent. It is still low in agriculture (24.6 per cent), veterinary science (30.8 per cent), and law (32.0 per cent) (Government of India 2014: T50–51). The last four subjects remain predominantly male domains, with women occupying less than or around 30 per cent of seats. Medical education in India has been preferred for women so that secluded women patients can be treated by women doctors, so this subject stands between the boundaries of feminine and masculine subjects. Therefore, the enrolment of women in medicine, though a professional subject, has passed the halfway mark. It is an increase from 48.9 per cent in 2011–12 (Government of India 2013).

The transition from postgraduation to doctoral research shows that in the four subjects in which the proportion of women was either more than 50 per cent or close to the 50 per cent mark, their proportions reduce substantially. For example, in social sciences the proportion of women reduces from 51.1 to 40.8 per cent; in science it goes up from 48.8 at the undergraduate level to 52.4 per cent at the postgraduate level, and then decreases to 39.9 per cent; in medical science it goes down from 60.8 per cent at the undergraduate level to 51.8 per cent and further reduces to 42.8 per cent; and in education from 60.5 per cent at the undergraduate level it reduces to 53.7 per cent at the postgraduate level and further decreases to 52.3 per cent at the doctoral level (Government of India 2014: T52–54).

Looking at the specialisations or substreams of these subjects at the undergraduate level and comparing the enrolment to the postgraduate and PhD levels, women do not retain their position of advantage. For example, out of 16 substreams in engineering at the undergraduate level, women outnumbered men (51 per cent) in only one of them, namely architecture. However, their proportion reduces at the postgraduate (42.3 per cent) and PhD levels (34.6 per cent). Women outnumber men in seven of the nine allopathic substreams or specialisations[3] in medical science. In three of them they comprise more than 60 per cent – dentistry (60.5), microbiology (66.1), and physiotherapy (69.7). In biotechnology, too, their proportion is close to 60 per cent

(58.3). There are more men in pharmacy (56.4 per cent) and general medicine (51.8 per cent). They outnumber women in these two specialisations at both the postgraduate and PhD levels – in pharmacy they comprise 57.3 and 72.6 per cent respectively, and in general medicine they account for 63.8 per cent and 56.9 per cent respectively. On the other hand, the proportion of women in dentistry at the postgraduate level reduces to 49.1 per cent and at the PhD level to 44.8 per cent. Even if they are able to retain their position at the postgraduate level, as for example in biotechnology (62.2 per cent), they lose it at the PhD level (49.1 per cent). This situation is the same in physiotherapy, where they are 59 per cent at the postgraduate level and only 42.9 per cent at the PhD level (Government of India 2014: T52–54).

Thus, gender inequality in participation has not declined – e.g. in enrolment men are over-represented in engineering, agriculture, and computer sciences, and women in biology-related sciences, both in the educational and occupational spheres (Chanana 2006). This is also reflected in the choice of subfields or specialisations. This is confirmed by a report on completed PhDs in India (Kurup and Arora 2010).

Conclusion

There is no doubt that access has increased for women and is reflected in the higher enrolment, GER, number of higher education institutions, and proportions of women in new professional subjects that are applied and market-driven. However, layers of disadvantage are uncovered when data are disaggregated by level and specialisation. For instance, the gaps by gender and subject choice continue. Again, the proportions of women decrease as one moves from one level to the other, especially from the undergraduate to postgraduate to doctoral level. This indicates lower transition rates and participation. Moreover, specialisations are replacing subjects in terms of clustering of women students. Therefore, and as mentioned above, while the *vertical dimension of unequal participation* may be declining, the *horizontal dimension* relating to specialisations, especially at the doctoral level, remains resistant to change.

As already mentioned, a very important function of the higher education system in social change is to assess the extent of educational opportunities for women. This is a very critical question but is hampered by very limited data. For example, although enrolments in Indian higher education have increased substantially and the student community is diversified, we do not know about the distribution of women students in the public and private HEIs and in the increasingly diversified institutional contexts. Additionally, their clustering in subjects leading to low-end jobs with low salaries indicates that they are unlikely to move to higher positions. What is needed is gender-desegregated data about the rapidly expanding private sector.

Moreover, while the private higher education institutions have remapped the educational arena and increased the institutional and subject options for students, they limit access due to high costs and so are likely to be beyond the reach of women students, especially those from the Scheduled Castes and Scheduled Tribes and from lower middle and lower strata. Thus, higher education fails to promote equality and be more inclusive.

In this scenario, education has once again been projected as a critical instrument of social change as well as for cultural reproduction. Classic sociological questions about the relationship between education, on the one hand, and economy and society, on the other, are being raised again. In the context of marginal groups and women, questions about simultaneous inclusion and exclusion are also being asked.

> Inclusion and exclusion both appear to pose dangers and opportunities. Women are simul-
> taneously constructed as winners and losers. Winners, because they are gaining access, as

students, in significant numbers, but losers because of their lack of entitlement to leadership and prestigious disciplines.

(Morley 2009: 384)

Therefore, the role of the state in pushing higher education for promoting change and equality through subject choices in the age of globalisation and privatisation is critical. This is more so when gender, marginality, race, caste, class, and ethnicity are pushed to the background. It is time to frame a policy that will evolve strategies and procedures to encourage women to shift subject choices and specialisations at school and in higher education and to initiate steps to plug the leaky pipeline from undergraduate/postgraduate to doctoral level so that higher education becomes inclusive and equitable.

Notes

1 This is a substantially revised and updated version of the paper published as 'Higher Education in and for a Changing World', *Journal of Educational Planning and Administration*, 2: 141–155, 2013.
2 From a very early age the toys and the clothing for the children encourage and reinforce gender stereotyping at home and later on in school through games, participation in extracurricular activities and subject choices. Boys are encouraged to play with cars and mechanical toys while girls play with dolls. This has been typical of the Western world, but is happening in India with the opening of the market economy and rise of consumerism.
3 I have excluded homoeopathy, Ayurvedic and Unani, and nursing. The last one because it is well known that a majority of nursing students are women.

References

Acker, Sandra. 1994. *Gendered Education: Sociological Reflections on Women, Teaching and Feminism*, Milton Keynes: Open University Press.
American Association of University Women (AAUW). n.d. Building a STEM Pipeline for Girls and Women, www.aauw.org/what-we-do/stem-education/?gclid=CLXip-2BncMCFVUsvQodiJIAGw (accessed on 20 March 2015).
Bacchi, Carol. 2001. Managing Equity: Mainstreaming and 'Diversity' in Australian Universities. In Ann Brooks and A. McInnon (eds) *Gender and the Restructured University*, Milton Keynes: The Society For Research into Higher Education and the Open University Press, pp. 119–135.
Becher, T. 1981. Towards a Definition of Disciplinary Cultures. *Studies in Higher Education*, 6 (2), pp. 109–122.
Bourdieu, P. 1977. Cultural Reproduction and Social Reproduction. In J. Karabel and A.H. Halsey (eds) *Power and Ideology in Education*. Oxford: Oxford University Press.
Bowles, Samual and Herbert Gintis. 2002. Schooling in Capitalist America Revisited. *Sociology of Education*, 75, (1): 1–18. www.jstor.org/stable/3090251.
Brennan, John and Rajani Naidoo. 2006. Managing Contradictory Functions: The Role of Universities in Societies Undergoing Radical Social Transformation. In Guy Neave (ed.) *Knowledge, Power and Dissent: Critical Perspectives on Higher Education and Research in Knowledge Society*. Paris: UNESCO Publishing, pp. 221–233.
Brown, Phillip, Hugh Lauder and David Ashton. 2011. *The Global Auction: The Broken Promises of Education, Jobs, and Incomes*. Oxford: Oxford University Press.
Chanana, Karuna. 2006. Gender and Disciplinary Choices: Women in Higher Education in India. In Guy Neave (ed.) *Knowledge, Power and Dissent: Critical Perspectives on Higher Education and Research in Knowledge Society*. Paris: UNESCO Publishing, pp. 267–294.
Couch, Robbie. 2015. No, Science Isn't 'A Boy Thing'. And These Genius Girls Prove It. *The Huffington Post* in association with the *Times of India* group, posted on 11 March. www.huffingtonpost.com/2015/03/10/microsoft-ad-girls-stem_n_6839424.html?utm_hp_ref=women-in-tech&ir=India (accessed on 28 March 2015).
David, Miriam, E. 2014. *Feminism, Gender and Universities: Politics, Passion and Pedagogies*. Aldershot: Ashgate.

Deem, Rosemary. 1978. *Women and Schooling*. London: Routledge and Kegan Paul.

Donald, Athene. 2013. Reinforcing Gender Stereotypes: How Our Schools Narrow Children's Choices, 9 December. www.theguardian.com/science/occams-corner/2013/dec/09/gender-stereotypes-schools-children-choices (accessed on 20 March 2015).

European Students' Union. 2008. Policy Paper on Gender Equality in Higher Education. www.esu-online.org/news/article/6064/100/ (accessed on 11 January 2015).

Gautam, Meenakshi. 2015. Gender, Subject Choices and Higher Education in India: Exploring 'Choices' and 'Constraints' of Women Students. *Contemporary Education Dialogue*, 12 (1): 31–58.

Government of India. 2013. *All India Survey of Higher Education*. New Delhi: Ministry of Human Resource Development, Government of India.

Government of India. 2014. *All India Survey of Higher Education*. New Delhi: Ministry of Human Resource Development, Government of India.

Harding, J. 1986. *Perspectives on Gender and Science*. London: Falmer Press.

Harvey, D. 1993. *The Condition of Postmodernity: An Enquiry into the Origins of Cultural Change*. Oxford: Blackwell.

Hudson, L. 1972. *The Cult of the Fact*. London: Cape.

Institute of Physics. 2013. Closing Doors: Exploring Gender and Subject Choice in Schools: A Statistical Study Exploring the Links Between Gender and Subject Choice. www.iop.org/education/teacher/support/girls_physics/closing-doors/page_62076.html (accessed on 21 January 2015).

Keller, E.F. 1983. Gender and Science. In S. Harding and M.B. Hintikka (eds) *Discovering Reality: Feminist Perspectives in Epistemology, Metaphysics, Methodology and Philosophy Science*. Reidel: Dordrecht, pp. 187–206.

Kurup, Anitha and Jagdish Arora. 2010. *Trends in Higher Education: Creation and Analysis of a Database of PhDs*. Bangalore: National Institute of Advanced Studies.

Leslie, Sara-Jane, Andrei Cimpian, Meredith Meyer, and Edward Freeland. 2015. Expectations of Brilliance Underlie Gender Distributions Across Academic Disciplines. *Science*, 347 (6219): 262–265.

McDonnell, Mary Byrne. 2008. Toward a Globally Connected, Public Social Science. In Tessa Morris-Suzuki (ed.) *Contradictions of Globalisation: Democracy, Culture, and Public Sphere*. Tokyo: International House of Japan, pp. 143–154.

Mackinnon A. and Ann Brooks (eds). 2001. Introduction. In Ann Brooks and A. Mackinnon (eds) *Gender and the Restructured University*, Milton Keynes: The Society For Research into Higher Education and the Open University Press, pp. 1–12.

Millett, K. 1983. *Sexual Politics*, London: Virago.

Morley, Louise. 2009. Momentum and Melancholia: Women in Higher Education Internationally. In Michael W. Apple, Stephen J. Ball and Luis Armando Gandin (eds) *The Routledge International Handbook of the Sociology of Education*. http://media.routledgeweb.com/pdf/9780415486637/toc.pdf (accessed on 5 August 2012).

Mukul, Akshaya 2015. Raj Girls Have Limited Access to Math, Science: Study Shows Paucity of Women Teachers, *Times of India*, 30 January.

Penner, Andrew M. 2015. Gender Inequality in Science. *Science*, 347 (6219): 234–235. www.sciencemag.org/content/347/6219/234 (accessed on 20 March 2015).

Sawer, M. 1989. Efficiency, Effectiveness … and Equity? In G. Davis, P. Weller, and C. Lewis (eds), *Corporate Management in Australian Government: Reconciling Accountability and Efficiency*. Melbourne: Macmillan.

Sharpe, Rachel. 1976. *Just Like A Girl*. London: Pelican.

Slaughter, Sheila and Larry L. Leslie. 1997. *Academic Capitalism: Politics, Policies, and the Entrepreneurial University*. Baltimore, MD: Johns Hopkins University Press.

Snow, C.P. 1961. *The Two Cultures and the Scientific Revolution*. New York: Cambridge University Press. http://en.wikipedia.org/wiki/The_Two_Cultures (accessed on 10 March 2015).

Thomas, Kim. 1990. *Gender and Subject in Higher Education*, Milton Keynes: Society For Research in Higher Education and Open University Press.

UNESCO. 2012. *UNESCO World Atlas of Gender Equality in Education*. Paris: UNESCO.

Wolpe, Ann Marie. 1978. Education and the sexual division of labour. In A. Kuhn and A.N. Wolpe (eds), *Feminism and Materialism: Women and Modes of Production*. Boston, MA: Routledge and Kegan Paul.

Yeatman, A. 1990. *Bureaucrats, Technocrats, Femocrats*. Sydney: Allen and Unwin.

15
Caste quotas and formal inclusion in Indian higher education[1]

Satish Deshpande

Both Dr Ambedkar's famous question and his succinct description of the Indian society that precedes it remain as relevant today as they were 64 years ago.[2] No one was more aware of the irony that the egalitarian Constitution he had helped draft was itself the cornerstone of the 'life of contradiction'. By superimposing formal equality on a highly unequal society – while guaranteeing property rights and refusing positive constraints on social capital – the Constitution actually empowered the rich and socially dominant 'haves'. But it also offered the 'have-nots' something: one egalitarian principle of universal adult franchise; one established precedent of protective discrimination otherwise known as reservations; and many good intentions of a progressive kind. In essence, the history of post-Independence India is the story of the intertwined efforts to cash in on these constitutional legacies, each constrained by the other, albeit in unequal and asymmetrical ways.

This situation, where deep inequalities persist under a thin veneer of formal equality decorated with progressive rhetoric, has also been described as a 'passive revolution'. As is well known, the Gramscian term refers to an incomplete or truncated revolution, a 'revolution from above', and it fits the Indian context very well because Independence was essentially a 'transfer of power' from a foreign to a local elite. It is because Independence was indeed something of a revolution that the Constitution of our 'sovereign socialist secular democratic republic' promises to secure for all its citizens 'justice social economic and political' as well as 'equality of status and of opportunity'. But because the revolution was passive and partial, these promises are endlessly deferred, being redeemed only in slow and grudging instalments. Madhav Prasad captures the essence of the matter when he writes that 'there is no militant class backing the Constitution with its iron will', so that '[w]hen we rue the absence of the will to change, we are merely acknowledging the fact that we have the letter of the law, in the form of the Constitution, without the spirit' (Prasad 2011: 45).

The story of reservations is part of this larger saga of the interplay between formal good intentions and substantive change. But because they are a major balancing item in the account between the haves and the have-nots, they become the focus of attention for both sides. Indeed, so great is the emphasis on reservations that the policy acts like a giant magnet dragging virtually all discussion about social justice and equality of opportunity into its force field. The excessive emphasis on reservations raises the risk of a metonymic slide that ends up equating reservations with social justice. Whereas reservations, especially in higher education, can only provide protected entry or formal inclusion – they cannot deliver social justice. While formal access is obviously an essential precondition, it is still a long way from ensuring that inclusion is 'full' or substantive, which is what social justice requires. Moreover, reservations policy urgently needs to adapt to recent changes such as the restructuring of higher education; the deepening differentiations within the groups eligible for reservations; and the shifts in the stances and capabilities of the state.[3] Whether and to what extent it is able to do so will depend, once again, on the political legacy of the Constitution and the ongoing tussles between the haves and the have-nots.

This chapter provides an overview of the conceptual, historical, and policy dimensions of the reservations policy in Indian higher education. The first section looks at the policy perspectives on equality of access in higher education. The second provides a summary of the history of modalities and justificatory frameworks. The third outlines the major changes that have transformed higher education in the past two decades and speculates on the possible directions that reservations policy could take in their wake.

Higher education and equality of access: policy perspectives

The specific features that make higher education a particularly challenging field for the theory and practice of social justice policy may be quickly summarised.[4] First, higher education is 'naturally elitist' in the sense that it is a downstream field that presupposes prior qualifications, which have a filtering effect on aspirants so that relatively few reach it. This filtering may be due to 'merit discrimination' based on the need for high levels of skill or competence, and/or 'resource discrimination' due to the unequal distribution of the material and non-material resources required to acquire skills. This leaves room for 'social discrimination' (based on prejudices related to race, caste, gender, etc.) to disguise itself as, or to work through, the other kinds of discrimination. The need for merit discrimination in particular may be ideologically exaggerated by the claim that higher education (or at least part of it) is engaged in knowledge production and must therefore cultivate 'excellence' to the exclusion of all other objectives (such as those of equity), or even that it must be exempted from such social responsibilities. The key point here is that the road to higher education passes through many kinds of 'discrimination' where very different types of distinctions are being made for a variety of different reasons backed by divergent moral or social values.

Second, the nature and force of the right to higher education is a contextual matter rather than a self-evident and universal axiom, such as the fundamental right to basic education or medical care. Third, higher education is also a highly desirable asset because it offers the possibility of social mobility and generally carries the promise of high material and non-material rewards. For this reason, the demand for higher education usually exceeds its supply, which means that yet another form of 'discrimination' must be practised due to sheer scarcity and the consequent need for rationing. Finally, higher education is usually a strongly contested field because, generally speaking, it is the most legitimate means for sustaining or justifying the existing social order as well as for changing or overthrowing it. Consequently, higher education is a field where equal access is hard to define, and policies for equalising access are always controversial.

Of course, higher education has been elitist not only 'naturally' (because it necessarily presupposes high levels of prior competences), but primarily socially or 'traditionally' (because of customs or norms that systematically include and exclude particular social groups). The important point here is that the major burden of excluding 'unsuitable' candidates is shifted to the upstream

229

levels of the educational system, i.e. to schooling. As Bourdieu and Passeron (1990)[5] have shown in their classic work, the 'differential educational mortality rate of the different social classes' (p. 154) that is responsible for filtering the candidate pool ensures that 'social advantages and disadvantages are progressively retranslated, through successive selections, into educational advantages or disadvantages' (p. 160). The overall effect from the point of view of higher education is that

> the combination of the educational chances of the different classes and the chances of subsequent success attached to the different sections and types of schools constitutes a mechanism of deferred selection which transmutes a social inequality into a specifically educational inequality, i.e. an inequality of 'level' or success, concealing and academically consecrating an inequality of chances of access to the highest levels of education.
>
> (p. 158)

Bourdieu and Passeron have also argued that the social filtering of the candidate pool as it advances up the education ladder is achieved more through induced self-exclusion rather than explicit elimination through failure in examinations. They even claim that the social purpose of the examination in this context has been misunderstood or exaggerated:

> The opposition between the 'passed' and the 'failed' is the source of a false perspective on the educational system as a selecting agency ... this opposition between the two sub-sets separated by selection in the examination from within the set of candidates hides the relation between this set and its complement (i.e., the set of non-candidates), thereby ruling out any inquiry into the hidden criteria of the election of those from whom the examination ostensibly makes its selection.
>
> (pp. 153–154)

This perspective fits the Indian case fairly well as a broad overview. It is well known, for example, that dropout rates in school are inversely related to class and caste status. The most recent official figures on dropout rates and examination pass rates are shown in Table 15.1. The data are shown separately for 'All' and for the Scheduled Castes (SC) and Scheduled Tribes (ST). The dropout rates are cohort-specific, that is, the three columns show the cumulative percentage of dropouts from the cohort that began at Class I. By the time this cohort reaches Class V, about 26 per cent of all students have dropped out, but the figure for SCs is about 33 per cent and that for STs close to 40 per cent. By the time Class X is reached the respective dropout rates are (in round figures) 62 per cent, 71 per cent, and 79 per cent. These figures show that the gap between dropout rates for 'All' and for the SCs and STs dips slightly (by one percentage point) at the Class VIII level relative to the Class V level, but rises by two percentage points between the Class VIII and Class X levels. This suggests that more SC and ST students dropout between Class VIII and Class X than those from other caste groups. Considered as an absolute difference in percentages, the gap in the pass rate for the board examinations in Classes X and XII is slightly less than the gap in dropout rates in Class X. This suggests that although SC/ST students are less likely than others to reach Class X, once they reach this stage they 'catch up' slightly with others in terms of the pass percentage. Thus, while the data are much too fragile to bear much interpretive weight, they do seem to lend some plausibility to Bourdieu and Passeron's contention that

> previous performances being equal, pupils of working-class origin are more likely to 'eliminate themselves' from secondary education by declining to enter it than to eliminate

themselves once they have entered, and a fortiori more likely not to enter than to be eliminated from it by the explicit sanction of examination failure.

(Bourdieu and Passeron 1990: 153)

But the major problem with the data in Table 15.1 is that they seriously understate intercaste differences for two reasons. First, because the 'All' category includes the SC and ST categories, it obviously understates the difference between these categories and the upper castes. Second, the data, like most official datasets, are silent about the Other Backwards Classes (OBCs); even if the All category had excluded the SC and ST groups, it would still lump together the OBCs and the upper castes into one group, thus understating the differences between them. These limitations seem severe enough to create doubt as to whether they support the contention noted above, namely that it is not the examination but 'unexamined exclusion' which accounts for the underrepresentation of lower classes and (by extension) castes as we go up the educational ladder.

The major dataset that offers disaggregation by caste groups is based on the National Sample Survey Organisation's (NSSO) regular surveys, especially the big sample quinquennial ones. A number of studies (Basant and Sen 2010; Desai and Kulkarni 2008; Deshpande 2006; Sundaram 2006) use these data to look at educational inequalities across social groups, and they offer a much more sophisticated view of the problem of equality of access. In my own earlier work, I have compared shares in the population of graduate degree holders across castes to argue for the presence of significant inequalities of access, and hence for strong protective discrimination policies in higher education. Table 15.2 is based on unit-level data from the 55th Round of the NSSO of 1999–2000 for urban India. It makes the simple but important point that the thick horizontal line that separates the Hindu OBC and all the rows above it from those below is the major faultline in Indian society. Above the line are the lower-caste groups (except Dalit Sikhs and Dalit Christians) and Muslims, whose shares in the population of graduates of various disciplines are less than their shares in the total urban population (shown in the last column). The opposite is the case with the upper-caste groups below the line, whose shares of graduates are significantly higher than their share in the urban population. These disparities build a *prima facie* case for reservations (or similar interventions) to boost the presence of students from lower castes and the Muslim community in higher education.

However, other scholars have argued that over- or underrepresentation of social groups in higher education must be evaluated with reference to not their share in the total population, but rather to their share in the population of the higher education-eligible population, i.e. the population that has successfully completed the Class XII examination. Table 15.3 is excerpted from one such study, that by K. Sundaram (2006) based on the 55th Round data. These data are restricted to the 17–25 age group, and are further divided into the 'poor' (defined as households

Table 15.1 Dropout rates and pass percentages in school, 2005–06

Social groups	Dropout rates			Pass percentages	
	I–V	I–VIII	I–X	X class	XII class
All	25.7	48.8	61.6	67.9	72.7
SC	32.9	55.2	70.6	60.4	65.6
ST	39.8	62.9	78.5	53.0	59.6

Source: Selected Educational Statistics 2005–06, MHRD.

Table 15.2 Graduate degree-holders by caste and community, urban India, 1999–2000

Castes and communities	Share of graduates in various disciplines				Caste/community share of total urban population
	Agriculture	Engineering	Medicine	Other subjects	
Hindu ST	2.4	1.3	1.8	1.3	2.6
Hindu SC	3.8	2.2	1.8	3.6	12.9
All Muslim	9.4	5.0	10.0	5.7	17.0
Hindu OBC	10.0	14.9	10.4	13.7	24.2
Hindu UC	62.1	66.8	65.3	65.9	36.9
All Christian	8.4	5.2	6.6	4.0	2.8
All Sikh	1.7	2.2	2.1	2.4	1.6
All others	2.4	2.4	1.9	3.3	2.0
Total	100.0	100.0	100.0	100.0	100.0

Source: computed by the author from NSSO unit-level data on CD.

Note
Includes persons with postgraduate degrees. Cells show rounded proportions, and columns may not add up to 100 due to rounding.

Table 15.3 Group shares in school graduates and those currently enrolled in higher education: age group 17–25, urban India, 1999–2000

Social groups	Percentage shares of the population			
	Total urban population	Passed Class XII	Currently enrolled in college		
			Technical subjects	Other subjects	All subjects
ST	3.7	2.7	3.4	2.5	2.7
SC	14.6	8.6	7.2	8.5	8.3
OBC	32.1	26.5	22.6	25.9	25.2
Others	49.7	62.2	66.9	63.2	63.9
All	100.0	100.0	100.0	100.0	100.0

Source: adapted from Sundaram 2006, table 6.

Note
Data shown here are for all economic levels, i.e. for the urban population in general.

below the official poverty line) and the residual 'non-poor' apart from the 'all' category that is a superset of both the previous categories. In each of these three divisions, Sundaram looks at the caste-wise shares of the total population, the population that has passed the Class XII exam, and the one currently enrolled in higher education, distinguishing between technical-professional fields and others. His main contention is that once the reference group is the eligible population, then the underrepresentation of groups like the OBCs is negligible. From this perspective, and based on the above data, Sundaram argues that there is no case for reservations for OBCs in higher education because their share in the population enrolled in higher education is not significantly different from their share in the urban population (in the 17–25 age group). Moreover, according to him, if the argument is that the share in higher education of the OBCs is to be increased, then this is desirable for all groups, given the low level of overall enrolment ratios. However, it is difficult to see how the wide inter-group differences in current attainment can be ignored when making an argument for interventions that will raise enrolment rates in higher education.[6]

In a detailed econometric study focusing on 'transitions', Sonalde Desai and Veena Kulkarni (2008) have used the same NSSO data but from the period between 1983 and 1999–2000. Because the statistical separation of OBCs only began with the 55th Round of 1999–2000, the social groups they work with are SC, ST, Muslim, and a residual category of Others (which includes both upper castes and OBCs, as well as the minority religions like Christians, Sikhs, etc.). The study asks two main questions. First, how do caste-class differences matter in the transition points all along the educational spectrum, from entering primary schooling to success-fully completing an undergraduate degree? Second, have there been any changes in the inter-group inequalities over this 17-year period? They find that relative to the 'Others', all the disadvantaged groups – SC, ST, and Muslim – have a significantly lower probability of crossing each of the educational thresholds, but that the differences are highest at either end of the spectrum. Thus, it is in entering school education in the primary stage, and in completion rates in undergraduate degrees, that social differences are at their maximum. As for changes over time, Desai and Kulkarni find that although all groups have seen rising probabilities of educational success, along with some narrowing in differences, this is not true for Muslims. Moreover, they also find that college completion rates continue to be lower for Dalits, and that these are not affected by income level. In other words, higher socio-economic status does not significantly increase the chances of Dalits acquiring undergraduate degrees.[7]

In what is probably the most recent study of social justice initiatives in higher education, Basant and Sen (2010) use NSSO data from the 61st Round of 2004–05. They disaggregate participation in higher education in terms of different age groups in the population. The 'all generations stock' represents those who have a higher education degree above the age of 20; the 'current generation stock' represents those with degrees in the 22–35 age group; and a 'current generation flow' in the 17–29 or 18–25 age groups. They look at these three measures (two stock and one flow) in both the total population as well as the restricted set of the population eligible for higher education. Their econometric analysis yields roughly the same conclusion as Sundaram – namely, that 'deficits' in higher education participation narrow considerably when we move from all-generation to current-generation stock and especially to current generation flow. The effect is even stronger when the higher education-eligible population is considered (rather than the total population). Thus, Basant and Sen endorse the view that school is the crucial threshold; after crossing it, under-privileged social groups do not seem to be much behind privileged groups in accessing higher education, and are even doing better in some contexts. However, they also offer the significant insight that the strong motivation for accessing higher education may itself be driven by the incentive of reservations, both in higher education itself as well as in state sector employment.

If these recent studies all point to the critical nature of the school–college transition, this is not exactly a new discovery. Indeed, it has been one of the long-time staples of the sociology of education in post-colonial India that although school education began as a common state system shared by all castes and classes, it was rapidly segregated along class lines. Since the upper end of the class spectrum was at that time occupied exclusively by the upper castes, this also meant caste segregation in the sense that only the upper castes were found in expensive private English-medium schools, although not all upper castes could afford them. This obviated the need for strong overt forms of social selection at the college level, because entrance into college was mediated by the mass examination. More than a quarter-century ago, sociologist of education Krishna Kumar described this as the combination of 'early selection' and 'mass examination':

By maintaining a separate system of schooling on the basis of early selection, the urban elite pre-empted the development of a truly mass education system. The system of holding mass examinations did act as a symbolic corrective to a certain extent, but it could not prove sufficiently effective in upholding the myth of open competition and equal opportunity. Early selection impeded the erosion of ascription-based differentiation and also the emergence of an achievement-based differentiation in school and society.

(Kumar 1985: 1282)

Over time, the system of social selection has been adapted into a new arrangement based on the distinction between 'exit' and 'entrance' examinations.[8] Exit examinations, like the school leaving examination, are supposed to be generalised indicators of a certain standard minimum competence, and do not confer any specific entitlements. Entrance exams, on the other hand, are gate-keeping devices regulating entry into sought-after courses and institutions. Their ideological function is to act as competitive measures of merit, while their logistical function is to ration a scarce resource in a socially acceptable manner. In India, political pressures and administrative expedience have forced 'exit' examinations to become 'softer', while entrance examinations have become progressively 'harder' as competition increases.[9] Given that entrance examinations privilege incremental differences in relative marks over absolute levels of competence or aptitude, they serve as devices of social selection that (unduly) favour those with a better school education.[10]

Finally, before concluding this section on evidence-based policy perspectives, it is necessary to point to some critical shortcomings of aggregate data. Such data will tend to understate the case for active intervention on behalf of equalising access for at least two reasons. First, they don't take into account the specific manner in which entry into higher education is regulated, i.e. through rank or marks obtained in an examination. In the absence of reservation or similar preferential devices, this mode of selection will ensure that disadvantaged groups will be forever disadvantaged because merely acquiring a high school certificate will be insufficient – they will have to 'perform better' than the advantaged groups in order to gain entry into higher education. Second, aggregate data hide the enormous variations in the quality of higher educational institutions (on which more below). The rationale for reservations also includes the fair distribution of access to high-quality institutions, and this cannot be decided by aggregate data. While they are important long-run indicators of equality of access and representation, aggregate data need to be interpreted with care.

Reservations in higher education: modalities and justifications

The previous section discussed the general aspects of the question of equalising access in higher education. This section moves to the specifics of how protective discrimination policies actually work (modalities) and the implicit or explicit rationale (justifications) behind these interventions. Thus, modalities have to do with the specific manner of implementing programmes, while justificatory frameworks work at different levels to defend such programmes.

The modalities of caste quotas in higher education

Although positive interventions in favour of the 'weaker sections' take many forms, the most visible and consequential one has been the caste quota.[11] This basically 'reserves' or sets aside a specific number of 'seats' or places – usually expressed as a proportion of the total available – for eligible members of particular caste-groups legally recognised as legitimate claimants. In higher education, this takes the form of reserved seats for the SC, ST, and OBCs (and other groups such as the disabled or some other region-specific categories of entitlement) in educational institutions. Quotas have been heavily criticised recently, partly due to the strong reaction to the 93rd Amendment and the institution of OBC quotas in elite higher educational institutions, and partly to the influence of US affirmative action discourse. One can distinguish objections in principle – that is, to the very idea or form of quotas – from objections of a consequential kind – that is, those based on the practical failures of quotas.

The strongest and most common objections on principle have to do with the modality itself. Quotas are rigid and inflexible – they discourage or preempt more nuanced and graded responses to the problem of inequality. Being fixed before the fact, quotas may act as a disincentive to effort, at least until intra-group competition reaches the level where admission is no longer assured. Because they are very visible, quotas provoke strong reactions and impose a heavy social cost on beneficiaries in the form of the permanent stigma associated with them. This can insulate popular (upper caste) prejudices from scrutiny and can turn prejudice into a sort of self-fulfilling prophecy that will eventually produce the truth of the very 'facts' that were initially falsehoods. When applied to groups that are internally differentiated, quotas have the potential to turn into the very opposite of what they are supposed to be. Because they can be monopolised by the stronger or relatively privileged sections within the larger group designated as the beneficiary, quotas can help to deepen intra-group inequalities. Their visibility and application to specific social groups makes quotas vulnerable to 'tokenism', or what in India is referred to as 'vote bank politics'. Governments and political parties find it much easier to announce a quota than to undertake the difficult and long gestation programmes that will actually produce lasting results. Thus, quotas encourage tacit collusion between ruling parties and the leaders and privileged sub-groups within beneficiary categories, and become a favourite option for pre-election announcements. Finally, quotas tend to become self-perpetuating in a pathological rather than healthy fashion due to the vested interests they may cultivate as well as the real or imagined political costs associated with ending them.

Although they often tend to be used in bad faith by opponents, each of these arguments against quotas has some truth to it. But the problem is that there are no perfect alternatives – every programme has its inevitable weaknesses and it is a question of balancing these with their strengths. For instance, the contrasts between US-style affirmative action which shuns quotas and Indian-style reservations are often exaggerated and the similarities understated.[12] The strengths of quotas are often underestimated. They have the important practical virtues of being 'transparent, inexpensive to implement and monitor and therefore easily enforceable', as Jayati Ghosh points out (Ghosh 2006: 2431). It is because they are a relatively simple, robust, and tamper-proof administrative modality that quotas have been the mainstay of Indian programmes for social redress. By rendering explicit the specific identities of the beneficiaries, quotas discourage dissimulation via the use of more anonymous categories based on the presumptions of formal equality.[13] Their political visibility generates useful debate and activity, and engenders a form of accountability whose long-term value outweighs its short-term drawbacks.

Perhaps the most valuable function of quotas is that, by their invocation of the idea of 'shares' and proportions, they serve as a much-needed reminder of the social contract on which our republic is founded. It is hardly surprising, therefore, that dominant common sense conspires to suppress this crucial aspect, and presents quotas as special favours bestowed on electorally important groups by venal politicians. In fact, an interesting symptomatic feature of mainstream discourse on quotas is that it had, until recently, successfully repressed the implications of 'electoral importance'. In curious contrast to the 'fear of small numbers', the upper-caste mindset had so firmly internalised its own normative stature that it 'forgot' that the groups entitled to reservations accounted for at least two-thirds of the national population.[14] It is only in the post-Mandal era, effectively since the latter half of the 1990s, that the upper caste national elite have had to explicitly confront the fact that they are a tiny minority, and that even with their lower-class caste-fellows they will at best be between one-fifth and one-fourth of the population. Of course, number alone does not, and should not, always guarantee moral or political precedence. But reminders in this regard are surely welcome, if only because the dominant ideology is long-accustomed to conflating the national or 'general' interest with the interests of vocal minorities. This is revealed, for example, in terms like 'general category', which is the preferred antonym for 'reserved category' in everyday language, even though it is arguably the latter which serves the wider cause while the former is more of a sectional or particularistic interest.

Consequential or practical objections attack the performance of quotas rather than the principles behind them. They argue that quotas just don't work, i.e. they fail to produce the results that they are supposed to. In the context of higher education, for example, this could take the form of the argument that quotas set up beneficiaries for failure by forcibly placing them in classes or courses that they are not really prepared for. This leads to high dropout rates, low self-esteem, and the reinforcement of the prejudices of opponents. Once again, there is some truth to these complaints, but they may as well be taken as proof of the fact that quotas alone are insufficient to achieve the ends they are supposed to serve. In a sense, therefore, the manner of their implementation – without the additional supportive components that they require – dooms them to eventual failure. So, rather than doing away with quotas, these shortcomings demonstrate the need to do more with and for quotas.

This brings us back to the initial characterisation of the 'passive revolution'. Laws and the programmes that they mandate are by themselves never enough if the apparatus for their implementation has no stake in their success. In the Indian context, it is fair to say that, outside the affected groups themselves, the well-wishers of social justice programmes tend to be themselves part of the elite or at least the upper echelons of society. Thus, it is only at the highest levels of the bureaucracy and the leadership of political parties where one may reasonably expect to find some 'disinterested' supporters, while opponents are to be found at all levels. In such a context, the active sabotage or passive neglect of social justice programmes is an unsurprising outcome.

Justificatory frameworks

Given that social justice initiatives in higher education have received sustained scholarly attention, it is not surprising that the justificatory frameworks involved are only just beginning to be re-examined. The law is the most convenient site where the shaping of these frameworks can be observed. It is the space where the legislative intentions of the polity are challenged by the interests that they affect. To understand the part that the courts have played in mediating the impact of social justice legislation it is necessary to begin with the pre-Independence roots of these policies.

As is well known, the basic principle of special protection for the political, social, and economic interests of the 'depressed classes' emerged from the so-called 'Poona Pact' of 1932. Gandhi won the standoff with Ambedkar on the issue of separate electorates for the depressed classes by going on his first ever fast unto death, which brought unbearable pressure to bear on the latter. In return for giving up the demand for separate electorates and agreeing to let the Congress represent them, the depressed classes were assured of protection. This assurance took shape in the Government of India Act of 1935 which drew up the Schedules listing the castes and tribes that were to be given special protection. These schedules were incorporated into the Constitution with hardly any changes (other than the addition of four Dalit castes among the

Sikhs) in 1950. While there was some discussion in the Constituent Assembly about protections for the 'backward classes' as well, this was inconclusive. What emerged at the time of the adoption of the Constitution was thus the legislative and job reservations, along with the general commitment to the amelioration of the social and educational backwardness of all groups considered to be part of the 'weaker sections'.

As Rochana Bajpai's recent work on the conceptual basis of the political language used in the Constituent Assembly debates shows, the initial framework adopted for special treatment of lower castes, tribes, and weaker sections was that of the 'minority'. However, given the hegemonic dominance of ideas of national unity and the consequent reluctance to create group rights, an exception had to be made for the SCs and STs, and at a different and vaguer level for the OBCs.[15] Following from this, the eventual consensus on reservations was worked out in consequentialist terms – 'as a means of moving collectively towards desired national goals, rather than as a matter of rights of individuals or groups' (Bajpai 2011: 133). These national goals included social justice, or the effort to move towards a more just social order in the future. But the most common argument was in terms of national unity and development – ameliorating the 'backwardness' of various social groups would help the developmental effort by 'uplifting' the sections of society that were a drag on the nation.

Translated into the terms of the three main justificatory 'themes' identified by Marc Galanter in his monumental work *Competing Equalities* (1984), this implies the dominance of the 'general welfare' over the 'non-discrimination' and 'reparations' themes.[16] The general welfare justification is a group-based argument; it does not take individual deserts into account, but rather argues consequentially in terms of the beneficial effects to society that preferential treatment brings about. Thus preferential treatment could be intended to 'reduce group disparities, afford representation, encourage the development of talent and so on' (1984: 553). The main point is that the modes of selection chosen here 'might diverge from that which would be dictated merely by … individual performance on the job, because it defines the job to include the symbolic, representational, and educational aspects' (1984: 554).

The text of the Constitution in its pristine incarnation therefore saw reservations and other such group-based measures as a limited exception to what was otherwise taken to be the legitimate default norm, namely individual merit. The larger justificatory framework for social justice initiatives worked out before Independence implicitly advocated the 'mixing' of these social objectives with merit, and this is what the Constitution reflected, if somewhat ambiguously. However, the courts did not share this view initially, leading to what then appeared as a clash of wills between the legislature and the judiciary of the new republic.

Barely six months after the Constitution of the Republic of India was formally adopted, the Madras High Court upheld in July 1950 the plea of two Brahmin petitioners claiming that their fundamental rights to equality and non-discrimination guaranteed by the Constitution were being violated by social justice legislation.[17] Although the specific order being challenged predated Constitutional reservations, these petitions also impacted the new legislation. The unanimous verdict of the Full Bench of three judges striking down the order known as the Communal G.O. sent shockwaves through Parliament, which saw its much publicised social justice initiative nipped in the bud when the Supreme Court concurred with the High Court in April 1951. The Law Ministry (then headed by B.R. Ambedkar) and the government (headed by Pt Jawaharlal Nehru) responded swiftly with the First Amendment to the Constitution protecting reservations in higher education with the same special provision already included for job reservations. The First Amendment was passed in June 1951, less than two months after the Supreme Court verdict, but it was not able to prevent a defensive cast to subsequent efforts to pursue the social justice agenda.[18]

The *Dorairajan case* that provoked the First Amendment involved three articles of the new Constitution, 15(1), 29(2), and 46.[19] The state's case was that Article 46 enjoined it to take special measures on behalf of the 'weaker sections', and that this meant that the equality guaranteed in Articles 15 and 29 would have to be limited somewhat in contexts such as that of preferential admissions. This limitation on equality was not due 'only' to caste, but involved other considerations; moreover, the state was not prohibiting all members of a particular caste, but only wished to take into account its responsibilities towards the weaker sections. The courts disagreed vehemently, asserting that the fundamental rights were supreme since the Directive Principles (of which Article 46 is a part) were non-justiciable; and because merit ought to be the sole criterion for admissions, especially since no enabling clause had been added to Articles 15 or 29 as it had been for Article 16 on job reservations.

With the addition of this clause to Article 15 by the First Amendment,[20] the state's powers appeared to be restored, but it took about a decade for the courts to come around to the point of view of the framers of the Constitution. Ruling in favour of the petitioners in *Dorairajan*, Justice Vishwanatha Sastri of the Madras High Court explicitly noted that 'fortuitous' advantages accruing to any group 'by reason of their caste discipline, habits and mode of life' are not taken away by Article 15(1), and went on to declare that

> It would be strange if, in this land of equality and liberty, a class of citizens should be constrained to wear the badge of inferiority because, forsooth, they have a greater aptitude for certain types of education than other classes.
>
> *(Madras High Court 1950)*

Using this rationale to argue that the Brahmin petitioners had been denied admission solely due to their caste (because they were not admitted to seats reserved for other castes), the Madras High Court struck down the Communal G.O. A decade later, however, the courts had come round to accepting the state's view. Ruling against petitioners[21] whose case was quite similar to *Dorairajan*, Justices Pai and Hussain of the Karnataka (then Mysore) High Court offered what could well be seen as an admirably clear rebuttal of Justice Sastri's arguments 11 years earlier:

> If ... a group of persons clearly identifiable by their caste is really backward socially and educationally, and is on that basis given the benefit of certain reservations, the ineligibility of a person belonging to another caste to secure those reservations is clearly not based on the ground of caste but is a consequence of the reservation properly made in favour of a backward class.
>
> *(Karnataka High Court 1961)*

Having ceded ground on the legitimacy of quotas, the court shifted its scrutiny to the reasonableness of the criteria used to determine 'backwardness', and the scope of the preferential advantage given to the designated beneficiaries. These principles were established by the Supreme Court judgment in *Balaji v. State of Mysore*:

> Reservations under Arts. 15 (4) and 16 (4) must be within reasonable limits. The interests of weaker sections of society, which are a first charge on the States and the Centre, have to be adjusted with the interests of the community as a whole. Speaking generally and in a broad way, a special provision should be less than 50 per cent.
>
> *(Supreme Court 1962)*

Balaji and its precursor cases were the first instance where the courts evinced an interest in the details of the criteria used to determine 'social and educational backwardness'. This was followed up in the next major event to impact reservations, the Government of India's belated decision (in 1990) to implement the Mandal Commission Report of 1980.[22]

Although not directly concerned with higher education, the series of cases beginning with the 'Mandal Case' of 1992 (*Indira Sawhney & Others v. Union of India*), and what are referred to as 'Indira Sawhney-1' (1996) and 'Indira Sawhney-2' (1999), are important because they contain the Supreme Court's insistence that in order to be valid, reservations for the OBCs must exclude the 'creamy layer', or the relatively advanced section to be determined by tests of 'income, property or status'. The court also reiterated the *Balaji* suggestion, but this time as an order, that reservations should not exceed 50 per cent of the available seats.[23]

Reservations in higher education were responsible for the First Amendment in 1951, and for the 93rd Amendment of 2006, which extends OBC reservations to elite state-funded institutions that were previously exempt, and opens the door to reservation in private and unaided institutions. This is effectively the end of the road for reservations in public higher education as all institutions are now covered. The only step that remains to be taken is the extension of reservations to private unaided educational institutions, but it is likely that this move will either follow or accompany the extension of job reservations. As for the legal challenges to reservations in higher education, the last major case is *Ashok Kumar Thakur v. Union of India* and its derivatives, which were settled in August 2011. Despite being one of the less coherent judgments of the court, *Thakur* established that the 93rd Amendment was lawful, although it left open the question of whether the state was entitled to extend reservations to the private sector (Krishnaswamy and Khosla 2008).

Against this background, it is difficult to dispute Marc Galanter's overall assessment that the courts have acted more 'as a brake and a baffle, rather than as stimulant and energiser of the compensatory discrimination policy' (1984: 537–538). Despite some ups and downs, the basic doctrine has been stable – preferential policies can be permitted as a limited and closely monitored abridgement of the fundamental right to non-discrimination; the Directive Principles are relevant and they do place a responsibility on the state, but they cannot override the Fundamental Rights. It is noteworthy that throughout this eventful history, it is the 'backward classes' and the determination of their backwardness that has been the chief source of anxiety for the courts. The case for special treatment of SCs and STs is, after the initial hiccup of *Dorairajan*, quickly conceded. But the question of OBC reservations is constantly challenged by litigants and kept on a tight leash by the courts. This is understandable, given their numerical weight, and also given the fact that the relatively better-off sections of this group are much closer rivals for the upper castes than the scheduled groups. However, despite the insistence on the exclusion of the 'creamy layer', it is significant that the courts have endorsed the use of caste as one of the criteria for determining backwardness as long as it is one among many, and not the sole criterion.

One of the more disappointing features of the case law in this area is the relative lack of interest in details of implementation, or an inexplicably uneven distribution of such interest.[24] As Galanter points out,

> The courts have not equipped themselves with any doctrine by which they might reach the 'affirmative' problems of compensatory discrimination policy that is, by which they might assure that the deserving are included among the beneficiaries, that preferences are of sufficient scope and amount, that they are implemented in a timely and effective fashion, etc.
>
> *(Galanter 1984: 537)*

This raises, yet again, the question of what is possible or likely – and impossible or unlikely – in the context of a limited, largely 'top-down' process of social change.

Higher education and the future of equal access: critical contexts

Indian higher education has been changing so much and so fast lately that it makes the past an unreliable guide to the future. Since this is also, and perhaps especially, true for questions of equal access, there is no option but to review the recent changes even if we are unable, as yet, to estimate the nature or size of their impact.

Recent changes and possible impact

It is best to begin by noting that, though it may be both necessary and inevitable, the shorthand term 'Indian higher education' needs to be used with care because it aggregates a vast and vastly differentiated field.[25] There are two main axles of differentiation: (1) fields and disciplines, especially the division between the technical-professional and other streams; and (2) institutional types, beginning with the private-public distinction and overlapping with the hierarchies of reputation and perceived worth that rank the entire spectrum from elite 'institutions of national importance' to the most subaltern sub-regional institutions. Elite Indian institutions in the fields of engineering, medicine, and management have long enjoyed a reputation for excellence amplified by the global visibility of high-profile alumni in technology, business, and science. However, these institutions are exceptional in the strict sense, as are the high stakes in this segment. The vast majority of institutions in Indian higher education are playing for stakes of a rather different order, though these may be just as important for the players involved.

Decisive changes in the first decade of the twenty-first century have transformed the field and cemented its integration into global circuits. The most visible change is in size. Between 2001 and 2010, higher education more than doubled its institutions (from 254 to 544) and raised enrolment by 62 per cent (from 9 million to 14.6 million), which works out to an astonishing growth rate of more than one new university *per fortnight*, and a more modest but still impressive increase of about 1,500 students *every day*.[26] This growth is fuelled from the demand side by the 'demographic bulge' in the age structure; by expanded access to schooling; and by larger numbers being able to afford higher education.[27] On the supply side, higher education has grown mainly through the expansion of the private sector. What used to be a virtual state monopoly by default has changed during the last two decades with the swift growth of technical-professional education as a lucrative site for private investment. Overall, the private sector now accounts for a majority of both institutions (63.2 per cent) and total enrolment (51.5 per cent), but it really dominates the technical-professional fields where credentials command high to astronomical premiums.[28] At the other end of the spectrum, preliminary estimates suggest that absolute levels (and not just shares) of enrolment may be falling in some of the basic sciences.[29]

Ongoing processes of 'globalisation' have been consolidated during this period in three main ways: (1) the explicit recognition (visible in vigorous marketing efforts) now granted to India as one of the top 'customers' of global-Western higher education; (2) recognition as a site for investment in the form of franchises or local branches of foreign higher education providers (though not much has happened on this front so far); and (3) through the intensification and expansion of academic networks linking Indian institutions and individuals to foreign ones.

These changes are yet to be analysed in detail. Moreover, they have already outpaced the statistical database, which has to evolve procedures to catch up. Nevertheless, what can be said by way of a preliminary assessment of their impact on questions of access and equity?

As discussed above, it is largely undisputed that most of the recent expansion in higher education has been within the private unaided sector, which in turn is heavily concentrated in vocational and technical-professional fields. There are, broadly speaking, two kinds of partially conflicting equity effects at work in response to the privatised expansion of higher education. There is first the easing of the supply bottleneck as more capacity is created in the sector to help meet the pent up demand for higher education. The more affluent and privileged sections of all groups – including the lower castes and discriminated communities – benefit from this expansion. Because they already had the social and economic capital required to convert credentials into mobility, these sections were being hurt by the stagnation of the state sector and its inability to expand the supply of higher education. This might be termed the 'crowding-in' effect of the easing of supply constraints in a situation of considerable excess demand. In other words, the top echelons of the underprivileged communities are 'crowded-into' higher education along with the much larger upper caste and privileged communities. But there is also a countervailing 'crowding-out' effect at work: the less affluent sections of underprivileged communities that are dependent on the subsidised state sector are now crowded out of higher education because only private sector sources are available. The exclusion of the underprivileged occurs both through the straightforward pricing-out of the poor (of all communities, but among whom the lower castes and Muslims are over-represented), and through the absence or non-implementation of reservation and related policies.

The net effect on equity is hard to assess. One could argue that since the affluent sections of underprivileged groups are much thinner than the much thicker layer of affluence in privileged communities, any outcome that benefits only the affluent will, overall, harm the interests of the underprivileged. But it is important not to be imprisoned within the logic of shares and proportions – absolute numbers also matter, particularly in a gigantic country like India. It is arguable that significant synergies may be released when a critical mass of educated members is created within the underprivileged communities. Moreover, the state has also embarked on an ambitious programme of expansion in higher education, with an outlay in the 11th Five-Year Plan that is nine times higher than in the past. While the concrete results of this expansion are too close for analysis, there is no doubt that it will substantially increase the supply of reservation seats.

It has also been suggested that globalisation and the expanded possibilities for seeking foreign education and employment may have acted as a kind of 'safety valve' in the Indian context.[30] The departure of those who can afford, and are able to access, foreign higher educational options may seem to create more space in local educational markets. But whether this will help lower castes and other underprivileged groups is still an open question that can only be settled empirically. This needs to be done independently of other considerations like the reinforcement or expansion of hierarchies that rank various kinds of credentials (including foreign and domestic ones) by their perceived worth.

Finally, past patterns in the inter-generational trajectories of mobility among classes and communities suggest that the most safe and lucrative options in higher education are accessed first by upwardly mobile communities. While this needs to be contextualised in terms of the inevitably localised tradeoffs among the probability of securing employment, the probable size of earnings, and the investment required, one could hazard a guess that the current preponderance of professional-technical courses favours this pattern. Indeed, it is itself a consequence of such patterned preferences. Depending on the resources they can command, underprivileged groups will tend to access the best technical-professional training first and liberal arts-based credentials last. As they gain in relative prosperity and acquire greater generational depth in higher education, along with the confidence that these bring, these groups will move across the educational spectrum more or less like their predecessors have done. But for the present, the relevant fact is that the supply of higher educational opportunities seems to be increasing in the very areas that are likely to be the first choices of the underprivileged communities.

The possible futures of quotas in higher education

What do these trends portend for the future of quotas in particular? At a general level, it is clear that, regardless of the transformations that higher education has gone through, the modality of the quota is not in any immediate danger. It is also safe to assume that the size of the quota (i.e. the sum total of all seats available under various schemes for reservation) will increase along with higher education as a whole, though probably not in the same proportion. But while its existence may not be in danger, the quota will certainly have to adapt and change according to the particular pressures and problems it is already facing or is likely to encounter. Some of the more important of these issues are outlined below.

Intra-group disparities and the 'creamy layer'

Among the more intriguing and consequential anomalies in the interpretation of social justice legislation is the simultaneous insistence of the courts on the decisive importance of internal disparities within the 'backward classes' and their irrelevance among the SCs and STs. In the form of the 'creamy layer' argument put into play by the Mandal judgment of the Supreme Court in 1992, internal disparities have acquired a critical legal status for the OBCs since they are grounds for excluding the economically better-off sections from the benefits available to this category.

But in the very different context of internal disparities among the SCs, the courts have held that the Constitution does not permit the state to make distinctions within the overall category, which must be treated as a single homogeneous collectivity. So they have struck down attempts by state governments to create sub-quotas reserved for sub-groups that have remained severely underrepresented in government employment. The most advanced case of this sort emerges from Andhra Pradesh, where the state tried to create a sub-quota within the larger SC quota for the left-behind segments of SC communities such as the Madigas and Rellis, etc. Since the sub-quotas would exclude relatively privileged SC sub-groups like Malas in exactly the same manner as the reservation quotas themselves exclude all non-SCs, the Malas went to court with merit-based arguments identical to those commonly used by the upper castes against reservations.[31] There are several other states where internal disparities within the SC or ST categories have crossed the point of no return in terms of political visibility. Given that this is happening in big and electorally important states like Maharashtra, Uttar Pradesh, and Rajasthan (where Mahars, Jatavs or Chamars, and Meenas among the STs are the respective dominant groups), it is unlikely that the problem will simply go away. In one form or another, sub-quotas are bound to appear on the political horizon very soon.

When it comes to the 'creamy layer' (where the courts are enforcers rather than impediments), the main issue of concern is the context-blindness of the injunction to exclude. In higher education, for example, it is mostly the 'creamy layer' of every social group that dominates, and for reasons that are quite transparent. In such a context, on what grounds would it be justified to prohibit the creamy layer of one group and permit that of another just because the former is availing of reservations? Put differently, what precise aspect or principle of the general legal argument for reservations would support the position that availing them requires the sacrifice of the (relative) economic advantages that a person or group may possess? If reservation policy is intended to address social, educational, and other kinds of 'backwardness' – including but not limited to poverty or economic backwardness – then the absence of (severe) economic disadvantage cannot be turned into a disqualification in an axiomatic, context-independent manner.

For example, it would be understandable if creamy layer exclusion occurred in the context of, say, a fee waiver or a textbook grant or some other clearly economic component of a broader reservation programme in higher education. But to deny admission to the programme itself suggests that OBC reservation is only about economic disadvantage and not about social disadvantage or discrimination. Otherwise we are left to defend the claim that social discrimination or disadvantage only operates below a certain economic threshold, a claim that would seem to empty the term 'social' of almost all its content.[32] This is quite apart from the possible pragmatic objections to the principle of creamy layer exclusion, such as the argument that, in contexts like higher education, this eliminates precisely the best prepared and most likely to succeed segment of the entitled group.[33]

Though they represent very different problems and contexts, the creamy layer OBCs and the relatively advanced sub-castes or tribes within the SCs and STs point to the difficulties of working exclusively with caste as a criterion when designing social policy. It is reasonable to expect some innovation in this direction in the near future, even if there are difficult conceptual and practical puzzles to be solved.[34]

The mismeasurement and misrecognition of merit

As the first line of offence and defence adopted by opponents since the time that reservations were first introduced, notions of 'merit' have always been central to the working of compensatory discrimination policies. There is also a growing literature on this link, so the basic arguments can be quickly summarised. In most higher education contexts, and especially in India, ideas of merit are plagued by two related problems. The first is the conflation of *rationing* and *selection*, and the second is the slide from *eligibility* into *excellence*. Rationing refers to the entirely non-academic imperative for restricting entry that is created by the shortage of higher education places relative to demand, while selection refers to the academic process of choosing from a candidate pool according to standards and indices of merit. Eligibility represents the minimum levels of academic competence or skill required for undertaking a course of study, whereas excellence refers to the highest levels of skill or competence associated with a field or discipline.

Whether it is unconscious or deliberate, shifting from one of these paired concepts to the other generally aids the anti-reservation cause and adds to avoidable confusion. Because of the ideological need to present rationing as selection, extravagant claims are made on behalf of devices like the competitive examination and the rank ordering it can be forced to yield. The way forward here would be to recognise the rationing component and introduce transparent methods of dealing with it, such as a lottery. However, this can only be done within a group that is recognised to be of broadly equal 'merit', measured in whatever way. To identify such a group – that is, to carry out genuine selection – requires two things: first, the definition of an honest and academically defensible standard of eligibility; and second, strenuous efforts to prevent this discrete threshold of eligibility from being converted into a continuous scale that claims to measure excellence.

The key step in the procedure outlined above is the definition of an honest eligibility threshold. This should be such that candidates below it will not profit from the given course of study because they are simply not prepared for it. That is why it is crucial that this be an honest standard, because the typical tendency in elite Indian institutions is to cheat by setting much higher standards than are reasonable simply because the huge demand for the course will ensure that enough candidates will meet them.[35] This allows the institution to 'free ride' on its highly selective entrance exam because the candidates selected will require little or no support from the institution to pass the exit examinations. As the reverse of the 'garbage in, garbage out' principle, this kind of free riding can be addictive because there is hardly any auditing of the actual value added by elite institutions in India (Mehta 2006; Mohanty 2006).

However, even if an epidemic of honest eligibility standards were to somehow infect all our institutions overnight, it is still possible that we would be left with a sizeable problem of unequal access to higher education across social groups. But this would be a real problem, shorn of the artificial complications added by active sabotage or passive apathy. And our attempts to tackle a real problem would always take us forward, even if progress were slow and painful. A concrete example might help, and here is one thrown up by the litigation around the 93rd Amendment mandating 27 per cent OBC reservations in centrally funded educational institutions. The Jawaharlal Nehru University (JNU) decided to interpret the somewhat ambiguous term 'cut-off mark' (for OBC candidates admitted under the new quota) in the *Ashok Kumar Thakur* judgment to mean 10 per cent less than the marks scored (in the JNU entrance examination, for which the pass mark was 40 per cent) by the last general category candidate to be admitted. Although the students' union and other student groups contested this interpretation, the JNU administration stuck to it, resulting in 54, 88, and 277 OBC quota seats remaining unfilled in 2008–09, 2009–10, and 2010–11 respectively.[36] Since alternative (equally or more plausible) interpretations were being used in other institutions, and since the JNU administration had made no secret of its antipathy to this quota, it is fair to say that the choice was probably influenced by the fact that this interpretation would be more restrictive than others.

The main issue here is the nature of the 'cut-off mark' which controls access to this elite institution. This cut-off has *no intellectual or academic content whatsoever* because it is determined solely by the number of seats available, which in turn is determined by administrative, financial, and logistical considerations.[37] In other words, a cut-off determined in this manner belongs to the realm of *rationing* rather than academic selection. On the other hand, the pass mark in the entrance exam does have academic and intellectual content, because the exam will presumably be designed in a way that *makes* the score of 40 per cent a meaningful threshold. This threshold will not change in response to extraneous factors like the number of seats available, and it has the added virtue of being a pre-declared benchmark known to all candidates before the examination.[38] But the decisive reason for the academic validity of the pass mark is still the first one relating to exam design. By comparison, it is impossible, even absurd, to think of designing an exam in such a way that the 'last qualifying candidate' will have a particular score.

The Supreme Court eventually did what it had to do and clarified that the cut-off mark means a pre-announced eligibility threshold, but it also fixed the cut-off mark for OBC candidates as 10 per cent less than the level for the general category (Supreme Court 2011). This last move illustrates once again the lack of clarity about eligibility thresholds. An honestly determined eligibility threshold should be at or near the minimum level of 'teachability' for a course of study. It does not make sense to move this goalpost for any group no matter how disadvantaged it may be. Problems of access at this level must be dealt with by raising capabilities, not by lowering thresholds. But in a situation where bad faith abounds, stakes are high and key concepts muddled, outcomes depend on the contingent balance of power rather than institutional logic.

The challenges of agency

By far the most difficult of the many challenges facing quotas is that of cultivating agency among the entitled. For it is true, as critics have long insisted, that the quota often takes away more than it gives. All the more so in a hostile environment, which is what quotas and their incumbents invariably face. But what makes agency the most challenging of challenges is that it is *not* a matter of 'policy'. This is despite the fact that policy matters (such as the quotas themselves, and their design and manner of implementation) are quite relevant to the development of agency. Though they might be close to each other on other planes, an immeasurable distance separates a policy-object – a 'target group' – from a political subject on the plane of agency. Even the law, which is supposed to bridge this gap, is only able to do so rarely because it is itself the product of a specific political compromise negotiated in a specific historical context.

As some insightful scholars with long involvement in social justice issues have suggested, the emergence of agency can be best facilitated by a 'return to politics' in the discourse on reservations (Tharu *et al.* 2007). But this is precisely the most difficult direction to take today when reservations discourse is dominated by perspectives that presuppose their own 'ownership' of the nation, and see quotas as generous concessions that they, the 'general category', are gifting to the 'reserved categories' representing narrow particularistic interests. This discourse is unable to conceive of the 'reserved categories' as possessing an equal or stronger claim to being the 'owners' of the nation. But the real difficulty is not of *replacing* the policy or legal perspective with a 'political' perspective, but of enabling a minimal collegiality between the two. The momentum necessary to leap from object to subject – some gaps cannot be bridged, they can only be jumped – can be generated only if both policy and the law make room for a new and unfamiliar political sensibility.

The irony is that, in the final analysis, despite its many layers of complexity, the case for quotas in higher education is simple and strong. Jayati Ghosh puts it well:

> [W]e still need reservations for different groups in higher education – not because they are the perfect instruments to rectify long-standing discrimination, but because they are still the most workable method to move in this direction. And most of all, because the nature of Indian society ensures that without such measures, social discrimination and exclusion will only persist and be strengthened.
>
> *(Ghosh 2006: 2432)*

Notes

1 An earlier version of the chapter entitled 'Social Justice and Higher Education in India Today: Markets, Ideologies, and Inequalities in a Fluid Context' appeared in Zoya Hasan and Martha Nussbaum (eds), *Equalising Access: Affirmative Action in Higher Education in India, United States, and South Africa* (New Delhi: Oxford University Press, 2012), pp. 212–238. I would like to thank an anonymous reviewer for suggestions and comments that have helped to clarify and strengthen the argument of this chapter. The responsibility for the errors and weaknesses that remain is mine.

2 This was Ambedkar's last speech to the Constituent Assembly before the final version of the Constitution prepared by the Drafting Committee (of which he was the Chairman) was passed the next day, on 26 November 1949. The Constitution was formally adopted by Parliament on 26 January 1950.

3 For example, if the state encourages the privatisation of higher education, then the equity impact of this policy shift will depend on the relative efficiency of the state as a regulator of private enterprise compared to its earlier role as direct provider of 'merit goods' like education. Arguments for privatisation are often predicated on the assumption that the state is a better regulator than provider. Such assumptions need to be explicitly investigated rather than taken for granted.

4 A longer earlier version of the following argument is found in Deshpande (2009a, pp. 41ff.).

5 Subsequent page references are to this work unless indicated otherwise.

6 It should also be noted that Sundaram's category of 'Others' includes Muslims, whose enrolment ratios are very different from the other groups (Hindu upper castes as a residual, and other minority religious groups like Christians, Sikhs, etc., in so far as these groups are not part of the SC or ST categories). This would tend to understate the difference between the 'forward' groups like the latter and the rest of society.

7 Desai and Kulkarni treat this as evidence against the popular prejudice among the upper castes that relatively well-off lower castes are gaining places in higher education at their expense.

8 A more detailed discussion of the social functions of 'exit' and 'entrance' examinations is available in Deshpande (2010); see specially the respective subsections on these types of examination, pp. 26ff.

9 In other words, pass percentages in 'exit' exams have been rising steadily, whereas they have been falling in 'entrance' examinations (where 'pass' actually means 'selection' or being above the 'cut-off').

10 Or those who can afford the effective but extremely expensive 'coaching' targeted at precisely these entrance examinations. These issues will be discussed further in the last section.

11 Other forms of preferential policies could include scholarships, remission of fees, relaxation of age limits, or other eligibility conditions, special hostels or institutions, and in some cases state-subsidised orientation or coaching programmes.

12 This is particularly true in the context of the fact that reservations in India have to cater to the majority of the population, whereas in the USA affirmative action is a minority issue. For a balanced and painstakingly researched perspective on this particular comparison, see Thomas Weisskopf (2004); for an overview on quotas in the Indian context, see K.S. Chalam (2007).

13 One of the curious aspects of popular opinion (as reflected in the media) is that the occasional instance of quota fraud (when persons who do not belong to the entitled groups falsely claim that they do) are seen as proving the axiom that 'quotas are bad' rather than the more logical conclusion that 'fraud is bad'.

14 Arjun Appadurai's (2006) argument is about the anxieties of majorities that feel irrationally threatened by small (often *very* small) minorities. See also Deshpande (2009b) for more on this theme.

15

> In nationalist arguments, the case for special treatment of Untouchables was constantly distinguished from that of religious minorities through an emphasis on their poverty and 'backwardness'. What separated these groups from the majority was not so much religio-cultural difference, but socio-economic inequality, it was argued. Group representation aimed not at the recognition of group difference, but the rectification of 'backwardness'.
>
> (Bajpai 2011: 125).

16 According to the non-discrimination argument, the main intent of compensatory preferences is to 'counter the residues of discrimination and to overcome structural arrangements which perpetuate the effects of past selections in which invidious discrimination was a major determinant'. This argument is linked to the notion of deserts and the unit of analysis here is the individual, even though group membership is used to identify those individuals who may be suffering from the resilient forms of discrimination mentioned above. The reparations argument is like the non-discrimination one in basing itself on fairness; but unlike the latter, it sees the group rather than the individual as the appropriate unit; and the timeframe it employs is different from both of the other principles in that it seeks to redress a past wrong in the present (Galanter 1984: 553).

17 Though it was named for its first petitioner, the *Champakam Dorairajan v. State of Madras* case actually rested on the second petitioner, C.R. Srinivasan, who (unlike Dorairajan) had actually applied for admission to the government engineering college in Guindy and been turned down because the Brahmin quota was already filled by candidates with higher marks. Srinivasan's case was that he had scored higher marks than many of those who had been admitted under the quotas for other communities (such as the non-Brahmins, backward Hindus, Muslims, Indian Christians, etc.), and that therefore he had been discriminated against solely because of his caste, since he would have been admitted on merit criteria. See Supreme Court of India 1951.

18 As Marc Galanter has noted, in spite of the government's swift response through the First Amendment, 'the *status quo ante* was not restored; the post-amendment State policies were more constricted than those that prevailed earlier.' (1984: 527).

19 Article 15.(1) – The State shall not discriminate against any citizen on grounds only of religion, race, caste, sex, place of birth or any of them. Article 29.(2) – No citizen shall be denied admission into any educational institution maintained by the State or receiving aid out of State funds on grounds only of

religion, race, caste, language or any of them. Article 46. – The State shall promote with special care the educational and economic interests of the weaker sections of the people, and, in particular, of the Scheduled Castes and the Scheduled Tribes, and shall protect them from social injustice and all forms of exploitation.

20 Article 15, Clause (4): 'Nothing in this article or in clause (2) of article 29 shall-prevent the State from making any special provision for the advancement of any socially and educationally backward classes of citizens or for the Scheduled Castes and the Scheduled Tribes.'

21 In *S.A. Partha v. State of Mysore*, one of the cases responsible for the more famous *M.R. Balaji & Others v. State of Mysore* judgment of the Supreme Court in 1962.

22 To go directly to Mandal is to ignore a major intervening case, *N.M. Thomas v. State of Kerala*, decided by the Supreme Court in September 1975. *Thomas* is important because its seven-judge bench proposed a major change in doctrine through a five–two majority. It argued that Articles 15(4) and 16(4) were of equal status to Articles 15(1) and 16(1). In other words, the court saw preferential treatment for SCs and STs as a sort of fundamental right in itself. However, I am skipping this case because (1) it had little to do with education; and (2) the doctrinal change it proposed, though extremely significant, may have been an aberration provoked by the Emergency and seems to have been shortlived. See Galanter (1984: 382–395).

23 This is how the government arrived at the 27 per cent figure for OBC reservations – added to the existing 22.5 per cent for the SCs and STs, it makes for a total of 49.5 per cent, which is in compliance with the court's rule of 'below 50 per cent'.

24 This is especially noticeable, for example, in the contrast between the blind acceptance of 'merit' arguments that take examination marks and ranks at face value, and the insistent scrutiny of measures of backwardness. It is not that the latter is unnecessary, but that the former also deserves comparable application of mind.

25 The following paragraphs are borrowed from Deshpande (2011).

26 Figures for 2010 are from MHRD (2011: 86), and for 2001 from MHRD (2008: Statement 1, C-1). Remarkable though they are, these growth rates are still insufficient, at least in aggregate terms. At 12.4 per cent, India's gross enrolment ratio (GER) for higher education in 2006 was well below the average for the world (23.2 per cent) or for Asia (22 per cent), and far behind the average for developed countries (54.6 per cent). Sources: figures in brackets: Planning Commission (2008: 22); figure for India: MHRD (2010: 27).

27 Both in the narrow sense of being able to pay fees as well as the broader sense of being able to defer entry into paid employment.

28 Figures in brackets are for 2006 and taken from Planning Commission (2008: 23). Powar and Bhalla (2004) estimate the share of private institutions in engineering, medicine, management, and teacher training as 78, 76, 64, and 67 per cent respectively.

29 This is suggested by the time series data in the *Selected Educational Statistics* of the MHRD, but some definitional issues need clarification before firm claims can be made.

30 See the study by Devesh Kapur (2010).

31 The Supreme Court found in favour of the Malas on the grounds that schemes addressing intra-SC inequalities (even though they did not change the schedules in any way) amounted to 'disturbing' the constitutionally decreed list of SCs, something which only the President was authorised to do on the advice of Parliament. For a lucid critique of this particular decision and an insightful discussion of the larger issues involved, see Balagopal (2005).

32 This argument may be misunderstood because we intuitively expect that (taking caste as an instance of social status) very poor people of a higher caste will find it difficult to discriminate against very rich people of a lower caste. This may or may not be true empirically, but even if it is, this does not rule out the equally intuitive probability that higher caste people of similar or higher economic standing would have no trouble at all in discriminating against our hypothetical very-rich-but-low-caste person.

33 This is argued in detail in Deshpande (2015). See also Mohanty (2006) and Ghosh (2006).

34 It may be relevant here to mention one such attempt to suggest more composite modes of addressing disadvantage and discrimination with which I am associated, and the criticisms that it has attracted (Deshpande and Yadav 2006). Speaking only for myself and without implicating my co-author, I am convinced that the modalities we proposed then need more careful specification, including empirical simulations, before they can hope to serve as models for concrete programmes. However, I am not able to share Mrityunjay Mohanty's conviction that social and economic disabilities should and more

importantly can always be kept separate (2006: 3788). Even policies that do not 'conflate' the two will surely have to respond to the fact that each impacts the other *in its own domain*, i.e. for real people in real-life situations, poverty exacerbates the disabilities of low caste status and vice versa. Both creamy layer and intra-Dalit disparities are cases in point. The data deficits that Ghosh (2006: 2431) mentions are problems of a different order and their impact may perhaps be clarified through realistic simulations.

35 There is anecdotal evidence that political pressure forces many (non-elite) institutions to do the opposite, i.e. set standards that are unreasonably low. In my view this is just as dishonest as a too-high standard.

36 I thank Tapas Saha of the All India Students' Association (AISA) for this information.

37 One could argue that the mark obtained by the last admitted non-reservation candidate is an academically *relevant* number in the sense that, along with other numbers showing the performance of the reserved categories, it would offer one measure of the 'academic range' of the admitted cohort. But note that this relevance comes *after* reservation candidates have been admitted by some other criteria. It is very difficult to defend it in a gate-keeping role with academic or intellectual pretensions.

38 This is the argument that seems to have swayed the court: 'A factor which is neither known nor ascertained at the time of declaring the admission programme cannot be used to disentitle a candidate to admission, who is otherwise entitled for admission.' (Supreme Court 2011).

References

Appadurai, Arjun. 2006. *Fear of Small Numbers: An Essay on the Geography of Anger*, Duke University Press, Durham.

Bajpai, Rochana. 2011. *Debating Difference: Group Rights and Liberal Democracy in India*, Oxford University Press, New Delhi.

Balagopal, K. 2005. 'Justice for Dalits among Dalits', *The Economic and Political Weekly*, 40(29): 3128–33.

Basant, Rakesh and Gitanjali Sen. 2010. 'Who participates in higher education in India? Rethinking the role of affirmative action', *The Economic and Political Weekly*, 45(39): 62–70.

Bourdieu, Pierre and Jean-Claude Passeron. 1990 [1970]. *Reproduction in Education, Society and Culture*, second English edition (original French edition published 1970), Sage Publications, London.

Chalam, K.S. 2007. *Caste-Based Reservation and Human Development in India*, Sage Publications, New Delhi.

Desai, Sonalde and Veena Kulkarni. 2008. 'Changing educational inequalities in India in the context of affirmative action', *Demography*, 45(2): 245–270.

Deshpande, Satish. 2009a. 'Inclusion versus excellence: caste and the framing of fair access in Indian higher education', *South African Review of Sociology*, 40(1): 127–147.

Deshpande, Satish. 2009b. 'The moral meanings of majorities', *Seminar*, 602: 20–24.

Deshpande, Satish. 2010. *Pass, Fail, Distinction: The Examination as a Social Institution*, Third Marjorie Sykes Memorial Lecture, NCERT, New Delhi.

Deshpande, Satish. 2011. 'Revisiting the basics', *Seminar*, 624.

Deshpande, Satish. 2015. 'Social justice and higher education in India today: markets, states, ideologies and inequalities in a fluid context', in Martha Nussbaum and Zoya Hasan (eds), *Equalising Access: Affirmative Action in Higher Education in India, the United States and South Africa*, Oxford University Press, New Delhi.

Deshpande, S. and Yogendra Yadav. 2006. 'Redesigning Affirmative Action', *The Economic and Political Weekly*, 41(24): 2419–2424.

Galanter, Marc. 1984. *Competing Equalities: Law and the Backward Classes in India*, University of California Press, Berkeley.

Ghosh, Jayati. 2006. 'Case for caste-based quotas in higher education', *The Economic and Political Weekly*, 41(24): 2428–32.

High Court of Karnataka. 1961. Judgment, *S.A. Partha v. State of Mysore*, AIR 1961 Mys 220, 16 January.

High Court of Madras. 1950. Judgment, *Srimathi Champakam Dorairajan v. State of Madras*, CMP No. 5255, 27 July.

Kapur, Devesh. 2010. *Diaspora, Development, and Democracy: The Domestic Impact of International Migration From India*. Princeton, NJ: Princeton University Press.

Krishnaswamy, Sudhir and Madhav Khosla. 2008. 'Reading *Ashok Kumar Thakur vs. Union of India*: legal effect and significance', *The Economic and Political Weekly*, 43(29): 53–60.

Kumar, Krishna. 1985. 'Reproduction or change? Education and elites in India', *The Economic and Political Weekly*, 20(30): 1280–1284.

Madras High Court. 1950. Judgment, *Champakam Dorairajan v. State of Madras* (CMP 5255) and *C.R. Srinivasan vs. State of Madras* (CMP 5340), 27 July.

Mehta, Pratap Bhanu. 2006. 'Democracy, disagreement and merit', *The Economic and Political Weekly*, 17 July: 2425–27.

MHRD (Ministry of Human Resource Development). 2008. *Selected Educational Statistics: Time Series Data 2005–06*, Government of India, New Delhi.

MHRD. 2010. *Report to the People on Education*, July, Government of India, New Delhi.

MHRD. 2011. *Annual Report 2010–11*, Government of India, New Delhi.

Mohanty, Mrityunjay. 2006. 'Social inequality, labour market dynamics and reservations', *The Economic and Political Weekly*, 41(24): 3777–89.

Planning Commission. 2008. *Eleventh Five Year Plan 2007–12; Vol. 2, Social Sector*. Government of India, New Delhi.

Powar, K.B. and V. Bhalla. 2004. 'Private professional higher education in India', *New Frontiers in Education* 34(2): 126–127.

Prasad, Madhav. 2011. 'Language, education and political existence', *Seminar*, 624.

Sundaram, K. 2006. 'On backwardness and fair access to higher education: results from the NSSO 55th Round surveys, 1999–2000', *The Economic and Political Weekly*, 41(50): 5173–5182.

Supreme Court of India. 1951. Judgment, *Champakam Dorairajan v. State of Madras*, Case Nos. 270 and 271 of 1951, 9 April.

Supreme Court of India. 1962. Judgment, *M.R. Balaji v. State of Mysore*, Case No. 649, 29 September 1962.

Supreme Court of India. 2008. Judgment, *Ashok Kumar Thakur v. Union of India*, 10 April.

Supreme Court of India. 2011. Judgment, *P.V. Indiresan v. Union of India*, Civil Appeal No. 7084, 18 August 2011.

Tharu, Susie, Madhav Prasad, Rekha Pappu, and K. Satyanarayana. 2007. 'Reservations and the return to politics', *The Economic and Political Weekly*, 42(49): 39–45.

Weisskopf, Thomas. 2004. *Affirmative Action in the United States and India: A Comparative Perspective*. Routledge, New York.

16

Tribes and higher education in India

Virginius Xaxa

On the eve of Independence, what marked the situation of tribals in India were poor economic conditions, social backwardness, and geographical and physical isolation. Such a state of being was attributed to their overall isolation from the larger Indian society. However, even in instances where this geographical and physical isolation was broken through roads, railways, and other means of communications, the economic and social condition of tribes hadn't changed for the better. Rather, it had become worse. With the improvement in means of communication, the general scenario was the movement of people from the plains, especially traders and money-lenders to begin with, and later land-hungry peasants, to tribal areas. With this began the process of dispossession of tribes from their lands through force, fraud, forgery but more importantly, usury. This alienation of land from tribes to non-tribes, widespread in the early phase of colonial rule, continued all through the colonial period. Alongside, there was another kind of dispossession. This had to do with the denial of rights over access to forest and forest resources that the tribes had traditionally exercised and enjoyed for generations. The forest, along with its land, was the life support system of the tribal population. These new developments had far-reaching implications – economic, social, and cultural – for tribal societies. Tribes, on the eve of Independence, were thus marked by physical and social isolation, on the one hand, and massive exploitation on the other due to their contact with the outside population.

The scenario noted above led to heated debates on the policy to be adopted towards tribes preceding India's Independence in 1947. The debate was led by Verrier Elwin and G.S. Ghurye. The former made a plea for their isolation, citing things that had happened to tribes following their contact with the outside world. The latter, on the other hand, attributed the overall social and economic backwardness of tribes to their geographical and social isolation which, he argued, needed to be overcome by their assimilation into the larger Indian society (Elwin 1943; Ghurye 1943). These two lines of thought found an echo among others. While the former had the support of the colonial administrators, the latter found resonance among nationalist leaders and social workers.

In fact, at the time of the constituent assembly's deliberation on the policy for tribes, the nationalist leadership was fully aware of its dual lines of debate as well as the situation prevailing in tribal India. Strangely still, neither of the two lines seemed to have fully convinced the leaders, who nowhere made any clear statements as to what the policy was. In fact, if one were to take the Constitution and the provisions laid down therein for tribes, it would be clear that post-Independence India has adopted neither a policy of isolation nor of assimilation towards them. The provisions for tribes in the Constitution take what may be termed as the middle path. And these are broadly of three types. The first are the provisions for protection, especially against their dispossession from land, which is evident in the fifth and sixth Schedule of the Constitution. The second are the provisions for safeguarding of their language and culture. This is what the policy of isolation envisaged by Elwin aimed at protecting, among many others. The third set of provisions guarantee reservation for them in state employment and higher educational institutions and development aimed at improving their economic and social conditions. These provisions in the Constitution were oriented to ensure access to employment as well as improvement of their socio-economic status as espoused by the policy of assimilation articulated by Ghurye.

Underlying policy and higher education

The policy of reservation has been identified as one of the most important institutional mechanisms for addressing the aspects of social isolation or exclusion, thereby initiating the integration of tribes with the larger Indian society. State employment and politics are the two sites where reservation has been identified as key to the process of integration. But reservation in state employment, unlike reservation in the sphere of politics, is conditional, as it is contingent on a level of educational attainment. For employment of certain kinds, mere school education of a certain level is necessary. However, there are employments that require qualification above high/higher secondary education. But even the movement to higher education is not automatic, dependent as it is on attainment of prerequisites – namely, the minimum qualification without which admission to a higher educational institution is not possible. Within school education, mobility to higher classes until the introduction of the Right of Children to Free and Compulsory Education Act, 2009 (RTE Act) was contingent on attainment of educational achievement in the form of passing the preceding classes. Hence, education of a certain level and kind is much more important today than education per se. Much of the employment available today either in the public or private sector requires qualification that goes beyond school level, underscoring the importance of higher education. In addition to qualification, a certain level of competence too is almost mandatory.

Modern education in India was introduced under the British, and so was higher education. Since then, both school and higher education have witnessed manifold expansion, especially in the post-Independence phase of the national reconstruction process. And yet the position of higher education in India is still far from adequate, not only in terms of number, but, more importantly, in quality. The existing higher educational institutions have scarce resources and hence entry to higher education is competitive. The greater the reputation of the institution, the fiercer the competition. For those who compete for entry into higher educational institutions, though in principle they are treated as equals in terms of the opportunities for entry, the ground reality is far different. The level of the playing field for the competitors varies greatly on account of disadvantages such as colour, ethnicity, status, class, sex, etc. The Indian Constitution has taken cognisance of this and has tried to address the problem with special provisions in the form of what is generally termed as 'protective discrimination'. Thus in higher educational institutions there is reservation of seats for the most deprived and disadvantaged – the Scheduled Tribes (STs) and Scheduled Castes (SCs). There is also relaxation in qualification for their entry to higher educational institutions. In addition, financial support in the form of scholarship, book grants, and others facilities is extended to students from this section of society.

Modern education and tribes

The tribal society did not have the tradition of reading and writing. Knowledge and values were passed from one generation to another orally. It was the Christian missionaries who introduced reading and writing skills among them. The educational institutions introduced by the Christian missionaries cannot be understood independent of their agenda and objectives. They were historically tied to the larger objective of evangelisation, which has now almost become autonomous. Thus, with the coming of the Christian missionaries a distinct and specialised institution emerged in tribal society, which took upon itself the role of imparting knowledge, values, and skills that were alien to them. It was directed primarily towards change and transformation in society. Its emergence to a certain degree undermined the place of the traditional institution but did not replace it. Thus both the traditional institution as well as the one introduced by the Christian missionaries existed side by side. One was oriented to change and the other to maintaining traditional social order, giving rise to much stress and strain in society.

This being the case, the missions did not generally go for education beyond primary- or at best middle-school level. The missionary agenda was just to equip tribes enough to read and write so that they could read and understand religious texts. If there was ever any student who was keen to move beyond this, such a case was rare; he had no alternative but to go to far-away towns/cities/hill stations where such institutions were available. Often the converts that the missionaries found bright were sent to higher schools elsewhere so that on their return they could be used to aid the work of the missions. Tribal students going for higher education was rare but not altogether absent.

Paradoxically enough, though the colonial government extracted enormous revenue by exploiting resources in the tribal region and exacting taxes of various kinds, it did little to improve their lives through extension of modern education and health services. It was left to the Christian missionaries to do this work. The educational institutions introduced by the Christian missions initially touched upon only some tribal pockets and tribes. Gradually, their work spread to other parts and tribes, and that is how more and more tribes and regions came under the influence of the missionary activity. A sizeable section of tribes today are Christians. While Christian presence in some tribes and regions is substantial and visible, a large chunk notably remain outside this religious fold. In Nagaland, Mizoram, Meghalaya, and Manipur, for example, Christians form the dominant segment of the tribal population, elsewhere in the region, they are present though are not as visible. This has also been the case in other parts of tribal India. However, even with respect to these regions, it is in some tribes and pockets that they are relatively more visible than the others.

Hence, on the eve of Independence, tribes and tribal regions outside the sphere of missionary activity still had no exposure to reading and writing. This began only after India's Independence. And in post-Independence India, the situation has changed significantly due to the role of the state – not discounting the significant role of the Christian missions and other nongovernmental organisations that have joined the venture. If one were to look at the status of the tribal population today, one would find the tribes and regions under the Christian mission influence better placed on social development indicators, literacy being the most notable among them.

Higher education and tribes

As noted earlier, entry into higher education is contingent on a level of educational attainment. And although literacy is linked to higher education, mere literacy is not sufficient for entry into higher education. There are people who are literate but may not have even completed primary education – a large chunk fall within this definition. Others have either completed primary, middle, high, or higher-secondary education. The last is the minimum requirement for entry into higher education. As one moves from one level of education to another, the total number keeps falling. This is a trend for all categories of social groups, but the fall in size is the largest in the case of tribes. The lower the literacy late, the lower the chance for entry into higher education and vice versa. This has been true in the case of tribes as well. In 1961, tribal literacy was a mere 8.54 per cent. It saw a steady rise through the decades and stood at 47.10 per cent in 2001. With a rise in literacy, the number of students obtaining higher education has also seen a steady increase. However, in comparison with other social categories, enrolment is still low – not so much due to literacy as to the level of educational attainment. Tribal literacy share keeps declining as they move from one level of education to another, and tends to become miniscule by the time they reach secondary level education. This has to do with dropouts, the most serious problem confronting school education among tribes today. Dropout happens to be a common problem facing all categories of school students. However, it is extremely severe among tribes, who have very high dropout rates – 57.36 per cent in Classes I–V, 72.80 per cent in Classes I–VIII, and 82.96 per cent in Classes I–X during 1998–99. Also, the gap between the general population and tribes was found to be widening from 13.67 per cent in 1990–91 to 15.52 per cent in 1998–99 at the secondary level (Government of India 2007). Hence, though eligible candidates for higher education have increased in recent years, the enrolment of tribes into it is still low and the gap vis-à-vis other social groups is still large. According to the higher education statistics for 2010–11, ST enrolment in higher education stood at 1.209 million out of a total of 27.5 million, of which 0.689 million were male and 0.52 million were female.

This constituted a mere 4.39 per cent of the total tribal population in the country. However, at 11.21 per cent the tribal gross enrolment ratio (GER) was relatively better in comparison to the 19.41 per cent GER of all social categories (Government of India 2013).[1] This was a marked improvement on the 1.43 per cent GER of 1991 for the tribes as compared to 2.4 per cent for the SCs and 4.72 per cent for other social categories. The corresponding figure was 3.13 per cent for STs, 4.78 per cent for SCs, and 7.81 per cent for others in 2000, and 7.33, 9.18, and 12.24 per cent in 2006 (Rout 2014: 110).

Reference was made earlier of high dropout rates among tribes as they move from one level of education to another. This is more evident in girls than boys, indicating a male gender preference. However, girls who have moved to a higher level of school education have been performing better than boys and moving to higher educational institutions. In fact, in terms of eligibility they fare better than boys in higher educational institutions more so at the postgraduate level. The percentage of girls passing out from Class XII is relatively higher compared to their male counterparts for all social groups, including tribes. However, their transition to Class XIII falls abysmally both in proportion to their pass percentage as well in comparison to their male counterparts except in the case of ST girls, where it is beyond 100 per cent (Rout 2014: 106). But even this exceptional pattern of the tribes has now taken a turn similar to the other social categories (Rout 2014: 107). At state levels, it is similar to the all-India pattern. For example, in the high-school pass results the percentage of girls was 38.1 per cent as compared to 40.1 per cent for boys in Chhattisgarh, 84.2 per cent as compared to 85.4 per cent for boys in Jharkhand, and 43.4 per cent as compared to 54.6 per cent for boys in West Bengal. At the higher secondary-school level, it was 70.27 per cent against 67.50 per cent for boys in Chhattisgarh, 68.82 per cent against 60.08 per cent for boys in Jharkhand, and 66.89 per cent against 62.30 per cent for boys in West Bengal. It was 85.66 per cent against 79.34 per cent for boys in Madhya Pradesh and 48.69 per cent against 48.79 per cent for boys in Orissa (Birua 2012: 10).

Thus, though girls have a higher pass percentage than boys, their enrolment in higher education is lower in comparison, showing prejudices against them even in the tribal society. As per higher education statistics 2010–11, the share of tribal girls in higher education was 4.32 per cent as compared to 4.45 per cent for boys. This was most evident in the GER. Tribal GER in higher education was 11.21 per cent, but the share of males and females were 12.95 per cent and 9.52 per cent respectively. However, once this initial bias has been overcome, the share of women going for higher education was better than that of men. This is evident if one takes looks at postgraduate education.

The studies on enrolment in higher education point out that once the threshold of higher education has been crossed, the entry of tribes to higher education in respect of enrolment is not very different from other social categories. The question is whether this equal chance of going to college is due to equality of opportunity or the policy of reservation of seats in higher education, which earlier remained unfilled either due to absence of eligible candidates or other constraints. Is the bridging in the gap in enrolment between SC/ST and non-SC/ST and others due to the openness of the system and the ability of tribal students to compete, or due to provision of reservation? Of course, there is much difference across social groups in terms of their share in the total senior secondary pass. The percentage of SCs and STs is relatively low. Yet their transition to higher education is much higher compared to other social categories. In 1996, for example, the pass figures for STs, SCs, and others stood at 36.3, 40.3, and 48.6 per cent respectively, but their enrolment share in the first year of higher education was as high as 117.4, 79.1 and 66.8 per cent respectively (Rout 2014: 106).

Higher education and unevenness in access

There is considerable regional variation among tribes and their access to higher education due to factors, such as the absence/presence of high/higher secondary schools, which in turn boost enrolment and literacy level – this being the most important. Tribes and regions with higher literacy rate have greater participation in higher education. The north-east participation in higher education in comparison to peninsular India's indicates this fairly well. In north-east India, those who aspire to higher education have no option but to go to schools run by the Christian missions in Shillong. In the tribal regions of what was once popularly known as Chhota Nagpur, aspirants either move to Ranchi or Jabalpur for higher education.

The point is that tribal regions even today suffer from lack of access to higher education. In this respect, north-east India stands as an exception, for given its size of tribal population, it has a higher density of higher educational institutions in comparison to other parts of tribal India. Almost every state in north-east India has a central university, other than those in Assam, Tripura, and Manipur, which primarily caters to the tribal population. In addition, many other higher educational institutions have arisen, offering aspirants space for different kinds of higher education. While stating so, it is important to note that there is also a relatively fair presence of candidates eligible for entry into higher education. This is linked to the relatively higher level of literacy in the region. The presence of higher educational institutions in the region in turn induces secondary school passing students to go for higher education.

The setting up of the North-Eastern Hill University at Shillong in Meghalaya in the 1970s, with campuses in Nagaland and Mizoram, acted as a catalyst for higher education among tribes in north-east India. As it is, Shillong had been and still is the centre of educational institutions, including some of the best colleges that attract students from different parts of the region. Since the inception of North-Eastern Hill University, many new institutions have arisen in different states. For example, in Mizoram, with a population of over one million, there were as many as

22 colleges and one university in 2009–10 administered either by governments (central and state) or private individuals. The same is true for other states of the region. This has resulted in manifold increase in the number of tribal students in higher educational institutions. In fact, unlike elsewhere in the country, they dominate the higher educational institutions in the region except in Assam, Tripura, and Manipur.

In the rest of the tribal regions, higher education is marked by an absence of infrastructure facilities and poor literacy rates and it is only since the mid-2000s that there seems to be some change taking place. The setting up of the Indira Gandhi Tribal University at Amarkantak in Madhya Pradesh with a vision of campuses in other tribal regions has been an important initiative. Situated on the border of Madhya Pradesh and Chhattisgarh, Amarkantak is inhabited by a tribal population. However, it is too short a time to ascertain the university's influence and impact. I have visited the university a couple of times and I must say that though it has lent the tribals an opportunity to gain higher education, their presence on the campus is far from visible. The university, largely, remains confined to students hailing from the vicinity and has not moved beyond this. In recent years, some more central universities have come up in some other tribal regions of peninsular India, such as the Central University of Koraput and the Central University of Gujarat. The latter, though located in Gandhinagar, has become a hub for tribal students from different parts of Gujarat. And unlike other universities in the state, they are quite visible in this one.

State universities and central universities

Tribes moving to higher education may thus be located at two levels: in the state they are born in and inhabit; and in other states that they move to. Students moving to other states either enrol in central government-run institutions or private institutions, particularly run by Christian organisations. Their entry into state-run institutions in states other than their own has an inherent constraint. They are not eligible for reservation, which is meant only for tribes belonging to that state, and can enter those institutions only as general candidates. At the same time, the state-run institutions are inadequately equipped in terms of infrastructure and faculty. This is not to say there are no exceptions.

Hence a large chunk of students who have been going for higher education are concentrated in their own states. Yet their share of enrolments within higher educational institutions in those states fall far short of the size of their population, excepting some states in the north-east. This has been so mainly due to high dropout rates as students reach higher level of school education. Hence, though in principle seats are available for them in higher educational institutions because of a quota in proportion to the size of the tribal population, the intake falls short due to the unavailability of students. Further, even those who are eligible often do not go for higher education either due to poor economic conditions or the distance of higher educational institutions or a combination of both. Often this is also due to a lack of people in the community or around them who could guide, encourage, and mentor them for higher education. The state governments are hardly proactive in addressing the issue of higher education of tribes. Neither are they proactive in dissemination of information nor in disbursement of facilities such as scholarship, book-grants, uniform, hostel facilities, etc. Even when these are in place, it is next to impossible to make use of them, as the process tends to be too cumbersome.

Despite the spread of higher educational institutions in regions especially the north-east, there is a wave of migration of students for higher education to other parts of India, particularly to metropolises such as Delhi, Mumbai, Bangalore, Hyderabad, and Chennai. Again this is most glaring in the case of north-east India. In the 1980s, the number of tribal students at a college or university in Delhi or elsewhere was small and could be counted. This is no longer the case. Since the early 1990s, there has been an exodus of students for admission to institutions of higher learning, especially central universities and colleges run by the central ministries, which are cosmopolitan in character (like the Delhi University and its colleges, the Jawaharlal Nehru University and the University of Hyderabad). There is also movement to state universities but enrolments there are relatively low. The private colleges and institutions are the other attractions, especially among those who can afford these, and this segment of the population among tribes has grown too. West Bengal, Jharkhand, Orissa, Chhattisgarh, and their adjoining areas have also seen heavy migration of tribal students to metropolises, especially Delhi, for higher education.

The rush to central institutions is for varied reasons. One that seems to stand out is the diversity they offer. They are open to students and faculties from across the country and more sensitive in complying with the reservation policy. Besides, they are also better than state institutions in terms of infrastructure facilities, reputation, and the standard of higher education. The cleavage between tribes and non-tribes (tacit and open) in various forms has been a part of the tribal situation throughout colonial India and continues to this day. The general tendency among tribes is to avoid institutions where groups/communities dominate. Most state institutions typify this, making tribal students feel uncomfortable as they are generally discriminated against, looked down upon, and treated as unwanted. It is also a fact that in state-level institutions of higher learning there is least interest in implementing reservations and other provisions of affirmative action. But then, if there are no options for the students due to a variety of constraints, which is the case with most, they do continue with these institutions. And this remains true even for central universities or institutions that disregard affirmative provisions, the Central University of Manipur being an example. The participation of tribal students here is hardly noticable even when they form nearly 30 per cent of the total state population. At the same time, there has long been an exodus of tribal students from Manipur to other parts of India. In fact, the scale of the movement of tribal students from the north-east to metropolises is much greater compared to other tribal regions.

However, there is great regional variation in their enrolments. Tribal students from the north-east far outnumber students from other parts of India, and their movement is far beyond Delhi. Students from Jharkhand, on the other hand, are mainly confined to Delhi. This pattern is visible in university departments. However, tribal student enrolment in these universities is predominantly in social sciences. Their numbers in basic science departments and related centres are abysmally low. Hence, while tribes have been competing for space in higher educational institutions in some institutions and some disciplines, from others they are conspicuously absent perhaps due to their inability to fulfil the minimum cut-off requirement for entry into these institutions and disciplines.

Inter- and intra-tribe differences

Other than region, religion is the other aspect of variation in access to higher education among tribes. Tribes today belong to different religious groupings that have a bearing on their education. That tribal Christians are far ahead in education is too obvious not only in the north-east but elsewhere too. As for other religious groups such as those who adhere to their traditional religion or to Hinduism, the picture is not very clear. What is evident, though, is that they lag far behind tribal Christians. In the case of peninsular India, the advantages that tribal Christians have gained in the course of time have brought about a divide and tension between them and tribal non-Christians, which keep surfacing in different forms.

Though tribe is treated as a category distinct from other social categories such as caste and dominant linguistic groups such as Assamese, Bengali, Oriya, etc., tribes form a very heterogeneous group in terms of their languages, population size, habitats of ecological settings, livelihood making, and so on. Those inhabiting distant and difficult ecological settings make their living mainly by hunting, food gathering, or shifting agriculture, or a combination of one or more of them. They are generally referred to as priority tribal communities, earlier known as primitive tribal communities. These communities have poor access even to primary education and hence secondary education/higher education is beyond their reach. Most tribes having access to higher education hail from either regions close to towns or distant places with communication facilities. There are also variations in access to higher education among tribes irrespective of the region they come from. Even in the north-east, where literacy is high and more eligible candidates are available for higher education in comparison to other regions, there is much ethnic variation in the region or state itself. In the state of Meghalaya, for instance, of the three dominant tribal communities, the Khasis and Jaintias have a much stronger presence in higher education vis-à-vis the Garos. The other groups, which are numerically small, are hardly visible in higher education. This is also the case in Nagaland, Tripura, Mizoram, Arunachal Pradesh, and Assam. The Angamis, Aos, and Lothas in Nagaland have better representation than other tribal groups. In Assam, Boros and Deoris are better placed vis-à-vis Lalungs, Rabhas, Tiwas, etc. Similar patterns can be seen in Jharkhand, Odisha, Chhattisgarh, Andhra Pradesh, and Rajasthan. In Jharkhand there are about 29 tribal groups, but the Oraons, Munda, Santhal, Kharia, Ho, the dominant groups of the state, have fared better than the others. In Andhra Pradesh, the Lambadas; in Rajasthan, the Meenas; and in Himachal Pradesh, the Negis – these groups dominate higher education. Of course, among the major groups too there is variation. Santhals are numerically the largest group in Jharkhand, but their literacy is lower than that of the Kharias, Mundas, and the Oraons.

The answer to why north-east India has done better than other tribal regions in higher education is rooted in its history. The region had an early exposure to modern education due to a widespread presence of Christian missionaries. One of the key concerns of these missionaries was/is education, which could aid their evangelisation. Those tribes or parts that had an early exposure to Christianity had better literacy, which resulted in a relatively large number of people going for higher level school education, and some among them even for higher education outside of the region.

Those who converted to Christianity and got educated also adopted a lifestyle which was seen as different and sometimes better than that of the rest. Their entry into new occupations either within the institutions of the Christian mission as teachers, catechist, health workers, etc., or in the government as office workers, peons, attendants, and clerks gave them an added status. Thus, there came about a process of social differentiation in the tribal society, not only of beliefs but also of occupations, which began to pose a challenge to the traditional system that was based either on birth in a lineage or age. Ascription, which was earlier the source of honour and esteem, was gradually replaced by lifestyle, occupation, and status. The values and status associated with the emerging positions gained momentum as the missionary work spread to different parts of the region. Apart from the north-east, the role of the missionaries is most visible in the tribal belt of what was earlier known as Chhota Nagpur. This part of mainland India has a visible Christian population, though meagre in comparison to the tribes practising their traditional religion. These tribal Christians are also visible in schools as well as higher education, and they are conspicuous by their presence in government and other employment. This pattern is the same in other tribal regions, but in a less visible form.

The changes that followed the work of Christian missions took the form of a new aspiration in the tribal society. Tribes that embraced Christianity and became educated were driven initially by the urge to work for the spread of Christianity and aspired to join the work of Christian missionaries as clergies and pastors. They went for higher education to theological colleges located in different parts of India and were trained in philosophy (Indian and Western) and Christian theology. After completion of their training and education, they worked and still work as pastors, teachers, administrators, etc., and in more recent years as social workers, development practitioners, and human rights activists. Such works were and are still considered as noble, and many young tribal students with good minds and talent go for education of this nature.

Gradually, other avenues of work and employment became accessible and available to educated tribals. They joined the government in various capacities, but their presence in the colonial government was tiny. Post-Independence India's policies of rapid economic and social development and affirmative action, despite various limitations, boosted higher education, as jobs of varying kinds and ranks became available to tribes. The earlier educated tribal youth, more so with higher education and employment in government or as clergies/pastors, acted as role models for others who later followed into their footsteps. It is important to note that the Christian missions place a great deal of stress on education and health. Encouragement, guidance, and at times even financial support form an integral part of their pastoral work. Such support has aided the movement of tribes to higher education.

The early exposure to reading and writing made it possible for tribes to enter new occupations in government and missionary organisations. These new opportunities attracted others, leading to the spread of Christianity and literacy, which eventually had a bearing on higher education. The difference among tribes with respect to modern education and higher education is related to this historical advantage. Tribes and tribal areas that had an early exposure to modern education have higher literacy rates, larger numbers of people with higher levels of educational attainment, and hence a higher pool of students for higher education.

Although, there is a strong association between tribal Christians and higher education, there are also cases of tribal non-Christians doing fairly well. Groups such as the Meenas in Rajasthan, Negis in Himachal Pradesh, and Lambadas in Andhra Pradesh have done fairly well without any Christian help. And even among tribes in which Christians are more visible, non-Christians have done well. This may be due to their good economic standing, but more importantly it was due to their exposure and interaction with the wider world. The drive for education may have come from the reference groups with whom they interacted on a regular basis. The presence of a community or group treated as superior often turns out to be a reference point of emulation. Tribes with such locations have somewhat better educational attainment and hence better representation in higher educational institutions, provided their economic condition is not precarious.

Tribes and academic programmes

The enrolment of tribes in higher educational institutions, as has been noted earlier, has increased substantially in recent years, but it has not been uniform across disciplines. A large bulk of students enrolled in higher educational institutions are generally found in humanities and social sciences. This is followed by medicine, engineering, commerce, etc. The lowest participation has been in sciences. In the late 1970s, for example, tribes constituted 2.48 per cent of the total undergraduate students in humanities and social sciences. This was 1.82 and 1.20 per cent respectively in medicine and engineering. In sciences, it was as low as 0.83 per cent. Participation saw a further decline at the postgraduate level. While it was 1.93 per cent for humanities and social sciences, it was as low as 0.50 and 0.18 per cent respectively for medicine and engineering. Science remained at 0.79 per cent, which was almost the same as the graduate level (Xaxa 2014: 124). This pattern of participation continues to this day, except that there has been a steady increase at each level. For example, in 2000–01, the percentage share of tribes at the undergraduate level was 5.09 per cent in BA/BA (Hons), 2.01 per cent in BSc/BSc (Hons), 1.7 per cent in BCom/BCom (Hons), and 3.54 per cent in BE/BSc (Eng)/BArch. In all these, their participation was less than the SCs and the range varied from two to eight times. The pattern remained similar at the postgraduate level. The only programme in which the tribes had a slight edge over the SCs was medicine. Their participation stood at 11.49 per cent against the 10.84 per cent of the SCs (Rout 2014: 115).

Within each of these broad disciplines, there have been variations. In the humanities, for instance, one would find them mainly in languages and rarely in subjects such as philosophy or linguistics. In the social sciences, disciplines such as economics find fewer takers. Professional streams such as medicine and engineering are employment-oriented and hence have higher participation than sciences. Of sciences, botany, agriculture, and zoology have better representation than sciences such as physics, chemistry, and mathematics. This may be so due to their interest and aptitude for those disciplines in view of their lived world in which plants and animals assume an important place.

However, in this respect one finds somewhat interesting and conflicting patterns between premier institutions or central institutions and state-run institutions or institutions in the state of their domicile. Even today, very few tribal students opt for basic sciences. And while they are visible to a small extent in institutions located in their respective regions, their absence is stark in premier/central institutions. In institutions such as JNU, Delhi University, the Central University of Hyderabad, and so on, it is almost rare to find tribal students in basic science disciplines. In contrast, they are conspicuous by their presence in social science disciplines. While there is poor participation of tribal students in basic sciences even in state institutions, the pattern is not the same with respect to professional and social science programmes. Indeed, one finds professional education having an edge over social science education in state-level institutions. There is a sort of obsession for professional courses such as engineering, medicine, and so on, at least in mainland India. This is in contrast to the north-east, where the social sciences are still popular and a large number of students still pursue them. The contrast may be illustrated better with reference to Jharkhand, where STs formed 5.0, 2.00, and 0.56 per cent respectively of the total student enrolment in BA/BA (Hons), BSc/BSc (Hons), and BCom programmes as per the educational statistics 2006–07. Against this in the BE/BSc (Eng)/BArch programmes, the share of STs was as high as 24 per cent. In medicine, dentistry, nursing, and pharmacy, the share was 22 per cent and in polytechnic 23 per cent. However, in postgraduate programmes the share of social sciences went up to 37 per cent of the total in MA, followed by 10.61 per cent in commerce and 4 per cent in science. For the other disciplines, students going for postgraduation are hardly visible (Birua 2012: 22). There are, of course, strong biases against social science education in mainland states, which has afflicted the tribes as well. There is a general feeling among the educated, including tribes, that social sciences have no scope for employment and are only for students who are poorly endowed. Hence, with poor performance there is a strong tendency for professional education. As noted above, this is not the case in north-east India.

Academic performance

Once they have entered higher educational institutions, the lives of tribal students are far from smooth, both in academic and non-academic terms. Although institutions provide hostels prescribed under government policy, these facilities fall far short of the requirement, and a large chunk of students are forced to stay in rented accommodation or as paying guests. Those who find the costs of these unaffordable decide to withdraw from the institutions and go back to their homes to look for other opportunities.

The academic performance of students belonging to tribal communities has been on the whole inadequate, though there are exceptions. Over the years, I have observed and interacted with many tribal students in higher educational institutions and have invariably been made aware of their difficulties and inadequacy in coping with the demands of higher educational institutions. This stress is more evident in institutions and departments of repute. The inadequacies of the tribal students stem from varied sources – one being English language proficiency. Though this does not pose a serious problem to students from the north-east and those from English-medium schools as a majority of them aspiring to higher education are fairly proficient in the language, the same is not true for students coming from other parts of India. But more serious than the problem of English language is tribals' inadequacy in learning – conceptualisation, comprehension, articulation, and more important their writing inability. Thus, they enter premier institutions with disadvantages that, while some are gradually able to overcome them, others find difficult to cope with. The baggage of disadvantages is invariably linked to the nature and type of institutions that they come from. During my 23 years at the Delhi School of Economics, I rarely found a tribal student in the Department of Economics. Those who did make it dropped out in the course of time. In other departments of the school, especially sociology, they were present in substantial numbers, but their overall performance was comparatively dissatisfactory. This was evident in their rates of failure, repetition of courses, and relative marks/grades. This dimension of higher education has received wide attention in the context of technological institutions such as the IITs in view of the large-scale failure of SC/ST students.

To conclude, the participation of tribes in higher education has increased manifold. Yet enrolments remain the lowest and the gap between tribes and other social categories continues. Academic performance remains an issue of serious concern, whatever the discipline. At the root of it lies the disadvantages with which tribal students join the higher education programme. This has largely to do with the schools they come from, which suffer from lack of quality education on various counts. The disparities among tribes that exist across regions, ethnicities, sizes of population, levels of development, and geographical/ecological settings with regard to their participation in higher education therefore are in need of urgent attention.

Note

1 Gross enrolment ratio (GER) provides a viable estimate of participation in higher education of various social groups by taking their enrolment in proportion to their population for higher education.

References

Birua, Balbhadra. 2012. Assessment of Educational Policies for Tribals: A Case Study of Central India. Paper presented at the Centre for Tribal and Regional Languages, Ranchi University, 25 January.
Elwin, V. 1943. *The Aboriginals*. Bombay: Oxford University Press.
Ghurye, G.S. 1943. *The Aboriginals So Called*. Poona: Gokhle Institute of Economics and Political Science.
Government of India (Ministry of Tribal Affairs). 2007. *Report of the Working Group on Empowerment of Scheduled Tribes for the Eleventh Five Year Plan (2007–2012)*. New Delhi: Ministry of Tribal Affairs.
Government of India (Ministry of Human Development Resources). 2013. *All India Survey on Higher Education 2010–2011*. New Delhi: Ministry of Human Resource Development.
Rout, Bharat Chandra. 2014. Affirmative Action for Weaker Sections of Society in Institutions of Higher Education in India. PhD thesis submitted to the National University of Educational Planning and Administration, New Delhi.
Xaxa, V. 2014. *Report of the High Level Committee on Socio-economic, Health and Educational Status of Tribal Communities of India*. Ministry of Tribal Affairs, Government of India.

Part V
Underbelly

This part addresses an area that lies outside the received knowledge and discourse of education in India. It exists, and not just in pockets or as an aberration, but rather as a major and vast venue of educational activity, but the activity itself is such that it resists acknowledgement. The three chapters included in this section hardly exhaust this vast area, nor do they provide an adequate mapping. Far from it, they merely provide an indication of the nature of the activities that characterise the underbelly of the legitimate system of education. The three activities covered by the chapters included in this part are: waiting, cheating, and coaching. These are not the kind of topics normally covered in reference books like this one. And technically, the geography they represent lies outside the borders of the system of education. It is important to view this geography for the same reasons that economists recognise the black market in order to study the market better. All three activities, namely waiting (for work), coaching (for success), and cheating (for ensuring success) form the ethos in which the system of education works. All three activities are widespread, though we lack sufficient information about how they are carried out in different parts of a vast country like India. Each of the three chapters included in this part concerns a specific region or state.

The first refers to unemployed youth. In their study of jobless youth of Western Uttar Pradesh, Craig Jeffrey and Jane Dyson came across a phenomenon they call the 'politics of waiting'. These authors see it as a global phenomenon of this period of history, but their chapter portrays it in the specific contours of Meerut, a town in the prosperous belt of an otherwise economically backward state. Unemployment among educated youth is as old as the modern system of education itself. It is often seen in relation to the impact that education has on the aspiration, attitude, and preferences of young people who have gone through the schooling process. Historically, it seems that the experience of going to school and college, and the certification of their success in examination, shape their views of acceptable employment. Education was once associated with salaried jobs of the kind that only the government could give. The unemployed youth whose lives and thoughts are analysed by Jeffrey and Dyson have received higher education. They carry the burden of their own and their parents' aspirations, in an era when the state has changed its character and no longer wishes to be perceived as an avenue of permanent salaried employment. How these young men endure long years of unemployment, and how they develop, through engagement and interaction, a critique of the political world that surrounds them is the focus of Jeffrey and Jane Dyson.

Aspiration and stress are also the main ingredients of the ethos in which 'Vyapam' became a synonym for scam in the central Indian state of Madhya Pradesh. Vyapam is otherwise the Hindi acronym for the Professional Examination Board. Krishna Kumar's chapter examines a recent scam involving entrance tests for higher professional education in Madhya Pradesh. It argues that the intensely competitive circumstances form one aspect of professional education in areas like medicine and engineering; emergence of assisted cheating as a service industry forms the other aspect of contemporary higher education in a state that has demonstrated rather extraordinary warmth towards neoliberal policies in education. The chapter highlights the involvement of professionally educated youth in the scam that remained manageable for several years before it lost its hold on the secret operations necessary for its continuation. The chapter also attempts to address the question one might ask about this scam, whether this could have occurred anywhere in India. The cautiously negative answer offered in this chapter is based on the analysis of the specific historical and political conditions of Madhya Pradesh. The analysis draws our attention to the complexity of education as a field of study in a country whose regional diversity is not merely cultural. Political and administrative legacies and circumstances shape the systemic characteristics of education in remarkably specific ways.

This message is further corroborated by the last chapter in this section, which concerns private tuition and coaching from an early age as a pervasive social phenomenon in Bengal. Manabi Majumdar has studied this elusive subject in order to find out what impact it makes on the social goals of the educational policy. Parents invest in private tuition obviously because it improves their children's performance in examinations. As Disha Nawani's chapter explained, examinations have been at the heart of the culture of schooling in India since colonial times. Bengal is where this culture took root before it did so in other parts of India. It has resisted the various attempts made to reform it through new policies and the promotion of new practices. Many of these reform-oriented policies did not make much of a dent in Bengal; but that is hardly a sufficient explanation for the scale and social fervour associated with home tuition. Indeed, private tuition is recognised as a major aspect of child-rearing in many other Asian countries, particularly in the East Asian region. How it intersects with political commitment with social justice and equity through modern governance that Bengal is believed to practice is what Manabi Majumdar attempts to explain.

17

Active partners

Rethinking the educated unemployed in India

Craig Jeffrey and Jane Dyson

In January 2005, at Meerut College, about 40 miles north-east of Delhi, I met Lekhpal Singh. Singh had more the appearance of a professor than a student – his hair was flecked with grey and laugh lines spread out from the corners of his eyes. He had been living at the college for 13 years, during which time he had acquired a BA, a BEd, three MAs, and a PhD. He had applied unsuccessfully for many government jobs, but was still *'berozgaar'* (unemployed). 'There's been nothing suspect about my achievement', Lekhpal said. 'My results have all been first class. But the college is very poor. And unemployment is everywhere. Recently 12,000 people applied for three government jobs'.

So what do you do all day? I asked.

'We do nothing. Just kill time.'

There are millions of Lekhpals across the world. The World Bank (2011) reported that 202 million people were unemployed around the world, of which over one-third are youth aged 15–24. The rate of unemployment is particularly high in North Africa and the Middle East, but is also very significant in Southern Europe, sub-Saharan Africa, and South Asia. While the economic fortunes of many countries in these regions have recovered to some extent since the global recession of 2008–11, the recovery has not resulted in the creation of high-skilled jobs for graduates. Even before the recession, rapid economic growth in the 1990s and 2000s did not see the creation of a large number of well-paid formal-sector jobs in China and India (see Kaplinsky 2005). For example, the IT sector employed six million people in 2009 in India, a country with a working-age population of 500 million (Joshi 2009). At the same time, national governments have been under pressure to reduce the overall size of state bureaucracies.[1]

A meagre supply of graduate jobs has coincided with a huge increase globally in demand for high-skilled, well-paid formal-sector employment. Rapid population growth rates, especially in sub-Saharan Africa, the Middle East, and parts of South Asia, are increasing demand for work, and this 'youth bulge' is increasingly likely to be educated. Enrolment in tertiary education has increased markedly, from roughly 17 per cent of the global youth population in university in 1991 to 29 per cent in 2011. Paul Willis (1977) famously argued that schools in the UK persuaded students to align their ambitions with available jobs – working class children learned to aspire to working-class jobs, and scholars in the USA have argued that junior colleges perform the same 'cooling out function' among youth from marginalised backgrounds (young people enter with high ambitions and then scale back). But the majority of colleges and universities in the global South do not work in this manner. Education encourages young people to plot futures in well-paid, non-manual, permanent employment, and media images of middle-class success feed into this revolution of rising aspirations. At the same time, employers find that schools and universities are not providing young people with the skills and knowledge required for the job market. It follows that the apparent advantage to a developing country of having a large, educated youth population – the so-called 'demographic dividend' – can become instead a restive and demoralised 'demographic disaster' (World Bank 2011).

Young people often respond to unemployment by refusing to enter jobs, such as manual labour or unskilled service work, that they regard as beneath their status – at least in the short term. But not all young people can afford to remain jobless very long, and even youth from relatively wealthy backgrounds often find it difficult to remain 'unemployed' in the face of parental and other pressures. The most important indicator of graduate distress is therefore not outright unemployment but 'underemployment': 'part-time or insecure work that does not reflect young people's skills and ambitions' (Prause and Dooley 1997). In 2010, 536 million young people were underemployed according to figures released by the World Bank (2011). The state does not regulate the terms of this employment, there are few opportunities for collective bargaining, and such jobs typically offer training or opportunities for self-development (World Bank 2011). The prevalence of male breadwinner norms means that in many regions young men often experience the problem of graduate un/underemployment most acutely, and shifts in the labour market have sometimes placed a premium on skills coded as 'feminine'. But women also face un/underemployment in many regions, and may face a 'double subordination' as they grapple both with the poor economic environment and entrenched gender norms.

Unemployment and underemployment have social and cultural, as well as economic, consequences. Young people are often unable to acquire the adult status and savings that are prerequisites for marriage (Masquelier 2005), they often cannot afford to buy or rent independent living space (Hansen 2005), and in many areas of the world they face difficulties in negotiating with state officials, especially the police (Rogers 2008). A sense of gendered crisis may become apparent, for example, where men feel that they are unable to fulfil locally salient visions of masculinity. More generally, scholars have written of widespread feelings of hopelessness, negative introspection, and even self-harm, including suicide, among graduate youth (Mains 2007). In many cases young people feel alienated from their peers, family, and wider society (Jeffrey 2010).

A number of commentators have argued that alienated youth become involved in forms of action that are violent, reproduce dominant power, and occur within patron–client networks. The World Bank *Development Report* (2011) identified educated unemployed youth as one of the chief causes of political turmoil around the world. Educated un/underemployed youth are commonly imagined in the media as the dry tinder for the flame of fascist or other extremist forms of politics. At a more everyday level, scholars have referred to educated un/underemployed young people, sometimes especially graduates, as engaged in violent forms of consumption, including compulsive behaviour (Mains 2007). These studies often rest on older ideas of youth as a period of 'storm and stress' (Hall 1904) or 'protest-prone population' (Keniston 1971). Marx and Engels (1978) famously argued that educated un/underemployed are capable only of idiosyncratic forms of politics and social action; they called these youth 'alchemists of the revolution', with deliberate irony.

Ethnographic studies provide some support for these depictions of educated un/underemployed youth. Heuzé (1996) and Hansen (1996), in two different studies of youth and religious communal violence in India, point to the connections between unemployment and violent action. Cincotta (2003) links rising educated un/underemployment among young people to cross-border terrorism. Moreover, even the everyday level reports show that a rise in the number of educated un/underemployed youth may increase gender violence. In all these studies – which tend to focus on men rather than women – educated un/underemployed young people's actions appear to sustain practices of class and gender dominance and bolster existing patron–client networks. But from another perspective, we might imagine youth as well positioned to promote constructive political and social change within countries in Asia, Africa, and Latin America. Mannheim (1972 [1936]) argues that within any region, generations experience the same conditions at the same times during their lives and thus come to constitute social units. In particular moments, this generation 'in itself' can become a generation 'for itself', and Mannheim places particular emphasis on the potential transformative power of the youth.

This chapter addresses the issue of unemployed young people's action by examining the lives of educated unemployed youth in north India, drawing on 20 years of research mainly in western Uttar Pradesh and the neighbouring state of Uttarakhand (see also Dyson 2014; Jeffrey 2010; Jeffrey et al. 2008). It is written as a set of personal reflections, tracking the problem of educated unemployment through three key social projects that I have conducted in India since 1995.

In the first section of the chapter, we situate the problem of educated unemployment with reference to Craig Jeffrey's research on the rise of a rural middle class in rural western Uttar Pradesh in the 1990s. The second part examines the problem of educated unemployment among young people in Meerut in the mid-2000s. The final section of the chapter, which focuses especially on the politics of jobless youth, considers the issue from the perspective of a community living in a mountainous and remote region of Uttarakhand. Our overall argument is that educated unemployed youth can be 'active partners' in efforts to address the employment crisis.

A rural middle class: the origins of social congestion

Between 1995 and 1999, Craig Jeffrey carried out 13 months of ethnographic research on the investment strategies of rich Jat farmers in Meerut district, western Uttar Pradesh. Meerut district is known as a centre of wheat, sugarcane, and potato farming. The introduction of tubewell irrigation and new improved varieties of cane and wheat between the 1960s and 1980s had transformed the fortunes of the region's farmers. The Jats were only roughly midway up the ladder in terms of their caste status, but as landowners and people who had good access to the state administration, many Jats owning over 12 acres of land had become prosperous – a nascent rural middle class (see also Jeffrey et al. 2008).

Jeffrey's fieldwork examined how rich Jats had used the profits they acquired from farming. Were they investing in local business such that their wealth was trickling down to the poor? Or were rich Jats investing their money in ways that reproduce inequalities between them and the relatively poor lower caste, the ex-Untouchables also called Dalits? These questions were particularly important in the mid-1990s in the context of the rise of the Bahujan Samaj Party (BSP), led by a Dalit woman and former school teacher Mayawati, which sought to improve the position of Dalits relative to Jats.

There was no typical Jat rich farmer. But the case of Kishanpal is instructive. In 1996, Kishanpal was in his early fifties and had a son and a daughter. As I arrived at the family's large metal gate for the first time in May 1996, I remember Kishanpal springing from his chair, banishing a German shepherd dog to the corner of the compound and ushering me inside 'Aaiye, aaiye', 'Come, come', he said, as if he had been expecting a foreign researcher to arrive any moment.

Within five minutes he had changed into a smart pyjama suit and his wife, Leela, had bought tea.

Kishanpal spoke in rich tones of the problems connected to farming in western Uttar Pradesh – land degradation, the difficulty of finding labourers, and the diminishing profits from his crops of cane and wheat. He spoke angrily about how the Dalits were being 'pampered' by the new BSP government. He said that he was adopting a two-pronged strategy for the future of his family. The first was protecting his land and farm by strengthening his family's connections with politicians and government officials. He said: 'To get on here as a farmer you need to cultivate people as well as cultivate land. You need a network of help.' 'The Jats have a saying', he continued, 'A fist is stronger than five fingers' (Jeffrey 2001, 2002).

The second prong was to strike out into urban areas and try to get his son a position in government service. He had invested an enormous amount of money making sure his children went to an impressive private school on the edge of Meerut. Kishanpal was also saving money for a bribe to get his son a job as a police inspector. He planned to get his daughter married into a Meerut police family – that would strengthen his links inside the police and help his son get a job. I asked what would happen if his daughter did not like her proposed partner. Kishanpal replied, 'She will adjust.'

After a few months, I could trace the fine lines of cooperation that linked rich Jat farmers to the police, land revenue officers, judges, school principals, district development officials, agricultural marketing offices, and other local bigwigs. Rich Jats went to government offices to flatter bureaucrats and they organised 'chicken and whiskey parties' for their influential friends. Corruption involving the police was especially common, and a few Jat farmers even hired police officers as paid mercenaries. The police would carry out hits using homemade pistols. They could not use their official weapons because every bullet has to be accounted for. The pistols were crude weapons made out of the taps found in train washrooms. It cost Rs. 100,000 to arrange a killing through the police in 1999. This was equivalent to what farmers could make in a year from six acres of sugarcane.

As I learned more about these networks it became clear that rich farmers had been able to reproduce their agricultural dominance in the sphere of competition for state resources, and had done so through a set of strategies that had profoundly negative effects on poorer members of their caste, Jat women, and Dalits. Also, by investing in local state networks, rich farmers had effectively been able to defend their historical privileges against the threat posed by the political party, the BSP.

Just how effective Jats had been at reproducing their power became obvious when I spoke to the Dalits, who felt angry and depressed. They complained constantly of having to work on starvation wages, of police and Jat brutality, of their daughters and wives facing molestation in the fields. If the Dalits threatened to revolt, the Jats wouldn't let them collect cattle fodder from the fields or defecate on their land. When I asked the Dalits whether there was any hope of seeking redress from the state, they were downbeat. 'We still live in a feudal system', they said. 'No one listens to the poor.' I asked if the government could help, and the typical reaction was to quote a local saying, 'Even the dogs don't approach the empty-handed.'

Timepass

The direction of my research was to change radically, however, in 2004, when I began to receive plaintive letters from the sons of rich Jat farmers. It seemed that rich Jat farmers' strategy of attempting to place their sons in off-farm employment, especially government jobs, was misfiring. Many young men were writing about being 'berozgaar' (unemployed). The economic reforms of the 1990s had not created many new private positions. At the same time, under the reforms the state was not able to create a large number of new government jobs. A type of social congestion had emerged. A huge burgeoning rural middle class, including by this stage upwardly-mobile Dalits, were competing for a tiny pool of jobs. Many rich Jat farmers had seen their sons come back from university disconsolate. 'We couldn't get jobs', they said, 'But we don't want to work on the farm. It would be too shameful.' These young men felt marooned. They were stuck between the rural and urban, between youth and adulthood, and between what they understood to be 'tradition' and 'modernity'.

In 2004–05, I carried out a new research project on the political actions of educated unemployed youth in Meerut and the associated issue of student politics. I spent much of my research in a tea stall outside the gate of the town's oldest, but now run down, Meerut College. There, next to a vast cauldron of boiling fat, I would meet with students to discuss their ambitions, ideas, and experiences. For eight months this research continued, by the end of which I had interviewed over 200 students and participated in numerous political rallies, hostel parties, and trips to meet government bureaucrats.

Versions of the following conversation run through my field notes.

CJ: Hey, how's it going? What are you doing?
STUDENT: Nothing.
CJ: Really, nothing?
STUDENT: Yes.
CJ: It looks like something or other.
STUDENT: Yes, yes, it's something or other.
CJ: So what is that something or other?
STUDENT: It's nothing. Timepass.

Timepass was everywhere in Meerut in the 2000s. Oxford Dictionaries Online defines timepass as 'The action or fact of passing the time, typically in an aimless or unproductive way.' In contemporary India people commonly use the word 'timepass' to refer to a period of down time between bouts of work, and it is variously rendered as 'timepass', 'time pass', 'time-pass', and 'TP'.

While timepass could theoretically refer to any activity that passes the time, it usually denotes relatively meaningless, light, trivial activity, and it is counter-posed with 'serious' action in India. Timepass involves distraction, faint amusement, and it is productive only in so far as it staves off boredom, prevents negative introspection, and allows the body, mind, and soul some respite from ordinary life.

Historians of nineteenth-century Europe have traced the rise of boredom to the spread of ideas of clock time and growth of industrial labour (Thompson 1967; Zerubavel 1985). In India, too, linear notions of clock time – physically represented in the spread of calendars and time-pieces – came to compete during the late colonial period with older, cyclical experiences of time. The colonial government simultaneously introduced new forms of time-consciousness, for example through the construction of railways. 'Time' itself became an object of social comment, and multiple spaces emerged in which this time needed to be 'passed', from traffic jams to railway waiting rooms, clinics to post office queues. In India, a small industry has emerged around catering for people's boredom, including magazines, cheap fiction, snack vendors, street performers, and more recently mobile phone apps. 'Timepass, timepass, time-pass' is a common mantra for those hawking peanuts on train platforms, just as it was the name selected in 2002 by Britannia Industries for a new line of salty snacks. So ubiquitous has the term

'Timepass' become in modern India that it was chosen as the title of a Bollywood film in 2005.

Passing time and humour are closely linked, as Samuel Beckett recognised in his classic play *Waiting for Godot*. 'That passed the time', announces Vladimir at one point in the play. 'It would have passed anyway', Estragon replies. As timepass has proliferated in popular culture in India it has also become the subject of jokes. In many colleges across India, youth make reference to their 'serious' and 'timepass' boyfriends and girlfriends. Their serious partners are marriage candidates. The timepass ones are simply being entertained for the time being. Parents often use timepass semi-humorously, 'What do you mean that you are just doing timepass?' They ask their children angrily. 'Watermelons do timepass in the fields!'

For unemployed young people in many parts of India, 'timepass' signals dissatisfaction with poor schooling, unemployment, blocked mobility, and financial stress. Unemployed young men have a triply problematic relationship to time: they are not able to accord with general notions of what it is to be developed; they are unable to effect a life transition from youth to adulthood; and they also feel that they exist somehow outside the normal run of clock time. Hanging out at street corners or spending long periods simply 'doing nothing' becomes a means of advertising this sense of social and temporal anomie. Timepass serves three functions simultaneously. First, it suggests detachment from one's situation. I'm not really interested in my studies, many young people said, I'm just doing timepass. The French sociologist Pierre Bourdieu (1984: 235) famously wrote that the refusal to work is often the tactic of the unemployed youth and he called this strategy 'the one man strike'. Second, timepass suggests an overabundance of time that needs to be killed. Third, it suggests a sense of being left behind relative to the small number of those who do 'make it'.

Timepass is also productive, however (see Jeffrey 2010). The social act of timepass, for example standing about at bus stops or playing cards in tea stalls, provides opportunities to hear news, exchange ideas, and establish friendships. People who would otherwise regard each other with disdain may, through the shared experience of waiting to realise their aspirations, come to strike up friendships and develop shared goals.

While doing timepass, young men from Jat, Dalit, and Muslim backgrounds shared cigarettes, bought each other chai, and stood around on bus stops with their arms draped around each other's shoulders. They got into mock battles, played badminton, and exchanged news. Such cross-caste fraternising would not have happened at that time in rural areas. These cultures were powerfully gender specific, however. Young women felt doubly excluded – from good employment (like the men) and from the ability to participate in urban timepass.

Timepass was also leading to some positive forms of politics. There were certain moments in which the plight of the underemployed, poorly educated youth came strikingly to light, and in these situations people passing time at street corners or in hostels came out onto the streets. For example, in October 2004 it emerged that the Registrar of Meerut University was lining his pockets by sending master's degree examinations to be marked by school children. This happened fairly frequently in Uttar Pradesh at that time. But in this case the official had been sending the exams to be marked by children as young as 12 years old. Students took to the streets to burn their degrees.

Much more generally, young people across lines of class, caste, religion, and gender campaigned against corruption in the university administration, lobbied for students to obtain scholarships, and worked to address problems of police harassment. They tried to increase public understanding of the struggles of unemployed youth, worked to improve standards of tuition in the city, and even went back to rural areas to advise younger youth. There was a type of positive feedback at work here: educated underemployed youth were concerned that the generation coming after them would not have to suffer the same indignities.

Some of the student demonstrations took bizarre forms. On one occasion early in 2005, students protested about their right to cheat in examinations. Students argued that the educational system is cheating them by leading them to expect good jobs. Why shouldn't they also cheat? They also argued that influential students are already able to cheat. Students argued that mass copying in exams is a democratic form of cheating.

Student politics aimed at countering corruption was difficult to sustain, in part because a section of the student population, mostly the sons of rich Jat farmers, had developed lucrative careers as student brokers. I spent a lot of time with these brokers, who found niches in which to operate between the state and local society.

Umesh Singh was typical. A well-built, tall young man who came from a rich farming family close to Meerut, Umesh began by developing a reputation as an anti-corruption crusader. This helped him build a support base among students, who voted for him in the student union election. After winning a student union post, he got involved in corruption himself. He helped businessmen get the affiliation certificates for their new colleges from the university. He worked as a middleman between building contractors and the university administration, and even influenced appointments in university posts.

These students weren't just copying their seniors. Student brokers were adamant they were a cut above their fathers. Umesh said, 'We actually have to go back to the villages to advise our fathers. We tell them, "You've been giving that policeman mangoes for 10 years to keep him sweet. But you should make the relationship work for you. You should demand a share of the income he makes from taking bribes." We teach our fathers how to be brokers.' This is a telling comment on how a particularly pernicious type of hyper-entrepreneurial culture has taken hold in some parts of provincial India.

It was also evident that many educated unemployed young men with some degree of social support and financial backing entered the educational business. They set up coaching institutes, tutorial centres, or became board members in private colleges. One set of young men I came to know well responded to the experience of applying unsuccessfully for army officer positions by setting up a tutorial institute that specialised in preparing young people for the army officer examinations and interview. The vast penumbra of institutions and individual forms of tuition that comprise the unofficial educational sector in areas of western Uttar Pradesh is poorly understood (although see other contributions to this volume). Yet one point was very clear in my Meerut research: A section of the youth population were responding to demoralising employment outcomes by reproducing the system that produced them as underemployed youth.

Many of these brokers and educational 'fixers' also continued to protest against corruption. The morning might see Umesh staging a roadblock to protest about the corrupt university administration. The afternoon might then see him in the vice-chancellor's office doing secret deals behind students' backs. Umesh justified this by making a distinction between corruption and fraud. He said that corruption is when you pay a bribe and get something done. He said that this is how the world works. He said that fraud is when you pay a bribe and something still doesn't happen.

I once saw Umesh at the hustings for the student election. He was standing in front of his audience asking them 'You name one instance when I've been corrupt.' When the audience started providing examples, Umesh just stared back at them, smiling. I asked Umesh later, 'How did you have the nerve to do that?' 'Craig', he said, 'I'm total politics.'

In 2009, I became interested in broadening my focus to understand how unemployed youth are responding to joblessness in different parts of the world. This interest led to a new project on the social strategies of educated unemployed youth in the Indian Himalayas. Jane Dyson and I based ourselves in the village of Bemni, located at 12,000 feet in the remote Nandakini valley in Chamoli district in Uttarakhand. Jane has spent 15 months interviewing children about their working lives and social relationships in Bemni as part of her doctoral research in 2003 and 2004 (see Dyson 2014). Between 2012 and 2014, Jane and I carried out a total of 12 months of follow-up field research in Bemni on the social and political practices of educated unemployed youth, often working with young people whom Jane interviewed as children in the early 2000s.

The General Caste (GC) population in Bemni was roughly 69 per cent and Scheduled Castes (SC) constituted the remaining 31 per cent. GCs tended to be somewhat wealthier than SCs, who also suffered some discrimination in the village. But caste and class inequalities were less marked in Bemni than in Meerut. GCs lacked the assets and income of their counterparts on the plains, and even the richest GCs in the village in 2012 had modest landholdings and few consumer goods.

Unemployment is as pressing a problem in this remote rural location as it is in western Uttar Pradesh. Chamoli district lacks manufacturing industry. Since the mid-2000s, in particular, the Uttarakhand government has been under pressure to reduce the number of people in government employment in the state. Moreover, those government jobs that exist are concentrated in the major cities in the southern (plains area) of the state.

Our research pointed to a widespread demoralisation among young people in Bemni in 2012–14 that echoed the despondency of youth whom I had interviewed in Meerut in 2004–05. Youth in Bemni did not speak of themselves as engaged in 'timepass', reflecting the fact that this word is most common in urban areas. But they did frequently refer to themselves as '*khaali*', a word that means 'free' but also 'empty'. In addition, educated young people who had tried unsuccessfully to obtain government or private jobs frequently practised forms of self-denigration. For example, when we asked about their employment, they would say that they are 'just breaking stones' (*pathhar thorna*).

Our research showed that young people are not passive in the face of this difficulty. Unemployed youth – men and women – are crucial social actors in contemporary rural Uttarakhand. My Meerut research pointed to positive youth politics, but it tended to be based largely around the life of the university. In Uttarakhand, young men and women were active in a broad range of social and political projects, campaigning for improvements to local schools, helping to bring electricity to the village, campaigning for the construction of a telecommunications tower, giving school tutorials free of charge, motivating other youth, starting new business enterprises, and resolving thorny political disputes.

Young people were also developing a new philosophy of politics. Youth said that politics should not be imagined as competition for a share of the pie, but rather as about making the pie. Politics is not about the distribution of resources, in other words, but actually about what you can do collaboratively and through painstaking negotiation to create resources. It is a vision of generative politics. Young people's new imagination of politics also had a strong temporal element. They said that people should not be waiting for the government to help them. They should instead be trying to embody better practices in their own conduct.

We should not underestimate the challenges of linking up these small-scale forms of community activism to broader state and international development efforts. Many young people argued that their generative politics will only be effective if it remains wholly outside the ambit of the state and NGOs. Moreover, many young people regarded the whole political establishment as 'rotten to the core'.

There are resonances between these conclusions and work on youth movements of the 2010s, such as the Occupy Movement in the USA (Manilov 2013). Young people in north India, working on an everyday level to improve the lives of their communities, were in the process trying to 'be the change they wanted to see in the world': be polite, be fair, and in the process slowly transform their communities. Technology played a prominent role in this type of politics. Increased mobile phone ownership allowed young people to take photos of examples of corruption and send these to local officials. They also put their phones on speaker mode when talking to officials so that their friends knew they were not conducting deals in secret.

In sum, a social revolution is afoot in provincial India. Young people have been drawn into education in unprecedented numbers. They have come to accept and believe in the norms of liberal democracy and citizenship. And they have new forms of power and knowledge, in the form of an understanding of modernity and technology. Parents acknowledge this, and look to youth as change agents. Youth in their late teens and twenties are often those who understand the needs of children most carefully and have children's interests at heart. But youth themselves in places such as Bemni and Meerut say that their actions are often poorly institutionalised and understood. There is also a critical lack of basic social research on young people in South Asia and Asia more broadly.

Conclusions

We have shown that an intended consequence of the mobility strategies of both a rural middle class and upwardly mobile sections of the rural population in Uttar Pradesh and Uttarakhand in the 1990s/2000s has been the creation of a large and socially heterogeneous educated under-employed youth population. This process is likely to continue into the future, with over 100 million young people set to join the labour market over the next decade (2015–2025).

Negative depictions of educated unemployed youth proliferate both in the media, government reports, and scholarly work (e.g. Cincotta 2003). Our anthropological research in two provincial parts of north India suggest that a portion of the educated unemployed youth population in north Indian is indeed involved in nefarious forms of politicking. The figure of the youth 'broker' is prominent in everyday life in places as diverse as Meerut and Bemni.

Yet we also found many young people who were acting as community activists. These youth were not simply imitating the politics of the previous generation. Building on their education and new technological opportunities, they were developing novel means of engaging with each other and the state. Moreover, as people relatively familiar with educational and employment markets, they were often better positioned to advise younger youth than were older adults in their forties, fifties, and sixties. In Mannheim's (1972 [1936]) terms, educated unemployed youth in their late teens and twenties constituted an 'active generation'.

A key policy implication is that educated unemployed youth are part of the solution to the problem of widespread joblessness. That youth often have the interests of younger children at heart makes them willing and effective potential partners for organisations, including the state, seeking to address the issue of educated unemployment. A key challenge in this area, however, will be countering young people's deep mistrust of government and NGOs in many parts of provincial India. Another key challenge will be harnessing young people's energies in such a way as to encourage educational reform in a context where many underemployed young people, understandably, see opportunities to cash in on their experience by running low-quality tutorials or educational institutions of different types.

Note

1 In 2000, the World Bank made an annual 2 per cent cut of the state bureaucracy a condition of its continuing aid to Uttar Pradesh (Jeffrey et al. 2008).

References

Bourdieu, P. 1984. *Distinction: A Social Critique of the Judgement of Taste*. London: Routledge.

Cincotta, R.P., R. Engelman, and D. Anastasion. 2003. *The Security Demographic: Population and Civil Conflict after the Cold War*. Washington, DC: Population Action International.

Dyson, J. 2014. *Working Childhoods: Youth and Work in the Indian Himalayas*. Cambridge: Cambridge University Press.

Hall, G.S. 1904. *Adolescence: Its Psychology and its Relations to Physiology, Anthropology, Sociology, Sex, Crime, Religion, and Education (Vols. I and II)*. New York: D. Appleton and Co.

Hansen, Karen, T. 2005. 'Getting Stuck in the Compound: Some Odds Against Social Adulthood in Lusaka, Zambia'. *Africa Today*, 51, 4, pp. 3–16.

Hansen, Thomas B. 1996. 'Recuperating Masculinity: Hindu Nationalism, Violence, and the Exorcism of the Muslim "Other"', *Critique of Anthropology*, 16, 22, pp. 137–172.

Heuzé, Gerard. 1996. *Workers of Another World: Miners, the Countryside and Coalfields in Dhanbad*. Delhi: Oxford University Press.

Jeffrey, C. 2001. 'A Fist is Stronger than Five Fingers: Caste and Dominance in Rural North India', *Transactions of the Institute of British Geographers*, 25, 2, pp. 1–30.

Jeffrey, C. 2002. 'Caste, Class and Clientelism: A Political Economy of Everyday Corruption in Rural North India', *Economic Geography*, 78, 1, pp. 21–42.

Jeffrey, C. 2010. *Timepass: Youth, Class and the Politics of Waiting in India*. Stanford, CA: Stanford University Press.

Jeffrey, C., P. Jeffery, and R. Jeffery. 2008. *Degrees Without Freedom: Education, Masculinities and Unemployment in North India*. Stanford, CA: Stanford University Press.

Joshi, Vijay. 2009. 'Economic Resurgence, Lop-sided Performance, Jobless Growth', in Heath, A. and Jeffery, R., editors, *Continuity and Change in Contemporary India: Politics, Economic, and Society*. Delhi: Oxford University Press.

Kaplinsky, Raphael. 2005. *Globalization, Poverty and Inequality: Between a Rock and A Hard Place*. Cambridge: Polity.

Keniston, K. 1971. *Youth and Dissent: The Rise of a New Opposition*. New York: Harcourt Brace Jovanovich.

Mains, Daniel. 2007. 'Neoliberal Times: Progress, Boredom, and Shame among Young Men in Urban Ethiopia', *American Ethnologist*, 34, 4, pp. 659–673.

Manilov, M. 2013. 'Occupy at One Year: Growing the Roots of a Movement', *The Sociological Quarterly*, 54 (2), 206–213.

Mannheim, K. 1972 [1936]. 'The Problem of Generations'. In Altbach, P. and Laufer, R., editors, *The New Pilgrims: Youth Protest in Transition*. New York: David McKay and Company, pp. 101–138.

Marx, K. and F. Engels. 1978. *Collected Works, Volume 10: 1849–51*. London: Lawrence and Wishart.

Masquelier, Adeline, M. 2005. 'The Scorpion's Sting: Youth, Marriage and the Struggle for Social Maturity in Niger', *The Journal of the Royal Anthropological Institute*, 11, 1, pp. 59–83.

Prause, J. and D. Dooley. 1997. 'Effects of Underemployment on School-leavers' Self-esteem', *Journal of Adolescence*, 20, pp. 243–260.

Rogers, Martyn. 2008. 'Modernity, "Authenticity", and Ambivalence: Subaltern Masculinities on a South Indian Campus', *Journal of the Royal Anthropological Institute*, 14, pp. 79–95.

Thompson, Edward P. 1967. 'Time, Work Discipline and Industrial Capitalism', *Past and Present*, 38, pp. 56–97.

Willis, Paul. 1977. *Learning to Labour: How Working Class Kids Get Working Class Jobs*. Farnborough: Saxon House.

World Bank. 2011. *Conflict, Security and Development: World Development Report*. Washington, DC: World Bank.

Zerubavel, E. 1985. *Hidden Rhythms: Schedules and Calendars in Social Life*. Berkeley, CA: California University Press.

18

Access, success, and excess

Debating shadow education in India

Manabi Majumdar

'Nothing is your own except the spelling mistakes.' This was what a legendary teacher in Kolkata once commented in the answer-script of a student studying in a highly reputable college of the city. What this remark underlines, above all, is the necessity to envision the purpose of learning as that of cultivating an ability to think on one's own, and in that sense to be creative, curious and independent in either solving an academic puzzle or thinking critically as a citizen and tending 'imaginative empathy' for others in a democratic society. Our intellectual and individual develop-ment and our social flourishing are contingent upon the promotion of such deeper learning.

No doubt, education is also a route to a decent career path, a 'positional good' likely to improve one's social status, and a key to economic accomplishment. The right balance between these instrumental motivations of education and the more intrinsic values that are stated above is not easy to strike. This is particularly so at a time when we observe a growing conviction around us that presumes instrumental purposes to be the only driving engine of education, thereby engendering a great deal of potential to harm the creative process of learning.

It is well to note that education as an innovative process is also, quintessentially, a collective and connected human endeavour to produce and promote what Boyle (2002) describes as the 'commons of the mind' – a public domain of ideas that should not be fenced off. In an inequality-sequestered country like India, however, the social system of education was and to a consider-able extent still is not an open and inclusive space that is accessible to all. That is why the more recent equity-enhancing education initiatives in the country, such as the Right to Education Act, have focused on the first-order question of educational access. However with such steps towards massification of basic educational opportunities, there has also grown, especially among the privileged social classes, an anxious competition to stay ahead of the masses, to be the 'coun-try's first boy', and to succeed in tomorrow's test as well as in those to follow for a better career, higher status, and more and more social and cultural capital. Even the interest of international donors has shifted from access to learning outcomes measured mainly in terms of test scores and success in examinations. This swing from access to success in educational goals and practices has captured the popular imagination to produce, in turn, a homogeneous thinking across social classes about the credence of education's instrumental purposes, to the relative neglect of its intrinsic values. And all this, we proceed to argue below, has engendered various forms of excesses in education, including excessive commercialisation in education, creating in turn a new ethos of teaching and learning that is individuated and isolated rather than collective and collaborative. Teachers and students, tutors and tutees are driven to 'bowl alone' rather than work as a team. It is against this backdrop of competing pressures of educational access, success, and excess that we attempt to analyse in the remainder of the chapter the extent, effectiveness, and equity implications of supplementary private tutoring in India – a widespread practice that is described as the 'shadow' (Bray 2007, 2009; Marimuthu *et al.* 1991) of mainstream schooling. The analysis remains limited as it focuses mainly on the school education sector in the country to the relative neglect of higher levels of education; its West Bengal-centric empirical focus constitutes another source of its limitation.

Isn't private tutoring old news?

Amrita Bazar Patrika – a leading newspaper that used to be published from Calcutta (now Kolkata), the premier city of British India – regularly carried advertisements in the late nineteenth and early twentieth centuries either seeking private tutors or offering tutoring services for students studying in schools and colleges. A small sample of these notices shown below displays aspirations, preferences and prejudices that characterised familial as well as social educational strategies in those days.

> **Notice:** Required a private tutor to take charge of two boys, one of whom is preparing for the next Entrance. Hours of attendance 10–30 A.M. to 5–30 P.M. He must be graduate, and possessed of experience in the art of teaching. Certificate of good moral character required. Any reasonable pay will be allowed. Apply to undersigned, stating terms. Chunder Narain Singh, 1, Elysium Row, The 22nd August, 1897.
>
> *(Amrita Bazar Patrika 23 August 1897)*

> **Notice:** Wanted a private tutor for the grandson of Babu Cally Kissen Tagore. Pay handsome according to qualifications. None need apply who has no experience in coaching up sons of noblemen. Preference will be given to those who served under court of wards as guardian tutor. For further particulars candidates may apply personally to the Manager. Applications should be addressed to Babu Hem Chandra Chatterjee, Manager to the Estate of C.K. Tagore Esqr., No-1, and Darponarayan Tagore Street, Calcutta. Narendranatha Gupta, Astt. Manager.
>
> *(Amrita Bazar Patrika 15 March 1899: 3)*

> Wanted a graduate qualified in Mathematics as a private tutor. Apply to Kanay Lall Mukherjee, Hurtokeebagan, Calcutta.
>
> *(Amrita Bazar Patrika 29 October 1900: 13)*

It is quite evident that the demand for home tutors, attuned understandably to economic wherewithal, came mainly from the privileged classes of society. Furthermore, the educated elite were not hesitant in exhibiting their class, caste, and community biases while looking for a prospective home tutor. There were clear-cut statements like the following: 'An elderly Brahmin or Baidya graduate strong in English with considerable experience in teaching will be preferred' (28 March 1905) or 'A "Shea" Mahomedan will be preferred' (23 January 1913: 3) and so on. Alongside class, caste, and community biases, there was a palpable gender bias; of those advertisements sifted, not a single one asked for extra coaching for girl students. On the contrary, perhaps to prevent any unwelcome possibility of romance between the prospective resident private tutor and the young wife or daughter of the family, some advertisements categorically mentioned that 'Only men ... of advanced age, good health and morals, and wearing gray beard, need apply' (13 July 1906).

These advertisements, at the same time, indicated a clear preference for professionally qualified people, having experience in 'the art of teaching'. Those who offered themselves as potential private tutors also stressed their professional background and competence: For example, 'A gentle-man (Indian) educated at an English University is open to engagement as Private tutor to a wealthy man's son in Calcutta or neighbouring suburbs on reasonable terms' (*Amrita Bazar Patrika*, 2 May 1905: 2). No doubt, paid private lessons were the preserve of the privileged and the privileged sought the help of trained practitioners for their children's educational development.

Clearly, there is a long history of private tutoring in this country.

What is new about the present paradigm of private tuition?

Over the last several decades the demand for private tutoring has been growing around the world, and India is no exception in this respect. On the one hand there are large private tutoring industries that are now known to exist in the country; at the other end of the spectrum there exist home-based small outfits comparable to cottage industries. What is new about the recent incarnation of shadow education are its scale, scope, and salience at almost every level of educa-tion – starting from pre-school education to postgraduate level. Also, it is considered essential for students of all abilities – from underachievers to class-toppers. Parents from all social strata consider it 'essential' to have private tutors for their children, even to master the basics in educa-tion (Sen 2002), irrespective of their children's needs and abilities, of the type of school they attend, and of the quality of teaching-learning available in these schools. So it is not that the students who take private tuition are only from 'poorly' performing state schools; rather, the majority of them are from private schools.

What is the reason behind this 'there is no alternative' (TINA) mentality? To boost exam results is the most truthful and straightforward answer. Also, the mainstream and its shadow increasingly look and function alike (which was not the case earlier), suggesting how education itself is being 'recast' (Macpherson *et al.* 2014), under the weight of commercial interests. More-over, both mainstream and shadow schooling have become excessively test-centric; the pressure on students to perform well in examinations has become intense. They are drawn into a fierce battle to stay ahead of other students. These excesses have led in turn to an intensification of the coaching culture. Interestingly, though schools and coaching classes seem to mimic each other, at times the out-of-school supplementary tutoring service appears to create a substitution effect, that is to say, it works to reduce the formal school to a mere certification centre. This over-shadowing quality of the shadow is a relatively recent change.

Again, while the well-to-do parents in the past had (as they do now) the resources and information to judge the professional competence of tutors, less-affluent parents internalise the pressure to hire tutors for their school-going children but are constrained by information asym-metry and limited means to ascertain the quality of such services. As a result, though parents across the social spectrum seem to harbour homogenised thinking about the need for paid coaching, since their choice sets and their actual choices remain highly stratified – parents from disadvantaged backgrounds often employ high-school graduates or high-school 'fails' as tutors – homogenisation of family strategies still does not hold promises of equalisation of opportun-ities, let alone outcomes. So today's massification of the culture of tutoring, which was strictly the preserve of the privileged in the past, cannot be straightforwardly taken to have an equity-enhancing potential. Wealthy parents still have the advantage to 'buy' better results for their children. The fresh inequalities that such a system is likely to generate and its pervasive nature and many forms thus rationalise the need to examine this phenomenon afresh.

It would be myopic, of course, to start with the premise that any form of private tutoring is necessarily and straightforwardly bad. Not all tutoring is about exam preparation and there can be some academic benefits of private lessons for some students. Still, it would be limiting not to pay heed to the serious negative implications of this steadily maturing phenomenon for the education system as a whole.

The scope of private tutoring

Estimates of the number of pupils going for paid supplementary coaching are not easy to come by, partly because the private domain in which transactions between tutors and tutees take place is an unregulated zone, lying beyond the ambit of any formal documentation. A handful of available studies suggest that in many parts of India, particularly in states like West Bengal and Tripura, private tuition is now considered an 'essential'. The statistics in the Pratichi Education Report I and II (2002 and 2009) show the picture of dependence on tuition in Bengal quite clearly. Between 2002 and 2009, private tutor-dependent students in primary education have increased from 57 per cent to 64 per cent, and among those going to the Shishu Shiksha Kendras, from 24 per cent to 54 per cent. According to this report, 78 per cent of parents (62 per cent in 2002) think there is no deliverance except via private tutors. Of the few children who are not obtaining extra help, 54 per cent of parents said it was because they could not afford coaching centres.

The India Human Development survey data show that in 2004–05, 20 per cent of children in the age group 6–14 years reported that they had received private tutoring in the previous year (Desai *et al.* 2010). The Annual Status of Education Report (ASER) surveys are another source of data on the scope of the so-called shadow education system. As Banerji and Wadhwa (2012: 54) state, drawing on ASER figures, 'The phenomenon of additional education inputs through tuition classes and coaching centres is very widespread and visible in India especially in secondary and post-secondary education'. ASER Centre (2007) figures indicate that at the level of elementary education, 20 per cent of government school children and 24 per cent of private school children in rural India went for additional coaching (Banerji and Wadhwa 2012).

The more recent National Sample Survey on household expenditure on education (Government of India 2015) provides figures on proportions of pupils, attending mainstream school, that also receive extra coaching, at various levels of school education (see Table 18.1). For the

Table 18.1 Percentage of students (5–29 years) using private tuition, 2014

	Level of education	Rural	Urban
India	Primary	18.2	32.5
	Upper primary	23	36.2
	Secondary	33.3	46.1
	Higher secondary	31.2	44.9
	All	23.2	37.4
West Bengal	Primary	63.9	78.3
	Upper primary	85.3	91.3
	Secondary	89.7	93.1
	Higher secondary	88.1	95.5
	All	76.8	87.3

Source: calculated from Social Consumption in India: Education, NSS 71st Round, January–June 2014.

country as a whole, in urban India in particular, a little less than 40 per cent of students enrolled in formal school go for private lessons. In rural areas of the country the incidence of this supplementation at different levels of the school sector is comparatively lower, ranging between roughly 20 and 30 per cent. Strikingly, in states like West Bengal and Tripura, such dependence on extra coaching is near-universal among the pupils enrolled in formal school. The extent to which 'shadow education' has broken into the school life of a child in Bengal in our time is rather exceptional.

Private tutoring effect on learning outcomes and school processes

The impact of private tutoring on students' achievement is not easy to ascertain, since it is particularly hard to disentangle its effects from those like family and school effects; in particular, estimating heterogeneous effects of extra coaching from abilities and efforts of tutees who gain differentially from the same tutor is a challenge. Supposing we are able to take care of these methodological issues, still the available evidence of its effectiveness is mixed. Some studies indicate positive but short-term effects in improving students' test scores, but not necessarily bettering scores on the university entrance examination (Lee 2013).

In India, among the handful of available studies, scholarly analyses based on recent ASER data allude to a 'divide' between those who go to private school or coaching classes and those who do not, implicitly suggesting an advantage of privatisation in education. However, only a small proportion of that advantage, as per the same source of data, is attributable to private schooling or coaching (Wadhwa 2015).

This admitted, some studies (Banerji and Wadhwa 2012; Desai *et al.* 2010) suggest that private inputs into children's education – private schooling as well as private tutoring – have a positive influence on children's learning outcomes. It is claimed that private educational support helps weaker students to catch up and strong students to achieve more. Our preliminary classroom observations in a few coaching centres, however, reveal that the pedagogy followed is mostly instruction- and study material-driven. It is passive listening and cramming rather than stimulating activities that the tutees do at these coaching classes.

We therefore pause here to ask the first-order question of what we are measuring in the name of academic achievement. As Kumar (2012) forcefully argues, the crude measures that usually make up the standard assessments 'mask the epistemic sterility of the curriculum, the pedagogic process and examination'. So the anxiety that our children are not learning much, even after attending school for years together, is a real concern, partly because the measuring rod itself fails to assess deeper learning. As a result, those who succeed in tests may still remain 'know-nots' in a substantive sense, let alone those who do not. And yet, the formal schools as well as out-of-school tuition classes increasingly look like mere test preparation centres. Consequently, and unsurprisingly, 'coaching to the test' may prove 'effective' as far as improving scores is concerned, but in the process can discourage 'imaginative learning'.

What effects does private tuition have on the school system and school processes? One way in which the impact can be assessed is with respect to students' attention to lessons in class. Lee's (2013) study shows some positive though nominal influence of private tutoring on students' attentiveness in class, especially in the low-ability group of students. In other words, low-achievers pay more attention to lessons in class if they go for extra coaching. Supplementary private lessons may help improve their confidence level and interest to participate in classroom activities. There are, however, counter-examples of students losing interest in classroom activities when they feel confident that they have out-of-school support to guarantee their examination success.

Similarly, teachers' attention to classroom activities, their pedagogic practices and their 'learning by doing' are likely to be affected by their engagement as private tutors, when they are so engaged. The practice of growing private tuition by teachers employed in private as well as public educational institutions is not uncommon. Some teachers maintain that tutoring improves their classroom teaching. However, a number of concerns have been raised in this respect in the scholarly literature that is available. Some claim that the parallel informal system disrupts the school system; it has a negative influence on teacher development and effectiveness when school teachers double up as private tutors. It is alleged that these teachers do not spend sufficient time teaching in the school but virtually compel the students to attend tuition classes. The Tripura High Court recently observed that 'even in government colonies where the teachers have been provided accommodation, they are running "teaching shops"' (*The Shillong Times* 21 June 2015). Indeed, private coaching is likely to create a conflict of interest between the official duty of a school teacher and his/her private practice, when during private lessons she/he offers for a fee to his/her own pupils for what she/he is supposed to provide anyway.

One relatively understudied concern relates to the extent to which school teachers stand to lose on 'peer learning' owing to their private solitary practices. To be sure, at many coaching centres there are usually a host of tutors coaching several batches of tutees. But the structure of these sessions is such that these tutors are like ships that pass in the night, coexisting but hardly interacting with each other and missing the 'camaraderie of the staff room'. But, evidence – national and international – suggests that to improve teaching and learning it is imperative to give teachers time and encouragement to collaborate to improve their work, and to receive feedback from their peers about how to teach specific concepts and content to particular students (Batra 2015; Darling-Hammond 2014–15; Kumar 1994). Such cooperative practices are harder to cultivate and sustain in an environment of competitive striving that defines the core of a privatised solution such as paid coaching in order to address what are quintessentially public deficiencies (for example, gaps in teacher preparation and teaching, in curricular and examination reforms, and so on). What a public community of teachers and educators can ideally attempt to do to improve the quality of education in the country is rendered an isolated strategy. Teaching and learning activities in mainstream school thus fail to flourish under the spell of 'shadow education'.

Two related dimensions of the mainstream education system that may be shortchanged as a result of the predominance of shadow education are the importance of teacher preparation on the one hand and of lessening of teacher isolation on the other. While a majority of policy-makers and parents view frequent testing as a means of enhancing quality of learning in schools, few pay attention to the fact that to reduce the learning gap it is essential to focus on the teaching gap and by extension on teacher preparation (Batra 2015).

If the mainstream debate on the quality of education remains rather indifferent to the critical need to examine 'curriculum and pedagogic processes that prepare and support teachers' (ibid.) to not only deal with their professional challenges but also become sensitive to their social justice mission, it is found utterly mute and unconcerned about the quality of supplementary tutoring that is available in the market in myriad forms and price ranges. It is as though the market is the final arbiter of quality. As a result, if school teachers are expected to go through at least some training, anybody is accepted as a tutor – a professional or a greenhorn or even a dropout – as long as there is a semblance of a drill that the drill master compels tutees to perform ostensibly to improve their test scores. The limitation of rote methods as a pedagogical practice is not much of a concern. Anyone, thus, can set up as a tutor by simply putting up an advertisement on the school walls, in a local shop window, at the railway or bus station, or in the newspaper.

Again, teaching is a 'team sport' (Darling-Hammond 2014–15). In particular, those teachers who have to teach children in poverty, and children from disadvantaged backgrounds, can benefit from working together, since there is a need for concerted thinking about how to address both pedagogical and social challenges that are involved in such instances. If the formal education system appears lukewarm to this need for professional interactions and exchanges among teachers, the structure of tutoring is thoroughly frozen to the idea of common effort. The individual tutors and coaching centres as well as the attending tutees are all engaged in isolated and fiercely competitive striving, away from opportunities for peer learning. Admittedly, learning and teaching involve a lot of personal slogging and struggle, but that is quite different from the form of isolation and cut-throat competition that private tutoring entails. Reducing the isolation of tutors and tutees does not appear to be the focus of the education bazaar. On the contrary, the private path to success that it advocates devalues learning from each other.

Choice, constraint, and compulsion

Parental choice as either school choice for their children or choice of tutors and coaching centres for them is being celebrated these days as a mark of consumer sovereignty that parents ostensibly enjoy in the education bazaar so much so that our time is defined as the age of 'parentocracy' (Nogueira 2010). Two issues deserve special attention here. First, is parental choice sovereign or manufactured? Second, is the choice set free from class differences? Some scholars find that the demand for private tutoring is not being manufactured by teachers, but rather by households (Brehm and Silova 2014). A few studies indicate that sometimes school teachers are approached by parents to give extra tuition to children they already teach at school, particularly in rural areas where the tutoring business is still less active.

But on the other hand, there are instances in which school teachers gently and not so gently nudge parents and suggest that their children would benefit from coaching, or more menacingly that they would fail to make the passing grade without private lessons. There is a demonstration effect and peer pressure too. The promise of personal tutoring, especially of training in English language, is regarded as highly desirable by families of all classes. Many parents feel the pressure, including marginalised families that are at risk of becoming prey to commercial exploitation. Admittedly, the middle-class households that can afford the extra lessons have some say in the matter; hence traces of a model of middle-class control over schooling processes are indeed evident. But for a large section of parents, private coaching is a kind of compulsion – a choice under constraint, since ranking in examinations determines educational future of their children and mobility later on in life.

In a response to a recent order banning private tuition by the High Court in the state of Tripura – the incidence of private tutoring is found to be among the highest in Tripura and West Bengal according to recent data – a section of students and parents came out on the street protesting against the move and demanding legitimisation of private tuition. Allegedly, teachers involved in private tutoring had urged them to demonstrate (*The Shillong Times* 21 June 2015). It is, therefore, hard to unequivocally establish that parents are calling the shots, certainly not the disadvantaged parents; rather, the demand for paid coaching is to a considerable extent supply-induced. There exist well-thought-out strategies that are often skilfully deployed to generate parental demand for supplemental help for their children. That it is mere spontaneity of parental choice behind the power that the culture of tutoring wields does not, therefore, induce full confidence.

Furthermore, the set of tuition options available to parents, i.e. the choice set from which they choose, unsurprisingly differs along lines of class, caste, religion, and location. Simply put, as inequalities in social capital and social network across different social groups in India suggest, there exist social class differences in resources in constructing choice sets and hence in choices. Consequently, the children of socially underprivileged may still remain trapped in inferior schools and inferior tuition classes, raising doubts about the inevitability of positive outcomes of choice. Also, there is a risk of overestimating the average parent's agency in the choice of school (Jennings 2010) as also of tuition classes, since many private schools as well as 'star' coaching centres (for example, FIITJEE) conduct screening tests for prospective tutees.

Is private tutoring equity-enhancing?

Since there seems to be a massification of supplementary private tutoring at least in states like West Bengal, it is apt to ask whether this is an 'egalitarian' supplement and whether the market is a means to enhance equity. Lee (2013) contends that private tutoring exacerbates educational inequality between 'high' and 'low' achievers in middle school but contributes to narrowing the achievement gap in high school. That is to say, low achievers benefit more from private tutoring in high school compared to high achievers. Given the widely yawning quality gap between various tutoring services and their instructional resources and study materials (Majumdar 2014), it is, however, hard not to suggest that the privately paid supplement, determined by the size of the purse, creates new inequality along class lines and compounds the advantages of the upper middle classes. The recent data show that the incidence of private tutoring increases with the ability to pay. Recent estimates also show that the cost of tutoring makes up a huge percentage of private expenditure of schooling. It imposes a substantial burden on low-income families. Yet, parents appear 'willing' to spend a substantial amount to 'top up' their children's education. Does it mean that schools – all sorts of schools for that matter – are uniformly deficient and that parents are frustrated with them? Or is it that parents want the 'best' for their children and hence the concerted private efforts? Or perhaps there is a larger process at work that normalises the hegemonic culture of coaching in the interest of commerce and profit-making such that both schools and families are swayed to recast and reduce the idea of education into a commodity and a paper certificate. With such a level and manner of commodification, education loses much of its equalising potential.

How much parents spend on buying private lessons for their children is difficult to gauge, as this is often deliberately kept hidden – more by the tutors – for reasons that are far from straight-forward. Some estimates are, however, available from field-based studies (Banerji and Wadhwa 2012; Desai et al. 2010; Pratichi 2002, 2009) on this phenomenon. The recent NSSO (2015) statistics on private expenditure on extra coaching in the state of West Bengal is indicative of the substantial burden that families seem to bear on this account. On average in urban West Bengal the per capita annual expenditure on private tuition at the primary level is in the order of Rs. 2,780. Probing deeper, social and economic inequalities in private spending on educational supplement become palpable; relatedly its unequalising effect becomes easily imaginable. For the pupils of government school, this amount is roughly Rs. 1,980, whereas for those studying in private aided and private unaided schools, the corresponding figure is Rs. 3,650 and Rs. 4,790 respectively. It is common knowledge that in West Bengal, and for that matter most parts of the country, government schools are peopled mainly with children from marginalised background, whereas fee-charging (with the exception of low-fee private schools) private schools are the preserve of the privileged. And the latter group of children also spends a much larger sum on private tutoring. It is, therefore, not a secret that the wealthy parents have an advantage, as far as the ability to 'buy' better results is concerned. The more general argument that can be made is that if the culpability for educating children is largely laid at the door of the family rather than in the public domain, then the egalitarian promise of education is that much compromised, because the actualisation of that promise is contingent upon social commitment to individual educational freedom.

Equity issues are also germane to the employment generation aspect of private tuition. Private tutoring has for a long time served as a source of self-employment for the educated but unemployed youth in the country that, however, are paid a fraction of what professionally trained and qualified teachers receive. Any reservations about the system of private tutoring are often countered from this standpoint. Two quick responses may be considered. First, the culpability for unemployment cannot be laid solely at the door of the education system and its policies. Macroeconomic policies and labour market policies all have their roles to play in creating job opportunities sufficient to absorb the fresh supply of job seekers. The lacklustre performance of the economy and the state sector on that front, particularly in this era of corporate capitalism – epitomised in the pithy phrase of 'jobless growth' – cannot be lost sight of. This is indeed a concern. But need we translate this concern into an argument for informalisation and causalisation of the profession of teaching – a drift palpable in the coaching bazaar? Second, and relatedly, there is both a surfeit of untrained and half-trained self-employed private tutors (sometimes glorified as 'micro-entrepreneurs') in the deregulated and informal tutoring market as well as a shortage of professionally trained teachers in the formal school sector. There is a clear case, therefore, to be made in favour of teacher preparation and their professional development and of their absorption in the formal sector such that the country's children – especially those who are trapped in poor-quality schools and casual coaching shops – get proper training. On the other hand, if we get too swayed by the larger neoliberal politics of the avowal of informality as a solution to the problem of jobless growth, we may end up suggesting, with a bit of a stretch of the argument, that uneducated (un)employment is better than educated unemployment, for certain social classes at least.

Commerce and corruption

Karl Polanyi (1957) wrote in *The Great Transformation* that the commodity description of labour, land, and money is 'fictitious' and that their commodification will destroy human society. With the rise of education as a commercially profitable business, it is apt to ask whether knowledge too has become a 'fictitious commodity' today rather than remaining as 'the intellectual commons'. This change in the value system has certainly affected the ethos of the formal institutions of learning, perhaps corrupting even more the centres of 'learning' that operate in the informal domain. It is against this backdrop of the growing hold of the logic of the market on education that we discuss the issues of commercialisation and informalisation of the tutoring market.

Of relevance here is also the emerging global education scenario wherein we find a steady expansion of for-profit education firms offering various kinds of services including testing and school improvement services, short-term teacher preparation kits, school chains, software, etc. National education markets are more and more open to such trans-local service provision. Even the state is being used to the aid of the market at times. The formal school system itself seems to be veering towards the principles of the market, let alone the informal tutoring sector.

The tuition market, however, is graded, offering widely divergent services, at times with quality no bar. There are home tutors, tutors supplied through micro-entrepreneurial agencies – who function as a go-between and provide tutors' details to parents and charge a commission from the tutor – full-time teachers who offer private lessons outside of school hours, university students, and the staff attached to full-scale business enterprises – 'professionals' for whom tutoring is the main source of income. Several dubious business practices swirl around the operations of such a highly variegated tuition market. Book publishers are seen to approach popular private tutors and offer them adequate incentives so that they recommend and endorse their books for the tutees. The private coaching system in general seems to gain increasing control over the market for textbooks, study guides, question paper banks, and even over the examination system. Corrupt business practices sometimes take starker forms such as sheer profiteering, outright violation of norms and ethics, such as impersonation at examination halls and the leaking of question papers, etc. In the Vyapam scam that is currently rocking the country, a large number of 'solvers' – candidates who appeared on behalf of real candidates in medical entrance exams and who have appeared on the radar of the investigative agencies – teach at coaching centres. As a newspaper report states,

> Most solvers were either medical students or doctors. Some were unsuccessful candidates who could not crack the pre-medical test and later lost on the eligibility criteria because of the age factor but started teaching in coaching centres and became solvers.... The middlemen offer 'solvers' amounts ranging from Rs 200,000–300,000 for one exam.
>
> *(The Hindu 24 August 2015)*

All these deeply disturbing practices disproportionately harm the already disadvantaged and restrict rather than expand their educational opportunities. A few more general concerns are powerfully articulated by Sandel (2012) and Delbanco (2013) with respect to the triumph of the market in education. They contend that the increasingly dominant social preference 'to remake the public enterprise of education on the model of private corporations', to infuse the allegedly overbureaucratised education system with 'entrepreneurial energy' may lead us to valuing education in the wrong way, as an individuated consumption activity rather than as a civic, collective, and social citizenship enterprise. It may change a 'public activity' into 'business', into a pure 'market commodity'. The corrupting and degrading effects of commercialisation are surely not confined to tuitions alone; rather, these tend to eclipse and deform the education system in general.

Concluding remarks: private solution as a social priority?

No doubt, there are deficiencies in the public system of education; no doubt, there are learning gaps among students; and no doubt, parents are bound to address these trouble spots according to their ability and means. This is the right diagnosis. But what is the right treatment? Is seeking a strictly private solution – inequitable and expensive – to this public deficiency the correct response? In her recent book, Nussbaum (2010) compellingly argues that education is not for profit. Hence, distributing education as a market commodity in a profit-driven delivery system is likely to lead to a number of distortions. Simply put, educating children is an activity that has to be pursued in a predominantly non-profit system.

This is by no means to suggest that private efforts have no place in this scheme of things. The moot point is one of maintaining a sense of proportion and balance. If societal commitment to education evaporates in the face of individualised aspirations of families for a 'good-quality' education, and of their arduous pursuit to access personal tutoring services for their children's educational success, then there is a problem. The excesses that we allude to in the discussion above relate to this loss of balance between a strictly 'family strategy approach' on the one hand and an idea of common effort to professionalise, de-commercialise, and equalise educational opportunities on the other.

More concretely, proposals for egalitarian educational reform must aim at improving and amending both the mainstream and its shadow (Majumdar 2014). What is urgently needed is an improvement in the quality of what is offered in schools. Reducing the weight of the curricula is another primary aspect of educational reform as the Indian school education system suffers from the crippling weight of what Pritchett and Beatty (2012) describe as an 'over-ambitious curriculum'. Reducing the pressure of success in examinations could also be a part of essential reforms. Examinations too need to be modelled differently to discourage passive memorisation drills for the students and to encourage instead their active and creative engagement with the learning process. There are indeed many time-tested proposals of innovative examinations reform that energise rather than enervate the education system. What is critical, of course, is the actualisation of such ideas.

So far as the long-established tradition of supplementary tutoring is concerned, it would be hard to eliminate or ban it altogether (Bray 2003, 2009), although the Right to Education Act of India does ban such practices. One reasonable and feasible action would be to prevent school teachers from tutoring their own students privately – a measure that has been adopted in many states in India and in many parts of the globe.

Above all, a balance has to be restored at the level of public discourse and popular imagination itself. That education has to be a cooperative endeavour seems to be steadily fading away from public consciousness. The limits imposed by the dominant discourse of individuated choice for a 'fictitious commodity' of education seems to be detracting from bringing people together around a common project of improving and reforming the public delivery of education. Excessive focus on educational success seems to be weakening the common and united effort to solve the first-order problem, namely, the lack of creativity and critical thinking in teaching-learning processes that the college teacher in Kolkata, whom we have quoted at the beginning of this chapter, so succinctly and poignantly articulated several decades ago. To secure individual and social flourishing through education, the urgent task is to resist the modern-day enclosure of the commons of the mind.

References

ASER Centre. Various years. *Annual Status of Education Report*, New Delhi: facilitated by PRATHAM.

Banerji, Rukmini and Wilima Wadhwa. 2012. 'Every Child in School and Learning Well in India: Investigating the Implications of School Provision and Supplemental Help', in *India Infrastructure Report*, New Delhi: Routledge.

Batra, Poonam. 2015. 'Quality of Education and the Poor: Constraints on Learning', TRG Poverty & Education Working Paper 4, Max Weber Stiftung.

Boyle, James. 2002. 'Fencing Off Ideas: Enclosure & the Disappearance of the Public Domain', *Daedalus*, 131:2, 13–25.

Bray, Mark. 2003. *Adverse Effects of Private Supplementary Tutoring: Dimensions, Implications and Government Responses*, Paris: International Institute of Educational Planning, UNECSO.

Bray, Mark. 2009. *Confronting the Shadow Education System: What Government Policies for What Private Tutoring?*, Paris: UNESCO Publishing.

Bray, Mark. 2007. 'Governance and Free Education: Directions, Mechanisms, and Policy Tensions'. *Prospects: Quarterly Review of Comparative Education*, 37:1, 23–35.

Brehm, William C. and Iveta Silova. 2014. 'Ethical Dilemmas in the Education Marketplace: Shadow Education, Political Philosophy and Social (In)justice in Cambodia', in Ian Macpherson, Susan Robertson, and Geoffrey Walford (eds) *Education, Privatisation and Social Justice: Case Studies from Africa, South Asia and South East Asia*, Oxford: Symposium Books, pp. 159–178.

Darling-Hammond, Linda. 2014–15. 'Want to Close the Achievement Gap? Close the Teaching Gap', *American Educator* 38:4, 14–18.

Delbanco, Andrew. 2013. 'The Two Faces of American Education', *New York Review of Books*, 60, 15.

Desai, Sonalde B., Amaresh Dubey, Brij Lal Joshi, Mitali Sen, Abusaleh Sharif, and Reeve Vanneman. 2010. *Human Development in India: Challenges for a Society in Transition*, New Delhi: Oxford University Press.

Government of India. 2015. *Social Consumption in India: Education*, January–June 2014, NSS 71st Round, New Delhi: Government of India.

The Hindu. 2015. 'Over 100 Vyapam "solvers" are from U.P.', 24 August.

Jennings, Jennifer L. 2010. 'School Choice or Schools' Choice? Managing in an Era of Accountability', *Sociology of Education*, 83:3 227–247.

Kumar, Krishna. 1994. 'Textbooks, Spaces and Examination', in *The Child's Language and the Teacher: A Handbook*, New Delhi: National Book Trust India.

Kumar, Krishna. 2012. 'Universities: Ours and Theirs', *The Hindu*, 9 August 2012.

Lee, Ji Yun. 2013. 'Private Tutoring and Its Impact on Students' Academic Achievement, Formal Schooling, and Educational Inequality in Korea', PhD, Columbia University. http://hdl.handle.net/10022/AC:P:20461, (accessed on 16 August 2015).

Macpherson, Ian, Susan Robertson, and Geoffrey Walford (eds). 2014. *Education, Privatisation and Social Justice: Case Studies from Africa, South Asia and South East Asia*. Oxford: Symposium Books.

Majumdar, Manabi. 2014. 'The Shadow School System and New Class Divisions in India', TRG Poverty and Education Working Paper Series Paper 2, Max Weber Stiftung.

Marimuthu, T., J.S. Singh, K. Ahmad, L.H. Kuan, H. Mukherjee, S. Osman, T. Chelliah, J.R. Sharma, and S.M. Salleh. 1991. *Extra School Institutions, Social Equity and Educational Quality*, report prepared for the International Development Research Centre.

Nogueira, Maria Alice. 2010. 'A Revisited Theme: Middle Classes and the School', in Michael W. Apple, Stephen J. Ball, and Luis Armando Gandin (eds) *The Routledge Handbook of the Sociology of Education*, New York: Routledge, pp. 253–263.

Nussbaum, Martha C. 2010. *Not For Profit: Why Democracy Needs the Humanities*, Princeton: Princeton University Press.

Polanyi, K. 1957. *The Great Transformation*, Boston: Beacon.

Pratichi (India) Trust. 2002. *The Pratichi Education Report I*, New Delhi: TLM Books.

Pratichi (India) Trust. 2009. *Pratichi Education Report II, Primary Education in West Bengal: Changes and Challenges*. Kolkata: Pratichi Publication.

Pritchett, Lant and Amanda Beatty. 2012. 'The Negative Consequences of Overambitious Curricula in Developing Countries', Center for Global Development Working Paper 293. www.cgdev.org/.../1426129_file_Pritchett_Beatty_Overambitious_FINA... (accessed on 1 March 2014).

Sandel, Michael J. 2012. *What Money Can't Buy: The Moral Limits of Markets*, London: Allen Lane and Penguin Books.

Sen, Amartya. 2002. 'Introduction', in *The Pratichi Education Report I*, New Delhi: TLM Books.

The Shillong Times. 2015. 'Tripura Students, Guardians Take to Street to Legalise Private Tuition', 21 June.

Wadhwa, Wilima. 2015. 'Government vs Private Schools: Have Things Changed?', in *Annual Status of Education Report (Rural) 2014*, New Delhi: ASER Centre.

19

Understanding Vyapam

Krishna Kumar

If we had specialists in corruption studies, Vyapam would have given them a new realm to explore. This is not because of its scale, measured in terms of money or the number of people involved, or the length of time over which the scam was in the shade of urban gossip. The electronic media are treating Vyapam as a unique scam because of the serial deaths associated with it. This dimension should interest and worry the judiciary. However, blocking investigation by destroying evidence and killing witnesses is a familiar method in cases of corruption. This method has come into use in Vyapam on a scale that makes Madhya Pradesh (MP) look like Guatemala. But MP is not Guatemala, nor is Vyapam a story of drug mafia. It is a story of education, and that is what makes Vyapam so remarkable and worthy of deeper social – not merely police – inquiry. The public scandal surrounding Vyapam (an acronym for *Vyavasayik Pareeksha Mandal* or Board of Professional Examination) concerns the sale of seats in medical colleges and jobs in the lower order of government service. Though the idea of sale is not new, its strategy in the Vyapam case is new in the pervasive planning it involved. Instead of outright sale of seats in medical colleges, Vyapam enabled exam cheating to evolve into a service industry. Cheating became a facility to be purchased by youth; those who hesitate to buy the facility dread they may be taking a risk.

The logic of Vyapam alters the moral codes that govern competition for scarce opportunities. The investigation that is now underway will hopefully reveal the networks – of individuals and institutions – that enabled Vyapam's fraudulent operations to be sustained year after year. But how these networks became so robust and why the fraud did not cause public outrage or stir up politics are questions that demand a wider search for answers. Institutional decay in education and a political equilibrium that defies ideological categories are two important clues for understanding Vyapam. The last quarter-century has seen radical changes in state–market relations across the country. How these changes unfolded in the specific socio-political landscape of MP needs to be taken into account. Before we embark on drawing this larger picture, let us first recognise the change in the meaning of cheating implicit in Vyapam.

Mutation of cheating

The key word used in news about the Vyapam scam is 'cheating'. A simple summary of the scam might say that it enabled thousands of students to enrol in medical colleges by cheating in the pre-medical or entrance exam. This summary is, of course, accurate. It induces us to use an old and familiar frame of cheating in exams to respond to the complex narrative of the scam. But this frame will not suffice to understand Vyapam. As a theme, cheating in exams is part of the annual coverage of exam-related news by the media between March and June. It follows a set pattern: in the first round, items about stress on students appear, and how parents are coping with it. A little later, when exams start, we get news about instances of cheating. And finally, when results are declared, news about suicides by students completes the annual round of exam coverage. This year, news about cheating came with visuals from Bihar in which high-school examinees were shown receiving help-material through the windows of a multi-storey exam centre. A short while later came the news about the Supreme Court's order to cancel the All India Pre-Medical Test (PMT) conducted by the Central Board of Secondary Education (CBSE) for 15 per cent of seats in all government medical colleges across the country. This news had some exotic items in it, such as the use of hi-tech means of cheating by the organisers to enable their clients to get high scores. When the national media started to report sudden, mysterious deaths in different parts of MP, readers and television viewers framed Vyapam as an exam-cheating story gone a bit too far. To see why such a frame is not appropriate for Vyapam, we need to take a brief look at the history of exam cheating.

Terms like 'cheating' and 'unfair means' invoke a record that began with the advent of the modern exam system in India in the late nineteenth century. 'Unfair means' covered a practice more directly denoted by the Hindi/Urdu term 'nakal', which literally means copying. It conveys the basic idea that an examinee who copies from material brought into the exam hall illegally is cheating. The distinction between an honest examinee and the one who cheats in this conventional usage is that the former has access to no external help. The term 'nakal' tells us what the most familiar form of help was. It meant concealing in one's dress a book or paper in order to copy from it. How widely prevalent the practice was can be guessed from a comment made on it by Rabindranath Tagore in 1919. Tagore saw no distinction between those who cheat and the rest who do not. 'If it be cheating to take a book into the examination hall hidden in one's clothes, why not when the whole of its contents is smuggled in within the head?' (Tagore 1919). The culture of cramming that Tagore decried remains the core of education and the examination system, but competitive entrance exams of the kind that Vyapam conducts present a new dimension.

Cheating under Vyapam is not an act we can attribute to individual candidates who appear in a mass test. Both the nature of the test they take and the enabling role played by the test-conducting authorities need to be comprehended. Organised cheating of the kind we see in Vyapam (and also in the PMT taken by the CBSE in which the Supreme Court asked for a re-test) involves the services of question-solvers who have access to the exam questions in advance and who are financially compensated for the risky service they provide. Their services are used by examinees in two ways. First, the solvers can act as proxy candidates by actually taking the exam in the place of a candidate. For this, they require a fake identity card which must be arranged by those who pay them, and this arrangement needs the tacit approval of designated authorities of the government who will also get a fee or cut for this risk-taking behaviour. The second or alternative method by which solvers' services can be availed is to equip the genuine candidates with electronic devices that permit the transmission of correct answers without drawing the attention of invigilators. This second method may require financial compensation for people performing functions like invigilation, guarding of entry doors, and checking identity cards, etc. An inclusive plan that ensures all such people do the needful and keep their mouths shut is necessary.

Another dimension of the difference between conventional exam cheating and present-day, organised cheating is the design of test items. Appreciating this dimension helps us to bring into the orbit of analysis a set of players that the official probe into Vyapam may not cover. Conventional cheating worked for essay-type questions; the new mode is meant for tests consisting of multiple choice questions (MCQs). In MCQ-style testing, cheating involves ticking off the correct choice in hundreds of items at considerable speed. Indeed, speed is a critical factor of success. Examinees keen on success cannot afford to leave any items unattempted due to lack of time or choose wrong answers due to hurrying: both incur negative marking. Unlike the conventional exam which asked a few questions covering a limited number of patches of the syllabus, an MCQ-based examination calls for mastery of the entire corpus of knowledge included in a syllabus, for mastery alone can give the honest examinee sufficient speed to cover the vast number of items that such exams carry. This academic attraction of an MCQ-based test is precisely what makes it vulnerable to organised cheating. We can appreciate this vulnerability by revisiting our earlier discussion of the roles involved in organised cheating.

Link industries

The key role played by 'solvers' is crucial for organised cheating. This role, in turn, depends on their access to the question paper in advance. Thus, if we wish to understand how cheating has mutated into a service industry, we must focus on these two factors: one, availability of solvers in sufficient numbers; two, solvers' access to the question paper in advance, i.e. its leakage. The Vyapam scam has brought out into the public domain, so to say, the full landscape of organised cheating. The attention this industry is currently receiving is somewhat new; otherwise, its operative presence in professional, especially medical and engineering, exams has been a part of post-secondary education in many states. The role of linking organised cheating with the system of education has been performed for decades by the coaching industry. How this industry operates, along with certain ancillary industries, is just beginning to be researched, but its emergence as a challenge to the state's system of education has been noted in many countries. In India, coaching and private tuition are closely associated with the mainstream system. Both prepare the young to improve their performance in competitive settings. Consumers of the coaching industry pay in order to buy an advantageous position in open contests organised by the public education system.

The stake that coaching institutions and their cartels have in competitive exams such as entrance tests for medical and engineering courses is high. The volume of money that coaching institutions generate from among their clients is vast enough for investment in building strong bridges between their personnel and state functionaries involved in entrance tests. One of the crucial merchandise passing through these bridges is the content of the question paper designed for school-leaving examinations and entrance tests for further education. Ancillary industries that facilitate this trafficking include publishing of exam guides, simplified textbooks, compendia of past exam questions along with answers, and provision of online exam-related services. The coaching industry and these ancillaries operate under the shelter of the public education system and assist it, often by sharing roles or even spaces. The two systems collaborate in maintaining the popular belief that children need the services of both – attendance at school for legitimacy and enrolment in a coaching institution for preparation for entrance exams. Along with coaching, the ancillary industry of exam-focused guidebooks acquires its credibility because they closely anticipate the actual exam papers at frequent intervals, thereby conveying their resourcefulness. The market value of individual companies involved in the ancillary industries keeps changing, but the industry as a whole retains its value for its young clients, who notice sufficient evidence to believe that the industry is linked to the exam process.

The awareness that cheating prevails has a very different psychological meaning for examinees appearing in today's mass entrance tests. Conventional cheating offers a very limited advantage to its beneficiary. In the conventional exam in which such cheating works, the scope for marks is, in any case, limited. Someone who cheats by copying faces a serious disadvantage arising out of the time it takes to give an essay-type answer by copying. Cheating by copying can seldom result in more than a pass score for the examinee. Therefore, the honest examinee does not feel threatened by those who cheat. This is not so in the case of organised cheating. Success in a competitive MCQ-based exam demands high scores. Someone who has used the aforementioned services of the organised cheating industry can obtain the highest scores. Genuine examinees may be weeded out entirely if the number of beneficiaries of organised cheating is substantial. For this reason, the genuine examinees feel the threat of being at a disadvantage. Some of them may well feel sufficiently stressed by their fear of failure and yield to the offers made by the service providers representing the organised cheating industry.

Their incursion into the routine of exam preparation has to be viewed as a significant cultural inversion. The idea that one must pay to ensure selection replaces the belief that tests for professional courses and state employment require hard work. This seems to have happened in MP. Conditions congenial to this change in popular perception have been coming together for a long time. There are districts where certain exam centres were given out to contractors to arrange uninterrupted cheating for candidates, many of whom were drawn from other states. The new set-up of organised exam fraud involves more meticulous arrangements and planning networks. In the networks so far revealed in the Vyapam case, ground-level help by proxy candidates and solvers was supplemented and scaffolded by computer experts who had access to score sheets and lists of selected examinees yet to be finalised. These high-layer functionaries had bureaucratic and political patrons. Private medical colleges also had a role in this multi-layered arrangement.

Systemic context

Growth of organised cheating as a service industry in MP has a larger, systemic context. The public system of education has been hollowed out over the last 25 years. This process covered all stages of education. From the early 1990s, MP's system of education followed the path recommended under the structural adjustment programme. The doctrine of neoliberal governance on which the structural adjustment policies were based demanded the substitution of welfarism with a thin social safety net to cover the risk of social unrest. This was a general prescription for all states, but while other states compromised on many aspects and negotiated the broad doctrine with partial compliance, MP adopted the vision with rigour and went further than any other state in implementing it. MP carried out a thorough dismantling of its welfare apparatus in education and health. Powers to appoint and monitor teachers were transferred to village *panchayats*, using the rhetoric of grassroot democracy to provide political underlining for the social safety net regime. Legal and administrative scaffolding enabled MP to drastically streamline its budget on teachers and schools while negotiating the goal of systemic expansion. Decentralisation, community participation, and other such discourses facilitated the dismantling of the old public system at all levels of school education. MP became the darling of global donors by launching populist programmes such as the Education Guarantee Scheme. They served to conceal the impoverishment of schools and teachers, and the promotion of low-cost private schooling.

The voice of civil society in MP was limited and the state had no difficulty in co-opting it. Appointments of permanent teaching staff at all levels of education froze and mutated. In colleges it happened in the late 1980s; in schools it happened through stages over the next decade. The old pool of school teachers – from primary to senior secondary – was declared a 'dying cadre', which meant that when teachers of the existing pool retire, their posts will be abolished and fresh, downgraded posts will be created in their place. Thus, the entire system got transformed and hollowed out. At the college level, guest and ad hoc appointments became the norm. Even as teachers were de-professionalised, infrastructure like libraries and laboratories was starved of funds. Demand for privately owned institutions of higher – especially professional – education grew, resulting in the establishment of links between edu-business and politicians. New networks were forming even as products of impoverished schools were struggling with entrance tests to claim eligibility for further education in a scarcity market. Ill-prepared for MCQ-based competitive tests, they turned to service providers promising a seat. The situation was becoming ripe for a scam.

Political consensus

Over the long period of this overhaul of education, political power oscillated smoothly between MP's two main parties. Consensus on the structural adjustment-related policies across party lines was not unique to MP. However, the vivacity and determination with which MP proceeded to embrace these policies call attention to MP's specific social and political history. The Vyapam scam is not incidental to this heartland region of India. The same can be said about the scam's aftermath in which the state has attempted to label a long series of unnatural deaths as incidental. Familiar terms such as 'backward' and 'underdeveloped' that are used to describe the social landscape of the Hindi Belt blind us to the specific histories of the regions this area comprises. These histories are important in as much as they remind us of the functions of the modern state that the new economic policies seek to redefine. The discourse of these policies also tends to establish the correctness of general prescriptions. How they will unfold in different regions invites little interest or attention.

'Self-financing' is one such prescription. It has been offered as the right approach to making education cost-effective as opposed to being a big burden on the exchequer. The self-financing model has been offered not merely for schools and colleges, but also for regulatory bodies such as the ones that control professional education in medicine, engineering, teacher training, and so on. Indeed, the self-financing model now covers examining bodies like the CBSE and Vyapam as well. Vyapam generates its resources from the vast number of aspirants who compete for a small number of seats. Technically, no test can distinguish between those who have potential and others who lack it when the contest is so keen – involving more than 1,000 for each single seat. But public testing does generate impressive revenue under the self-financing model. As a public utility, therefore, Vyapam is trusted to work with competence and technologically monitored transparency, irrespective of the socio-political terrain it serves. Mass poverty, illiteracy, sharp income disparities, and caste hierarchies are characteristic of this terrain. Too little time has passed since modern statehood and citizenship started to replace loyalty to princely structures. In such a terrain, a self-financing institution charged with selection of a few hundred out of millions can easily become a conduit for the distribution of patronage by networks of power and new businesses.

As an administrative territory, MP was sculpted nine years after Independence by merging some of the older units and jettisoning some others. Much of the area consisted of princely states of different sizes. They catapulted into democracy straight from princely rule. The area that came under Central Provinces in the colonial period consisted of culturally distinct populations. Princely loyalties prevailed in this area as well. Administrative unification could hardly mean that social cohesion and civic identities would soon follow. A social ethos marked by entrenched poverty and extremely limited opportunities for education enabled local orbits of feudal-style patronage to survive. Diaspora of the educated unemployed from neighbouring states also got assimilated into the dominant cultural system. Political expression of social and economic aspirations remained confused and weak, as the ideological alternatives represented by the two main political parties – the Congress and the Bharatiya Janata Party (BJP; formerly Jan Sangh) – stayed deceptive. As a renowned MP journalist, the late Rahul Barpute, once told me, it is unnecessary to look for stable ideological distinctions behind party loyalties in MP.

Political occult

Vyapam presents a modern political occult that failed to contain its secrecy. The moment of failure came after success sustained over many years, along with the growth of confidence among collaborators. The fraud pervaded the entire system of selection for distribution of opportunities for professional education and lower-level state employment. Its immanence and continued growth is currently passing through the phase in which the participants are doing whatever is possible to destroy the evidence that might reveal the fraud – its dimensions and the diverse identities of players. A series of unnatural deaths of young people and several others is part of this phase of the scam (*The Hindustan Times* 2015). The social world of MP has taken these deaths laconically, as yet another episode in the familiar story of power plays. On the specific identity and life stories of those who were found dead at some point, brevity has guided the regional Hindi media.

Although this melodrama had set in a while ago, the specific death that made Vyapam a national media story this summer was that of a TV journalist who had travelled from Delhi to interview the father of a medical student whose body was reportedly found on a railway track three years previously. The young journalist died soon after completing the interview. Despite the high number of unexplained deaths – figures reported exceed 40 – the state government's investigating team initially saw no point in treating this phenomenon as a relevant matter. The political brass of MP repeatedly asserted that the deaths should not be viewed as being necessarily related to the scam. The news of deaths, as indeed all Vyapam-related news, had become normalised by the time the national media suddenly smelled something unusually meaty in the scam. In MP itself, neither the fraudulent enrolments and appointments in jobs, nor the series of mysterious deaths aroused public outcry or political stirrings. The only voice of anxiety was that of four individuals who were identified in the media as whistle-blowers. They had used their limited means to collect certain details to bring the fraud to public attention. They have faced threats and harassment since.

In the context of Vyapam, an apparent tussle has broken out between the two main parties. The focus of this tussle is corruption, an omnibus term that covers a wide range of behaviours, from abuse of power to incompetence. As a corruption story, Vyapam also includes a cover-up attempt. There is plenty of material here for allegations to be exchanged. Only if we see the scam as a systemic failure can we notice the longer story of state-sponsored institutional decay and the rise of cheating as a service industry. In that longer story, neither of the two political parties can hope to remain clean. Indeed, the entire political apparatus – including the office of the governor – has to be held responsible for the abuse of education, both as a system and as a social resource. The project of education, both as a means of human resource development – its official aim since the mid-1980s – and as a means of nurturing civil society, has miserably failed in MP. Failure of this kind is hardly ever dramatic, so it cannot be dated, but the Vyapam scam has revealed it in a dramatic manner. Whether such a revelation will create the desire and energy needed for embarking on the road to reform is a different matter.

References

The Hindustan Times. 2015. 'HT Exclusive: In Vyapam Scam, 10 Dead in Mishaps and 4 Suicides', 30 June.

Tagore, Rabindranath. 1919. 'The Centre of Indian Culture'. Lecture, Madras, 9 February 1919.

Index

Page numbers in *italics* denote tables, those in **bold** denote figures.